COMMUNICATION
in Everyday Life

SELECTED READINGS

DALTON A. KEHOE
York University

Excerpts taken from:

Social Psychology, Third Canadian Edition
by Elliot Aronson, Timothy D. Wilson, and Robin M. Akert

Mastering Human Relations, Second Edition
by Anthony Falikowski

Messages. Building Interpersonal Communication Skills, Second Canadian Edition
by Joseph A. DeVito, Rena Shimoni, and Dawne Clark

Interpersonal Communication and Human Relationships, Fifth Edition
by Mark L. Knapp and Anita L. Vangelisti

The Interpersonal Communication Book, Ninth Edition
by Joseph A. DeVito

Person to Person: Positive Relationships Don't Just Happen, Third Edition
by Sharon L. Hanna

Messages: Building Interpersonal Communication Skills, Fifth Edition
by Joseph A. DeVito

Interpersonal Communication: Relating to Others, Third Canadian Edition
by Steven A. Beebe

PEARSON
Custom
Publishing

Taken from:

Social Psychology, Third Canadian Edition
by Elliot Aronson, Timothy D. Wilson, and Robin M. Akert
Copyright © 2007 by Pearson Education Canada
Published by Prentice Hall
Toronto, Ontario

Mastering Human Relations, Second Edition
By Anthony Falikowski
Copyright © 1999 by Pearson Education Canada
Published by Prentice Hall

Messages: Building Interpersonal Communication Skills,
Second Canadian Edition
By Joseph A. DeVito, Rena Shimoni, and Dawne Clark
Copyright © 2005 by Pearson Education Canada
Published by Allyn & Bacon
Toronto, Ontario

Interpersonal Communication and Human Relationships, Fifth
Canadian Edition
By Mark L. Knapp and Anita L. Vangelisti
Copyright © 2005 by Pearson Education Canada
Published by Allyn and Bacon

The Interpersonal Communication Book, Ninth Edition
By Joseph A DeVito
Copyright © 2000 by Pearson Education Canada
Published by Allyn & Bacon

Person to Person: Positive Relationships Don't Just Happen,
Third Edition
by Sharon L. Hanna
Copyright © 1999 by Pearson Education Canada
Published by Prentice Hall

Messages: Building Interpersonal Communication Skills,
Fifth Edition
by Joseph A. DeVito
Copyright © 2002 by Allyn and Bacon
A Pearson Education Company
Boston, Massachusetts 02116

Interpersonal Communication: Relating to Others, Third
Canadian Edition
by Steven A. Beebe
Copyright © 2003 by Pearson Education Canada
Published by Allyn & Bacon

Copyright © 2007 by Pearson Custom Publishing
All rights reserved.

Printed in Canada

4 5 6 DPC 12 11 10

ISBN 0-536-48036-2

2007560131

ED/LD

Please visit our web site at *www.pearsoncustom.com*

PEARSON
Custom
Publishing

PEARSON CUSTOM PUBLISHING
501 Boylston Street, Suite 900, Boston, MA 02116
A Pearson Education Company

TABLE OF CONTENTS

FOREWORD

This reader is an essential companion to the text *Communication in Everyday Life*. Each reading has been carefully selected and edited to provide you with more information, engaging exercises, and hopefully, deeper insight into the communication models and concepts described in overview form in the text. As you read through a chapter in *Communication in Everyday Life* you will come across an "Additional Reading" box and within each box you will find one of these readings referred to by number, title and author. I have tried to place this link in exactly the place in *Communication in Everyday Life* where I think it would effectively provide support to the points being made. I would suggest that you review the linked reading before continuing your reading in the text.

THE UNIVERSALS OF INTERPERSONAL COMMUNICATION

Excerpts from: Devito, J. (2001). *The Interpersonal Communication Book, 9ᵗʰ Ed.* Toronto: Addison Wesley Longman, Inc., pp. 8 -15.

The following excerpts from Unit One of the Joseph DeVito's book will explain not only the key concepts in the IP model but also its dynamics, that is, how the concepts flow together around the three levels of complexity mentioned in chapter one of *Communication In Everyday Life.*

Figure 1.1   The Interpersonal (IP) Model of Talk

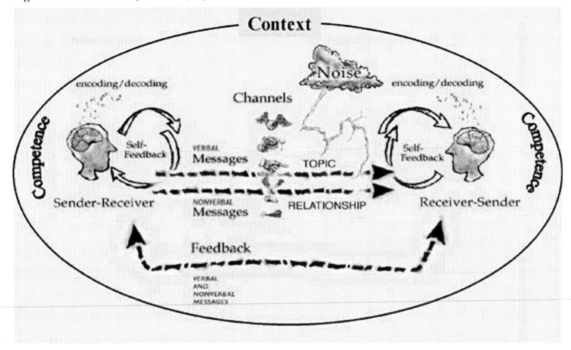

***

ELEMENTS OF INTERPERSONAL COMMUNICATION

The model presented in Figure 1.1 is designed to reflect the circular nature of interpersonal communication; both persons send messages simultaneously rather than as a linear sequence where communication goes from person 1 to person 2 to person 1 to person 2 and on and on. Each of the concepts identified in the model and discussed here may be thought of as a **universal of interpersonal communication**, in that it's present in all interpersonal interactions.

Source-Receiver

Interpersonal communication involves at least two persons. Each person formulates and sends messages (**source** functions) and also perceives and comprehends messages (**receiver** functions). The hyphenated term source-receiver emphasizes that both functions are performed by each individual in interpersonal communication.

Who you are, what you know, what you believe, what you value, what you want, what you have been told, what your attitudes are all influence what you say, how you say it, what messages you receive, and how you receive them. Each person is unique; each person's communications are unique.

Encoding-Decoding

Encoding refers to the act of producing messages—for example, speaking or writing. *Decoding* is the reverse and refers to the act of understanding messages—for example, listening or reading. By sending your ideas via sound waves, you're putting these ideas into a code, hence encoding. By translating sound waves into ideas, you're taking them out of a code, hence decoding. Thus speakers and writers are called **encoders**, and listeners and readers **decoders**. The hyphenated term encoding-decoding is used to emphasize that the two activities are performed in combination by each participant. For interpersonal communication to occur, messages must be encoded and decoded. For example, when a parent talks to a child whose eyes are closed and whose ears are covered by stereo headphones, interpersonal communication does not occur because the messages sent are not being received.

Competence

Your ability to communicate effectively is your interpersonal **competence** (Spitzberg and Cupach 1989). Your competence includes, for example, the knowledge that in certain contexts and with certain listeners one topic is appropriate and another isn't. Your knowledge about the rules of nonverbal behavior—for example, the appropriateness of touching, vocal volume, and physical closeness—is also part of your competence. In short, interpersonal competence includes knowing how to adjust your communication according to the context of the interaction, the person with whom you're interacting, and a host of other factors discussed throughout this text.

You learn communication competence much as you learn to eat with a knife and fork—by observing others, by explicit instruction, by trial and error. Some have learned better than others, though, and these people are generally the ones with whom you find it interesting and comfortable to talk. They seem to know what to say and how and when to say it.

Not surprisingly there's a positive relationship between interpersonal competence on the one hand and success in college and job satisfaction on the other (Rubin and Graham 1988, Wertz, Sorenson, and Heeren 1988). So much of college and professional life depends on interpersonal competence—meeting and interacting with other students, teachers, or colleagues; asking and answering questions; presenting information or argument—that you should not find this connection surprising. Interpersonal competence also enables you to develop and maintain meaningful relationships in friendship, love, family, and work which, in turn, contribute to the lower levels of anxiety, depression, and loneliness observed in interpersonally competent people (Spitzberg and Cupach 1989).

Messages

Messages—signals that serve as **stimuli** for a receiver—may be auditory (hearing), visual (seeing), tactile (touching), olfactory (smelling), gustatory (tasting), or any combination. You communicate interpersonally by gesture and touch as well as by words and sentences. The clothes you wear communicate to others and, in fact, to your self as well. The way you walk communicates, as does the way you shake hands, cock your head, comb your hair, sit, smile, or frown. These signals are your interpersonal communication messages. Interpersonal communication can take place by telephone, through prison cell walls, through videophone hookup, or face-to-face. Increasingly, it's taking place through computers.

Messages may be intentional or unintentional. They may result from the most carefully planned strategy as well as from the unintentional slip of the tongue, lingering body odor, or nervous twitch.

Messages may refer to the world, people, and events as well as about other messages. Messages that are about other messages are called **metamessages** and represent many of your everyday messages, for example: "Do you understand?" "Did I say that right?" "What did you say?" "Is it fair to say that...?" "I want to be honest." "That's not logical." Two particularly important types of metamessages are feedback and feedforward.

Feedback Messages

Throughout the interpersonal communication process, you exchange **feedback**—messages sent back to the speaker concerning reactions to what is said (Clement and Frandsen 1976). Feedback tells the speaker what effect she or he is having on listeners. On the basis of this feedback, the speaker may adjust, modify, strengthen, de-emphasize, or change the content or form of the messages.

Feedback may come from yourself or from others. In the diagram of the universals of communication (Figure 1.1), the arrows from source-receiver to effect and from one source-receiver to the other source-receiver go in both directions to illustrate the notion of feedback. When you send a message— say, in speaking to another person—you also hear yourself. That is, you get feedback from your own messages; you hear what you say, you feel the way you move, you see what you write. In addition to this self-feedback, you get feedback from others. This feedback can take many forms. A frown or a smile, a yea or a nay, a pat on the back or a punch in the mouth are all types of feedback.

Feedback can be looked upon in terms of five important dimensions: positive-negative, person focused-message focused; immediate-delayed; low monitoring-high monitoring; and supportive-critical. (Figure 1.2).

Figure 1.2 Five Dimensions of Feedback

Using these five dimensions of feedback, how would you describe the feedback that longtime and happy lovers would exchange? What kinds of feedback would be exchanged between casual acquaintances? What kinds would be exchanged between two people who disliked each other?

Positive	___:___:___:___:___:___	Negative
Person Focused	___:___:___:___:___:___	Message Focused
Immediate	___:___:___:___:___:___	Delayed
Low Monitoring	___:___:___:___:___:___	High Monitoring
Supportive	___:___:___:___:___:___	Critical

Positive-Negative Feedback may be positive (you compliment or pat someone on the back) or negative (you criticize someone or scowl). **Positive feedback** tells the speaker that he or she is on the right track and should continue communicating in essentially the same way. **Negative feedback** tells the speaker that something is wrong and that some adjustment should be made.

Person Focused-Message-Focused Feedback may center on the person ("You're sweet" or "You have a great smile"). Or it may center on the message ("Can you repeat that number?" or "Your argument is a good one").

Immediate-Delayed In interpersonal situations, feedback is often sent immediately after the message is received; you smile or say something in responses almost simultaneously with your receiving

3

the message. In other communication situations, however, the feedback may be delayed. Instructor evaluation questionnaires completed at the end of the course provide feedback long after the class began. When you applaud or ask questions of a public speaker at the end of a lecture, the feedback is delayed. In interview situations, the feedback may come weeks afterward. In media situations, some feedback comes immediately through Nielsen ratings, and other feedback comes much later through viewing and buying patterns.

Low Monitoring—High Monitoring Feedback varies from the spontaneous and totally honest reaction (low-monitored feedback) to the carefully constructed responses designed to serve a specific purpose (high-monitored feedback). In most interpersonal situations, you probably give feedback spontaneously; you allow your responses to show without any monitoring. At other times, however, you may be more guarded, as when your boss asks you how you like your job or when your grandfather asks what you think of his new earring.

Supportive-Critical Supportive feedback accepts the speaker and what the speaker says. It occurs, for example, when you console another, encourage him or her to talk, or otherwise confirm the person's definition of self. Critical feedback, on the other hand, is evaluative, it's judgmental. When you give critical feedback (whether positive or negative), you judge another's performance, as in, for example, coaching someone learning a new skill.

Feedforward Messages

Feedforward is information you provide before sending your primary messages (Richards 1951). Feedforward reveals something about the messages to come. Examples of feedforward include the preface or table of contents of a book, the opening paragraph of a chapter, movie previews, magazine covers, and introductions in public speeches. Feedforward may serve a variety of functions: to open the channels of communication, to preview the message, to disclaim, and to altercast.

To Open the Channels of Communication In his influential essay "The Problem of Meaning in Primitive Languages," anthropologist Bronislaw Malinowski (1923) coined the phrase phatic communion to refer to messages that open the channels of communication rather than communicate information. Phatic communion is a perfect example of feedforward. It's information that tells you that the normal, expected, and accepted rules of interaction will be in effect. It tells you another person is willing to communicate.

To Preview the Message Feed forward messages frequently preview other messages. They may, for example, preview the content ("I'm afraid I have bad news for you"), the importance ("Listen to this before you make a move"), the form or style ("I'll tell you all the gory details"), and the positive or negative quality of subsequent messages ("You're not going to like this, but here's what I heard").

To Disclaim The disclaimer is a statement that aims to ensure that your message will be understood as you want it to be and that it will not reflect negatively on you. For example, you might use a disclaimer when you think that what you're going to say may be met with opposition. Thus, you say "I'm not against immigration, but…" or "Don't think I'm homophobic, but..." …

To Altercast Feedforward is often used to place the receiver in a specific role and to request responses in terms of this assumed role, a process called **altercasting** (Weinstein and Deutschberger 1963, McLaughlin 1984). For example, you might alter cast by asking a friend, "As an advertising executive, what would you think of corrective advertising?" This question casts your friend in the role of advertising executive …

Channel

The communication **channel** is the medium through which messages pass. It's a kind of bridge connecting source and receiver. Communication rarely takes place over only one channel; two, three, or four channels are often used simultaneously. For example, in face-to-face interaction, you speak and listen (vocal-auditory channel), but you also gesture and receive signals visually (gestural-visual channel), and you omit odors and smell those of others (chemical-olfactory channel). Often you communicate through touch (cutaneous-tactile channel). Another way to think about channels is to consider them as the means of communication: for example, face-to-face contact, telephone, e-mail and snail mail, film, television, radio, smoke signal, fax or telegraph.

Noise

Noise interferes with your receiving a message someone is sending or with someone receiving your message. Noise may be physical (others talking loudly, cars honking, illegible handwriting, "garbage" on your computer screen), physiological (hearing or visual impairment, articulation disorders), psychological (preconceived ideas, wandering thoughts), or semantic (misunderstood meanings). Technically, noise is anything that distorts the message, anything that prevents the receiver from receiving the message (Table 1.2).

Table 1.2 Four Types of Noise

Types of Noise	Definition	Examples
Physical	Interference that is external to both speaker and listener and that prevents accurate transmission of the signal or message	Screeching of passing cars, hum of computer, sunglasses
Physiological	Physical barriers within the speaker or listener	Visual impairments, hearing loss, articulation problems, memory loss
Psychological	Cognitive or mental interference	Biases and prejudices in senders and receivers, closed-mindedness, inaccurate expectations, extreme emotionalism (anger, hate, love, grief)
Semantic	Speaker and listener assigning different meanings	People speaking different languages, use of jargon or overly complex terms not understood by listener, dialectical differences in meaning

A useful concept in understanding noise and its importance in communication is *signal-to-noise ratio*. *Signal* refers to information that you'd find useful, and *noise* refers to information that is useless (to you). So, for example, a mailing list or newsgroup that contains lots of useful information would be high on signal and low on noise; those that contain lots of useless information would be high on noise and low on signal. One of the most important skills in communication is to recognize the types of noise and to develop ways to combat them. Consider, for example, what kinds of noise occur in the classroom. What kinds of noise occur in your family communication? What kinds occur at work? What can you do to combat these kinds of noise?

Since messages may be visual as well as spoken, noise too may be visual. The sunglasses that prevent someone from seeing the nonverbal messages from your eyes would be considered noise, as would blurred type on a printed page.

All communications contain noise. Noise cannot be totally eliminated, but its effects can be reduced. Making your language more precise, sharpening your skills for sending and receiving nonverbal messages, and improving your listening and feedback skills are some ways to combat the influence of noise.

Context

Communication always takes place in a **context**, which influences the form and content of your messages. At times this context isn't obvious or intrusive; it seems so natural that it's ignored—like background music. At other times the context dominates, and the ways in which it restricts or stimulates your messages are obvious. Compare, for example, the differences between communicating in a funeral home, in a football stadium, in a formal restaurant, and at a rock concert. The context of communication has at least four dimensions, all of which interact and influence each other.

The *physical dimension* is the tangible or concrete environment in which communication takes place—the room, hallway, or park, the boardroom or the family dinner table. The size of the space, its temperature, and the number of people present in the physical space would also be part of the physical dimension.

The *temporal dimension* refers not only to the time of day and moment in history but also to where a particular message fits into the sequence of communication events. For example, a joke about illness told immediately after the disclosure of a friend's sickness will be received differently than the same joke told in response to a series of similar jokes.

The *social-psychological dimension* includes, for example, status relationships among the participants, roles and games that people play, norms of the society or group, and the friendliness, formality, or gravity of the situation.

The *cultural context* refers to the cultural beliefs and customs of the people communicating. When you interact with people from different cultures, you may each follow different rules of communication. This can result in confusion, unintentional insult, inaccurate judgments, and a host of other miscommunications. Similarly, communication strategies or techniques that prove satisfying to members of one culture may prove disturbing or offensive to members of another.

Purpose

Interpersonal communication serves a variety of purposes, for example, to learn, to relate, to influence, to play, and to help. Interpersonal communication enables you to learn, to better understand the external world—the world of objects, events, and other people. Although a great deal of information comes from the media, you probably discuss and ultimately learn or internalize information through interpersonal interactions. In fact, your beliefs, attitudes, and values are probably influenced more by interpersonal encounters than by the media or even formal education.

Most important, however, interpersonal communication helps you learn about yourself. By talking about yourself with others, you gain valuable feedback on your feelings, thoughts, and behaviors. Through these communications, you also learn how you appear to others—who likes you, who dislikes you, and why.

Interpersonal communication helps you relate. One of the greatest needs people have is to establish and maintain close relationships. You want to feel loved and liked, and in turn you want to love and like others. Such relationships help to alleviate loneliness and depression, enable you to share and heighten your pleasures, and generally make you feel more positive about yourself.

Very likely, you *influence* the attitudes and behaviors of others in your interpersonal encounters. You may wish them to vote a particular way, try a new diet, buy a new book, listen to a record, see a movie, take a specific course, think in a particular way, believe that something is true or false, or value some idea—the list is endless. A good deal of your time is probably spent in interpersonal persuasion.

Talking with friends about your weekend activities, discussing sports or dates, telling stories and jokes, and in general just passing the time are *play* function. Far from frivolous, this purpose is an extremely important one. It gives your activities a necessary balance and your mind a needed break from all the seriousness around us. Everyone has an inner child, and that child needs time to play.

Therapists of various kinds serve a helping function professionally by offering guidance through interpersonal interaction. But everyone interacts to *help* in everyday interactions: you console a friend who has broken off a love affair, counsel another student about courses to take, or offer advice to a colleague about work. Success in accomplishing this helping function, professionally or otherwise, depends on your knowledge and skill in interpersonal communication.

The purposes of interpersonal communication can also be viewed from two other perspectives (see Figure 1.3). First, purposes may be seen as motives for engaging in interpersonal communication. That is, you engage in interpersonal communication to satisfy your need for knowledge or to form relationships. Second, these purposes may be viewed in terms of the results you want to achieve. That is, you engage in interpersonal communication to increase you knowledge of yourself and others or to exert influence or power over others.

***

This figure identifies some of the reasons you listen. The innermost circle contains the general purposes of interpersonal communication. The middle circle contains the motivations that lead you to communicate. The outer circle contains the results that you might hope to achieve by engaging in interpersonal communication. A similar typology of purposes comes from research on motives for communicating. In a series of studies, Rubin and her colleagues (Rubin, Fernandez-Collado, and Hernandez-Sampieri 1992, Rubin and Martin 1994, Rubin, Perse, and Barbato 1988, Rubin 1992, Graham 1994, and Graham, Barbato, and Perse 1993) have identified six primary motives for communication: pleasure, affection, inclusion, escape, relaxation, and control. How do these compare to the five purposes discussed here?

Figure 1.3 Why You Engage in Interpersonal Communication

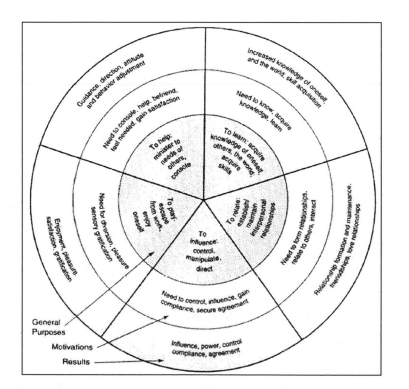

7

Ethics

Because communication has consequences, interpersonal communication also involves ethics; each communication act has a moral dimension, a rightness or wrongness (cf. Jaksa and Pritchard 1994, Johannesen 1990). Communication choices need to be guided by ethical considerations as well as by concerns with effectiveness and satisfaction. The ethical dimension of communication is complicated by the fact that because it's so closely interwoven with your own philosophy of life—heavily influenced by the culture in which you were raised—it's difficult to propose universal guidelines....

***

Axioms Of Interpersonal Communication

Excerpts from: Devito, J. (2001). *The Interpersonal Communication Book, 9th Ed.* Toronto: Addison Wesley Longman, Inc., pp.

These excerpts from Unit Two of DeVito's book will explain the dynamics of the IP model by explaining the six axioms – or fundamental rules – that seem to govern how interpersonal communication works at the three levels of complexity mentioned in chapter one of *Communication In Everyday Life.* These axioms are:

1. **Interpersonal Communication Is a Transactional Process**
2. **Interpersonal Relationships May Be Viewed as Symmetrical or Complementary**
3. **Interpersonal Communications Have Content and Relationship Dimensions**
4. **Interpersonal Communication Is a Process of Adjustment**
5. **Interpersonal Communication Is a Series of Punctuated Events**
6. **Interpersonal Communication Is Inevitable, Irreversible, and Unrepeatable**

***

INTERPERSONAL COMMUNICATION IS A TRANSACTIONAL PROCESS

A transactional perspective views interpersonal communication as (1) a process (2) whose elements are *inter*dependent...

***

Interpersonal communication is best viewed as an ever-changing process. Everything involved in interpersonal communication is in a state of flux: you're changing, the people you communicate with are changing, and your environment is changing. Sometimes these changes go unnoticed, and sometimes they intrude in obvious ways. But they're always occurring.

The process of communication is circular: one person's message serves as the stimulus for another's message, which serves as a stimulus for the other person's message, which serves as a stimulus for the other person's message, and so on. Throughout this circular process, each person serves simultaneously as a speaker and a listener, an actor *and* a reactor. Interpersonal communication is a mutually interactive process.

Elements Are Interdependent

The elements in interpersonal communication are interdependent. Each element—each part of interpersonal communication—is intimately connected to the other parts and to the whole. For example, there can be no source without a receiver; there can be no message without a source; there can be no feedback without a receiver. Because of interdependency, a change in any one element causes changes in the others…

INTERPERSONAL RELATIONSHIPS MAY BE VIEWED AS SYMMETRICAL OR COMPLEMENTARY

Interpersonal relationships can be described as either symmetrical or complementary (Bateson 1972, Watzlawick, Beavin, and Jackson 1967). In a **symmetrical relationship**, the two individuals mirror each other's behavior (Bateson 1972). If one member nags, the other member responds in kind. If one member is passionate, the other member is passionate. If one member expresses jealousy, the other member also expresses jealousy. If one member is passive, so is the other. The relationship is one of equality, with the emphasis on minimizing the differences between the two individuals.

Note, however, the problems that can arise in this type of relationship. Consider the situation of a couple in which both members are very aggressive. The aggressiveness of one person fosters aggressiveness in the other, which fosters increased aggressiveness in the first individual. As this cycle escalates, the aggressiveness can no longer be contained, and the relationship is consumed by the aggression.

In a **complementary relationship**, the two individuals engage in different behaviors. The behavior of one serves as the stimulus for the other's complementary behavior. In complementary relationships, the differences between the parties are maximized. The people occupy different positions, one superior and the other inferior, one passive and the other active, one strong and the other weak. At times, cultures establish such relationship—for example, the complementary relationship between teacher and student or between employer and employee.

Early marriages are likely to be complementary relationships where each person tries to complete himself or herself. When these couples separate and form new relationships, these new ones are more likely to be symmetrical and involve a kind of reconfirmation of their own identity (Prosky 1992). Generally, research finds that complementary couples have a lower marital adjustment level than do symmetrical couples (Main and Oliver 1988, Holden 1991).

***

INTERPERSONAL COMMUNICATIONS HAVE CONTENT AND RELATIONSHIP DIMENSIONS

Messages may make reference to the real world, for example, to the events and objects you see before you. At the same time, however, they also refer to the relationship between the people communicating. For example, a judge may say to a lawyer, "See me in my chambers immediately." This simple message has both a content aspect, which refers to the behavioral response expected (namely, that the lawyer will see the judge immediately), and a relationship aspect, which says something about the relationship between the judge and the lawyer and, as a result of this relationship, how the communication is to be dealt with. Even the use of the simple command shows that there is a status difference between the two parties. This difference can perhaps be seen most clearly if you imagine the command being made by the lawyer to the judge. Such a communication appears awkward and out of place because it violates the normal relationship between judge and lawyer.

***

In any two communications, the content dimension may be the same, but the relationship aspect may be different, or the relationship aspect may be the same and the content dimension different. For example, the judge could say to the lawyer, "You had better see me immediately" or "May I please see you as soon as possible?" In both cases, the content is essentially the same; that is, the message about the expected behavioral response is the same. But the relationship dimension is quite different. The first message signifies a definite superior-inferior relationship; the second signals a more equal relationship, one that shows respect for the lawyer.

Similarly, at times the content may be different but the relationship is essentially the same. For example, a daughter might say to her parents, "May I go away this weekend?" or "May I use the car tonight?" The content of the two questions is clearly very different, but the relationship dimension is essentially the same. It clearly reflects a superior-inferior relationship in which permission to do certain things must be secured.

Implications of Content and Relationship Dimensions

The major implications of these content and relationship dimensions center on conflict and its effective resolution. Many problems between people result from failure to recognize the distinction between the content and the relationship dimensions of communication. For example, consider the couple arguing because Pat made plans to study with friends during the weekend without first asking Chris if that would be all right. Probably both would agree that to study over the weekend is the right decision. Thus, the argument isn't primarily concerned with the content level. It centers on the relationship level; Chris expected to be consulted about plans for the weekend. Pat, in not doing so, rejected this definition of their relationship....

Consider the following interchange:

Dialogue	Comments
HE: I'm going bowling tomorrow. The guys at the plant are starting a team.	He focuses on the content and ignores any relationship implications of the message.
SHE: Why can't we ever do anything together?	She responds primarily on a relationship level, ignores the content implications of the message, and expresses her displeasure at being ignored in his decision
HE: The guys at the plant are organizing a bowling team. I'd sure like to be on the team. Would it be a problem if I went to the organizational meeting tomorrow?	Although focused on content, he is aware of the relationship dimensions of his message and includes both in his comments—by acknowledging their partnership, asking if there would be a problem, and expressing his desire rather than his decision.
SHE: That sounds great, but I was hoping we could do something together.	She focuses on the relationship dimension but also acknowledges his content orientation. Note, too, that she does not respond as though she has to defend her emphasis on relationship aspects.
HE: How about your meeting me at Pizza Hut, and we can have dinner after the organizational meeting?	He responds to the relationship aspect without abandoning his desire to join the bowling team—and incorporates it
SHE: That sounds great. I'm dying for pizza	She responds to both messages, approving of his joining the team and their dinner date.

10

Arguments over the content dimension are relatively easy to resolve. Generally, you can look up something in a book or ask someone what actually took place. It is relatively easy to verify disputed facts. Arguments on the relationship level, however, are much more difficult to resolve, partly because you may not recognize that the argument is in fact a relational one. Once you realize that, you can approach the dispute appropriately and deal with it directly.

INTERPERSONAL COMMUNICATION IS A PROCESS OF ADJUSTMENT

Interpersonal communication can take place only to the extent that the parties communicating share the same system of symbols. This is obvious when dealing with speakers of two different languages. Your communication with another person will be hindered to the extent that your language systems differ. This principle takes on particular relevance when you realize that no two persons share identical symbol systems. Parents and children, for example, not only have very different vocabularies but also, even more important, have different meanings for some of the terms they have in common. Different cultures and social groups, even when they share a common language, often have greatly differing nonverbal communication systems. To the extent that these systems differ, communication will not take place.

Part of the art of interpersonal communication is learning the other person's signals, how they're used, and what they mean. People in close relationships—either as intimate friends or as romantic partners—realize that learning the other person's signals takes a long time and, often, great patience. If you want to understand what another person means—by a smile, by saying "I love you," by arguing about trivial matters, by self-deprecating comments—you have to learn their system of signals. Furthermore, you have to share your own system of signals with others so that they can better understand you....This principle is especially important in **intercultural communication**, largely because people from different cultures use different signals and sometimes the same signals to signify quite different things ...

Communication Accommodation

An interesting theory largely revolving around adjustment is communication accommodation theory. This theory holds that speakers will adjust to or accommodate to the speaking style of their listeners to gain, for example, social approval and greater communication efficiency (Giles, Mulac, Bradac, and Johnson 1987). For example, when two people have a similar speech rate, they seem to be more attracted to each other than to those with dissimilar rates (Buller, LePoire, Aune, and Eloy 1992). Speech rate similarity has also been associated with greater immediacy, sociability, and intimacy (Buller and Aune 1992). Also, the speaker who uses language intensity similar to that of listeners is judged to have greater credibility than the speaker who uses intensity different from that of listeners (Aune and Kikuchi 1993). Still another study found that roommates who had similar communication **attitudes** (both were high in communication competence and willingness to communicate and low in verbal aggressiveness) were highest in roommate liking and satisfaction (Martin and Anderson 1995).

***

INTERPERSONAL COMMUNICATION IS A SERIES OF PUNCTUATED EVENTS

Communication events are continuous transactions. There is no clear-cut beginning and no clear-cut end. As participants in or observers of the communication act, you segment this continuous stream of communication into smaller pieces. You label some of these pieces causes of stimuli and others effects of responses.

Consider an example. A married couple is in a restaurant. The husband is flirting with another woman, and the wife is talking to her sister on her cell phone. Both are scowling at each other and are obviously in a deep nonverbal argument. Recalling the situation later, the husband might observe that the wife talked on the phone, so he innocently flirted with the other woman. The only reason for his behavior (he says) was his anger over her talking on the phone when they were supposed to be having dinner together. Notice that he sees his behavior as a response to her behavior. In recalling the same incident, the wife might say that she phoned her sister when he started flirting. The more he flirted, the longer she talked. She had no intention of calling anyone until he started flirting. To her, his behavior was the stimulus and hers was the response; he caused her behavior. Thus, the husband sees the sequence as going from phoning to flirting, and the wife sees it as going from flirting to phoning. This example is depicted visually in Figure 2.2 and is supported by research which shows that, among marrieds at least, the individuals regularly see their partner's behavior as the cause of conflict (Schutz 1999).

This tendency to divide communication transactions into sequences of stimuli and responses is referred to as **punctuation** (Watzlawick, Beavin, and Jackson 1967). Everyone punctuates the continuous sequences of events into stimuli and responses for convenience. Moreover, as the example of the husband and wife illustrates, punctuation usually is done in ways that benefit the person and are consistent with his or her self-image.

Understanding how another person interprets a situation, how he or she punctuates, is a crucial step in interpersonal understanding. It is also essential in achieving empathy (feeling what the other person is feeling). In all communication encounters, but especially in conflicts, try to see how others punctuate the situation.

Figure 2.2 Punctuation and the Sequence of Events

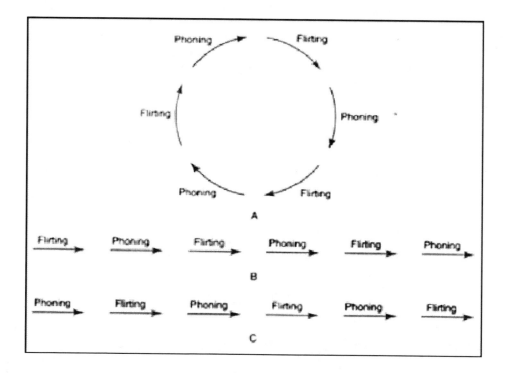

In the figure, (A) shows the actual sequence of events as a continuous series of actions with no specific beginning or end. Each action (phoning and flirting) stimulates another action, but no initial cause is identified. (B) shows the same sequence of events as seen by the wife. She sees the sequence as beginning with the husband's flirting and her phoning behavior as a response to that stimulus. (C) shows the same sequence of events from the husband's point of view. He sees the sequence as beginning with the wife's phoning and his flirting as a response to that stimulus...

***

INTERPERSONAL COMMUNICATION IS INEVITABLE, IRREVERSIBLE, AND UNREPEATABLE

Interpersonal communication cannot be prevented (is inevitable), cannot be reversed (is irreversible), and cannot be repeated (is unrepeatable). Let's look briefly at each of these qualities and their implications.

Inevitability

Often communication is thought of as intentional, purposeful, and consciously motivated. In many instances it is. But in other instances you're communicating even though you might not think you are or might not even want to communicate. Consider, for example, the new editorial assistant sitting at the desk with an "expressionless" face, perhaps staring out the window. Although this assistant might say that she or he is not communicating with the manager, the manager may derive any of a variety of messages from this behavior—for example, the assistant lacks interest, is bored, or is worried about something. In any event, the manager is receiving messages even though the assistant might not intend to communicate. In an interactional situation, all behavior is potentially communication. Any aspect of your behavior may communicate if the other person gives it message value…Even if you don't respond openly, that lack of response is itself a response and it communicates (assuming it is perceived by the other person).

Irreversibility

The processes of some systems can be reversed. For example, you can turn water into ice and then reverse the process by melting the ice. Moreover, you can repeat this reversal of ice and water for as long as you wish. Other systems, however, are irreversible. In these systems, the process can move in only one direction; it cannot go back again…

Interpersonal communication is irreversible. What you have communicated remains communicated; you cannot *un*communicate. Although you may try to qualify, negate, or somehow reduce the effects of your message, once it has been sent and received, the message itself cannot be reversed. In interpersonal interactions (especially in conflict), you need to be especially careful that you don't say things you may wish to withdraw later….

Face-to-face communication is evanescent; it fades after you have spoken. There is no trace of your communications outside of the memories of the parties involved or of those who overheard your conversation. In computer-mediated communication, however, the messages are written and may be saved, stored, and printed. Both face-to-face and computer-mediated messages may be kept confidential or revealed publicly. But computer messages may be made public more easily and spread more quickly than face-to-face messages…

Unrepeatability

In addition to being inevitable and irreversible, interpersonal communication is unrepeatable. The reason is simple: everyone and everything are constantly changing. As a result, you can never recapture the exact same situation, frame of mind, or relationship dynamics that defined a previous interpersonal act. For example, you can never repeat the experience of meeting a particular person for the first time, comforting a grieving friend on the death of his or her mother, or resolving a specific conflict…

❊ ❊ ❊

VERBAL MESSAGES

Excerpts from: Devito, J. A. (2002). *Messages: Building Interpersonal Communication Skills*, 5th Edition, Boston, MA: Allyn & Bacon, pp. 121-135.

***

THE NATURE OF VERBAL MESSAGES

In communication you use two major signal systems—the verbal and the nonverbal. This chapter focuses on the *verbal* system: how spoken and written **language** serves as a system for communicating meaning, how it can be used effectively, and how it creates problems when it isn't.

***

Messages Vary in Directness

Think about how you'd respond to the following verbal messages:

1a. I'm so bored; I have nothing to do tonight.
2a. I'd like to go to the movies. Would you like to come?

How would you describe this dinner scene in denotative terms? In connotative terms?

1b. Do you feel like hamburgers tonight?
2b. I'd like hamburgers tonight. How about you?

Statement 1a and 1b are relatively indirect; they're attempts to get the listener to say or do something without committing the speaker. Statements 2a and 2b are more direct—they state more clearly the speaker's preferences and then ask if the listener agrees.

Here we focus on the advantages and disadvantages of directness. For the most part, the advantages of indirect messages are the disadvantages of direct messages, and the disadvantages of indirect messages are the advantages of direct messages.

Advantages of Indirect Messages Indirect messages allow you to express a thought without insulting or offending anyone; they allow you to observe the rules of polite interaction. So instead of saying, "I'm bored with this group," you say, "It's getting late, and I have to get up early tomorrow." Instead of saying, "This food tastes like cardboard," you say, "I just started my diet" or "I just ate." In each instance you're stating a preference indirectly so as to avoid offending someone. Not all direct messages, however, should be considered impolite. In one study of Spanish and English speakers, for example, no evidence was found to support the assumption that politeness and directness were incompatible (Mir, 1993)....

Disadvantages of Indirect Messages Indirect messages, however, can also create problems. Consider the following dialogue:

Pat: You wouldn't like to have my parents over for dinner this weekend, would you?
Chris: I really wanted to go to the shore and just relax.
Pat: Well, if you feel you have to go to the shore, I'll make the dinner myself. You go to the shore. I really hate having them over and doing all the work myself. It's such a drag shopping, cooking, and cleaning all by myself.

Given this situation, Chris has two basic alternatives. One is to stick with the plans to go to the shore and relax. In this case Pat is going to be upset and Chris is going to be made to feel guilty for not helping with the dinner. A second alternative is to give in to Pat, help with the dinner, and not go to the shore. In this case Chris is going to have to give up a much desired plan and is likely to resent Pat's "manipulative" tactics. Regardless of which decision is made, this "win-lose" strategy creates resentment, competition, and often an "I'll get even" attitude. With direct requests, this type of situation is much less likely to develop. Consider:

Pat: I'd like to have my parents over for dinner this weekend. What do you think?
Chris: Well, I really wanted to go to the shore and just relax.

Regardless of what develops next, both individuals are starting out on relatively equal footing. Each has clearly and directly stated a preference. Although at first these preferences seem mutually exclusive, it may be possible to meet both persons' needs...

Gender and Cultural Differences in Directness

A popular stereotype in much of the United States holds that women are indirect in making requests and in giving orders—and that this indirectness communicates powerlessness, a discomfort with authority. Men, the stereotype continues, are direct, sometimes to the point of being blunt or rude. This directness communicates men's power and comfort with their own authority.

Deborah Tannen (1994b) provides an interesting perspective on these stereotypes. Women are, it seems, more indirect in giving orders; they are more likely to say, for example, "It would be great if these letters could go out today" rather than "Have these letters out by three." But Tannen (1994b, p. 84) argues that "issuing orders indirectly can be the prerogative of those in power" and in no way shows powerlessness. Power, to Tannen, is the ability to choose your own style of communication.

Men, however, are also indirect but in different situations (Rundquist, 1992). According to Tannen men are more likely to use indirectness when they express weakness, reveal a problem, or admit an error. Men are more likely to speak indirectly in expressing emotions other than anger. Men are also more indirect when they shrink from expressions of increased romantic intimacy. Men are thus indirect, the theory goes, when they're saying something that goes against the masculine stereotype.

Many Asian and Latin American cultures stress the values of indirectness, largely because indirectness enables a person to avoid appearing criticized or contradicted and thereby losing face. An example of a somewhat different kind of indirectness is the greater use of intermediaries to resolve conflict among the Chinese than among North Americans (Ma, 1992). In most of the United States, however, you're taught that directness is the preferred style. "Be up front" and "Tell it like it is" are commonly heard communication guidelines. Contrast these with the following two Japanese principles of indirectness (Tannen, 1994b):

omoiyari, a concept close to empathy, says that a listener needs to understand the speaker without the speaker's being specific or direct. This style obviously places a much greater demand on the listener than would a direct speaking style.

sassuru advises listeners to anticipate a speaker's meanings and use subtle cues from the speaker to infer his or her total meaning.

15

In thinking about direct and indirect messages, it's important to be aware of the ease with which misunderstandings can occur. For example, a person who uses an indirect style of speech may be doing so to be polite and may have been taught this style by his or her culture. If you assume, because of your own culture, that the person is using indirectness to be manipulative, then miscommunication is inevitable.

***

Message Meanings Are in People

If you wanted to know the meaning of the word *love,* you'd probably turn to a dictionary. There you'd find, according to *Webster's:* "the attraction, desire, or affection felt for a person who arouses delight or admiration or elicits tenderness, sympathetic interest, or benevolence." This is the denotative meaning.

But where would you turn if you wanted to know what Pedro means when he says, "I'm in love"? Of course, you'd turn to Pedro to discover his meaning. It's in this sense that meanings are not in words but in people. Consequently, to uncover meaning, you need to look into people and not merely into words.

Also recognize that as you change, you also change the meanings you created out of past messages. Thus, although the message sent may not have changed, the meanings you created from it yesterday and the meanings you create today may be quite different…

Message Meanings Depend on Context

Both verbal and nonverbal communications exist in a context, and that context to a large extent determines the meaning of any verbal or nonverbal behavior. In terms of verbal messages, the same words may have totally different meanings when they occur in different contexts. For example, the greeting, "How are you?" means "Hello" to someone you pass regularly on the street but means "Is your health improving?" when said to a friend in the hospital. Similarly, the meaning of a given message depends on the other behavior it accompanies or is close to in time. Saying "This stinks to high heaven" in reaction to the behavior of a politician means something quite different from that same comment in reaction to a piece of overripe cheese. Divorced from the context, it's often impossible to tell what meaning words are intended to convey. Of course, even if you know the context in detail, you still may not be able to decipher the meaning of some messages.

****

Sexism

One widespread expression of sexism is **sexist language:** language that puts down someone because of his or her gender (a term usually used to refer to language derogatory toward women). The National Council of Teachers of English has proposed guidelines for nonsexist (gender-free, gender-neutral, or sex-fair) language. These guidelines concern the use of the generic word *man,* the use of generic *he* and *his,* and sex role stereotyping (Penfield, 1987).

Generic *Man* The word *man* refers most clearly to an adult male. To use the term to refer to both men and women emphasizes maleness at the expense of femaleness. Similarly, the terms *mankind or the common man* or even *cavemen* imply a primary focus on adult males. Gender-neutral terms can easily be substituted. Instead of *mankind,* you can say *humanity, people,* or *human beings.* Instead of *the common man, you can say the average person or ordinary people.* Instead of *cavemen,* you can say *prehistoric people* or *cave dwellers.*

***

LISTEN TO THIS
Listening to Gender Differences

The best way to start thinking about gender differences in languages is to think about your own beliefs. These beliefs influence what you hear (or think you hear) and the interpretations you give to what you hear. Here are 10 statements about the "differences" between the speech of women and men. For each of the following statements, indicate whether you think the statement describes women's speech (W), men's speech (M), or women's and men's speech equally (W/M).

____   1.   This speech is logical rather than emotional.
____   2.   This speech is vague.
____   3.   This speech is endless, is not concise, and jumps from one idea to another.
____   4.   This speech is highly businesslike.
____   5.   This speech is more polite.
____   6.   This speech uses weaker forms (for example, weak intensifiers like so and such) and fewer exclamations.
____   7.   This speech contains more tag questions (questions appended to statements that ask for agreement, such as "Let's meet at ten o'clock, OK?").
____   8.   This speech uses more euphemisms (contains more polite words as substitutes for taboo or potentially offensive terms) and uses fewer swear terms.
____   9.   This speech is generally more effective.
____   10.   This speech is less forceful and less in control.

These statements were drawn from the research of Cheris Kramarae (1974a, 1974b, 1977, 1981; also see Coates & Cameron, 1989), who argues that with the exception of statements 5 and 8 (women's speech is often more "polite") these "differences" are actually stereotypes of women's and men's speech that are not in fact confirmed in analyses of actual speech. According to Kramarae, then, you should have answered "women's and men's speech equally" (W/M) for statements 1, 2, 3, 4, 6, 7, 9, and 10 and "women's speech" (W) for statements 5 and 8. Perhaps we see these "differences" in cartoons or on television and so form the impression that they actually characterize real speech.

***

…Consider using nonsexist alternatives for these and similar terms; make these alternatives (for example, *police officer* and *firefighter*) a part of your active vocabulary. Offer alternatives for each of these terms: *man, mankind, countryman, manmade, the common man, manpower, repairman, doorman, fireman, stewardess, waitress, salesman, mailman,* and *actress.*

Generic He and His The use of the masculine pronoun to refer to any individual regardless of sex is certainly declining…. There seems to be no legitimate reason why the feminine pronoun cannot alternate with the masculine pronoun to refer to hypothetical individuals … Alternatively, you can restructure your sentences to eliminate any reference to gender. For example, the NCTE Guidelines (Penfield, 1987) suggest that instead of saying, "The average student is worried about his grades," you say, "The average student is worried about grades." Instead of saying, "Ask the student to hand in his work as soon as he is finished," say, "Ask students to hand in their work as soon as they're finished."

Sex Role Stereotyping The words you use often reflect a sex role bias—the assumption that certain roles or professions belong to men and others belong to women. To eliminate sex role stereotyping from verbal communication, avoid, for example, making the hypothetical elementary school teacher female and the college professor male. Avoid referring to doctors as male and nurses as female. Avoid noting the sex of a professional with terms such as "female doctor" or "male nurse." When you're referring to a specific doctor or nurse, the person's gender will become clear when you use the appropriate pronoun: "Dr. Smith wrote the prescription for her new patient" or "The nurse recorded the patient's temperature himself."

17

Heterosexism

A close relative of sexism is heterosexism—a relatively new addition to the list of linguistic prejudices. As the term implies, *heterosexism* refers to attitudes, behaviors, and language that disparage gay men and lesbians. As with racist language, **heterosexist language** includes derogatory terms used for lesbians and gay men. For example, recent surveys in the military show that 80 percent of those surveyed heard "offensive speech, derogatory names, jokes or remarks about gays" and that 85 percent believed that such derogatory speech was "tolerated" (*New York Times,* March 25, 2000, p. A12). You also see heterosexism in more subtle forms of language usage; for example, when you qualify a professional—as in "gay athlete" or "lesbian doctor"—and, in effect, say that athletes and doctors are not normally gay or lesbian. Further, this kind of expression highlights the affectional orientation of the athlete or the doctor in a context where it may have no relevance. This practice, of course, is the same as qualifying by gender, already noted.

Still another instance of heterosexism—and perhaps the most difficult to deal with—is the presumption of heterosexuality. Usually, people assume the person they're talking to or about is heterosexual. And usually they're correct, because most people are heterosexual. At the same time, however, note that this presumption denies the lesbian or gay identity a certain legitimacy. The practice is very similar to the presumption of whiteness and maleness that we have made significant inroads in eliminating. Here are a few additional suggestions for avoiding heterosexist or what some call homophobic language.

***

- When talking about gay men and lesbians, avoid offensive nonverbal mannerisms that parody stereotypes.
- Avoid "complimenting" gay men and lesbians by saying that they "don't look it." To gay men and lesbians, this is not a compliment. Similarly, expressing disappointment that a person is gay— often thought to be a compliment, as in comments such as "What a waste!"—is not really a compliment.
- Avoid making the assumption that every gay or lesbian knows what every other gay or lesbian is thinking. It's very similar to asking a Japanese why Sony is investing heavily in the United States or, as one comic put it, asking an African American, "What do you think Jesse Jackson meant by that last speech?"
- Avoid denying individual differences. Saying things like "Lesbians are so loyal" or "Gay men are so open with their feelings," which ignore the reality of wide differences within any group, are potentially insulting to all groups.
- Avoid overattribution, the tendency to attribute just about everything a person does, says, and believes to the fact that the person is gay or lesbian. This tendency helps to recall and perpetuate stereotypes …

***

Racism

According to Andrea Rich (1974), "any language that, through a conscious or unconscious attempt by the user, places a particular racial or ethnic group in an inferior position is racist." **Racist language** expresses racist attitudes. It also, however, contributes to the development of racist attitudes in those who use or hear the language.

Racist terms are used by members of one culture to disparage members of other cultures, their customs, or their accomplishments. Racist language emphasizes differences rather than similarities and separates rather than unites members of different cultures. Generally, racist language is used by the dominant group to establish and maintain power over other groups…

Many people feel that it's permissible for members of a culture to refer to themselves in racist terms. That is, Asians may use the negative terms referring to Asians, Italians may use the negative terms referring to Italians, and so on. This issue is seen clearly in rap music, in which performers use derogatory racial terms (*New York Times,* January 24, 1993, 1, 31). The reasoning seems to be that groups should be able to laugh at themselves.

***

One possible problem, though, is that such terms may not lose their negative connotations and may simply reinforce the negative stereotypes that society has already assigned to certain groups. By using these terms, members may come to accept the labels with their negative connotations and thus contribute to their own stereotyping.

It has often been pointed out (Ossie Davis, 1973; Bosmajian, 1974) that there are aspects of language that may be inherently racist. For example, one examination of English found 134 synonyms for *white*. Of these 44 had positive connotations (for example, "clean," "chaste," and "unblemished"), and only 10 had negative connotations (for example, "whitewash" and "pale"). The remaining were relatively neutral. Of the 120 synonyms for *black,* 60 had unfavorable connotations ("unclean," "foreboding," and "deadly"), and none had positive connotations.

Cultural Identifiers

Perhaps the best way to avoid sexism, heterosexism, and racism in language is to examine the preferred cultural identifiers to use (and not to use) in talking about members of different cultures. As always, when in doubt, find out. The preferences and many of the specific examples identified here are drawn largely from the findings of the Task Force on Bias-Free Language of the Association of American University Presses (Schwartz, 1995). Do realize that not everyone would agree with these recommendations; they're presented here—in the words of the Task Force—"to encourage sensitivity to usages that may be imprecise, misleading, and needlessly offensive" (Schwartz, 1995, p. ix)....

Generally: The term *girl* should be used only to refer to a very young female and is equivalent to *boy.* Neither term should be used for people older than say 13 or 14. *Girl* is never used to refer to a grown woman; nor is *boy* used to refer to persons' blue-collar positions, as it once was. *Lady* is negatively evaluated by many, because it connotes the stereotype of the prim and proper woman. *Woman or young woman* is preferred. *Older person* is preferred to *elder, elderly, senior,* or *senior citizen* (technically, someone older than 65).

***

Generally, *Gay* is the preferred term to refer to a man who has an affectional preference for other men, and *lesbian* is the preferred term for a woman who has an affectional preference for other women. (*Lesbian* means "homosexual woman," so the phrase *lesbian woman* is redundant.) This preference for the term *lesbian* is not universal among homosexual women, however, in one survey, for example, 58 percent preferred *lesbian,* but 34 percent preferred *gay* (Lever, 1995). *Homosexual* refers to both gay men and lesbians but more often merely denotes a sexual orientation to members of one's own sex. *Gay* and *lesbian* refer to a lifestyle and not simply to sexual orientation. *Gay* as a noun, although widely used, may prove offensive in some contexts; for example, "We have two gays on the team." Although used within the gay community in an effort to remove the negative stigma through frequent usage, the term *queer*—as in "queer power"—is often resented when used by outsiders. Because most scientific thinking holds that one's sexuality is genetically determined rather than being a matter of choice, the term *sexual orientation* rather than *sexual preference* or *sexual status* (which is also vague) is preferred.

***

Generally: Most African Americans prefer *African American to black* (Hecht, Collier, & Ribeau, 1993), though *black* is often used with *white* and is used in a variety of other contexts (for example, Department of Black and Puerto Rican Studies, *Journal of Black History,* and Black History Month). The

American Psychological association recommends that both terms be capitalized, but *The Chicago Manual of Style* (a manual used by most newspapers and publishing houses) recommends using lowercase. The terms *Negro* and *colored,* although used in the names of some organizations (for example, the United Negro College Fund and the National Association for the Advancement of Colored People), are not used outside of these contexts.

Generally: *White* is used to refer to those whose roots are in European cultures, but not to Hispanics. A parallel to *African American* is the phrase *European American.* Few European Americans, however, would want to be called that; most would prefer to specify their national origins; for example, to use *German American* or *Greek American.* This preference may well change as Europe becomes a more cohesive and united entity. *People of color*—a somewhat literary-sounding term appropriate perhaps to public speaking but awkward to use in most conversations—is preferred to *nonwhites,* which implies that whiteness is the norm and nonwhiteness is a deviation from that norm. The same is true of the term *non-Christian.*

Generally: *Hispanic* is used to refer to anyone who identifies himself or herself as belonging to a Spanish-speaking culture. People born in Spain prefer to be called *Spanish* rather than *Hispanic. Latina* (female) and *Latino* (male) refer to persons whose roots are in one of the Latin American countries, such as the Dominican Republic, Nicaragua, or Guatemala. *Hispanic American* refers to United States residents from Spanish-speaking cultures and includes people from Mexico, the Caribbean, and Central and South America… *Chicana* (female) and *Chicano* (male) refer to persons with roots in Mexico, though these terms often connote a nationalist attitude (Jandt, 1995) and are considered offensive by many Mexican Americans. *Mexican American* is preferred.

***

Inuk (plural, *Inuit*) was officially adopted at the Inuit Circumpolar Conference to refer to the indigenous peoples of Alaska, Northern Canada, Greenland, and Eastern Siberia. *Inuk* is preferred to *Eskimo* (a term the U.S. Census Bureau uses), which was applied to the indigenous peoples of Alaska by Europeans and derives from a word that means "raw meat eaters" (Maggio, 1997).

Indian refers only to someone from India and is incorrectly used when applied to members of other Asian countries or to the indigenous peoples of North America. *American Indian* or *Native American* is preferred, even though many Native Americans refer to themselves as *Indians* and *Indian people.* The term *native American* (with a lowercase *n*) is most often used to refer to persons born in the United States. Although the term technically could refer to anyone born in North or South America, people outside the United States generally prefer more specific designations such as *Argentinean, Cuban,* or *Canadian.* The term *native* means an indigenous inhabitant; it's not used to mean "member of a less developed culture."

Muslim is the preferred form (rather than the older *Moslem*) to refer to a person who adheres to the religious teachings of Islam. *Quran* (rather than *Koran*) is the preferred term for the scriptures of Islam. The terms "Mohammedan" or "Mohammedanism" are not considered appropriate; they imply worship of Muhammad, the prophet, which is "considered by Muslims to be a blasphemy against the absolute oneness of God" (Maggio, 1997, p. 277).

Although there is no universal agreement, *Jewish people* is often preferred to *Jews;* and *Jewess* (a Jewish female) is considered derogatory. *Jew* should be used only as a noun and is never correctly used as a verb or an adjective (Maggio, 1997).

When history was being written with a European perspective, Europe was taken as the focal point and the rest of the world was defined in terms of its location relative to that continent. Thus, Asia became the East or the Orient, and Asians became *Orientals*—a term that is today considered inappropriate or "Eurocentric." People from Asia are *Asians,* just as people from Africa are *Africans* and people from Europe are *Europeans.*

***

USING VERBAL MESSAGES EFFECTIVELY AND CRITICALLY

A chief concern in using verbal messages is to recognize what critical thinking theorists call "conceptual distortions": mental mistakes, misinterpretations, or reasoning fallacies. Avoiding these distortions and substituting a more critical, more realistic analysis is probably the best way to improve your own use of verbal messages....

Messages Symbolize Reality (Partially)

Language symbolizes reality; it's not the reality itself. Of course, this is obvious. But consider: Have you ever reacted to the way something was labeled or described rather than to the actual item? Have you ever bought something because of its name rather than because of the actual object? If so, you were probably responding as if language were reality, a distortion called intentional orientation.

Intensional Orientation

Intensional orientation (the s in *intensional* is intentional) refers to our tendency to view people, objects, and events in the way they're talked about—the way they're labeled. For example, if Sally were labeled "uninteresting" you would, responding intensionally, evaluate her as uninteresting even before listening to what she had to say. You'd see Sally through a filter imposed by the label "uninteresting." **Extensional orientation,** on the other hand, is the tendency to look first at the actual people, objects, and events and only afterwards at their labels. In this case, it would mean looking at Sally without any preconceived labels, guided by what she says and does, not by the words used to label her. ...

The way to avoid intentional orientation is to extensionalize. Recognize that language provides labels for things and should never be given greater attention than the actual thing. Give your main attention to the people, things, and events in the world as you see them and not as they're presented in words. For example, when you meet Jack and Jill, observe and interact with them. Then form your impressions. Don't respond to them as "greedy, money-grubbing landlords" simply because Harry labeled them this way. Don't respond to Carmen as "lazy and inconsiderate" because Elaine told you she was.

THINKING CRITICALLY ABOUT
Weasel Words

A weasel is a slippery beast; just when you think you're going to catch it, it slips away. Weasel words are words whose meanings are difficult to pin down, words that allow the speaker to weasel out of an implied commitment or agreement (Larson, 1998; Wrighter, 1972). For example, a medicine that claims to work better than Brand X doesn't specify how much better or in what respect it performs better. Is it possible that it is better in one respect and less effective on nine other measures? *Better* is a weasel word. *Like* is another word often used for weaseling, as when a claim is made that "Brand X will make you feel like a new man"—or, with the *like* only implied, that "Brand X makes you feel young again." Exactly what these claims mean in specific terms would be impossible to pin down. Other weasel words are *helped, virtually, as much as,* and *more economical.* Try looking for weasel words; you'll often find them lurking in the promises of advertisers and politicians.

Allness

A related distortion is to forget that language only symbolizes a portion of reality, never the whole. When you assume that you can know all or say all about anything, you're into a pattern of behavior called **allness.** You never see all of anything. You never experience anything fully. You see a part, then conclude what the whole is like. You have to draw conclusions on the basis of insufficient evidence (because you always have insufficient evidence). A useful **extensional device** to help combat the tendency to think that all can or has been said about anything is to end each statement mentally with **etcetera**—a reminder that there is more to learn, more to know, and more to say; that every statement is inevitably incomplete (Korzybski, 1933). Some people overuse "et cetera." They use it not as a mental reminder but as a substitute for being specific. This obviously is to be avoided and merely adds to the distortions in communication.

To avoid allness, recognize that language symbolizes only a part of reality, never the whole. Whatever someone says—regardless of what it is or how extensive it is—is only part of the story.

***

Messages Express Facts and Inferences

You can construct statements of both facts and inferences without making any linguistic distinction between the two. Similarly, when you articulate or listen to such statements, you often don't make a clear distinction between statements of facts and statements of inference. Yet there are great differences between the two. Barriers to clear thinking can be created when inferences are treated as facts, a tendency called **fact-inference confusion.**

For example, you can say, "She's wearing a blue jacket," and you can say, "He's harboring an illogical hatred." Although the sentences have similar structures, they're different. You can observe the jacket and the blue color, but how do you observe "illogical hatred"? Obviously, this is not a **factual statement** but an **inferential statement.** It's one you make on the basis not only of what you observe, but of what you infer. For a statement to be considered factual, it must be made by the observer after observation and must be limited to what is observed (Weinberg, 1959).

There is nothing wrong with making inferential statements. You must make them to talk about much that is meaningful to you. The problem arises when you act as if those inferential statements are factual. You may test your ability to distinguish facts from inferences by taking the self-test below (based on tests constructed by Haney, 1973).

To avoid fact-inference confusion, phrase inferential statements not as factual but as tentative. Recognize that they may prove to be wrong. Inferential statements should leave open the possibility of alternatives. If, for example, you treat the statement "Our biology teacher was fired for poor teaching" as factual, you eliminate any alternatives. When making inferential statements be psychologically prepared to be proved wrong. If you're prepared to be wrong, you will be less hurt if you're shown to be wrong. Be especially sensitive to this distinction when you're listening. Most talk is inferential. Beware of the speaker who presents everything as fact. Analyze closely and you'll uncover a world of inferences.

Messages Are Relatively Static

Language changes only very slowly, especially when compared to the rapid change in people and things. **Static evaluation** is the tendency to retain evaluations without change even if the reality to which they refer is changing. Often a verbal statement you make about an event or person remains static ("That's the way he is; he's always been that way") while the event or person may change enormously. Alfred Korzybski (1933) used an interesting illustration. In a tank you have a large fish and many small fish, the natural food for the large fish. Given freedom in the tank, the large fish will eat the small fish. If you partition the tank, separating the large fish from the small fish by a clear piece of glass, the large fish will continue to attempt to eat the small fish but will fail, knocking instead into the glass partition.

Eventually, the large fish will learn the futility of attempting to eat the small fish. If you now remove the partition, the small fish will swim all around the big fish, but the big fish will not eat them. In fact, the large fish will die of starvation while its natural food swims all around. The large fish has learned a pattern or "map" of behavior, and even though the actual territory has changed, the map remains static.

While you'd probably agree that everything is in a constant state of flux, do you act as if you know this? Do you act in accordance with the notion of change or just accept it intellectually? Do you realize, for example, that even if you've failed at something once, you need not fail again? Your evaluations of yourself and of others must keep pace with the rapidly changing real world; otherwise your attitudes and beliefs will be about a world that no longer exists.

The mental **date** is an extensional device that helps to keep language (and thinking) up to date and helps guard against static evaluation. The procedure is simple: Mentally date your statements and especially your evaluations. Remember that Pat Smith 1984 is not Pat Smith 1996; academic abilities 1992 are not academic abilities 1996. T. S. Eliot, in *The Cocktail Party,* said, "What we know of other people is only our memory of the moments during which we knew them. And they have changed since then… at every meeting we are meeting a stranger." In listening, look carefully at messages that claim that what was true still is. It may or may not be. Look for change.

Messages Can Obscure Distinctions

Messages can obscure distinctions, both by generalizing about people or events that are covered by the same label but are really quite different (indiscrimination) and by making it easy to focus on extremes rather than on the vast middle ground (polarization).

Indiscrimination

Each word in the language can refer to lots of things; most general terms refer to a wide variety of individuals. Words such as *teacher* or *textbook* or *computer program* refer to lots of specific people and things. When you allow the general term to obscure the specific differences (say, among teachers or textbooks), you're into a pattern called indiscrimination.

Indiscrimination refers to the failure to distinguish between similar but different people, objects or events. It occurs when you focus on classes and fail to see that each phenomenon is unique and needs to be looked at individually.

Everything is unlike everything else. Our language, however, provides you with common nouns such as *teacher, student, friend, enemy, war, politician,* and *liberal.* These lead you to focus on similarities—to group together all teachers, all students, all politicians. At the same time, the terms divert attention away from the uniqueness of each person, each object, and each event.

THINKING CRITICALLY ABOUT

Snarl and Purr Words

Semanticist S. I. Hayakawa (Hayakawa & Hayakawa, 1989) coined the terms *snarl words* and *purr words* to further clarify the distinction between denotative and connotative meanings. Snarl words are highly negative: "She's an idiot." "He's a pig." "They're a bunch of losers." Sexist, racist, and heterosexist language and hate speech provide lots of other examples. Purr words are highly positive: "She's real sweetheart." "He's a dream." "They're the greatest."

Snarl and purr words, although they may sometimes seem to have denotative meaning and to refer to the "real world," are actually connotative in meaning. These terms do not describe people or events in the real world but rather the speaker's feelings about these people or events.

Examples?

Give examples of recent interactions you've had in which someone made snarl or purr statements that were used or interpreted as if they had denotative meaning.

This misevaluation is at the heart of stereotyping on the basis of nationally, race, religion, gender, and affectional orientation. A stereotype, you'll remember from Chapter 3, is a fixed mental picture of a group that is applied to each individual in the group without regard to his or her unique qualities.

Most stereotypes are negative and denigrate the group to which they refer. Some, however, are positive. A particularly glaring example is the popular stereotype of Asian American students as successful, intelligent, and hardworking.

Whether stereotypes are positive or negative, they create the same problem: They provide you with shortcuts that are often inappropriate. For instance, when you meet a particular person, your first reaction may be to pigeonhole him or her into some category—perhaps religious, national, or academic ("She's typical academic: never thinks of the real world"). Then you assign to this person all the qualities that are part of your stereotype. Regardless of the category you use or the specific qualities you're ready to assign, you fail to give sufficient attention to the individual's unique characteristics. Two people may both be Christian, Asian, and lesbian, for example, but each will be different from the other. Indiscrimination is a denial of another's uniqueness.

A useful antidote to indiscrimination (and stereotyping) is the **index.** This mental subscript identifies each individual as an individual even though both may be covered by the same label. Thus, $politician_1$ is not $politician_2$; $teacher_1$ is not $teacher_2$. The index helps you to discriminate among without discriminating against. Although a label ("politician," for example) covers all politicians, the index makes sure that each politician is thought about as an individual.

Polarization

Another way in which language can obscure differences is in its predominance of extreme terms and its relative lack of middle terms, a situation that often leads to **polarization.** You can appreciate the role language plays in fostering polarization by trying to identify the opposites of the following terms: *happy, long, wealth, life, healthy, up, left, legal, heavy, strong.* This should have been relatively easy; you probably identified the opposites very quickly. Now, however, identify the middle terms, the terms referring to the middle ground between the italicized terms and the opposites you supplied. These terms should have been more difficult to come up with and should have taken you more time and effort. Further, if you compare your responses with those of others, you'll find that most people agree on the opposites; most people would have said *unhappy, short, poverty,* and so on. But when it comes to the middle terms, the degree of agreement will be much less. Thus, language makes it easy to focus on opposites and relatively difficult to talk about the middle areas.

Polarization, then, is the tendency to look at the world in terms of opposites and to describe it in extremes—good or bad, positive or negative, healthy or sick, intelligent or stupid. Polarization is often referred to as the fallacy of "either/or" or "black and white." Most of life exists somewhere between the extremes. Yet there's a strong tendency to view only the extremes and to categorize people, objects, and events in terms of these polar opposites.

Problems are created when opposites are used in inappropriate situations. For example, "The politician is either for us or against us." These options do not include all possibilities. The politician may be for us in some things and against us in other things, or may be neutral. During the Vietnam War people were categorized as either hawks or doves. But clearly many people were neither, and many were hawks on certain issues and doves on others.

To correct this polarizing tendency, beware of implying (and believing) that two extreme classes include all possible classes—that an individual must be one or the other; with no alternatives ("Are you pro-abortion or pro-life?"). Most people, most events, most qualities exist between polar extremes. When others imply that there are only two sides or two alternatives, look for the middle ground.

Summary of Concepts and Skills

In this chapter we considered verbal messages. The chapter discussed the nature of language and the ways in which language works; the concept of disconfirmation and how it relates to sexist, hetero-sexist, and racist language; and the ways in which language can be used more effectively.

1. Language meanings are in people, not in things.
2. Meanings are context based; the same message in a different context will likely mean something different.
3. Language is both denotative (conveying meanings that are objective and generally agreed upon) and connotative (conveying meanings that are subjective and generally highly individual).
4. Language varies in directness; you can use language to state exactly what you mean or to hedge and state your meaning very indirectly.
5. Language is a cultural institution; each culture has its own rules identifying the ways in which language should be used.
6. Language varies in abstraction; words can vary from extremely general to extremely specific.

7. Disconfirmation is the process of ignoring the presence and the communications of others. Confirmation is accepting, supporting, and acknowledging the importance of the other person.
8. Sexist, heterosexist, and racist language puts down and negatively evaluates various cultural groups.
9. Using language effectively involves eliminating conceptual distortions and substituting more accurate assumptions about language, the most important of which are;
10. Language symbolizes reality; it's not the reality itself.
11. Language can express both facts and inferences, and distinctions need to be made between them.
12. Language is relatively static; because reality changes so rapidly, you need to constantly revise the way you talk about people and things.
13. Language can obscure distinctions in its use of general terms and in its emphasis on extreme rather than middle terms.

The nature of language, disconfirmation, and popular conceptual distortions have important implications for the skills of effective communication.

READING THREE

NON-VERBAL MESSAGES

Excerpts from: Devito, J. A. (2002). *Messages: Building Interpersonal Communication Skills*, 5th Edition, Boston, MA: Allyn & Bacon, pp.152-173.

***

THE CHANNELS OF NONVERBAL MESSAGES

Body Messages

Two aspects of the body are especially important in communicating messages. First, the movements you make with your body communicate; second, the general appearance of your body communicates.

Body Movements Nonverbal researchers identify five major types of body movements: emblems, illustrators, affect displays, regulators, and adaptors (Ekman & Friesen, 1969; Knapp & Hall, 1996).

TABLE 6.1 Five Body Movements

NAME AND FUNCTION	EXAMPLES
EMBLEMS directly translate words or phrases	"OK" sign, "come here" wave, hitchhiker's sign
ILLUSTRATORS accompany and literally "illustrate" verbal messages	Circular hand movements when talking of a circle; hands far apart when talking of something large
AFFECT DISPLAYS communicate emotional meaning	Expression of happiness, surprise, fear, anger, sadness, disgust/contempt
REGULATORS monitor, maintain, or control the speaking of another	Facial expressions and hand gestures indicating "keep going," "slow down," or "what else happened?"
ADAPTORS satisfy some need	Scratching head

Body Appearance Your general body appearance also communicates. Height, for example, has been shown to be significant in a wide variety of situations. Tall presidential candidates have a much better record of winning the election than do their shorter opponents. Tall people seem to be paid more and are favored by interviewers over shorter applicants (Keyes, 1980; Devito & Hecht, 1990; Knapp & Hall, 1996; Jackson & Ervin, 1992).

Your body also reveals your race (through skin color and tone) and may also give clues as to your more specific nationality. Your weight in proportion to your height will also communicate messages to others, as will the length, color, and style of your hair.

Your general **attractiveness** is also a part of body communication. Attractive people have the advantage in just about every activity you can name. They get better grades in school, are more valued as friends and lovers, and are preferred as coworkers (Burgoon, Buller, & Woodall, 1995)…

Facial Messages

Throughout your interpersonal interactions, your face communicates many things, especially your emotions. Facial movements alone seem to communicate the degree of pleasantness, agreement, and sympathy felt; the rest of the body doesn't provide any additional information. But for other emotional messages—for example, the intensity with which an emotion is felt—both facial and bodily cues are used (Graham, Bitti, & Argyle, 1975; Graham & Argyle, 1975).

Some researchers in nonverbal communication claim that facial movements may express at least the following eight emotions: happiness, surprise, fear, anger, sadness, disgust, contempt, and interest (Ekman, Friesen, & Ellsworth, 1972). Others propose that in addition, facial movements may also communicate bewilderment and determination (Leathers, 1997).

***

Of course, some emotions are easier to communicate and to decode than others. For example, in one study, participants judged happiness with 55 to 100 percent accuracy, surprise with 38 to 86 percent accuracy, and sadness with 19 to 88 percent accuracy (Ekman, Friesen, & Ellsworth, 1972). Research finds that women and girls are more accurate judges of facial emotional expression than men and boys (Hall, 1984; Argyle, 1988).

Facial Management As you grew up, you learned your culture's nonverbal system of communication. You also learned certain **facial management techniques;** for example, to hide certain emotions and to emphasize others. Table 6.2 identifies four types of facial management techniques that you will quickly recognize (Malandro, Barker, & Barker, 1989).

We learn these facial management techniques along with display rules that tell us what emotions to express when; they're the rules of appropriateness. For example, when someone gets bad news in which you may secretly take pleasure, the display rule dictates that you frown and otherwise nonverbally signal your displeasure. If you violate these display rules, you will be judged insensitive.

Facial Feedback The **facial feedback hypothesis** holds that your facial expressions influence physiological arousal (Lanzetta, Cartwright-Smith, & Kleck, 1976; Zuckerman, Klorman, Larrance, & Spiegel, 1981). In one study, for example, participants held a pen in their teeth to simulate a sad expression and then rated a series of photographs. Results showed that mimicking sad expressions actually increased the degree of sadness the participants reported feeling when viewing the photographs (Larsen, Kasimatis, & Frey, 1992).

Further, support for this hypothesis comes from a study that compared participants who (1) felt emotions such as happiness and anger with those who (2) both felt and expressed these emotions. In support of the facial feedback hypothesis, subjects who felt and expressed the emotions became emotionally aroused faster than did those who only felt the emotion (Hess, Kappas, McHugo, Lanzetta, et al., 1992).

28

TABLE 6.2 Facial Management Techniques

Can you identify a specific situation in which you or someone with whom you interacted used one of these techniques?

TECHNIQUE	FUNCTION	EXAMPLE
Intensifying	To exaggerate a feeling	Exaggerating surprise when friends throw you a party, to make your friends feel better
Deintensifying	To underplay a feeling	Covering up your own joy in the presence of a friend who didn't receive such good news
Neutralizing	To hide a feeling	Covering up your sadness so as not to depress others
Masking	To replace or substitute the expression of one emotion for another	Expressing happiness in order to cover up your disappointment at not receiving the gift you had expected

Generally, research finds that facial expressions can produce or heighten feelings of sadness, fear, disgust, and anger. But this effect does not occur with all emotions; smiling, for example, doesn't seem to make us feel happier (Burgoon, Buller, & Woodall, 1995)... facial expressions can influence some feelings but not all (Burgoon, Buller, & Woodall, 1995; Cappella, 1993).

Eye Messages

From Ben Jonson's poetic exhortation "Drink to me only with thine eyes, / And I will pledge with mine" to the scientific observations of modern researchers (Hess, 1975; Marshall, 1983), the eyes have long been regarded as the most important nonverbal message system.

Research on communication via the eyes (a study known technically as oculesis) shows that these messages vary depending on the duration, direction, and quality of the eye behavior. For example, in every culture there are strict, though unstated, rules for the proper duration for eye contact. In our culture the average length of gaze is 2.95 seconds. The average length of mutual gaze (two persons gazing at each other) is 1.18 seconds (Argyle & Ingham, 1972; Argyle, 1988). When eye contact falls short of this amount, you may think the person is uninterested, shy, or preoccupied. When the appropriate amount of time is exceeded, you may perceive the person as showing unusually high interest.

The direction of the eye glance also communicates. In much of the United States, you're expected to glance alternately at the other person's face, then away, then again at the face, and so on. The rule for the public speaker is to scan the entire audience, not focusing for too long on or ignoring any one area of the audience. When you break these directional rules, you communicate different meanings—abnormally high or low interest, self-consciousness, nervousness over the interaction, and so on...

Eye Contact With eye contact you send a variety of messages. One such message is a request for feedback. In talking with someone, we look at her or him intently, as if to say, "Well, what do you think?" ... Another type of message informs the other person that the channel of communication is open and that he or she should now speak. … Eye contact may also send messages about the nature of the relationship. For example, if you engage in prolonged eye contact coupled with a smile, you'll signal a positive relationship. … Eye contact messages enable you to psychologically lessen the physical distance between yourself and another person. When you catch someone's eye at a party for example, you become psychologically close though physically far apart.

Eye Avoidance The eyes are "great intruders," observed sociologist Erving Goffman (1967). When you avoid eye contact or avert your glance, you help others to maintain their privacy. You may do this when you see a couple arguing in public: You turn your eyes away (though your eyes may be wide open) as if to say, "I don't mean to intrude; I respect your privacy." Goffman refers to this behavior as **civil inattention.**

***

Space Messages

Your use of space to communicate—an area of study known technically as **proxemics**—speaks as surely and as loudly as words and sentences. Speakers who stand close to their listener, with their hands on the listener's shoulders and their eyes focused directly on those of the listener, communicate something very different from speakers who stand in a corner with arms folded and eyes downcast. Similarly, for example, **territoriality**—the territory you occupy or own and the way you protect this territory—also communicates. The executive office suite on the top floor with huge windows, private bar, and plush carpeting communicates something totally different from the six-by-six foot cubicle.

Spatial Distance Messages Edward Hall (1959, 1966) distinguishes four distances that define the type of relationship between people and the type of communication in which they're likely to engage. In **intimate distance,** ranging from actual touching to 18 inches, the presence of the other individual is unmistakable. Each person experiences the sound, smell, and feel of the other's breath. You use intimate distance for lovemaking, comforting, and protecting. This distance is so short that most people do not consider it proper in public.

Personal distance refers to the protective "bubble" that defines your personal space, ranging from 18 inches to 4 feet. This imaginary bubble keeps you protected and untouched by others… At **social distance,** ranging from 4 to 12 feet, you lose the visual detail you have at personal distance. You conduct impersonal business and interact at a social gathering at this social distance… **Public distance,** from 12 to more than 25 feet, protects you. At this distance you could take defensive action if threatened. …

Influences on Spatial Distances Several factors influence the way you relate to and use space in communicating. Here are a few examples of how status, culture, subject matter, gender, and age influence space communication (Burgoon, Buller, & Woodall, 1995).

People of equal *status* maintain shorter distances between themselves than do people of unequal status. When status is unequal, the higher-status person may approach the lower-status person more closely than the lower-status person would approach the higher-status person.

Members of different *cultures* treat space differently. For example, those from northern European cultures and many Americans stand fairly far apart when conversing; those from southern European and Middle Eastern cultures tend to stand much closer. …

When discussing personal *subjects* you maintain shorter distances than with impersonal subjects. Also, you stand closer to someone who is praising you than to someone criticizing you.

Your *gender* also influences your spatial relationships. Women generally stand closer to each other than men. Similarly, when someone approaches another person, he or she will come closer to a woman than to a man. With increasing *age* there is a tendency for the spaces to become larger.…

***

Touch Messages

Touch communication, or **tactile communication,** is perhaps the most primitive form of communication (Montagu, 1971). Touch develops before the other senses; even in the womb the child is stimulated by touch. Soon after birth the child is fondled, caressed, patted, and stroked. In turn, the child explores its world through touch and quickly learns to communicate a variety of meanings through touch.

The Meanings of Touch Researchers in the field of **haptics**—the study of touch—have identified the major meanings of touch (Jones & Yarbrough, 1985):

- *Positive emotion.* Touch may communicate such positive feelings as support, appreciation, inclusion, sexual interest or intent, and affection.
- *Playfulness.* Touch often communicates our intention to play, either affectionately or aggressively.
- *Control.* Touch may direct the behaviors, attitudes, or feelings of the other person. To get attention, for example, you may touch a person as if to say, "Look at me" or "Look over here."
- *Ritual.* Ritualistic touching centers on greetings and departures; for example, shaking hands to say hello or goodbye or hugging, kissing, or putting your arm around another's shoulder when greeting or saying farewell.
- *Task-relatedness.* Task-related touching occurs while you're performing some function, such as removing a speck of dust from another person's face or helping someone out of a car.

***

Paralanguage Messages

The term **paralanguage** refers to the vocal but nonverbal dimensions of speech. It refers to how you say something, not what you say. A traditional exercise students use to increase their ability to express different emotions, feelings, and attitudes is to repeat a sentence while accenting or stressing different words. One popular sentence is, "Is this the face that launched a thousand ships?" Significant differences in meaning are easily communicated depending on where the speaker places the stress. Consider the following variations:

1. *Is* this the face that launched a thousand ships?
2. Is *this* the face that launched a thousand ships?
3. Is this *the face* that launched a thousand ships?
4. Is this the face *that launched* a thousand ships?
5. Is this the face that launched *a thousand ships*?

Each sentence communicates something different; in fact, each asks a different question, although the words are the same. All that distinguishes the sentences is stress, one aspect of paralanguage.

In addition to stress and **pitch** (highness or lowness), paralanguage includes such **voice qualities** or vocal characteristics as **rate** (speed), **volume** (loudness), and rhythm as well as the vocalizations you make in crying, whispering, moaning, belching, yawning, and yelling (Trager, 1958, 1961; Argyle, 1988). A variation in any of these features communicates. When you speak quickly, for example, you communicate something different from when you speak slowly. Even though the words may be the same, if the speed (or volume, rhythm, or pitch) differs, the meanings people receive will also differ.

Judgments About People Paralanguage cues are often used as a basis for judgments about people; for example, evaluations of their emotional state or even their personality. A listener can accurately judge the emotional state of a speaker from vocal expression alone, if both speaker and listener speak the same language…

***

Judgments About Communication Effectiveness The rate or speed at which people speak is the aspect of paralanguage that has received the most attention (MacLachlan, 1979). Rates of speech are of interest to the advertiser, the politician, and, in fact, anyone who tries to convey information or influence others. They are especially important when time is limited or expensive.

In one-way communication (when one person is doing all or most of the speaking and the other person is doing all or most of the listening), those who talk fast (about 50 percent faster than normal) are more persuasive. People agree more with a fast speaker than with a slow speaker and find the fast speaker more intelligent and objective.

***

Silence Messages

Like words and gestures, **silence,** too, communicates important meanings and serves important functions (Johannesen, 1974; Jaworski, 1993). Silence allows the speaker *time to think,* time to formulate and organize his or her verbal communications. Before messages of intense conflict, as well as before those confessing undying love, there is often silence. Again, silence seems to prepare the receiver for the importance of these messages.

Some people use silence as a *weapon* to hurt others. We often speak of giving someone "the silent treatment." After a conflict, for example, one or both individuals may remain silent as a kind of punishment…

Sometimes silence is used as a *response to personal anxiety,* shyness, or threats. You may feel anxious or shy among new people and prefer to remain silent. By remaining silent you preclude the chance of rejection…

Silence may be used *to prevent communication* of certain messages. In conflict situations silence is sometimes used to prevent certain topics from surfacing and to prevent one or both parties from saying things they may later regret….

Like the eyes, face, or hands, silence can also be used *to communicate emotional responses* (Ehrenhaus, 1988). Sometimes silence communicates a determination to be uncooperative or defiant; by refusing to engage in verbal communication, you defy the authority or the legitimacy of the other person's position. Silence is often used to communicate annoyance, particularly when accompanied by a pouting expression, arms crossed in front of the chest, and nostrils flared…

***

CULTURE AND NONVERBAL MESSAGES

Not surprisingly, nonverbal communication is heavily influenced by culture. Consider a variety of differences. At the sight of unpleasant pictures, members of some cultures (American and European, for example) will facially express disgust. Members of other cultures (Japanese, for example) will avoid facially expressing disgust (Ekman, 1985b; Matsumoto, 1991).

Although Americans consider direct eye contact an expression of honesty and forthrightness, the Japanese often view this as a lack of respect. The Japanese will glance at the other person's face rarely and then only for very short periods (Axtell, 1990). Among some Latin Americans and American Indians, direct eye contact between, say, a teacher and a student is considered inappropriate, perhaps aggressive; appropriate student behavior is to avoid eye contact with the teacher. Table 6.4…presents a variety of other nonverbal signals, identified by Axtell (1993), that can get you into trouble if used in certain cultures.

32

TABLE 6.4 A Few Nonverbal Behaviors That Can Get You into Trouble

Can you identify other behaviors that can create cultural problems?

COMMUNICATION BEHAVIOR	MAY BE CONSIDERED
Blinking your eyes	Impolite in Taiwan
Folding your arms over your chest	Disrespectful in Fiji
Waving your hand	Insulting in Nigeria and Greece
Gesturing with the thumb up	Rude in Australia
Tapping your two index fingers together	An invitation to sleep together in Egypt
Pointing with the index finger	Impolite in many Middle Eastern countries
Bowing to a lesser degree than your host	A statement of superiority in Japan
With a clenched fist, inserting your thumb between your index and middle finger	Obscene in some southern European countries
Pointing at someone with your index and third fingers	A wish that evil fall on the person in some African countries
Resting your feet on a table or chair	Insulting in some Middle Eastern countries

In the United States living next door to someone means that you're expected to be friendly and to interact with that person. This cultural expectation seems so natural that Americans and members of many other cultures probably don't even consider that it is not shared by all cultures. In Japan, the fact that your house is next to another's does not imply that you should become close or visit each other. Consider, therefore, the situation in which a Japanese person buys a house next to an American. The Japanese may see the American as overly familiar and as taking friendship for granted. The American may see the Japanese as distant, unfriendly, and unneighborly. Yet each person is merely fulfilling the expectations of his or her own culture (Hall & Hall, 1987).

Different cultures also assign different meanings to colors. Some of these cultural meanings are listed in Table 6.5—but before looking at the table, think about the meanings your own culture gives to such colors as red, green, black, white, blue, yellow, and purple.

TABLE 6.5 Some Cultural Meanings of Color

This table, constructed from research reported by Henry Dreyfuss (1971), Nancy Hoft (1995), and Norine Dresser (1996), illustrates only some of the different meanings that colors may communicate in different cultures. As you read this table, consider the meanings you give to these colors and where your meanings came from.

COLOR	CULTURAL MEANINGS AND COMMENTS
Red	In China red signifies prosperity and rebirth and is used for festive and joyous occasions; in France and the United Kingdom, it signifies masculinity; in many African countries, blasphemy or death; and in Japan, anger and danger. Koreans, especially Korean Buddhists, use red ink only to write a person's name at the time of death or on the anniversary of the person's death; this creates lots of problems when American teachers use red ink to mark homework.
Green	In the United States green signifies capitalism, "go ahead," and envy; in Ireland, patriotism; among some Native Americans, femininity; to the Egyptians, fertility and strength; and to the Japanese, youth and energy.
Black	In Thailand black signifies old age, in parts of Malaysia courage, and in much of Europe death.
White	In Thailand white signifies purity; in many Muslim and Hindu cultures, purity and peace; but in Japan and other Asian countries, death and mourning.
Blue	In Iran blue signifies something negative, in Egypt truth, and in Ghana joy; among the Cherokee it signifies defeat, and for Egyptians virtue and truth.
Yellow	In China yellow signifies wealth and authority, in the United States caution and cowardice, in Egypt happiness and prosperity; and in many countries throughout the world, femininity.
Purple	In Latin America purple signifies death, in Europe royalty, in Egypt virtue and faith, in Japan grace and nobility, and in China barbarism.

***

Touching too varies greatly across cultures. For example, African Americans touch one another more than do whites. Similarly, touching declines from kindergarten to the sixth grade for white but not for African American children (Burgoon, Buller, & Woodall, 1995). Similarly, Japanese touch one another much less than do Anglo-Saxons, who in turn touch one another much less than do southern Europeans (Morris, 1977; Burgoon, Buller, & Woodall, 1995).

***

Not surprisingly, the role of silence is seen differently in different cultures (Basso, 1972). Among the Apache, for example, mutual friends do not feel the need to introduce strangers who may be working in the same area or on the same project. The strangers may remain silent for several days. During this time the individuals look each other over, trying to determine if the other person is all right. Only after this period do the individuals talk. When courting, especially during the initial stages, the Apache remain silent for hours; if they do talk, they generally talk very little. Only after a couple has been dating for several months will they have lengthy conversations. These periods of silence are generally attributed to shyness or self-consciousness. But the use of silence is explicitly taught to Apache women, who are especially discouraged from engaging in long discussions with their dates. Silence during courtship is a sign of modesty to many Apache.

34

In Iranian culture there's an expression, *qahr,* which means not being on speaking terms with someone, giving someone the silent treatment. For example, when children disobey their parents, or are disrespectful, or fail to do their chores as they should, they are given this silent treatment. With adults *qahr* may be instituted when one person insults or injures another. After a cooling-off period, *ashti* (making up after *qahr*) may be initiated. *Qahr* last for a relatively short time when between parents and children but longer when between adults. *Qahr* is more frequently initiated between two women than between two men, but when men experience *qahr* it lasts much longer and often requires the intercession of a mediator to establish *ashti* (Behzadi, 1994).

Time is another communication channel with great cultural differences. Two types of cultural time are especially important in nonverbal communication: formal and informal. In U.S. culture, *formal time* is divided into seconds, minutes, hours, days, weeks, months, and years. Other cultures may use seasons or phases of the moon to delineate time periods…As these examples illustrate, formal time units are arbitrary. The culture establishes them for convenience.

Informal time terms are more general—for example, expressions such as "forever," "immediately," "soon," "right away," "as soon as possible." Informal time creates the most communication problems, because the terms have different meanings for different people.

Another interesting distinction is that between **monochronic** and **polychronic time orientations** (Hall, 1959, 1976; Hall & Hall, 1987). Monochronic people or cultures (the United States, Germany, Scandinavia, and Switzerland are good examples) schedule one thing at a time. Time is compartmentalized; there is a time for everything, and everything has its own time. Polychronic people or cultures (Latin Americans, Mediterranean people, and Arabs are good examples), on the other hand, schedule multiple things at the same time. Eating, conducting business with several different people, and taking care of family matters may all be conducted at the same time. No culture is entirely monochronic or polychronic; rather, these are general tendencies that are found across a large part of the culture. Some cultures combine both time orientations; Japanese and parts of U.S. culture are examples in which both orientations are found.

Attitudes toward time vary from one culture to another. One study, for example, measured the accuracy of clocks in six cultures—Japan, Indonesia, Italy, England, Taiwan, and the United States. Japan had the most accurate clocks, Indonesia the least accurate. And a measure of the speed at which people in these six cultures walked found that the Japanese walked the fastest, the Indonesians the slowest (LeVine & Bartlett, 1984).

***

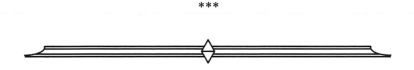

READING FOUR

SOCIAL COGNITION:
HOW WE THINK ABOUT THE SOCIAL WORLD

Excerpts from Chapter 3 of Aronson, E., Wilson, T., Akert, R., Fehr, B. (2007) *Social Psychology, 3rd Canadian Edition.* Toronto, Pearson Education.

***

In this chapter we will explore social cognition, which is the way people think about themselves and the social world-how they select, interpret, remember, and use social information to make judgments and decisions. Not only are we able to recognize chairs and other physical objects without any apparent effort, but we are also able to make complex judgments about people at lightning speed. Of course, we also occasionally make mistakes, and sometimes these mistakes are costly. In this chapter you will see how sophisticated we are as social thinkers, as well as the kinds of mistakes we are prone to make.

To understand how people think about the social world and how accurate their impressions are likely to be, one needs to distinguish between two different kinds of social cognition. One kind of thought is quick and automatic - as when we effortlessly classify an object as a chair. Other times, we pause and think about ourselves and our environment, and think carefully about what is going on around us. You may have spent hours deliberating over important decisions in your life, such as where to go to university or college, what to choose as your major, and whether to break up with your boyfriend or girlfriend. This is the second kind of social cognition-controlled thinking, which is more effortful and deliberate. Often the automatic and controlled modes of social cognition work very well together. Think of a plane that can fly on automatic pilot, that monitors hundreds of complex systems and adjusts instantly to changes in atmospheric conditions. The autopilot does just fine most of the time, though occasionally it is important for the human pilot to take over and fly the plane manually. Humans, too, have an "automatic pilot" that monitors their environment, draws conclusions, and directs their behaviour. But people can also "override" this automatic type of thinking and analyze a situation slowly and deliberately. We will begin by examining the nature of automatic thinking.

On Automatic Pilot: Low-Effort Thinking

People typically size up a new situation very quickly: they figure out who is there, what is happening, and what might happen next. Often these quick conclusions are correct. When you attended your first university class, for example, you probably made quick assumptions about who people were (the person standing at the lectern was the professor) and how to behave. We doubt that you confused the class with a birthday party. And you probably reached these conclusions without even being aware that you were doing so.

Imagine a different approach. Every time you encounter a new situation, you stop and think about it slowly and deliberately, like Rodin's statue The Thinker. When you are introduced to someone new, you have to excuse yourself for fifteen minutes while you analyze what you have learned and how much you like the person. When you drive down an unfamiliar road, you have to pull over and analyze its twists and turns before knowing how to proceed. Sounds exhausting, doesn't it? Instead, we form impressions of people quickly and effortlessly, and navigate new roads without much conscious analysis of what we are doing. We see an object with two dark lenses attached to curved arms and immdiately know that those are sunglasses. We do these things by engaging in an automatic analysis of our environments, based on our past experiences and knowledge of the world. Automatic thinking is thought that is nonconscious, unintentional, involuntary, and effortless. While different kinds of automatic thinking meet these criteria to varying is nonconscious, degrees (Bargh & Ferguson, 2000; Wegner & Bargh, 1998), for our purposes we can define automaticity as thinking that satisfies all or most of these criteria.

People as Everyday Theorists: Automatic Thinking with Schemas

Automatic thinking helps us understand new situations by relating them to our prior experiences. When we meet someone new, we don't start from scratch to figure out what he or she is like; we categorize the person as "an engineering student" or "like my cousin Helen." The same goes for places, objects, and situations. When we walk into a fast-food restaurant we've never visited, we know, without thinking, not to wait at a table for a waiter and a menu. We know that we have to go to the counter and order because our mental "script" automatically tells us that this is what we do in fast-food restaurants, and we assume that this one is no different.

More formally, people use schemas, which are mental structures that organize our knowledge about the social world. These mental structures influence the information we notice, think about, and remember (Bartlett, 1932; Markus, 1977; Taylor & Crocker, r1981). The term schema is very general; it encompasses our knowledge about many things other people, ourselves, social roles (e.g., what a librarian or an engineer is like), and specific events (e.g., what usually happens when people eat a meal in a restaurant). In each case, our schemas contain our basic knowledge and impressions that we use to organize what we know about the social world and interpret new situations.

There is evidence that information relevant to a particular schema will be processed more quickly than information unrelated to it. For example, in one study, Gardner, MacIntyre, and Lalonde (1995) asked English-speaking students living in Quebec to rate the characteristics of various groups (e.g., English Canadians, French Canadians, males, females). Participants were faster when rating the stereotypical characteristics of each group than when rating its nonstereotypical characteristics; for example, when the target group was males, characteristics such as rugged, impatient, and talkative were rated more quickly than characteristics such as irreligious, artistic, and impolite.

We also tend to "fill in the blanks" with schema-consistent information. In a study by Kunda, Sinclair, and Griffin (1997), students at the University of Waterloo were told that Michael was either a salesperson or an actor, and that his friends described him as very extroverted. They were then asked, "What kinds of behaviours do you suppose they have in mind when they describe him this way?" The researchers found that when told that Michael was a salesperson, participants generated pushy descriptions (e.g., loud speaking, monopolizes conversations), whereas when Michael was described as an actor, they generated descriptions such as "life of the party" and "not afraid of the spotlight." In another study by these researchers, participants read about John the lawyer versus John the construction worker, and were asked to generate examples of aggressive behaviour that John might perform. John the lawyer was seen as more likely to argue, whereas John the construction worker was seen as more likely to punch and fight (Kunda, Sinclair, & Griffin, 1997). In other words, given a label, we fill in the blanks with all kinds of schema-consistent information.

Stereotypes About Race And Weapons

When applied to members of a social group such as gender or race, schemas are commonly referred to as stereotypes... [S]tereotypes can be applied rapidly and automatically when we encounter other people; for example, recent experiments have tested whether people's stereotypes about African Americans can influence their perception of whether a person is holding a weapon. In one U.S. study, non-Black college students saw pairs of pictures in rapid succession on a computer screen (Payne, 2001). The first picture was always of a face, whereas the second picture depicted either a tool or a gun. Participants were told to pay attention only to the second picture and to press one key if it was a tool and another if it was a gun, as rapidly and as accurately as they could. In fact, they had only half a second to identify the picture and press a key.

It just so happened that half of the faces in the first picture were of Whites and half were of Blacks. The question was, did the race of the face influence people's perception of whether they saw a gun or a tool in the second picture? Indeed it did; people were significantly more likely to misidentify a tool as a gun when it was preceded by a Black face than when it was preceded by a White face.

In another study that resembled real-life situations, people performed a task that was even closer to the dilemma faced by police officers (Correil et al., 2002). Participants played a video game in which they saw photographs of young men in realistic settings, such as in a park, at a train station, and on a city sidewalk. Half of the men were Black and half were White. And half of the men in each group were holding a handgun and half were hold a non-threatening object such as a cell phone, wallet, or camera. Participants were instructed to press a button labeled "shoot" if the man in the picture had a gun and a button labeled "don't shoot" if he did not. Like a real police officer, they had very little time to make up their minds (just over half a second). Participants won or lost points on each round of the game, modeled after the risks and benefits faced by officers in real life. Participants earned 5 points for not shooting someone who did not have a gun and 10 points for shooting someone who did have a gun. They lost 20 points if they shot someone who was not holding a gun and lost 40 points if they failed to shoot someone who was holding a gun (which, in real life, would be the most life-threatening situation for a police officer).

The results? Participants were especially likely to pull the trigger when the person in a picture was Black, whether or not he was holding a gun. This "shooter bias" meant that people made relatively few errors when a Black person was in fact holding a gun but also that they made the most errors, shooting an unarmed person, when a Black person was not holding a gun…Sadly, these effects are not limited to the laboratory. In 1999, police officers in the Bronx mistakenly thought that Amadou Diallo, a Black man, was reaching for a gun when he was simply reaching for his wallet. Police fired a total of 41 shots at Diallo, killing him instantly. Before leaving this study, we should note that when the men in the picture were White, participants made about the same number of errors whether the men were armed or unarmed.

In research along the same lines, it was found that when a crime object, such as a gun, was displayed on a computer screen, White university students and police officers were quicker to identify Black faces (also presented on a computer screen) than White faces (Eberhardt, et al., 2004). Similarly, a study conducted at the University of British Columbia found that when participants were seated in a dark room, the negative stereotype of Blacks, particularly traits relevant to danger (e.g., crime), came to mind more quickly than when participants were seated in a brightly lit room (Schaller, Park, & Mueller, 2003). This tendency was particularly pronounced among those who regard the world as a dangerous place.

In all these studies, people had to respond so quickly that they had little time to control their responses or think about what they were doing. The errors they made were the result of automatic thinking that is rooted, perhaps, in the pervasive stereotypes in American culture about Black people and violence. Correll and colleagues (2002) found that the people who were most likely to show the shooter bias were those who believed the strongest that there was a cultural stereotype linking Black people to violence even when they did not personally endorse this stereotype. The authors argue that knowledge of a 'cultural stereotype can influence people in insidious ways, even if the people are not themselves prejudiced.

Obviously, the effects we have been discussing are not limited to stereotypes about Black people and violence. In the summer of 2005, news headlines focused on the police shooting of Jean Charles de Menezes, a 27-year-old Brazilian man living in London, England. De Menezes was shot five times in the head at close range as he approached a subway station. Members of Britain's Muslim community expressed alarm and concern that police were targeting men whose race or physical characteristics resembled those accused of the July 7, 2005, subway bombings. The response from the head of police was that tragic mistakes such as this occur because officers are forced to make "incredibly difficult fast-time decisions in life-threatening situations" (Frankel, 2005).

We should keep in mind that stereotypes, such as the American police officers' assumptions about Amadou Diallo and the London police officers' assumptions about Jean Charles de Menezes-based on their race-are a special case of a more general phenomenon: people's organization of the world into schemas

(Kunda, 1999). In addition to schemas about classes of people, for example, we have schemas about specific individuals (e.g., what Aunt Jane is like), social roles (e.g., how mothers are supposed to behave), or how people act in specific situations (e.g., at a party or in a restaurant). We now turn to properties of schemas more generally.

The Function Of Schemas: Why Do We Have Them?

We have been focusing on the negative consequences of schemas, cases in which people "fill in the blanks" in erroneous ways (e.g., assuming a Brazilian man on his way to a subway train is a suspected terrorist). However, we should point out that the consequences of "filling in the blanks" are not always negative. A few years ago, one of your authors, Beverley Fehr, attended a fundraising breakfast for a counseling centre. Guest speaker Pamela Wallin described an early incident that nearly cost her her broadcasting career - or so she thought. The setting was the G-7 economic summit in Quebec, and CTV had managed to arrange interviews with the British prime minister and the chancellor of West Germany. Wallin excitedly announced to viewers that they should stay tuned, because after the commercial break they would be interviewing then prime minister Margaret Thatcher and chancellor Helmut "Shit." Convinced that she had just committed career suicide, Wallin left the studio. The first few people she ran into commented that, for a moment, they thought she had mispronounced Chancellor Schmidt's name but then realized that the vacuum cleaner had been on, or that they hadn't had their morning coffee yet, or .... In short, the fact that Pamela Wallin said "shit" on television was so inconsistent with people's schemas of her that they convinced themselves they must have heard wrong - that she really must have said "Schmidt."

If schemas can sometimes make us misperceive the world, why do we have them? Schemas are typically very useful for helping us organize and make sense of the world and to fill in the gaps of our knowledge…. What would it be like to have no schemas about the social world? What if everything you encountered was inexplicable, confusing, and unlike anything else you'd ever known? Tragically, this is what happens to people who suffer from a neurological disorder called Korsakov's syndrome. People who suffer from Korsakov's syndrome also have difficulty forming schemas…This can be so unsettling even terrifying that some people with Korsakov's syndrome go to great lengths to try to impose meaning on their experiences. The neurologist Oliver Sacks gives the following description of a Korsakov patient named Mr. Thompson:

> He remembered nothing for more than a few seconds. He was continually disoriented. Abysses of amnesia continually opened beneath him, but he would bridge them, nimbly, by fluent confabulations and fictions of all kinds. For him they were not fictions, but how he suddenly saw, or interpreted, the world. Its radical flux and incoherence could not be tolerated, acknowledged, for an instant-there was, instead, this strange, delirious, quasi-coherence, as Mr. Thompson, with his ceaseless, unconscious, quick-fire inventions, continually improvised a world around him, for such a patient must literally make himself (and his world) up every moment (Sacks, 1987).

In short, it is so important to us to have continuity, to relate new experiences to our past schemas that people who lose this ability invent schemas where none exist.

Schemas are particularly important when we encounter information that can be interpreted in a number of ways, because they help us reduce ambiguity. Consider a classic study by Harold Kelley (1950), in which students in different sections of an economics class were told that a guest lecturer would be filling in that day. In order to create schema about what the guest lecturer would be like, Kelley told the students that the economics department was interested in how different classes reacted to different instructors and that the students would therefore receive a brief biographical note about the instructor before he arrived. The note contained information about the instructor's age, background, and teaching experience. It also gave one of two descriptions of his personality. One version said, "People who know him consider him to be a rather cold person, industrious, critical, practical, and determined." The other version was identical, except that the phrase "a rather cold person" was replaced with "a very warm person." The stunts were randomly given one of these personality descriptions.

The guest lecturer then conducted a class discussion for 20 minutes, after which the students rated their impressions of him. How humorous was he? How sociable? How considerate? Given that there was some ambiguity in this situation - after all, the students had seen the instructor for only a brief time - Kelley hypothesized that they would use a schema provided by the biographical note to fill in the blanks. This is exactly what happened. The students who expected the instructor to be warm gave him significantly higher ratings than did the students who expected him to be cold, even though all of the students had observed the same teacher behaving in the same way. Students who expected the instructor to be warm were also more likely to ask him questions and to participate the class discussion.

It is important to note that there is nothing wrong with what Kelley's students did. As long as people have reason to believe their schemas are accurate, it is perfectly reasonable to use them to resolve ambiguity. If a suspicious-looking character approaches you in a dark alley and says, "Take out your wallet," your schema about such encounters tells you the person wants to steal your money, not admire pictures of your family. This schema helps you avert a serious, and perhaps deadly, misunderstanding. The danger comes when we automatically apply schemas that are not accurate, such as assuming that every dark-skinned person boarding a subway train with a backpack is a terrorist carrying explosives.

Schemas As Memory Guides

Human memory is reconstructive, and people generally fill in the blanks with information that is consistent with their schemas. We don't remember exactly what occurred in a given setting as if our minds were a film camera recording precise images and sounds. Instead, we remember some information that was there-particularly information our schemas lead us to notice and pay attention to, and we remember other information that was never there but that we have unknowingly added later (Darley & Akert, 1993; Markus & Zajonc, 1985)…

Not surprisingly, memory reconstructions tend to be consistent with people's schemas. For example, participants in a study by Linda Carli (1999) read a story about a woman named Barbara and her relationship with a man named Jack. After dating for a while, Barbara and Jack went to a ski lodge for a weekend getaway. In one condition, the story ended with Jack proposing to Barbara; in the other condition, the story ended with Jack sexually assaulting Barbara. Two weeks later, participants took a memory test in which they read several facts about Jack and Barbara, and judged whether these facts had appeared in the story. In the marriage-proposal condition, people were likely to misremember details that were consistent with a proposal schema, such as "Jack wanted Barbara to meet his parents" and "Jack gave Barbara a dozen roses." Neither of these details had been in the story, but people in the proposal condition tended to think they were…. Similarly, people in the sexual assault condition were likely to misremember details that were consistent with a sexual assault schema, such as "Jack liked to drink" and "Jack was unpopular with women."

The fact that people filled in the blanks in their memory with schema-consistent details suggests that schemas become stronger and more resistant to change over time….

Which Schemas Are Applied? Accessibility And Priming

The social world is full of ambiguous information that is open to interpretation. Imagine for example that, while you are riding on a city bus, a man gets on and sits beside you. He mutters incoherently to himself, stares at everyone on the bus, and repeatedly rubs his face with one hand. How would you make sense of his behaviour? You have several schemas you could use. What dictates your choice? Your impression of the man on the bus can be affected by accessibility, defined as the extent to which schemas and concepts are at the forefront of our minds and therefore are likely to be used when we are making judgments about the social world (Ford & Thompson, 2000; Higgins, 1996; Todorov & Bargh, 2002; Wyer & Srull, 1989).

There are two kinds of accessibility. First, some schemas can be chronically accessible because of past experience (Chen & Andersen, 1999; Dijksterhuis & van Knippengerg, 1996; Higgins & Brendl, 1995; Rudman & Borgida, 1995). This means that these schemas are constantly active and ready to use to interpret ambiguous situations. For example, if there is a history of alcoholism in your family, traits describing an alcoholic are likely to be very accessible to you, increasing the likelihood that this schema will come to mind when you are thinking about the behaviour of the man on the bus. If someone you know suffers from mental illness, however, then thoughts about how the mentally ill behave are more likely to be accessible than are thoughts about alcoholics, leading you to interpret the man's behaviour very differently.

Second, traits can also become temporarily accessible for more arbitrary reasons (Bargh, 1990, 1996; Higgins & Bargh, 1987; Stapel & Koomen, 2000). This means that a particular schema or trait is not always accessible but happens to be primed by something people have been thinking about or doing before encountering an event. Suppose, for example, that right before the man on the bus sat down, you were reading Ken Kesey's One Flew over the Cuckoo's Nest, a novel about patients in a mental hospital. Given that thoughts about mental patients are at the forefront of your mind, you would probably assume that the man's strange behaviour was attributable to mental illness. If, on the other hand, thoughts about alcoholism were fresh in your mind - for example, you had just looked out the window and seen a person leaning against a building drinking a bottle of wine - you would probably assume that the man on the bus had had a few too many drinks... These are examples of priming, whereby a recent experience such as reading Kesey's novel increases the accessibility of certain traits (i.e., those describing the mentally ill), making it more likely that you will use these traits to interpret a new event - such as the behaviour of the man on the bus-even though this new event is completely unrelated to the one that originally primed the traits.

Tory Higgins, Stephen Rholes, and Carl Jones (1977) illustrated this priming effect, in the following experiment. Research participants were told they would take part in two unrelated studies. The first was a perception study, in which they would be asked to identify different colours while at the same time memorizing a list of words. The second was a reading comprehension study, in which they would be asked to read a paragraph about someone named Donald and then give their impressions of him. This paragraph is shown in Figure 3.4. Take a moment to read it. What do you think of Donald?

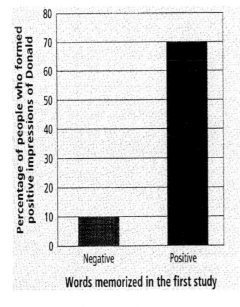

Description of Donald

Donald spent a great deal of time in his search for what he liked to call excitement. He had already climbed Mt. McKinley, shot the Colorado rapids in a kayak, driven in a demolition derby, and piloted a jet-powered boat—without knowing very much about boats. He had risked injury, and even death, a number of times. Now he was in search of new excitement. He was thinking, perhaps, he would do some skydiving or maybe cross the Atlantic in a sailboat. By the way he acted, Donald seemed well aware of his ability to do many things well. Other than business engagements, Donald's contacts with people were rather limited. He felt he didn't really need to rely on anyone. Once Donald made up his mind to do something it was as good as done no matter how long it might take or how difficult the going might be. Only rarely did he change his mind even when it might well have been better if he had.

You might have noticed that many of Donald's actions are ambiguous, interpretable in either a positive or a negative manner. Take the fact that he piloted a boat without knowing much about it and wants to sail across the Atlantic Ocean. It is possible to put a positive spin on these acts, and decide that Donald has an admirable sense of adventure. It's just as easy, however, to put a negative spin on these acts, and assume that Donald is a rather reckless and foolhardy individual.

How did the participants interpret Donald's behaviour? Higgins, Rhodes, and Jones (1977) found, as expected, that it depended on whether positive or negative traits were primed and accessible. In the first study, the researchers divided people into two groups and gave them different words to memorize. People who had first memorized the words adventurous, self-confident, independent, and persistent later formed positive impressions of Donald, viewing him as a likeable man who enjoyed new challenges. People who had first memorized reckless, conceited, aloof, and stubborn later formed negative impressions of Donald, viewing him as a stuck-up person who took needlessly dangerous chances.

But it was not memorizing just any positive or negative words that influenced people's impressions of Donald. In other conditions, research participants memorized words that were also positive or negative, such as neat or disrespectful. However, these traits did not influence their impressions of Donald because the words did not apply to Donald's actions. Consequently, thoughts have to be applicable before they will act as primes, exerting an influence on our impressions of the social world. Priming is a good example of automatic thinking because it occurs quickly, unintentionally, and unconsciously. When judging others, people are usually not aware that they are applying concepts or schemas that they just happened to be thinking about earlier.

Schemas Can Persist Even After They Are Discredited

Sometimes we hear something about an issue or another person that later turns out not to be true. For example, a jury might hear something in the courtroom about a defendant that is untrue or labelled as inadmissible evidence, and be told by the judge to disregard that information. The problem is that, because of the way schemas operate, our beliefs can persist even after the evidence for them proves to be false.

Imagine, for example, that you were a participant in a study by Lee Ross, Mark Lepper, and Michael Hubbard (1975). You are given a stack of cards containing both real and fictitious suicide notes. Your job is to guess which ones are real, supposedly to study the effects of physiological processes during decisionmaking. After each guess, the experimenter tells you whether you are right or wrong. As the experiment progresses, you find out that you are pretty good at this task. In fact, you guess right on 24 of the 25 cards, which is much better than the average performance of 16 correct.

At this point, the experimenter tells you that the study is over and explains that it was actually concerned with the effects of success and failure on physiological responses. You learn that the feedback you received was bogus; that is, you had been randomly assigned to a condition in which the experimenter said you were correct on 24 of the cards, regardless of how well you actually did. The experimenter then gives you a final questionnaire, which asks you how many answers you think you really got correct and how many times you think you would guess correctly on a second, equally difficult test with new cards. What would you say? Now pretend you were in the other condition of the study. Here, everything is identical, except you are told that you got only 10 of the 25 answers correct, which is much worse than average. How would you respond to the questionnaire after you found out the feedback was bogus?

Depending on which condition you were in, you would have formed a schema that you were either very good or very poor at the task. What happens when the evidence for this schema is discredited? Ross, Lepper, and Hubbard (1975) went to some pains to ensure that the participants realized the feedback had been randomly determined and had nothing to do with their actual performance. Even though the participants believed this, those who had received the "success" feedback still thought they had gotten more of the items correct and would do better on a second test than did people who had received, the "failure" feedback. In addition, when asked how they would do on a new test, success participants said they would do better than failure participants did....

This result is called the perseverance effect because people's beliefs persisted even after the original evidence was discredited. When people received the feedback, they explained to themselves why they were doing so well or so poorly, bringing to mind evidence from their past that was consistent with their performance (e.g., "I am really very perceptive. After all, last week I was the only one who realized that Jennifer was depressed" or "Well, I'm not so good at this stuff, my friends always say I'm the last to know"). Even after learning that the feedback was false, these thoughts were still fresh in people's minds, making them think they were particularly good or poor at the task (Anderson, 1995; Anderson & Lindsay, 1998; Davies, 1997; Sherman & Kim, 2002).

Making Our Schemas Come True: The Self-Fulfilling Prophecy

We have seen that, when people encounter new evidence or have old evidence discredited, they tend not to revise their schemas as much as we might expect. People are not always passive recipients of information, however-they often act on their schemas and, in doing so, can change the extent to which these schemas are supported or contradicted. In fact, people can inadvertently make their schemas come true by the way they treat others. This is called a self-fulfilling prophecy, and it occurs when people have an expectation about what another person is like that influences how they act toward that person, which in turn causes that person to behave consistently with their original expectations-making the expectations come true. Figure 3.6 illustrates this self-perpetuating cycle.

Figure 3.6

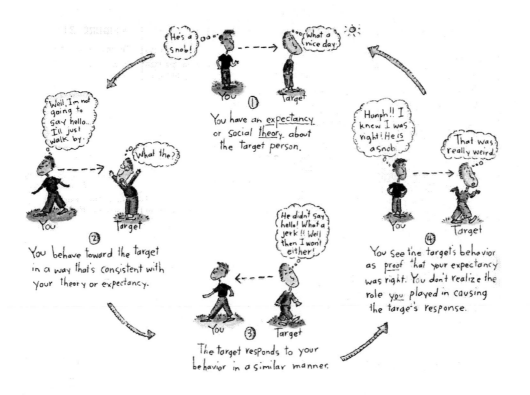

In what has become one of the most famous studies in social psychology, Robert Rosenthal and Lenore Jacobson (1968) examined whether teachers expectations for students can have self-fulfilling effects. They administered an IQ test to all students in an elementary school and told the teachers that some of the students had scored so well that they were sure to "bloom" academically in the upcoming year. In fact, this was not necessarily true; the students identified as "bloomers" were chosen randomly by the researchers. As we discussed [earlier] the use of random assignment means that, on average, the students designated as bloomers were no smarter or more likely to bloom than any of the other kids. The only way in which these students differed from their peers was in the minds of the teachers. (Neither the students nor their parents were told anything about the results of the test.)

After creating the expectation in the teachers' minds that some of the kids would do especially well, Rosenthal and Jacobson waited to see what would happen. They observed the classroom dynamics periodically over the school year, and at the end of the year they tested all of the children again with an actual IQ test. Did the prophecy come true?

Indeed it did. The students in each class who had been labelled as bloomers showed significantly higher gains in their IQ scores than did the other students.... The teachers' expectations had become reality. Rosenthal and Jacobson's findings have since been replicated in a number of both experimental and correlational studies (Babad, 1993; Blank, 1993; Brattesani, Weinstein, & Marshall, 1984; Jussim, 1989, 1991; Madon, Jussim, & Eccles, 1997; Smith, Jussim, & Eccles, 1999).

Did the teachers in the Rosenthal and Jacobson (1968) study callously decide to give more encouragement and attention to the bloomers? Not at all. Most teachers are quite dedicated and try not to treat some students in a more advantageous manner than others. Far from being a conscious, deliberate act, the self-fulfilling prophecy is instead an example of automatic thinking (Chen & Bargh, 1997). Interestingly, the teachers in the Rosenthal and Jacobson (1968) study reported that they spent slightly less time with the students who were labelled as bloomers. In subsequent studies, however, teachers have been found to treat bloomers (i.e., the students they expect to do better) differently in four general ways:

a) They create a warmer emotional climate for bloomers, giving them more personal Attention, encouragement, and support
b) They give bloomers more material to learn and material that is more difficult
c) They give bloomers more and better feedback on their work, and
d) They give bloomers more opportunities to respond in class and give them longer to respond (Brophy, 1983; Jussim, 1986; Rosenthal, 1994; Snyder, 1984).

A distressing implication of research on the self-fulfilling prophecy is that our schemas may be resistant to change. Suppose a teacher has the schema that boys possess innate ability that makes them superior in math to girls. "But Mr. Jones," we might say, "how can you hold such a belief? There are plenty of girls who do very well in math." Mr. Jones would probably be unconvinced because he would have data to support his schema. "In my classes over the years," he might reply, "nearly three times as many boys as girls have excelled at math." His error lies not in his characterization of the evidence but in his failure to realize his role in producing it. Robert Merton referred to this process as a "reign of error," whereby people can "cite the actual course of events as proof that [they were] right from the very beginning" (1948)…

Cultural Determinants Of Schemas

***

Clearly, an important source of our schemas is the culture in which we grow up. In fact, schemas are a very important way in which cultures exert their influence-namely, by instilling mental structures that influence the very way we understand and interpret the world…we will see that across cultures there are fundamental differences in people's schemas about themselves and the social world, with some interesting consequences. For now, we point out that the schemas our culture teaches us have a large influence on what we notice and remember about the world. One researcher, for example, interviewed a Scottish settler and a local Bantu herdsman in Swaziland, a small country in southeast Africa (Bartlett, 1932). Both men had been present at a complicated cattle transaction that had transpired a year earlier. The Scottish man had little memory about the details of the transaction; he had to consult his records to remember how many cattle were bought and sold and for how much. The Bantu man, when asked, promptly recited from memory every detail of the transaction, including from whom each ox and cow had been bought, the colour of each ox and cow, and the price of each transaction. The Bantu people's memory for cattle is so good that they do not bother to brand them; if a cow happens to wander away and get mixed up with a neighbour's herd, the owner simply goes over and takes it back - having no trouble distinguishing his cow from dozens of others,

It is not the case that the Bantu simply have better memories overall. Each of us has a superb memory, in the areas that are important to us, areas for which we thus have well-developed schemas. Cattle are a central part of the Bantu economy and culture, and, as a result, the Bantu have well-developed schemas about cattle. To a person who grew up in a different culture, one cow might look like any other; this person undoubtedly has well- developed schemas about, and an excellent memory for, things that are quite foreign to the Bantu, such as transactions on the Toronto Stock Exchange, foreign movies, or, for that matter, the reasons why people wear braces on their teeth.

To summarize, we have seen that the amount of information we face every day is so vast that we have to reduce it to a manageable size. In addition, much of this information is ambiguous or difficult to decipher. One way we deal with this "blooming, buzzing, confusion," in William James's words, is to rely on schemas, which help us reduce the amount of information we need to take in and help us interpret ambiguous information. These schemas are applied quickly, effortlessly, and unintentionally; in short, they are one form of automatic thinking. Another form of automatic thinking is to apply specific rules and shortcuts when thinking about the social world. These shortcuts are, for the most part, extremely useful, but as we will see, they too can sometimes lead to erroneous inferences about the world.

Mental Strategies and Shortcuts: Heuristics

How did you decide which university to apply to? One strategy would be to investigate thoroughly each of the more than 70 universities in Canada as well as all of the community colleges. You could read every catalogue from cover to cover, visit every campus, and inter- view as many faculty members, deans, and students as you could find. Getting tired yet? Such a strategy would, of course, be prohibitively time-consuming and costly. Instead of considering every university and college, most high school students narrow down their choice to a small number of options and find out what they can about these schools.

This example is like many decisions and judgments we make in everyday life. When deciding which job to accept, what car to purchase, or whom to marry, we usually do not conduct a thorough search of every option ("Okay, it's time for me to get married; I think I'll consult the census lists of unmarried adults in my city and begin my interviews tomorrow"). Instead, we use mental strategies and shortcuts that make the decision easier, allowing us to get on with our lives without turning every decision into a major research project. These shortcuts do not always lead to the best decision…Mental shortcuts are efficient, however, and usually lead to good decisions in a reasonable amount of time (Gigerenzer, 2000; Gilovich & Griffin, 2002; Nisbett & Ross, 1980).

What kinds of shortcuts do people use? One, as already discussed, is to use schemas to understand new situations. Rather than starting from scratch when examining our options, we often apply previous knowledge and schemas. We have many such schemas, out everything from colleges and universities (e.g., what community colleges are like versus what universities are like) to other people. When making specific kinds of judgments and decisions, however, we do not always have a ready-made schema to apply. At other times, there are too many schemas that could apply, and it is not clear which one to use. What do we do?

At times like these, people often use mental shortcuts called judgmental heuristics. The word heuristics comes from the Greek word meaning "to discover"; in the field of social cognition, heuristic refers to the mental shortcuts people use to make judgments quickly and efficiently. Before discussing these heuristics, we should note that they do not guarantee people will make accurate inferences about the world. In fact, we will document many mental errors in this chapter. However, keep in mind that people use heuristics for a reason: most of the time, they are highly functional and serve as well.

How Easily Does It Come To Mind? The Availability Heuristic

Suppose you are sitting in a restaurant with several friends one night, when it becomes clear that the waiter made a mistake with one of the orders. Your friend Michael ordered he veggie burger with onion rings but instead got the veggie burger with fries. "Oh, well," he says, "I'll just eat the fries." This starts a discussion of whether he should have sent back his order, and some of your friends accuse Michael of being unassertive. He turns to you and asks, "Do you think I'm an unassertive person?" How would you answer this question?

One way, as we have seen, would be to call on a ready-made schema that provides the answer. If you know Michael well and have already formed a picture of how assertive he is, you can recite your answer easily and quickly: "Don't worry, Michael, if I ever need a used-car salesman, you'd be the first person I'd call." Suppose, though, that you've never really thought about how assertive Michael is and have to think about your answer. In such a situation, you might rely on how easily different examples come to mind. If it is easy to think of times when Michael acted assertively (e.g., "that time he stopped someone from butting in line in front of him at the movies"), you will conclude that Michael is a pretty assertive guy. If it is easier to think of times when Michael acted unassertively (e.g., "that time he let a phone solicitor talk him into buying an expensive long-distance calling plan"), you will conclude that he is pretty unassertive.

This mental shortcut is called the availability heuristic, which is basing a judgment on the ease with which you can bring something to mind (Dougherty, Gettys, & Ogden, 1999; Manis et al., 1993; Rothman & Hardin, 1997; Schwarz & Vaughn, 2002). The first studies demonstrating "the availability heuristic" were conducted by Tversky and Kahneman (1973). In one of their studies, participants were presented with the names of famous and non-famous people. When asked to recall the names, participants were more likely to remember the famous ones, even though there were fewer famous than non-famous names on the list. Presumably, the famous names were more available in memory. When other participants were asked to estimate the number of male and female names, they gave higher estimates for the gender that was famous…

There are many situations in which the availability heuristic is a good strategy. If you can easily bring to mind several times when Michael stood up for his rights, he probably is an assertive person; if you can easily bring to mind several times when he was timid or meek, he probably is not an assertive person. The trouble with the availability heuristic is that sometimes what is easiest to bring to mind is not typical of the overall picture, leading to faulty conclusions. When physicians are diagnosing diseases, for example, it might seem a relatively straightforward matter for them to observe people's symptoms and figure out what disease, if any, they have. Sometimes, though, medical symptoms are quite ambiguous and might be a sign of several different disorders. Do doctors use the availability heuristic, whereby they are more likely to consider diagnoses that come to mind easily? Several studies of medical diagnoses suggest that the answer is Yes (Eraker (e.g.& Politser, 1988; Fox, 1980; Travis, Phillippi, & Tonn, 1989; Weber et al., 1993).

Consider Dr. Robert Marion's diagnosis of Nicole, a bright, sweet, nine-year-old patient. Nicole was normal in every way, except that once or twice a year she had strange, neurological attacks, characterized by disorientation, insomnia, slurred words, and strange mewing sounds. Nicole had been hospitalized three times, had seen more than a dozen specialists, and had undergone many diagnostic tests, including CT scans, brain-wave tests, and virtually every blood test there is. The doctors were stumped; they could not figure out what was wrong with her. Within minutes of seeing her, however, Dr. Marion correctly diagnosed her problem as a rare, inherited blood disorder called acute intermittent porphyria (AIP). The blood chemistry of people with this disorder often gets out of sync, causing a variety of neurological symptoms. It can be controlled with a careful diet and by avoiding certain medications.

How did Dr. Marion diagnose Nicole's disorder so quickly, when so many other doctors failed to do so? Dr. Marion had just finished writing a book on the genetic diseases of historical figures, including a chapter on George III of England, who -you guessed it -suffered from AIP. "I didn't make the diagnosis because I'm a brilliant diagnostician or because I'm a sensitive listener," reports Dr. Marion. "I succeeded where others failed because Nicole] and I happened to run into each other in exactly the right place, at exactly the right time" (Marion, 1995). In other words, Dr. Marion used the availability heuristic. AIP happened to be available in his memory, making the diagnosis easy. Though this was a happy outcome of the use of the availability heuristic, it is easy to see how it can go wrong. As Dr. Marion says, "Doctors are just like everyone else. We go to the movies, watch TV, read newspapers and novels. If we happen to see a patient who has symptoms of a rare disease that was featured on the previous night's 'Movie of the Week,' we're more likely to consider that condition when making a diagnosis" (Marion, 1995). That's all well and good if your disease happens to be the topic of last night's movie. It's not so good if your disease doesn't happen to be available in your doctor's memory, as was the case with the 12 doctors Nicole had seen previously.

Do people use the availability heuristic to make judgments about themselves? It might seem that we have well-developed ideas about our own personalities, such as how assertive we are. Often, however, people do not have firm schemas about their own traits (Kunda et al., 1993; Markus, 1977) and thus people might make judgments about themselves based on how easily they can recall examples of their own behaviour. To see if this is the case, Norbert Schwarz and his colleagues (1991) performed a clever experiment in which they altered how easy it was for people to bring to mind examples of their own past behaviours. In one condition, they asked people to think of 6 times they had acted assertively. Most people found this to be pretty easy; examples came to mind quickly. In another condition, the researchers asked people to think of 12 times they had acted assertively. This was much more difficult; people had to try hard to think of this many examples. All participants were then asked to rate how assertive they thought they really were.

The question was, did people use the availability heuristic (the ease with which they could bring examples to mind) to infer how assertive they were? …they did. People asked to think of 6 examples rated themselves as relatively assertive, because it was easy to think of 6 examples ("Hey, this is easy I guess I'm a pretty assertive person"). It might surprise you to learn that people asked to think of 12 examples rated themselves as relatively unassertive, because it was difficult to think of 12 examples ("Hmm, this is hard - I must not be a very assertive person").… In short, people use the availability heuristic - the ease with which they can bring examples to mind-when making judgments about themselves and other people.

How Similar Is A To B? The Representativeness Heuristic

Suppose, for example, that you attend a university in Alberta. One day you meet a student named Lyric standing in line for one of the food outlets on campus. Lyne is fashionably dressed, orders a café au lait and a croissant, and, from the way she pronounces croissant, it's apparent she speaks French. Which province do you think Lyne is from? Because Lyne seems similar to many people's stereotype of a Quebecer, you might guess Quebec, or at least seriously entertain this possibility. If so, you would be using the representativeness heuristic, which is a mental shortcut whereby people classify something according to how similar it is to a typical case - such as how similar Lyne is to your conception of Quebecers (Gilovich & Savitsky, 2002; Kahneman & Frederick, 2002; Kahneman & Tversky, 1973; Tversky & Kahneman, 1974).

Categorizing things according to representativeness is often a perfectly reasonable thing to do. If you did not use the representativeness heuristic, how else would you decide where Lyric comes from? Should you just randomly choose a province? Actually, there is another source of information you might use. If you knew nothing about Lyne, it would be wise to guess that she was from Alberta, because at Albertan universities there are more in-province than out-of-province students. If you guessed Alberta, you would be using what is called "base rate" information, or information about the relative frequency of members of different categories in the population (e.g., the percentage of students at information about the frequency Albertan universities who are from Alberta).

Taking Things At Face Value: The Anchoring And Adjustment Heuristic

Suppose you are a judge trying to decide what sentence to give a defendant who has been convicted of aggravated sexual assault. There are all kinds of relevant facts you could bring to bear on this important decision, such as the severity of the crime, sentencing guidelines from the Criminal Code of Canada, and your sense of how likely the defendant is to commit this offence again. Surprisingly, you might also be influenced by quite irrelevant numbers that happen to be on your mind, such as the sentence you gave to the previous defendant or the fact that you are attending someone's twenty-fifth birthday party that night. If you are thinking about the number 25, you might give a longer sentence than if the number 2 were on your mind. If so, you would be using the anchoring and adjustment heuristic (Tversky & Kahneman, 1974), a mental shortcut whereby people use a number or value as a starting point and then adjust their answer away from this anchor. If the number 25 is on your mind, you might begin by saying, "Hmm, 25 sounds a little long; I'll give the guy 10 years." If the number 2 was on your mind, you might start with this and adjust upward, ending with a substantially shorter sentence than if you had started out with 25.

Like all the other mental shortcuts we have considered, the anchoring and adjustment heuristic is a good strategy under many circumstances. If you have reason to believe that a starting value is valid and informative, then it can be a logical place to begin. Suppose, for example, that an experienced prosecutor whom you respect recommends a prison term of 25 years. Using this as a starting point would be quite reasonable, because the prosecutor probably knows more details about the case than you do and probably has good reason for this recommendation. This is in fact what judges did in a recent study (Englich & Mussweiler, 2001). They gave a significantly longer prison sentence in a hypothetical sexual assault case when the prosecutor recommended a longer sentence versus a shorter one.

The problem with anchoring and adjustment heuristics is that people are sometimes influenced by completely arbitrary anchor values. The same study, for example, found that judges gave higher sentences when they read that a first-year computer science student recommended a long sentence than when the computer science student recommended a short sentence, even though virtually all of the judges said that the computer science student's recommendation had no bearing on their decision. Similar anchoring effects have been found in many other studies (e.g., Chapman & Johnson, 2002; Epley & Gilovich, 2001; Mussweiler & Strack, 1999; Slovic & Lichtenstein, 1971; Wilson et al., 1996).

Anchor values can influence us in two ways. First, when we consider a starting point, we selectively retrieve from memory information that is consistent with it. A judge who initially considers 10 years as a possible sentence, for example, is likely to bring to mind information consistent with that number: "Well, it was a heinous crime, and the evidence suggests that he's very likely to reoffend." Because information consistent with a long prison term is in mind, the judge is likely to stick to a higher number when making the final decision ("Well, 25 years is a little long; but 10 years sounds about right") (Mussweiler & Strack, 1999). This effect of anchoring is related to the role of accessibility we discussed earlier. The starting point increases the accessibility of thoughts that are consistent with it (e.g., reasons why the criminal deserves a long sentence).

The problem is that sometimes the starting point can be wrong and, even though people may realize that, they do not adjust enough from their starting points (Epley & Gilovich, 2001). They stick too closely to the value they started with....

The Pervasiveness of Automatic Thinking

At this point, you might be wondering why we have spent so much time on the automatic, nonconscious type of social cognition. Didn't we say earlier that there are two modes of thinking, automatic and controlled? Isn't it possible to think about the social world slowly, carefully, and deliberately, such as when someone takes time to sit down and really think a problem through? Indeed it is. We spent so much time on automatic thinking, however, because it is so pervasive and dominates much of people's mental lives. Just as modern jetliners fly mostly on autopilot.

But how can this be when it seems as if so much of our life is governed by our conscious deliberations? Many decisions, such as where to go to university or whom to date, are accompanied by deliberative, conscious thinking. Yet, even big decisions like these can be influenced by automatic thinking, such as when we use judgmental heuristics when deciding where to apply to college. Obviously, conscious thinking is extremely important, though, especially when people try to correct or fix mistakes in their automatic thinking.

We cannot leave this topic, however, without pointing out that just because people think they are consciously controlling their actions does not necessarily mean that they are. Daniel Wegner (2002) argues

48

that the sense people have of consciously willing an action can be an illusion, a feeling that we create when our actions were really controlled by either our automatic thinking or the external environment.

Have you ever seen children in a video arcade furiously working the controls, believing that they are playing the game, when in fact they never put money in the machine and are watching the demonstration program? Occasionally, when the children push the controls in one direction, the game does appear to respond to the commands, making it hard for the children to realize that in fact they had no control over what was happening (Wegner, 2002). Adults are not immune from such illusions of control, either. People who are able to choose their lottery numbers, for example, are more confident that they will win than people who are assigned numbers (Langer, 1975). And what sports fans haven't felt that they helped a favourite team by crossing their fingers at a key moment in the game?

These examples illustrate that there can be a disconnect between our conscious sense of how much we are causing our own actions and how much we really are causing them. Sometimes we overestimate the amount of control we have, as when we believe that crossing our fingers will help our favourite sports team. Other times we underestimate the amount of control we actually do have (Wegner, 2002).

We turn now to the kind of thinking that people are most aware of: slow, deliberate, and conscious. The way in which controlled, conscious thinking interacts with automatic thinking is one of the most intriguing issues in social cognition, as we will now discuss.

Controlled Social Cognition: High-Effort Thinking

Racial profiling-official action toward people based on their race, ethnicity, or national origin instead of their behaviour has received a great deal of attention since the events on September 11, 2001. Because the terrorists who flew the planes into the World Trade Center towers, a field in Pennsylvania, and the Pentagon were of Middle Eastern descent, some people feel that anyone who looks as if he or she might be of a similar background should receive special scrutiny when flying on commercial airlines. On the New Year's Eve after the attacks, for example, Michael Dasrath and Edgardo Cureg boarded a Continental Airlines flight from New Jersey to Tampa. Dasrath was a U.S. citizen who was born in South America, and Cureg was a U.S. resident from the Philippines. Both had successfully passed through extensive security checks. Dasrath, seated in first class, was removed from the plane when a woman with a dog complained that he made her uncomfortable. Cureg was also removed from the flight, allegedly because he made other passengers nervous. Neither man posed a threat but, because they had brown skin, they were singled out and refused service. Both are suing the airlines for violating their civil rights (Judge Rules, 2002).

These examples of racial profiling bear some similarities to the recent tragedy of Jean Charles de Menezes, the Brazilian man gunned down by London police, as discussed earlier. In these cases, innocent people were suspected of a crime because of the colour of their skin. In other respects, however, the examples are quite different. In de Menezes' case, the police had very little time to react -seconds or less- as he approached a subway station. More than likely, the police officers' automatic thinking took over. In the case of the men removed from the airplane, however, the airline officials presumably had ample time to think about and consider their actions. Racial prejudice can thus be the result of automatic thinking or of conscious, deliberative thinking…

Controlled thinking is defined as thinking that is conscious, intentional, voluntary, and effortful. People can usually turn on or turn off this type of thinking at will and are fully aware of what they are thinking. Further, this kind of thinking is effortful in the sense that it requires mental energy. People have the capacity to think in a conscious, controlled way about only one thing at a time; they cannot be thinking about what they will eat for lunch today at the same time they are thinking through a complex math problem. Automatic thinking, in contrast, can occur in the background with no conscious effort at all.

One purpose of controlled thinking is to provide checks and balances for automatic thinking. Just as an airline captain can turn off the automatic pilot and take control of the plane when trouble occurs, controlled thinking takes over when unusual events occur. Unlike automatic thinking, however, controlled thinking requires motivation and effort. We have to want to do it, and we have to have the time and energy to devote to it. Consequently, when the stakes are low and we do not particularly care about the accuracy of a decision or judgment, we often let our automatic thinking do the job without bothering to check or correct it. If we are idly watching television after a long day, for example, we might be judging the people we see on the tube rather automatically. Similarly, we might react to the commercials in a mindless way, expending little mental effort to examine what is being said. The message that "nine out of ten doctors recommend this brand of pain reliever" might register automatically, without much critical thinking to evaluate the claim.

Sometimes, though, people have the motivation and mental capacity to analyze a particular commercial. Suppose that you have been looking around for a new car and have been considering all-wheel-drive station wagons. When a commercial for one of these cars comes on, you are likely to sit up and take notice, analyzing what is said in much more detail....there is considerable evidence that when people are motivated to analyze a message carefully and have the mental capacity to do so (i.e., if they are not tired or distracted), they go off automatic pilot and engage in more controlled thinking, paying closer attention to the merits of what is being said. When people are not very motivated … they remain on automatic pilot and are influenced more by the surface characteristics of the message (Chaiken, 1987; Petty & Cacioppo, 1986; Petty, Priester, & Brinol, 2002; Petty & Wegener, 1999).

When people care enough to analyze a problem thoughtfully, they can sometimes avoid the kinds of biases that result from automatic thinking. In some of the studies we reviewed earlier, the tasks were not all that important to people. Several studies show that when tasks have greater consequences, people make more complex and more accurate inferences (e.g., Kruglanski & Webster, 1996; Martin, Seta, & Crelia, 1990; Strack & Hannover, 1996). In one study, for example, female participants read about another student named Tom Ferguson. They learned how interested Tom was in dating each of several women and learned several things about these women, such as how good their sense of humour was. They were asked to judge the relationship between the qualities of the women (e.g., their sense of humour) and Tom's willingness to date them. As with many other studies that have examined people's ability to judge such relationships, the participants used simple strategies that were not particularly accurate (Harkness, DeBono, & Borgida, 1985) - unless, that is, they were highly motivated to make careful judgments. Some of the participants thought that they were taking part in a dating study and that they themselves would be dating Tom for several weeks. Then, the women cared more about what Tom liked and disliked in a dating partner, and they put their high-effort thinking into gear and made judgments that were more accurate. When the stakes are high, people use more sophisticated, effortful strategies than when the stakes are low and, hence, make more accurate judgments (Dunn & Wilson, 1990; Kruglanski, 1989; Stangor & McMillan, 1992; Tetlock, 1992; Trope & Lieberman, 1996).

We do not mean to imply that, with a little motivation, people become perfect reasoners...we'll discuss examples of people making erroneous judgments about the social world despite their best efforts and intentions. Human judgment is not like a car engine, where it is easy to tell when it breaks down and what is wrong with it. It is often hard for people to know exactly how they formed a judgment, whether it is biased, and how much, if at all, they should correct it (Martin, 1986; Schwarz & Bless, 1992; Wegener & Petty, 1997; Wilson & Brekke, 1994). Nonetheless, it is often true that the more motivated people are to form unbiased judgments, the greater the likelihood is that they will do so.

Automatic Believing, Controlled Unbelieving

There are other interesting ways in which controlled thinking provides checks and balances on automatic thinking. As we explained earlier, when people use the anchoring and adjustment heuristic, they use starting points in their judgments and fail to adjust sufficiently from these points. One explanation for this process is that people automatically use whatever they encounter as a starting point without even fully realizing that they are doing so and then attempt to adjust from this starting point with controlled thinking.

Three centuries ago, the philosopher Benedict Spinoza observed that when people initially see, hear, or learn something, they take it at face value and assume it is true. Only after accepting the veracity of a fact do they go to the effort of deciding whether it might be false. While other philosophers (e.g., René Descartes) have disagreed, recent research has shown that Spinoza was right (Gilbert, 1991, 2002; Krull &

Dill, 1996). Daniel Gilbert argues that people are programmed to believe automatically everything they hear and see. This automatic "seeing is believing" process is built into human beings, he suggests, because pretty much everything we hear and see is true. If we had to stop and deliberate about the truthfulness of everything we encountered, life would be difficult indeed. ("Let's see, it looks like a car careening toward me down the street, but maybe it's really an illusion"...CRASH!)

Occasionally, however, what we see or hear is not true; therefore, we need a checks-and-balances system to be able to assess and, if necessary, "unaccept" what we initially believed. When we hear a political candidate say, "If elected, I will lower your taxes, balance the budget, reduce crime, and wash your car every Sunday afternoon," we initially believe what we hear. However, the assessment and "unacceptance" part of the process quickly kicks in, making us doubt the truth of what we've just heard ("Now wait just a minute...")....

The interesting thing about this process is that the initial acceptance occurs automatically, which, as we have seen, means that it occurs nonconsciously and without effort or intention. The assessment and unacceptance parts of the process are the product of controlled processing, however, which means that people have to have the energy and motivation to do it. If people are preoccupied, tired, or unmotivated, the acceptance part of the process will operate unchecked, and this can lead to the acceptance of falsehoods. If we mindlessly watch television and do not think carefully about what is said, for example, we might mindlessly accept outlandish claims being made in commercials....

Thought Suppression and Ironic Processing

Being preoccupied and unable to engage in controlled thinking has another interesting consequence: it reduces our ability to engage in thought suppression - the attempt to avoid thinking about something we would just as soon forget, such as a lost love, an unpleasant encounter with one's boss, or a delectable piece of cheesecake in the refrigerator. According to Daniel Wegner (1992, 1994; Wenzlaff & Wegner, 2000), successful thought suppression depends on the interaction of two processes, one relatively automatic and the other relatively controlled. The first, automatic part, called the monitoring process, searches for evidence that the unwanted thought is about to intrude on consciousness. Once the unwanted thought is detected, the second, more controlled part, called the operating process, comes into play. This is the effortful, conscious attempt to distract oneself by finding something else to think about. These two processes operate in tandem, like two parents conspiring to keep their kids away from junk food outlets at a mall. One parent's job, akin to the monitoring process, is to keep a watch out for the food joints and let the other one know when they are in the vicinity ("McDonald's alert!"). The other parent's job, akin to the operating process, is to divert the kids' attention away from the fast-food places ("Hey, kids, look at the giant picture of SpongeBob in that store window"). This system works pretty well as long as each process (parent) does its job-one ever alert for the topic we want to avoid and the other diverting our attention from this topic.

What happens, though, when the controlled operating process is unable to do its job because the person is tired or preoccupied? The monitoring process continues to find instances of the unwanted thought, which then intrude on consciousness unchecked by the controlled process. A state of hyperaccessibility results in which the unwanted thought occurs with high frequency. If the parent whose job it is to distract the children falls down on the job, for example, the kids will become even more aware that fast-food joints are in the vicinity because they will keep hearing the monitoring parent point them out (Renaud & McConnell, 2002; Wenzlaff & Bates, 2000). The irony is that, when people are trying their hardest not to think about something (e.g., you are on guard not to think about jokes about short people because your 142 centimetre-tall boss is standing next to you), if people are tired or preoccupied that is, under cognitive load - these thoughts are especially likely to spill out unchecked.

Further, there can be an emotional and physical cost to thought suppression. In one study, medical school students wrote about a personal topic once a day for three days (Petrie, Booth, & Pennebaker, 1998). After each writing episode, some participants were asked to suppress all thoughts about what they had just written for five minutes. Compared to people who did not suppress their thoughts, people in the suppress condition showed a significant decrease in immune system functioning. In another study, women who had

had an abortion were asked how much they had tried to suppress thoughts about the abortion (Major & Gramzow, 1999). The more the women reported that they tried not to think about the abortion, the greater their reported psychological distress…it is generally better to open up about one's problems by writing about or discussing them than to try to suppress thoughts about the problems.

Thinking about What Might Have Been: Counterfactual Reasoning

There is one final condition under which people are likely to go off automatic pilot and think about things more slowly and consciously: when they experience a negative event that was a "close call," such as failing a test by just a point or two. Under these conditions, people engage in counterfactual thinking-mentally changing some aspect of the past as a way of imagining what might have been (Kahneman & Miller, 1986; Kahneman & Tversky, 1982; Markman et al., 1995; Roese, 1997; Roese & Olson, 1997). "If only I hadn't fallen asleep while studying the night before the test," you might think, "I would have gotten a better grade," or "If only I had worked up the courage to ask Michelle, she might be going out with me instead of my best friend." And if you had mustered up the courage to ask out Michelle and the two of you were now head over heels in love, chances are you probably wouldn't be spending much time agonizing over how the outcome could have been different.

There is considerable evidence that we are more likely to engage in counterfactual thinking when we were nearly able to avoid a negative event. For example, missing a plane by five minutes causes more counterfactual thinking ("If only I had driven a little faster," "If only I hadn't stopped to pick up a coffee") and more regret than missing a plane by half an hour (Kahneman & Miller, 1986; Miller, Turnbull, & McFarland, 1990), Similarly, if you sold a winning lottery ticket to your sister one hour before the draw, you would experience more regret than if you had sold the ticket two weeks before the draw (Miller & Taylor, 2002). As you might expect, people also feel greater sympathy for others in near-miss situations. To demonstrate this, Miller and McFarland (1986) had students at Simon Fraser University read a scenario in which a man attempted to walk to safety after his plane crashed in an isolated northern area. Those who were told that the man perished 0.4 kilometres from the nearest town awarded greater compensation to his family than did those who were told that he died 120 kilometres from the nearest town. The use of hypothetical scenarios such as these is common in counterfactual research….

The effects we have been discussing, however, are not limited to people's reactions to hypothetical scenarios (Branscombe et al., 1996; Davis & Lehman, 1995). Indeed, as Davis, Lehman, Wortman, Silver, and Thompson (1995) have demonstrated, counterfactual thoughts have a great impact on people's emotional reactions to actual events. These researchers interviewed people who had experienced the trauma of losing a spouse or child in a car accident or the death of an infant from Sudden Infant Death syndrome. They discovered that thoughts such as "If only I had done something differently, my spouse [child] would still be alive" were common. In fact, for half of their participants, these kinds of thoughts persisted four to seven years later. Sadly, the more people engaged in such counterfactual thinking, the greater their distress. Similar findings were obtained when Davis and colleagues (1996) interviewed spinal cord injury victims. As expected, the more people imagined ways in which the tragedy could have been averted, by mentally "undoing" the circumstances preceding it, the more distress they reported.

Counterfactual reasoning can also lead to some paradoxical effects on emotions. For example, who do you think would be happier: an Olympic athlete who won a silver medal (came in second) or an Olympic athlete who won a bronze medal (came in third)? Though you might think that the athlete who performed better (the silver medal winner) would be happier, that is not what Victoria Medvec, Scott Madey, and Tom Gilovich (1995) predicted. They reasoned that the silver medal winner should feel worse, because he or she could more easily imagine having won the event and would therefore engage in more counterfactual reasoning. To see if they were right, they analyzed videotapes of the 1992 Olympics. Both immediately after their event and while athletes received their medals, silver medal winners appeared less happy than bronze medal winners. And during interviews with reporters, silver medal winners engaged in more counterfactual reasoning, saying things such as "I almost pulled it off; it's too bad"…

Earlier we described controlled thinking as conscious, intentional, voluntary, and effortful, but different kinds of controlled thought meet these requirements to different degrees. Counterfactual reasoning is clearly conscious and effortful; we know we are obsessing about the past, and this kind of thinking can take up so much mental energy that we cannot think about anything else. It is not, however, always intentional or voluntary. Even when we want to stop dwelling on the past and move on to something else, it can be difficult to turn off the "if only" thinking that characterizes counterfactual reasoning. This is not so good if counterfactual thinking results in rumination, whereby people repetitively focus on negative things in their lives. Rumination has been found to be a contributor to depression (Lyubomirsky, Caldwell, & Nolen-Hoeksema, 1993). Thus, it is not advisable to ruminate constantly about a bad test grade to the point where you can't think about anything else.

Counterfactual thinking can be useful, however, if it focuses people's attention on ways that they can cope better in the future. For example, research conducted at the University of Western Ontario (Roese, 1994; Roese & Olson, 1997) and at the University of British Columbia (Mandel & Lehman, 1996) shows that counterfactual thinking involves thinking not only about why an event occurred but also about how various outcomes could have been avoided. In one study, Roese (1994) asked students at the University of Western Ontario to think of an exam they had written in the past year on which they had performed very poorly. Some participants were then asked to "list some specific actions that, in retrospect, could have been taken to have improved your exam score." These students subsequently expressed greater intentions to perform success-enhancing behaviours in the future (e.g., studying), and in fact, actually worked harder to improve their performance compared to students who were asked to focus actions that could have made the outcome even worse. …Thus, counterfactual thinking can be useful when it motivates us to take steps to prevent similar outcomes from occurring in the future.

A Portrayal of Social Thinking

By now you have seen two rather different modes of social cognition, one that is effortless, involuntary, unintentional, and unconscious (automatic thinking) and another that is more effortful, voluntary, intentional and conscious (controlled thinking). We have also discussed that both kinds of thinking can lead to consequential errors. Jean Charles de Menezes' death may have been the result of an automatic assumption made by the London police officers who shot him, based on his race. Other kinds of racial prejudice can be the result of more controlled thinking. So how good a thinker is the typical human being anyway? How can we reconcile the fact that human beings have amazing cognitive abilities that have resulted in dazzling cultural and intellectual achievements but at the same time humans are prone to making consequential mental errors like the ones documented in this chapter?

One way of addressing this question is to ask which kind of thinking - automatic or controlled - is more important in human functioning. The answer to this question has engendered a lively debate among social psychologists. It is fair to say that there has been an increasing appreciation of the role of automatic thinking in human thought; more and more research has shown that people operate on automatic pilot when thinking about the social world. Some researchers have gone so far as to argue that the role of conscious, controlled thinking may be quite limited in human functioning (Bargh & Chartrand, 1999; Wegner, 2002; Wilson, 2002). Others have argued that although it can be difficult, it is possible to gain conscious control over unwanted automatic responses, such as prejudiced ones (Devine, 1989b; Devine & Monteith, 1999; Fiske, 1989a). Debate over these fundamental issues, such as the role of consciousness in human functioning, is likely to generate a good deal of research in the next several years.

What is clear is that despite the troubles they can cause, both kinds of thinking are extremely useful. It would be difficult to live without the ability to process information about the social world automatically and make quick assumptions about our environment; we would be like a primitive, extremely slow computer, chugging away constantly as we tried to understand what was happening around us. And it is clearly to our advantage to be able to switch to controlled mode, where we can think about ourselves and our social world more slowly and carefully.

The following portrait of the social thinker is emerging. First, people are very sophisticated social thinkers who have amazing cognitive abilities. No one has yet been able to construct a computer that comes close to matching the power of the human brain. But there is plenty of room for improvement. The shortcomings of social thinking we have documented can be tragic, as demonstrated by the examples of racial prejudice in this chapter (Gilovich, 1991; Nisbett & Ross, 1980; Quattrone, 1982; Slusher & Anderson, 1989). Tim Wilson and colleagues have gone so far as to use the term mental contamina- tion to describe the kinds of biases that are pervasive in everyday life (Wilson & Brekke, 1994; Wilson, Centerbar, & Brekke, 2002). Perhaps the best metaphor of human thinking is that people are "flawed scientists"- brilliant thinkers who are attempting to discover the nature of the social world in a logical manner but do not do so perfectly. People are often blind to truths that don't fit their schemas and sometimes treat others in ways that make their schemas come true-something that good scientists would never do.

Improving Human Thinking

Given that human reasoning is sometimes flawed, and can have unpleasant and even tragic consequences, it is important to consider how these mistakes can be corrected. Is it possible to teach people to make better inferences, thereby avoiding the kind of mistakes we have discussed in this chapter? If so, what is the best way to do it?

One approach is to make people a little more humble about their reasoning abilities. Often we have greater confidence in our judgments than we should (Blanton et al., 2001; Buehler, Griffin, & Ross, 2002; Vallone, Griffin, & Ross, 1990). For example, research conducted in Canada and Great Britain has shown that if people are able to answer a few difficult questions correctly, they tend to overestimate just how much general knowledge they have (Griffin & Buehler, 1999). Anyone trying to improve human inference is thus up against an overconfidence barrier (Metcalfe, 1998). Many people seem to think that their reasoning processes are just fine the way they are..[however when] Lord, Lepper, and Preston (1984), … asked people to consider the opposite point of view to their own, people realized there were other ways to construe the world and were less likely to make errors in their judgments (see also Anderson, Lepper, & Ross, 1980; Hirt & Markman, 1995; Mussweiler, Strack, & Pfeiffer, 2000).

Another approach is to teach people directly some basic statistical and methodological principles about how to reason correctly, with the hope that they will apply these principles in their everyday lives. Many of these principles are already taught in courses in statistics and research design, such as the idea that if you want to generalize from a sample of information (e.g., a group of welfare mothers) to a population (e.g., all welfare mothers), you must have a large, unbiased sample. Do people who take such courses apply these principles in their everyday lives? Are they less likely to make the kinds of mistakes we have discussed in this chapter? A number of recent studies have provided encouraging answers to these questions, showing that people's reasoning processes can be improved by university statistics courses, graduate training in research design, and even brief one-time lessons (Fong, Krantz, & Nisbett, 1986; Malloy, 2001; Nisbett et al., 1983; Nisbett et al., 1987; Schaller et al., 1996). Thus, there is reason to be cautiously optimistic…

In summary, there is reason to be hopeful about people's ability to overcome the kinds of mistakes we have documented in this chapter. And you don't have to go to graduate school to do it. Sometimes it helps simply to consider the opposite, as participants in the Lord and colleagues' (1984) study did. Beyond this, formal training in statistics helps, at both the graduate and undergraduate levels-especially if your instructor illustrates how these principles apply in real-life situations. So, if you were dreading taking a university statistics course, take heart: it might not only satisfy a requirement for your major but improve your reasoning as well!

***

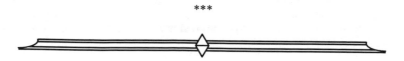

READING FIVE

SOCIAL PERCEPTION:
HOW WE COME TO UNDERSTAND OTHER PEOPLE

Excerpts from Chapter 4 of Aronson, E., Wilson, T., Akert, R., Fehr, B. (2007) *Social Psychology, 3rd Canadian Edition.* Toronto, Pearson Education.

***

Our desire to understand people is so fundamental that it carries over into our hobbies and recreational lives. We go to movies, read novels, watch soap operas, and 'people-watch" at airports because thinking about the behaviour of even strangers and fictional characters fascinates us. This basic aspect of human cognition has been exploited brilliantly by "reality TV" programmers, who have recently begun to cast television shows with real people instead of actors, and to place them in unusual or difficult situations. This new genre of television has proved a powerhouse. Why are these shows so popular? Because we enjoy figuring people out. We do it all day long, as a necessary part of social survival, and then we go home, turn on the television, and do it for fun and entertainment. Since the original version of Survivor, shot in 2000 on an island in the South China Sea, reality shows have crowded the top ten list of most- watched shows every year (Carter, 2000, 2003). In Survivor, the contestants scheme, lie, and form secret alliances as, one by one, they vote their fellow contestants off the show in hope of being the last survivor and collecting the reward of $1 million. A typical segment of the show featured one contestant confiding to another her plans and strategy for remaining on the island, then presenting a totally different story to another contestant, and finally, speaking directly into the camera to us, the television audience, telling yet a third version that contradicted the other two. What was the truth? What would she really do? And what was she really like as a person-a deceitful, manipulative opportunist or just someone who knows how to play the game? Why do we care? Why do we expend so much time and energy trying to explain the behaviour of others? Because doing so helps us understand and predict our social world (Heider, 1958; Kelley, 1967).

This chapter discusses social perception-the study of how we form impressions - of other people and make inferences about them. One important source of information that we use is nonverbal behaviour, such as facial expressions, body movements, and tone of voice.

Nonverbal Behaviour

What do we know about people when we first meet them? We know what we can see and hear, and, even though we know we should not judge a book by its cover, this kind of easily observable information is critical to our first impressions. Physical characteristics such as people's attractiveness and facial configuration (e.g., a "baby face") influence others' judgments of them (Berry & McArthur, 1986; Hatfield & Sprecher, 1986a; McArthur, 1990; Zebrowitz, 1997; Zebrowitz & Montepare, 1992). We also pay a great deal of attention to what people say. After all, our most noteworthy accomplishment as a species is the development of verbal language.

But people's words are not the full story. There is a rich source of information about people other than their words-the ways they communicate nonverbally (Ambady & Rosenthal, 1992,1993; DePaulo & Friedman, 1998; Gifford, 1991, 1994). Nonverbal communication refers to how people communicate, intentionally or unintentionally, without words. From the large body of research on this topic, we understand that facial expressions, tones of voice, gestures, body positions and movement, the use of touch, and eye faze are the most frequently used diagnostic channels of nonverbal communication Henley, 1977; Knapp & Hall, 1997).

***

...you can learn quite a lot about people from their nonverbal behaviour, including their attitudes, emotions, and personality traits. Nonverbal behaviour offers many bits of information - "data" that we then use to construct our overall impressions or theories about others. But nonverbal cues are just the beginning of social perception. We turn now to the cognitive processes people use when forming impressions of others.

Implicit Personality Theories: Filling in the Blanks

As we discussed in Chapter 3, when people are unsure about the nature of the social world, they use their schemas to fill in the gaps. An excellent example of this use of schemas is the way in which people form impressions of other people. If you know that someone is kind, you use an important type of schema called an implicit personality theory to determine what other qualities the person has. You might assume for example, that this person is also generous; similarly, you assume that a stingy person is also irritable. These theories consist of people's ideas about what kinds of personality traits go together (Asch, 1946; Schneider, 1973; Sedikides & Anderson, 1994; Sherman & Klein, 1994; Werth & Foerster, 2002).

These implicit theories about personality serve the same function as does any schema. You can extrapolate from a small to a much larger amount of information (Fiske & Taylor, - 1991; Markus & Zajonc, 1985). In this case, you can use just a few observations of a person as a starting point, and then, using your schema, create a much fuller understanding of what that person is like (Kim & Rosenberg, 1980). This way, you can form impressions quickly, without having to spend weeks with people to figure out what they are like.

However, this efficiency can come at some cost and in some cases could even be fatal. How could our implicit personality theories cost us our lives? A team of researchers in the United States and Canada found that university students relied on implicit personality theories to determine whether they should use condoms (Williams et al., 1992). If they knew their partner and liked their partner, participants assumed that he or she couldn't possibly be HIV positive. If participants didn't know their partner, they relied on superfi- cial characteristics, such as the person's age, the way he or she dressed, or even whether the person was from a large city versus a small town. For example, if a potential sexual partner didn't dress provocatively or wasn't from a large city, participants assumed that a condom wasn't necessary. The researchers concluded that young people are placing themselves at considerable risk by relying on such implicit personality theories, because these variables are not accurate indicators of whether a sexual partner actually has HIV or AIDS.

Culture and Implicit Personality Theories

Implicit personality theories are strongly tied to culture. Like other beliefs, they are passed from generation to generation in a society, and one culture's implicit personality theory might be very different from another culture's (Anderson, 1995; Chin, Morris, Hong & Menon, 2000). For example, a strong implicit personality theory in our culture involves physical attractiveness. We presume that "what is beautiful is good"-that people with physical beauty will also have a whole host of other wonderful qualities (Dion, Berscheid, & Walster, 1972; Eagly et al., 1991; Jackson, Hunter, & Hodge, 1995). For example, when Dion and Dion (1987) showed visitors to the Ontario Science Centre photographs of attractive and unattractive individuals, more positive qualities (e.g., kind, considerate, sincere) were attributed to the attractive individuals. Participants also predicted that attractive individuals would experience more successes in life.

Dion, Pak, and Dion (1990) wondered whether physical attractiveness stereotyping might be less likely to occur in collectivist cultures (e.g., China) where social judgments are more likely to be based on group related attributes (e.g., family, position in a social group) than on characteristics of the individual. Dion and colleagues tested this prediction in a sample of University of Toronto students of Chinese ethnicity. Indeed, students with a collectivist orientation-defined in this study as being highly involved in Toronto's Chinese community were less likely to assume that an attractive person possessed desirable personality traits than were students who did not have a strong collectivist orientation (i.e., were less involved in the Chinese community).

Cultural variation in implicit personality theories was also demonstrated in an intriguing study by Hoffman, Lau and Johnson(1986). They noted that different cultures have different ideas about personality types that is, the kinds of people for whom there are simple, agreed-on verbal labels. In Western cultures, for example, we agree that there is a kind of person who has an artistic personality: a person who is creative, intense, and temperamental, and who has an unconventional lifestyle. The Chinese, however, do not have a schema or implicit personality theory for an artistic type. Conversely, in China there are categories of personality that do not exist in Western cultures; for example, a shi gu person is someone who is worldly, devoted to family, socially skillful, and somewhat reserved. Hoffman, Lau, and Johnson (1986) hypothesized that these culturally implicit personality theories influence the way people form impressions of others. To test this hypothesis, they wrote stories that described a person behaving like an artistic type of person or a shi gu type of person, without using those labels to describe the person. These stories were written in both English and Chinese. The English versions were given to a group of unilingual English speakers and to a group of Chinese-English bilingual participants. Another group of Chinese-English bilingual participants received the versions written in Chinese. Participants were asked to write down their impressions of the characters in the stories. The researchers then examined whether the participants listed traits that were not used in the stories but did fit the artistic or shi gu personality type. For example, "unreliable" was not mentioned in the "artistic personality type" story but is consistent with that implicit personality theory.

…when the unilingual English speakers read about the characters, they formed an impression that was more consistent with the artistic type than with the shi gu type. This was also the case for the Chinese-English bilingual participants who read the descriptions in English. However, Chinese-English bilingual participants who read the descriptions in Chinese showed the opposite pattern of results. Their impression of the character was more consistent with the shi gu type than with the artistic type because the Chinese language provides a convenient label or implicit personality theory for this kind of person.

These results are consistent with a well-known argument by Whorf (1956) that the language people speak influences the way they think about the world. Character, although described identically, were perceived differently by the bilingual research participants, depending on the language and therefore the implicit personality theory used. Consequently, one's culture and one's language produce widely shared implicit personality theories, and these theories can influence the kinds of impressions people form of each other.

Causal Attribution: Answering the "Why" Question

We have seen that when we observe other people, we make guesses about their personalities, such as how friendly or outgoing they are. And once we get this far, we use our implicit personality theories to fill in the blanks. If a person is friendly, she must be sincere as well. Or, more disturbingly, if a person is likeable, he or she must not have AIDS.

However, nonverbal behaviour and implicit personality theories are not fail-safe indicators of what a person is really thinking or feeling. If you meet an acquaintance and she says, "It's great to see you!" does she really mean it? Perhaps she is acting more thrilled than she really feels, out of politeness. Perhaps she is outright lying. The point is that even though nonverbal communication is sometimes easy to decode and implicit personality theories can streamline the way we form impressions, there is still sub-stantial ambiguity as to what a person's behaviour really means. Why did that acquaintance behave as she did? To answer this "why" question, we use our immediate observations to form more elegant and complex inferences about what people really are like and what motivates them to act as they do. How we go about answering these questions is the focus of attribution theory, the study of how we infer the causes of other people's behaviour.

The Nature of the Attributional Process

Fritz Heider is frequently referred to as the father of attribution theory. His influential book defined the field of social perception, and his legacy is still very much evident in current research (Gilbert, 1998a; Ross, 1998). Heider (1958) discussed what he called "naive" or "common sense" psychology. In his view, people are like amateur scientists, trying to understand other people's behaviour by piecing together information until they arrive at a reasonable explanation or cause.

One of Heider's (1958) most valuable contributions is a simple dichotomy: we can make an internal attribution, deciding that the cause of the person's behaviour was something about that person - his or her disposition, personality, attitudes, or character - an explanation that assigns the causality of his or her behaviour internally. Conversely, we can make an external attribution, deciding that the cause of a person's behaviour was something about the situation...

This dichotomy was vividly illustrated in an incident that occurred in North Vancouver, British Columbia, on September 22, 1999. Nadia Hama made newspaper headlines when her 18-month-old daughter Kaya fell 47 metres from the Capilano Suspension Bridge. People in the media and on the street were quick to blame Hama. They accused her of intentionally throwing Kaya off the bridge. These accusations mounted as it came to light that her daughter had Down's syndrome and that Hama had looked into placing her daughter for adoption. In short, Hama was portrayed as a bad mother who intentionally tried to kill her child. Others agreed that Nadia Hama may have tried to kill her child but made external attributions for her behaviour. They pointed to extremely high levels of stress in her life raising a handicapped child, being embroiled in an ugly divorce, not receiving child-care payments from her estranged husband. Not surprisingly, Hama herself explained the situation in terms of external factors stating that baby Kaya's fall was accidental.

Whether we make internal or external attributions for someone's behaviour can have serious consequences. In Nadia Hama's case, those who made internal attributions concluded that she was a cold-hearted murderer; in contrast, those who made external attributions felt compassion, sympathy, and pity. Quite a difference! Perhaps even more important, the fate of Hama rested on the attributions made for baby Kaya's fall. In this case, police and Crown prosecutors did not find sufficient evidence to charge Hama with either attempted murder or criminal negligence causing bodily harm (D'Angelo, 2000).

Thus, attributions can play a pivotal role in determining whether someone is charged with a crime. As demonstrated in a study by Linda Coates (1997), attributions also play a role in the severity of sentencing when people are convicted of committing crimes. She recorded the kinds of attributions made by judges in transcripts of 70 cases of convictions of sexual assaults in British Columbia. The kind of attributions made had important implications for sentencing: if the assault was seen as the result of a decision to be violent or due to the offender's violent nature, the sentence was harsher than if situational or external attributions were made (e.g., the assault was attributed to stress or negative mood).

Another of Heider's (1958) important contributions was his observation that people generally prefer internal attributions over external ones. While either type of attribution is always possible, Heider noted that we tend to see the causes of a person's behaviour as residing in that person. We are perceptually focused on people-they are who we notice-while the situation, which is often hard to see and hard to describe, can be over- looked (Bargh, 1994; Carlston & Skowronski, 1994; Gilbert, 1998b; Newman & Uleman, 993; Pittman & D'Agostino, 1985; Uleman & Moskowitz, 1994).

The Covariation Model: Internal versus External Attributions

Harold Kelley (1967, 1973) developed a theory of attribution that focused on the first step in the process of social perception, namely how people decide whether to make an internal or an external attribution. Kelley's major contribution to attribution theory was the idea that we notice and think about more than one piece of information when we form an impression of another person. For example, let's say that you ask your friend to lend you her car, and she says no. Naturally, you wonder why. In formulating an answer, Kelley's theory, called the covariation model, states that you will examine multiple instances of behaviour, occurring at different times and in different situations. Has your friend refused to lend you her car in the past? Does she lend it to other people? Does she normally lend you other possessions of hers?

Kelley - like Heider before him - assumes that when we are in the process of forming an attribution, we gather information, or data, which will help us reach a judgment. The data we use, according to Kelley, are how a person's behaviour covaries across time, place, different actors, and different targets of the behaviour. By discovering covariation in people's behaviour (e.g., your friend refuses to lend you her car; she agrees to lend it to others), you are able to reach a judgment about what caused their behaviour.

When we are forming an attribution, what kinds of information do we examine for covariation? Kelley (1967, 1973) states that there are three important types of information: consensus, distinctiveness, and consistency. Let's describe these three types of information through an example. You are working at your part-time job in a clothing store and you observe your boss yelling at another employee, Hannah, telling her in no uncertain terms that she's an idiot. Without any conscious effort on your part, you pose the attributional question: "Why is the boss yelling at Hannah and being so critical - is it something about the boss, or is it something about the situation that surrounds and affects him?"

Now let's look at how Kelley's model of covariation assessment answers this question. Consensus information refers to how other people behave toward the same stimulus in this case, Hannah. Do other people at work also yell at Hannah and criticize her? Distinctiveness information refers to how the actor (the person whose behaviour we are trying to explain) responds to other stimuli. Does the boss yell at and demean other employees in the store? Consistency information refers to the frequency with which the observed behaviour between the same actor and the same stimulus occurs across time and circumstances. Does the boss yell at and criticize Hannah regularly and frequently, whether the store is busy with customers or empty?

According to Kelley's theory, when these three sources of information combine into one of two distinct patterns, a clear attribution can be made. People are most likely to make an internal attribution - deciding the behaviour was a result of something about the boss - when the consensus and distinctiveness of the act are low but its consistency is high…We would be pretty confident that the boss yelled at Hannah because he is a mean and vindictive person if we knew that no one else yells at Hannah, that the boss yells at other employees, and that the boss yells at Hannah every chance he gets. People are likely to make an external attribution (in this case, about Hannah) if consensus, distinctiveness, and consistency are all high. Finally, when consistency is low, we cannot take a clear internal or external attribution and so resort to a special kind of external or situational attribution, one that assumes something unusual or peculiar is going on in these circumstances for example, the boss just received very upsetting news and lost his temper with the first person he saw.

The covariation model assumes that people make causal attributions in a rational, logical fashion. People observe the clues, such as the distinctiveness of the act, and then draw a logical inference about why the person did what he or she did. Several studies have confirmed that people often do make attributions the way that Kelley's (1967) model says they should (Gilbert, 1998b; Hewstone & Jaspars, 1987; White, 2002)-with two exceptions. First, studies have shown that people don't use consensus information as much as Kelley's theory predicted; they rely more on consistency and distinctiveness information when forming attributions (McArthur, 1972; Wright, Luus, & Christie, 1990). Second, people don't always have the relevant information they need on all three of Kelley's dimensions; for example, you may not have consistency information because this is the first time you have ever asked your friend to borrow her car. In these situations, research has shown that people proceed with the attribution process using the information they do have, and, if necessary, making inferences about the "missing data" (Fiedler, Walther, & Nickel, 1999; Kelley, 1973).

***

Attributions also can be biased or distorted when people use mental shortcuts (see Chapter 3). In the next section, we will discuss some specific errors or biases that plague the attribution process. One shortcut is very common, at least in Western cultures: assuming that people do what they do because of the kind of people they are, not because of the situation they are in.

The Correspondence Bias: People as Personality Psychologists

Martha Stewart: the name conjures up images of domestic perfection that few mortals hope to attain. Over the past two decades, Stewart grew her small Connecticut catering business into a multimedia, billion-dollar company (Sorkin, 2003). Books, magazines, newspaper columns, television and radio shows, Internet commerce, and department store product lines communicate her vision of homemaking: meticulous, artistic, and time-consuming ways of doing everyday chores (Kahn, 2003a). While millions of people have embraced Stewart's vision of home life (hence the billion-dollar company), others have found her ripe for parody and criticism.

On June 4, 2003, Martha Stewart was indicted by the U.S. government on nine counts of conspiracy, obstruction of justice, and securities fraud. Following her indictment, a flurry of explanations appeared in the press, made by both reporters and the general public they interviewed. Their attempts to understand Stewart's behaviour offer an excellent real-life example of the prevalence of internal, or dispositional, attributions. Martha Stewart's detractors offered strong internal attributions. Described in the press as the "queen of micromanagement" (Sorkin, 2003, p. Cl), Stewart was "so detail oriented that, even with a net worth of hundreds of millions, she could not resist an illegal stock trade that netted her 145 000" (Martha Stewart's troubled world, 2003, p. A34). These critics note that she worked as a stockbroker on Wall Street in the 1960s and therefore cannot plead ignorance or naïveté (Robertson, 2003). Some feel that this is "the classic story of an extremely successful yet irritating person getting her comeuppance" (Kahn, 2003b, p. Dl).

Stewart's attorney - and her supporters - countered with a situational attribution to explain her troubles: innocent of the crime, she was being singled out because she was a celebrity and a highly successful woman in the predominantly male business world (Robertson, 2003). Thus, it wasn't anything about her personality or values that got her into this predicament (a dispositional attribution) but rather aspects of the situation, such as animosity toward her gender or occupation (a situational attribution), that caused her to be unfairly targeted. As you probably know, Martha Stewart was ultimately sentenced; in the summer of 2005, she was released from jail and resumed her career.

The pervasive, fundamental theory or schema most of us have about human behaviour is that people do what they do because of the kind of people they are, not because of the situation they are in. When thinking this way, we are more like personality psychologists, who see behaviour as stemming from internal dispositions and traits, than social psychologists, who focus on the impact of social situations on behaviour. This tendency to infer that people's behaviour corresponds to or matches their dispositions and personality has been called the correspondence bias (Fiske & Taylor, 1991; Gilbert & Malone, 1995; Jones, 1979, 1990). The correspondence bias is so pervasive that many social psychologists call it the fundamental attribution error (Heider, 1958; Jones, 1990; Ross, 1997; Ross & Nisbett, 1991).

***

Why is this correspondence bias - the tendency to explain behaviour in terms of people's dispositions - often called the fundamental attribution error? It is not always wrong to make an internal attribution; clearly, people frequently do what they do because of the kind of people they are. However, there is ample evidence that social situations can have a strong impact on behaviour; indeed, the major lesson of social psychology is that these influences can be extremely powerful. The point of the fundamental attribution error is that people tend to underestimate these influences when explaining other people's behaviour. Even when a situational constraint on behaviour is obvious, as in the Jones and Harris (1967) experiment, people persist in making internal attributions (Lord et al., 1997; Newman, 1996; Ross, 1977; Ross, Amabile, & Steinmetz, 1977; Ross & Nisbett, 1991).

The Role Of Perceptual Salience In The Fundamental Attribution Error

Why do we commit the fundamental attribution error? One reason is that when we try to explain someone's behaviour, our focus of attention is usually on the person, not on the surrounding situation

(Heider, 1958; Jones & Nisbett, 1972). In fact, as Daniel Gilbert and Patrick Malone (1995) have pointed out, the situational causes of another person's behaviour are practically invisible to us. If we don't know what happened to a person earlier in the day (e.g., she received an F on her midterm), we can't use that situational information to help us understand her current behaviour. Even when we know her "situation," we still don't know how she interprets it - for example, the F may not have upset her because she's planning to drop the course anyway. If we don't know the meaning of the "situation" for her, we can't accurately judge its effects on her behaviour. Thus, information about the situational causes of behaviour is frequently unavailable to us or difficult to interpret accurately (Gilbert, 1998b; Gilbert & Malone, 1995).

What information does that leave us? Although the situation may be close to invisible, the individual is extremely perceptually prominent-people are what our eyes and ears notice. And as Heider (1958) pointed out, what we notice seems to be the reasonable and logical cause of the observed behaviour.

Several studies have confirmed the importance of perceptual salience-in particular, an elegant one by Shelley Taylor and Susan Fiske (1975). In this study, two male students engaged in a "get acquainted" conversation. (They were actually both accomplices of the experimenters and were following a specific script during their conversation.) At each session, six actual research participants also took part. They sat in assigned seats, surrounding the two conversationalists (see Figure 4.5). Two of them sat on each side of the actors; they had a clear, profile view of both individuals. Two observers sat behind each actor; they could see the back of one actor's head but the face of the other. Thus, who was visually salient - that is, who the participants could see the best - was cleverly manipulated in this study.

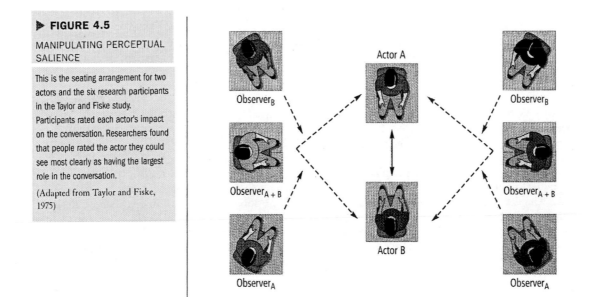

▶ **FIGURE 4.5**

MANIPULATING PERCEPTUAL SALIENCE

This is the seating arrangement for two actors and the six research participants in the Taylor and Fiske study. Participants rated each actor's impact on the conversation. Researchers found that people rated the actor they could see most clearly as having the largest role in the conversation.

(Adapted from Taylor and Fiske, 1975)

After the conversation, the research participants were asked questions about the two men - for example, who had taken the lead in the conversation, and who had chosen the topics to be discussed. As you can see in Figure 4.6, the person whom they could see the best was the person whom they thought had the most impact on the conversation. Even though all the observers heard the same conversation, those who were facing Actor A thought he had taken the lead and chosen the topics, whereas those who were facing Actor B thought he had taken the lead and chosen the topics. In comparison, those who could see both students equally well thought both were equally influential. Perceptual salience, or our visual point of view, helps explain why the fundamental attribution error is so widespread. We focus our attention more on people than on the surrounding situation because the situation is so hard to see or know; we underestimate -

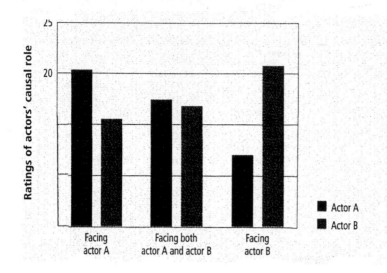

FIGURE 4.6

THE EFFECTS OF PERCEPTUAL SALIENCE

These are the ratings of each actor's causal role in the conversation. People thought that the actor they could see the best had the most impact on the conversation.

(Adapted from Taylor and Fiske, 1975)

or even forget about - the influence of the situation when we are explaining human behaviour. But this is only part of the story. Why should the simple fact that we are focused on a person make us exaggerate the extent to which that person is the cause of his or her actions?

The culprit is one of the mental shortcuts we discussed in Chapter 3: the anchoring and adjustment heuristic. In that chapter, we discussed several examples in which people began with a reference point when making a judgment and then did not adjust sufficiently away from this point. The fundamental attribution error is another by-product of this shortcut. When making attributions, people use the focus of their attention as a starting point; for example, when we hear someone argue strongly in favour of Castro's regime in Cuba, our first inclination is to explain this in dispositional terms: "This person must hold radical political views." We realize this explanation might not be the whole story, however. We might think, "On the other hand, I know he was assigned this position as part of a debate," and adjust our attributions more toward a situational explanation. However, the problem is that people often don't adjust their judgments enough. In the Jones and Harris (1967) experiment, participants who knew that the essay writer did not have a choice of topics nevertheless thought he or she believed what he or she had written, at least to some extent. They adjusted insufficiently from their anchor, the posi- tion advocated in the essay.

The Two-Step Process Of Making Attributions

In sum, we go through a two-step process when we make attributions (Gilbert, 1989, 1991, 1993; Krull, 1993). First, we make an internal attribution; we assume that a person's behaviour is caused by something about that person. Then we attempt to adjust this attribution by considering the situation the person was in. But we often don't make enough of an adjustment in this second step. Indeed, when we are distracted or preoccupied, we often skip the second step, making an extreme internal attribution (Gilbert & Hixon, 1991; Gilbert & Osborne, 1989; Gilbert, Peiham, & Krull, 1988). Why? Because the first step (making the internal attribution) occurs quickly and spontaneously, whereas the second step (adjusting for the situation) requires more effort and conscious attention…We will engage in this second step of attributional processing if we consciously slow down and think carefully before reaching a judgment, if we are motivated to reach as accurate a judgment as possible, or if we are suspicious about the behaviour of the target person, for example, believing that he or she is lying or has ulterior motives (Burger, 1991; Fein, 1996; Hilton, Fein, & Miller, 1993; Webster, 1993).

The Actor/Observer Difference.

An interesting twist on the fundamental attribution error is that it does not apply to our attributions about ourselves to the same extent that it applies to our attributions about other people. While we tend to see others' behaviour as dispositionally caused (through the fundamental attribution error), we are less likely to rely so extensively on dispositional attributions when we are explaining our own behaviour. Instead, we frequently make situational attributions about why we did what we did. Thus, an interesting attributional dilemma is created: the same action can trigger dispositional attributions in people observing the action and situational attributions in the person performing the action. This is called the actor/observer difference (Frank & Gilovich, 1989; Herzog, 1994; Johnson & Boyd, 1995; Jones & Nisbett, 1972; Robins, Spranca, & Mendelsohn, 1996). The letter to Rhona Raskin (see Figure 4.8) is an interesting demonstration of the actor/observer difference. The writer focuses on the external forces affecting her life and shaping her behaviour. Raskin, however, will have none of it. She responds with a strong, internal attribution the woman herself, not her situation, is the cause of her problems.

There have been countless demonstrations of the actor/observer difference in the laboratory. For example, a series of studies conducted at Memorial University found that people perceive more consistency in the attitudes of other people than in their own attitudes (Grant et al., 2003). University of British Columbia social psychologist, Peter Suedfeld (2003), compared the attributions made by survivors of the Holocaust (i.e., their explanations for why they survived) with those made by a control group of Jewish partic- ipants who had been safe from Nazi persecution. (Participants in the control group were asked to explain why some Jews survived the Holocaust.) Survivors were most likely to make external attributions, reporting that they had survived because of the help and support of other people, or because of luck, fate, or help from God. In contrast, those in the control group were more likely to mention internal factors, such as the survivors' determination and persistence.

Perceptual Salience Revisited

Why, at times, do the attributions made by actors and observers diverge so sharply? One reason for such divergence is our old friend perceptual salience (Jones & Nisbett, 1972). As we said earlier, just as we notice other people's behaviour more than their situation, so too do we notice our own situation more than our own behaviour. None of us is so egotistical or self-centered that we walk through life constantly holding up a full-length mirror in order to observe ourselves. We are looking outward; what is perceptually salient to us is other people, objects, and the events that unfold. We don't, and can't, pay as much attention to ourselves. As a result, when the actor and the observer think about what caused a given behaviour, they are swayed by the information that is most salient and noticeable to them: the actor for the observer, and the situation for the actor (Malle & Knobe, 1997; Nisbett & Ross, 1980; Ross & Nisbctt, 1991).

The Role Of Information Availability In The Actor/Observer Difference

The actor/observer difference occurs for another reason as well. Actors have more information about themselves than observers do (Greenwald & Banaji, 1989; Jones & Nisbett, 1972; Krueger, Ham, & Linford, 1996; Malle & Knobe, 1997). Actors know how they've behaved over the years; they know what happened to them that morning. They are far more aware than observers are of both the similarities and the differences in their behaviour across time and across situations. In Kelley's (1967) terms, actors have far more consistency and distinctiveness information about themselves than observers do. For example, if you are quiet and sit alone at a party, an observer is likely to make a dispositional attribution about you ("Gee, that person is quite an introvert"). In fact, you may know that this is not your typical way of responding to a party setting. Perhaps you are shy only at parties where you don't know anyone, or you might be tired or depressed by some recent bad news. Thus, it is not surprising that actors' self-attributions usually reflect situational factors, because they know more about how their behaviour varies from one situation to the next than do most observers, who see them in limited contexts.

So far, our discussion of the mental shortcuts people use when making attributions has covered the role of perceptual salience and information availability. But what about a person's needs, desires, hopes, and fears-do these more emotional factors also create biases in our attributions? Are you motivated to see the world in certain ways because these views make you feel better, both about yourself and life in general? The answer is yes. The shortcuts discussed below have a motivational basis; they are attributions that protect our self-esteem and our belief that the world is a safe and just place.

Self-Serving Attributions

Imagine that Alison goes to her chemistry class one day with some apprehension because she will find out how she did on the midterm. When the professor returns her exam, Alison sees that she has received an A. What will Alison think is the reason for her great grade? It probably will come as no surprise that people tend to take personal credit for their successes but explain away their failures as coming from external events that were beyond their control. Therefore, Alison is likely to think that her success came from her-she's good at chemistry and just plain smart.

How can we explain this departure from the typical actor/observer pattern? The answer is that when people's self-esteem is threatened, they often make self-serving attributions. Simply put, these attributions refer to our tendency to take credit for our successes (by making internal attributions) but to blame others (or the situation) for our failures (Miller & Ross, 1975). Many studies have shown that people make internal attributions when they do well on a task but make external attributions when they do poorly (Davis & Stephan, 1980; Elig & Frieze, 1979; McAllister, 1996; Pronin, Lin & Ross, 2002; Sedikides et al., 1998).

A particularly interesting arena for studying self-serving attributions is professional sports. Consider, for example, a headline that appeared in the sports section of the July 3, 2000, Winnipeg Free Press: "Injured Canadians tagged with ninth straight loss." The article describes yet another loss by Canada's men's volleyball team-this time in Argentina. How did the team explain this loss? One of the players, Jules Martens, offered this comment: "We get here and our major offensive players are injured; it's a different lineup again; it's a patch-work job." The coach added, "People back at home don't understand the extreme conditions, that you rarely get a call (in a close situation)…that can swing a match." The coach was referring to a call made by one of the officials that went against Canada. Thus, both the player and the coach made self-serving attributions blaming the loss on external factors, rather than on the team.

Consider now another story in the same sports section. In the U.S. Senior Open golf tournament, Hale Irwin defeated Bruce Fleisher, who led after the first three rounds. How did Irwin account for his victory? "I did what I wanted to do early on .... I let Bruce now I'm there, and put pressure on him."

These examples are consistent with the findings of social psychological research on the attributions made by professional athletes and coaches for why they or their team won or lost a game (Sherman & Kim, 2005), For example, Richard Lau and Dan Russell (1980) found that, when explaining their victories, the athletes and coaches overwhelmingly pointed to aspects of their own team or players; in fact, 80 percent of the attributions for wins were to such internal factors. Losses were more likely to be attributed to things external to their own team.

Who is more likely to make self-serving attributions? Roesch and Amirkhan (1997) wondered if a player's skill, experience, and type of sport (i.e., team sports versus solo sports such as singles tennis or golf) affected the type of attribution he or she made about a sports outcome. The researchers found that less experienced athletes were more likely to make self-serving attributions than were experienced ones. Experienced athletes realize that losses sometimes are their fault and that wins are not always because of them. The Winnipeg Blue bombers' dismal beginning to the 2005 season provides ample opportunity to observe such attributions in action. Following a loss to Regina, veteran slotback Milt Stegall commented: "Finger pointing? There will be no pointing of fingers. Everybody ought to point a thumb at their own selves. Nobody should be saying they played OK after...losing like that" (Tait, 2005a). In a subsequent loss to the Toronto Argonauts, Bombers' head coach, Jim Daley, made this attribution for the Bombers' poor performance: "We did not look sharp. We did not execute well and we did not tackle well" (Tait, 2005b).

64

Roesch and Amirkhan (1997) also found that highly skilled athletes made more self-serving attributions than did those with lower ability. The highly talented athlete believes that success results from his or her prowess, while failure or an unusual and upsetting outcome results from teammates or other circumstances of the game. Finally, athletes in solo sports made more self-serving attributions than did those in team sports. Solo athletes know that winning or losing rests on their shoulders. You can explore self-serving attributions by sports figures in the Try It! on page 120.

The self-serving bias has a number of important implications that extend well beyond the world of sports. For example, it leads people to believe that their actions are rational and defensible, but that the actions of others are unreasonable and unjustified. This phenomenon was demonstrated by Sande, Goethals, Ferrari, and Worth (1989), who found that American students attributed positive motives to the United States for both positive actions (e.g., saving whales trapped in ice) and negative actions (e.g., building more nuclear-powered submarines). However, these same actions were attributed to negative, self-serving motives if participants were told they had been performed by the former Soviet Union. Apparently one participant remarked that the only reason Soviets would save trapped whales was to slaughter and eat them later; another participant assumed that the whales must have been blocking Soviet shipping lanes! In contrast, Canadian students tended to attribute similar motives to American and Soviet actions.

Self-serving biases also tend to creep in whenever we work on tasks with others (Sande, Ellard, & Ross, 1986; Shestowsky, Wegener, & Fabrigar, 1998; Zanna & Sande, 1987). For example, in a classic study conducted at the University of Waterloo, Ross and Sicoly (1979) found that students working on a group project had very good memories when asked to recall their contributions to the project. However, their memories were considerably poorer when asked to recall the contributions of the other group members. Ross and Sicoly found that this tendency extends even to our closest relationships. They asked married couples living in student housing at the University of Waterloo to indicate the extent to which each spouse assumed responsibility for 20 different activities (e.g., cooking, deciding how money should be spent, resolving conflicts). Each person tended to overestimate his or her contribution, such that, when the husband's and wife's estimates of responsibility were added, the total was greater than 100 percent!

Defensive Attributions

People also alter their attributions to deal with other kinds of threats to their self-esteem. One of the hardest things to understand in life is the occurrence of tragic events, such as sexual assaults, terminal diseases, and fatal accidents. Even when they happen to strangers we have never met, they can be upsetting. They remind us that, if such tragedies can happen to someone else, they can happen to us. Of all the kinds of self-knowledge that we have, the knowledge that we are mortal and that bad things can happen to us is perhaps the hardest to accept (Greenberg, Pyszczynski, & Solomon, 1986; Greening & Chandler, 1997...). We therefore take steps to deny this fact. One way we do so is by making defensive attributions, which are explanations for behaviour that defend us from feelings of vulnerability and mortality.

One form of defensive attribution is unrealistic optimism, wherein people believe that good things are more likely to happen to them than to others, and bad things are less likely to happen to them than to others (Harris, 1996; Heine & Lehman, 1995; Klein, 1996; Regan, Snyder, & Kassin, 1995; Weinstein & Klein, 1996). Suppose we asked you to estimate how likely it is that each of the following will happen to you, compared to how likely it is that they will happen to other students at your college or university-owning your own home, liking your postgraduate job, living past age 80, having a drinking problem, getting divorced, and being unable to have children. When Neil Weinstein (1980) asked students these and similar questions, he found that people were too optimistic. Virtually everyone thought that the good things were more likely to happen to them than to their peers and that the bad things were less likely to happen to them than to their peers.

According to research conducted at the University of Waterloo, unrealistic optimism abounds when it comes to people's romantic relationships. For example, Murray and Holmes (1997) found that both dating and married couples claimed that they were unlikely to encounter the kinds of difficulties and conflicts that affect most relationships. They also believed that should problems arise, they were better equipped to deal with them than the average couple. When forecasting the fate of their relationship, these couples believed that their relationship had a brighter future than most.

Similarly, MacDonald and Ross (1999) found that University of Waterloo students who were in dating relationships expected that their relationship would last longer than at of the typical first-year student. In an interesting twist, they also asked each participant's parents and dormitory roommates how long they thought the participant's relationship would last. These "outsiders" were less optimistic about the longevity of these relationships than were the participants themselves. Who was right? To answer this question, MacDonald and Ross contacted the participants six months later and one year later to see whether their relationships were still intact. It turned out that the participants' rents and roommates were better at predicting how long these relationships would last an the participants were themselves. Why were the forecasts of "outsiders" more accurate than those of the people who were actually involved in these relationships? Apparently, when judging the likelihood of their relationship surviving, the participants tended to focus only on its positive aspects, whereas parents and roommates were more likely to take negative information into account. This more balanced approach resulted more accurate predictions. Thus, if you are in a dating relationship and are wondering whether it will last, your best bet is to ask your friend or your mother!

***

On a much sadder note, battered women have also been found to be unrealistically optimistic about the personal risks they run when they return to live with their abusive partners. They estimate that their own risk is significantly lower than the risk of most battered women even when the facts of their situation would suggest otherwise (Martin et al., 2000), Thus, although unrealistic optimism may help us feel better in the short term, in the long term it can be a potentially fatal attribution error.

Unrealistic optimism pervades all aspects of people's lives not just their romantic involvements. Indeed, research has indicated that unrealistic optimism describe women's attitudes about getting breast cancer and men's attitudes about getting prostate cancer (Clarke et al., 2000), heroin users' attitudes about the risk of overdosing (McGregor et al., 1998), gamblers' attitudes about winning the lottery (Rogers, 1998), and motorcyclists' attitudes about having a serious accident (Rutter, Quine, & Albery, 1998).

Unrealistic optimism undoubtedly explains what lies behind the popularity of "extreme" sports-athletic activities that take place under very dangerous conditions in which the chance of death is definitely present. How can these athletes take such risks? Wendy Middleton and her colleagues (1996) interviewed British bungee jumpers immediately before they jumped. (To bungee, a person ties a high-strength cord around one ankle, leaps off a very high tower or bridge, free falling, and then bounces at the end of the tether.) The researchers found strong support for unrealistic optimism among the jumpers. Each jumper perceived his or her own risk of injury to be less than that of the typical jumper.

It is important to point out that risk takers are not impulsive, reckless fools with no regard for danger. In a study on risk taking conducted in Kingston, Ontario, Trim op, Kerr, and Kirkcaldy (1999) found that among the young men interviewed, at least some planned ahead and carefully prepared for high-risk activities. Ironically, it may be just these "precautions" that fuel unrealistic optimism…

Blaming the Victim: An Unfortunate By-product of Attributional Processes

Earlier, we discussed people's tendency to make dispositional attributions for the behaviour of other people, even when those behaviours result from situational factors. This is known as the fundamental attribution error. Sadly, this error can lead to some tragic consequences, including a tendency to blame those who are victimized or stigmatized for their plight. Even if people are made aware of the situational factors responsible for the plight of disadvantaged members of our society (e.g., inadequate nutrition, disrupted family life), they may still see these individuals as responsible for their misfortune. Guimond and Dubé (1989), for example, found that Anglophone students viewed Francophones themselves, rather than situational factors, as responsible for their lower economic status in Quebec.

Even more unsettling, these kinds of attributions are prevalent in cases of sexual assault and domestic violence. For example, suppose a female student on your campus was the victim of a date rape by a male fellow student. How do you think you and your friends would react? Would you wonder if she'd done something to trigger the sexual assault? Was she acting suggestively earlier in the evening? Had she invited the man into her room?

Research by Elaine Walster (1966) and others has focused on such attributions (e.g., Burger, 1981; Lerner & Miller, 1978; Stormo, Lang, & Stritzke, 1997). In several experiments, they have found that the victims of crimes or accidents are often seen as causing their fate. For example, people tend to believe that rape victims are to blame for the sexual assault (Bell, Kuriloff, & Lottes, 1994; Burt, 1980; Lambert & Raichle, 2000). Researchers at the University of Manitoba recently found that those who believe in rape myths (e.g., "women falsely report rape to get attention") are especially likely to engage in victim blaming (Morry & Winkler, 2001). This was true for both women and men.

Similarly, battered wives are frequently seen as responsible for their abusive husbands' behaviour (Summers & Feldman, 1984). One way in which people justify blaming victims of violence is to assume that the victims must have done something to provoke the attack. Researchers at Carleton University (Kristiansen & Giulietti, 1990) and at Mount Saint Vincent University (Perrott, Miller, & Delaney, 1997) have found that women are especially likely to be blamed for domestic assaults if they are seen as having done some- thing to provoke their partner. (See, for example, Connections on page 11 in Chapter 1.)

The research we have been discussing focused on situations in which women have been the victims of violence. Are male victims of violence also blamed? To find out, Perrott and Webber (1996) presented students at Mount Saint Vincent University with scenarios in which a man or a woman was attacked. In some of the scenarios, the victim knew the attacker; in other scenarios he or she did not. The researchers found that there was greater blaming of female victims than of male victims. Moreover, different attributions were made for the assault, depending on the victim's gender. Female victims were blamed for being "too trusting" and for not having anticipated the assault. Male victims, on the other hand, were blamed for not having been able to fight off the attackers. Perrott and Webber found the extent of victim blaming quite disturbing, given that most of their participants were female students attending a university that has a strong women's issues focus.

Finally, another way in which the fundamental attribution leads to victim blaming is when people decide that victims could have exercised control over the situation but didn't. In a study conducted at the University of Manitoba, Menec and Perry (1998) constructed descriptions of people with stigmas (e.g., heart disease, AIDS) that varied in degree of controllability. For example, heart disease was attributed to the person's heredity (an uncontrollable factor) in one scenario and to excessive smoking and a high-cholesterol diet (controllable factors) in another scenario. When a stigma was seen as uncontrollable, participants felt pity for the person and expressed a willingness to help. However, when a stigma was seen as controllable, participants responded with anger. Similarly, a study conducted at the University of Windsor found that people who attributed serious illness (e.g., HIV and lung cancer) to controllable factors were more likely to blame victims for their illness (Mantler, Schellenberg, & Page, 2003). In yet another study, Rotenberg (1998) found that students at Lakehead University were less accepting of a lonely student if they attributed his or her loneliness to controllable factors. More recently, Lawson (2003) found that women who gave birth to a disabled child were blamed more when prenatal diagnostic testing had been available to them compared to mothers for whom this test had not been available. This held true for both a large sample of university employees and a group of Canadian doctors. And finally, there is evidence that prejudice against overweight people is greatest in cultures where people are seen as personally responsible for being fat (Crandall et al., 2001)…

Why are people so motivated to explain other people's misfortunes in dispositional terms, rather than to consider the situational factors that could have produced these negative outcomes? According to research on defensive attributions, one way we deal with these unsettling reminders that bad things happen is by explaining them, to make it seem as if they could never happen to us. We do so by believing that bad things happen only to bad people. Melvin Lerner (1980) at the University of Waterloo has called this belief in a just world-the assumption that people get what they deserve and deserve what they get. By using this attributional bias, the perceiver does not have to acknowledge that there is a certain randomness in life, that an accident or a criminal or unemployment may be just around the corner for an innocent person. Indeed, in an ingenious set of experiments, Carolyn Hafer (2000a) at Brock University demonstrated that the greater people's belief in a just world was threatened by hearing about an attack on an innocent person, the more likely they were to derogate the victim's character and to distance themselves from the victim. Presumably, by doing so they were able to convince themselves that bad things happen only to bad people-and since they themselves are good, surely no misfortune will befall them.

More recently, Hafer (2000b, 2002) has identified another reason why people subscribe to just world beliefs, namely that such beliefs motivate us to invest in our future. We will not be very motivated to plan ahead and make long-term investments if we believe that the world is an unfair, unjust place. To test this idea, Hafer (2000b) asked Brock University students to write an essay about their plans after graduation; other students were asked to write about their current university courses and activities. Later, all students saw a video of a young woman, named Sarah, who was seeing a counsellor because she had recently contracted a sexually transmitted disease. In the "innocent victim" version of the videotape, Sarah said that she and her partner had used a condom but it had broken during sex; in the "not innocent" version, Sarah admitted that no condom had been used. Who was most likely to blame Sarah for contracting the disease, even when she was portrayed as an innocent victim? You guessed it - the students who earlier had been asked to focus on their long-term goals and plans. Presumably, these participants most needed to be reassured that their long-term investments would be rewarded according to principles of fairness and justice. By blaming Sarah for her fate, they were able to maintain this belief.

***

Culture and Attributions

For decades, the attributional biases we've discussed (the fundamental attribution error, the actor/observer difference, and defensive attributions) were thought to be universal. People everywhere, it was thought, applied these cognitive shortcuts when forming attributions (Norenzayan, Choi, & Nisbett, 1999). But social psychologists are focusing more and more on the role of culture in many aspects of social behaviour. Given that social psychology is the study of how the situation affects the individual, we can think of culture as an all-encompassing, higher-level situational variable. You are born into a culture; as you grow up, you learn the rules, norms, and ways of labelling reality that define your culture. In short, culture is one of the biggest "situations" affecting your daily life. In the past decade, social psychologists have explored attributional biases across cultures, with very interesting results. For example, do people everywhere make the fundamental attribution error? Or is culture-specifically Western culture-a cause of the attributional biases we have been discussing? Let's look at the evidence.

Culture And The Fundamental Attribution Error

There is evidence that the fundamental attribution error is, in fact, more likely to occur in Western culture, which emphasizes individual freedom and autonomy and socializes us to prefer dispositional attributions over situational ones (Dix, 1993; Rholes, Newman, & Ruble, 1990). In comparison, collectivist (often Asian) cultures emphasize group membership, interdependence, and conformity to group norms (Fletcher & Ward, 1988; Markus & Kitayama, 1991; Newman, 1991; Triandis, 1990; Zebrowitz-McArthur, 1988). These cultural values suggest that people would be socialized to take situational factors into account. In a classic study, for example, Joan Miller (1984) asked people of two cultures - Hindus living in India and Americans living in the United States - to think of various examples of behaviours performed by their friends, and to explain why those behaviours occurred. Consistent with what we've said so far, the American participants preferred dispositional explanations for the behaviours; they were more likely to say that the causes of their friends' behaviours were the kinds of people they are, rather than the situation or context in which the behaviours occurred. In contrast, Hindu participants preferred situational explanations for their friends' behaviours (Miller, 1984).

"But," you might be thinking, "perhaps the American and Hindu participants generated different kinds of examples. Perhaps the Hindus thought of behaviours that really were more situationally caused, whereas the Americans thought of behaviours that really were more dispositionally caused." To test this alternative hypothesis, Miller (1984) took some of the behaviours generated by the Hindu participants and gave them to Americans to explain. The difference in internal and external attributions was again observed: American participants preferred dispositional causes for the behaviours that the Hindu participants had thought were situationally caused.

***

Finally, in a more recent study, Chin, Morris, Hong, and Menon (2000) asked members of the public in the United States and Hong Kong to read a scenario about patients who got sick because a pharmacy worker made an error while mixing medicines. As expected, Americans made more dispositional attributions (assigning responsibility to the worker), whereas the Chinese were more likely to assign responsibility to the clinic (e.g., poor management, incompetent training of workers). This cultural difference was even more pronounced in a follow-up laboratory study when some participants answered the questions while performing another task. Presumably under these conditions, participants engaged in automatic processing (see Chapter 3), with the result that American participants were especially likely to blame the worker and Chinese participants were especially likely to blame the clinic.

Thus, people in Western cultures appear to be more like personality psychologists, viewing behaviour in dispositional terms. When making attributions about others, the initial, automatic, and effortless attribution tends to be dispositional. Only if they are motivated to think more deeply will Westerners come up with situational explanations (Lee, Hallahan, & Herzog, 1996; Webster, 1993). In contrast, people in Asian (collectivist) cultures seem to be more like social psychologists, viewing behaviour in situational terms. Their initial, automatic, and effortless attribution tends to be situational and again, only if they are motivated to engage in more cognitive work will they come up with possible dispositional attributions (Lee, Hallahan, & Herzog, 1996; Krull, 1993).

Culture And Other Attributional Biases

Social psychologists have also examined the link between culture and the actor/observer difference (Van Boven et al., 2003). For example, Incheol Choi and Richard Nisbett (1998) examined the actor/observer difference among American and Korean research participants. These groups did not differ in the attributions they made to themselves -the "actors." They both made situational attributions for their behaviour. They differed only in the attributions they formed about another person, and in a familiar way. American participants were more likely to think that the other person's behaviour derived from his or her disposition (the fundamental attribution error), whereas Korean participants were more likely to think that the other person's behaviour was caused by the situation.

Recent research suggests that, like the other attributional biases we have discussed, the self-serving bias has a strong cultural component as well. For example, traditional Chinese culture values modesty and harmony with others. As a result, Chinese students are expected to attribute their successes to other people-such as their parents or teachers or to other aspects of the situation - such as the quality of their school - rather than to themselves (Bond, 1996; Leung, 1996). Indeed, in several experiments, researchers have found that Chinese participants take less credit for their successes and more blame for their failures than do American participants (Anderson, 1999; Lee & Seligman, 1997; Oishi, Wyer, & Colcombe, 2000)....

Finally, we also discussed unrealistic optimism in this chapter. This attributional bias, too, may be a Western phenomenon. In a study by Heine and Lehman (1995), students at the University of British Columbia showed classic unrealistic optimism. They assumed that negative events (e.g., contracting AIDS, becoming an alcoholic) were less likely to happen to them than the "average" UBC student, and that positive events were more likely to happen to them. However, when students at Nagasaki University in Japan were asked to make the same judgments, the opposite was true: Japanese students believed that bad things were more likely to happen to them and good things were less likely to happen to them than to the average student at their university.

How Accurate Are Our Attributions and Impressions?

When we make attributions, our goal is to be able to understand other people and predict what they will do. It is obviously to our advantage to make attributions that are as accurate as possible. But how accurate are we? The answer in a nutshell is that under many circumstances, we are not very accurate, especially compared to how accurate we think we are. For example, research has found that first impressions-the quick, attributional snapshots we form when we first meet someone-are not very accurate (DePaulo et al., 1987; Funder & Colvin, 1988). However, our impressions of others do become more accurate the more we get to know them (Wegener & Petty, 1995). At the University of British Columbia, Delroy Paulhus and his colleagues (Paulbus & Bruce, 1992; Paulhus & Reynolds, 1995) had students complete a variety of standard personality questionnaires. They then interacted in groups on a weekly basis for a seven-week period. Each group consisted of between five and seven students who did not previously know one another. After weeks 1, 4, and 7, the group members rated one another's personalities...the correlation between students' self-ratings and the group members' ratings of them increased over time, suggesting that people's perceptions of one another were becoming more accurate...the accuracy of the group members' perceptions was far from perfect....[b]ut it did increase significantly with increased acquaintance.

Thus, the evidence suggests that our impressions of others do become more accurate as we get to know them. However, it is also apparent that there is plenty of room for improvement. Sometimes our impressions of other people - even those we know well are just plain wrong. Why might that be?

The first culprit is our familiar friend, the fundamental attribution error. People are too ready to attribute others' actions to their personalities rather than to the situation. For example, suppose you meet Andrea at a party and she is acting in an outgoing, sociable manner. If you are like most people, you will conclude that Andrea is outgoing and sociable, rather than taking into consideration that you are meeting her in a situation where most people act sociably-a fun party. We don't mean to imply that people are always wrong when making dispositional attributions, but when they overlook situational causes of another person's behaviour they are likely to end up with faulty impressions.

To improve the accuracy of your impressions, remember that the fundamental attribution error, the actor/observer difference, and defensive attributions exist, and try to counteract these biases. Before deciding that another person is shy, for example, ask your self whether the situation that he or she is in might account for the seeming shyness. Even if a person actually is shy, try to resist the tendency to draw inferences about the other person's qualities based on your implicit personality theories. For example, University of British Columbia researchers Paulhus and Morgan (1997) found that if someone was shy, people also tended to assume that the person was unintelligent-an assumption that simply was not true. To reduce defensive attributions, it can be helpful to give our self- esteem a boost (e.g., via self-affirmation; see Chapter 5) so that we are less likely to feel threatened when we fail or when bad things happen (Sherman & Kim, 2005).

Let's cut to the chase. Yes, we are quite accurate perceivers of other people. We do very well most of the time. We are adept at reading and interpreting nonverbal forms of communication; in fact, most of us are actually better at this than we realize (Ambady, Bernieri, &Richeson, 2000; Archer & Akert, 1980). We become more accurate at perceiving others as we get to know them better, and since most of our truly important social interactions involve people we know well, this is good news. In short, we are capable of making both blindingly accurate assessments of people and horrific attributional mistakes.

***

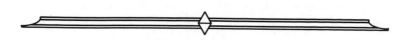

EMOTIONS AND INTERPERSONAL COMMUNICATION

Excerpts from Chapter 5 of Beebe, S.A., Beebe, S.J., Redmond, M. Geerlink, T. (2004). *Interpersonal Communication: Relating to Others*, 3rd Canadian Edition, Toronto: Pearson Education Canada.

***

"Oh, did you see that deer! I just about hit it! I think we have to pull over. I'm shaking like a leaf!" exclaimed Jenna.
"Okay, just take a couple of deep breaths. Thank goodness you missed it," replied Tia. "I'm shaking too!"

***

Interpersonal communication cannot be properly discussed without including the topic of emotions. Emotions are an integral part of communication. As the above scene depicts, the two women while communicating verbally are also communicating and experiencing emotions through non-verbal channels. During communication with others, we feel and react to the messages that we receive. Often we are surprised by others' reactions to what we say—what we intended and what was received are not always the same message. Or we may communicate in order to get a specific emotional reaction such as telling a joke to make another person laugh. Emotions are displayed non-verbally...

We begin by defining emotions and the physiological make-up and effects of emotion. Then we will turn our attention to examining the impact of emotions on interpersonal communication and the factors that influence our emotional expression. Third, skills in two areas: skills for recognizing and dealing with the emotions of others and skills for managing your own emotions will be explored including the managing of some difficult emotions.

There are several theories of emotions [to be outlined below]...Here we will not examine these theories but rather examine what all of these theories have in common. These theories all conclude that emotions are triggered by environmental stimuli and that we react to these stimuli both physically and cognitively. For example, Jenna and Tia almost hit a deer and, realizing how close they were to having an accident, experience both the fear of almost hitting something and the relief of not hitting something. Physically both women are shaking, and Jenna needs to pull over to regain her composure. Emotions, then, are reactions to the environment and consist of physiological reactions, subjective cognitive states, and behavioural reactions. Scientists generally agree on these three characteristics of emotions. Let's examine each of these three characteristics more closely.

Physiological Effects of Emotions

When we encounter a situation, our bodies respond physiologically. For example, you are walking home late at night and hear a noise behind you that sounds like footsteps. Your heart rate increases, the hair on the back of your neck stands up, and your mouth suddenly goes dry. These reactions are prompted by your autonomic nervous system—the part of your nervous system that connects internal organs, glands, and involuntary muscles to the central nervous system. Two parts of the autonomic nervous system are active in regulating the physiological reactions that accompany emotion. The activation of the *sympathetic nervous system* readies the body for vigorous action by performing such functions as increasing the heart rate, blood pressure, and respiration. The *parasympathetic nervous system* helps restore the body's resources through such actions as diverting blood from large muscles to the digestive organs for digestion. For the most part, you do not actively control these aspects of your nervous system, which include such activities as maintaining your heart rate, breathing, swallowing, digestion, and other more "automatic" physiological functioning. Part of these automatic reactions to a stimulus activated by the sympathetic nervous system is the fight or flight response, which prepares you for action in such situations as the example of being followed late at night or preparing the body for impact in a near car accident. While a rather simplistic explanation of the complex bodily reactions that occur during an event, it serves to illustrate the nature of emotions as having physical impact in the body that can range from extremes such as created by fear to other emotions such as happiness or sadness. For milder emotions, we may not feel that we are experiencing any physiological changes at all.

Heightened Arousal

When we are angry, frustrated, or upset, we experience physiological arousal. Recent research has examined more closely the relationship of heightened physiological arousal and emotions. In many situations the body prepares itself for "fight or flight," even though neither behaviour may be required. For example, you are rushing in your car to meet your sister at a restaurant. On the way, you are narrowly missed by a driver who swerves into your lane and barely misses you. Your heart pounds, your mouth goes dry, and your hands clench the steering wheel. If you are like many of us, you may also utter a few choice words! As you continue to drive, you feel less stressed. When you get to the restaurant 10 minutes late, your sister is not there. You wait another 10 minutes. You finally order a coffee and are still waiting. As your sister approaches, you say angrily, "It's about time you got here! What took you so long?" A growing body of research indicates that such emotional arousal lasts long after an incident and is very slow to dissipate. It also appears that under some conditions, heightened arousal can enhance aggressive responses, regardless of the source of the arousal. According to excitation transfer theory, because physiological arousal takes time to dissipate, this arousal can be transferred to other situations. Instead of becoming merely annoyed (a small increase in arousal) at a further small incident (your sister being late), you become enraged. You are unaware of the *residual arousal* from the car experience and therefore attribute the arousal to your sister's lateness: even when you are aware of this arousal, you attribute it to the current situation. In other words, past emotionally arousing events continue to affect you long after the event is over. This has many implications for communication. If we are not aware of this residual arousal, we may not understand why we are feeling the way we are later when we overreact to the next event. Have you ever been surprised at someone who you feel has overreacted to an event? One answer for such overreaction is the presence of this residual arousal.

Cognitive Effects of Emotion

The second characteristic is the subjective experience of emotions based on the personality and characteristics of the person. Who you are affects your experience and interpretation of an event. In other words, your cognitions or thoughts about an event affect how you feel. If you are over 180 cm tall and weigh over 90 kg, you do not even notice the sound of the footsteps, or if you do, you may think to yourself, "Hope this person does not want any trouble, because he is going to be messing with the wrong person." But if you are just over 150 cm tall, weigh 45 kg, and are terrified of being mugged, you may well perceive this as a threatening situation and experience fear. In the first example, the increased heartbeat of the person is the thrill of a possible fight, whereas in the second example, the increased heartbeat is the fear of possibly being hurt. In both cases, the physiological symptoms are the same, but the interpretations are different. Missing the deer was a great relief for both women in our opening example. Since their sympathetic nervous systems were activated so quickly, the shaking occurs after the event as their parasympathetic nervous systems attempt to calm them down again.

While there is often a direct connection between the body and emotions, the mind and our thoughts play an important role in determining our feelings in any situation. The body reacts similarly to both fearful and joyful situations. It is up to us to determine what the physiological changes mean, which is a large component of theories of emotion proposed by various researchers. Such theories concentrate on the role of cognition and use *cognitive labels* to describe what we are feeling as a result of our interpretation of the situation. When we are not sure how we are feeling, we look outward for clues to assist us in identifying our emotions. In other words, when we experience some sort of physiological arousal, we think about what we are feeling and then add the label. For example, if you win a large sum of money, you label the physiological effects as joy! External events and cues assist us in labeling how we are feeling.

Cognition also influences emotions through the activation of *schemas.* Schemas are organized mental representations or a system of cognitions about something such as an event, a role, a type of person, and so on. For example, you have schemas about weddings and the characteristics of a good teacher. These schemas are organized in our minds and help us to define and understand events. Emotions are also part of schemas. At a wedding you expect people to be happy; you expect yourself to be happy for the couple. But how would you react if everyone looked sad or if the bride and groom started fighting? Chances are you would try to figure out what is going on by looking at others around you and trying to determine how they are feeling about this turn of events.

Behavioural Effects and Emotions

In many cases, we end up guessing how a person feels by watching his or her behaviour. Most of this behaviour is non-verbal and we make assumptions about how someone is feeling based on non-verbal clues.... This is the third component of emotions: the behavioural expression of the internal feeling or state. If someone starts shouting at you, waves his or her arms, and stomps his or her feet, you would hazard the guess that the person is angry or very upset about something. We continually assess situations based upon the behaviour of the people involved—not an easy task, especially in situations that are ambiguous or that we have little information about. For example, your roommate is angry with you but you have no idea what she could be angry about. You know she is angry because she looks angry—a red face, tight lips, and refusing to speak to you. How do you know if someone is about to lose control? How do you know if your message is being well received or even understood? Paying close attention to non-verbal behavior and to other uncontrolled actions will become an important skill for you to learn. Emotions are communicated non-verbally…

It is often easy to interpret strong emotions as the internal physiological changes are also manifested outwardly. For example, if someone is angry his or her blood pressure increases, which may result in "going red in the face," an easily observable behaviour. Under the influence of strong emotions, people turn red in the face (blush), perspire, grit their teeth, clench fists, pout, cry, slump in posture, and engage in other readily observable behavioural manifestations of the emotion. But what about emotions that are not strong, or two or more emotions that can be illustrated by the same behaviours? Is the person who is red in the face angry, embarrassed, or experiencing high blood pressure? Is the person who is perspiring nervous or excited? People can also mask their emotions to some degree. We can smile even when we do not feel like it and pretend not to be angry when we are seething under the surface. In many public situations, we cannot demonstrate how we feel as social etiquette may dictate how we are to respond. Few of us yell at our bosses during a meeting. It goes against social norms and chances are it will also damage our career path… non-verbal behaviour can also be ambiguous and difficult to read….

***

The Depth and Breadth of Emotions

Before looking at the factors that influence emotional expression, we need to more closely look at two other characteristics of emotion: depth and breadth. We experience emotions on many different levels. You can be overjoyed or mildly amused. How does it feel when you are apprehensive, yet happy? Just how many emotions are there, and do they differ in intensity?

How Many Emotions

We can feel many, many emotions and even feel different emotions at the same time… there appear to be six universal emotions including happiness (joy), anger, sadness, surprise, fear, and disgust. One researcher has labeled these as primary emotions and adds to these two other emotions: acceptance and anticipation. [As outlined earlier] Plutchik defines these primary emotions as being simple or made up of just one feeling. Other emotions are more complex and are labelled as mixed emotions because they are blends of the primary emotions. For example, according to Plutchik, the emotion of love consists of joy and acceptance and the emotion of contempt is a combination of anger and disgust. These mixed emotions are more difficult to read accurately. The real key here is that there are a great number of emotions and emotional states that we experience and some are more complex than others....

Intensity of Emotions

Emotions also vary in intensity. Think of the difference between mild annoyance and rage. Mildly annoyed, you may tell a person what you think in a calm and cool manner; but, if in a rage, you may scream at the person. The more intense the emotions, the more likely you will feel the physiological effects of experiencing the emotion, and the chances are higher that others will recognize how you feel. It should be noted that people vary in how well they communicate or feel emotions. For some people, everything that happens leads to intense feelings. To them, everything is "absolutely wonderful" or, at the other extreme, everything is an "absolute disaster." Some people are very clear when they experience strong emotions, but may not be clear about how they feel when experiencing less intense emotions (hence the need to examine the situation to assist in identifying emotion).

Factors that Influence Emotional Expression

We all feel emotions, so why don't we just express them? Why is it that many of us readily give opinions, state facts and figures, but become tongue-tied and uncomfortable when asked to express how we feel? Obviously, people differ in this comfort level with some people telling you exactly how they feel (to the point where you want to leave the room) while others stay tight-lipped and rarely, if ever, express how they feel. There are many factors that influence how and when we express our emotions. Here we will briefly outline a few, including culture, gender, etiquette, and roles.

Culture

… [T]he influence of culture on the expression of emotion deserves some mention here. Your culture is your learned and shared system of knowledge, beliefs, values, and norms. Earlier, you learned that some emotions are universally experienced and expressed across all cultures and are easy to identify, whereas blends of emotions are more difficult for people to identify. The culture you were born into has had profound influence upon you in many ways; one of those ways is the rules or norms of acceptable emotional expression. Cultures vary in many ways, including expressiveness of emotions, non-verbal communication of emotions, and differences in what is emotionally pleasing or displeasing.

Some cultures are more emotionally expressive than others and display their emotions more openly than other cultures. For example, one study found evidence that people from warmer climates are more emotionally expressive than those who live in cooler places. Individualistic cultures (like Canada and the United States), which are more oriented toward the "self" rather than harmony, allow individuals to express their emotions more openly. More collectivistic cultures (such as Japan and China) with their emphasis on harmony, discourage members from overt displays, particularly of negative emotions such as anger or dislike. Another cultural dimension to take into consideration is the difference between high-context and low-context cultures. High-context cultures rely heavily on non-verbal cues for communication, whereas cultures classified as low-context rely more on verbal cues to communicate messages. People raised in low-context cultures may not be as adept at reading non-verbal behaviour as are individuals from high-context cultures. Since many non-verbal behaviours indicate emotions, members from these cultures may fail to recognize some emotions.

People from high-context cultures tend to spend less time speaking and use fewer words. High-context cultures include Japan, Greece, and Arab nations. Low-context cultures include the United States, Germany, and German-Swiss cultures.

Gender

Men and women are different in how they express emotions, at least in some major areas, according to research. Research continues to lend some credence to the stereotype of the male who displays few emotions and the more emotionally expressive female. Women tend to express how they feel, whereas men are less likely to do so. Women use more emotionally expressive words than men and are quicker to express how they feel. Women also tend to "show" how they feel more than men. For example, one research study found that women displayed more facial expression and had stronger physiological reactions to emotion-provoking films. Also, males who scored high in masculinity on a questionnaire to assess gender identity had much less facial expressiveness than males whose results were less masculine or androgynous. Regardless of sex, people who were classified as androgynous experienced the highest levels of arousal and displayed more emotion. Interestingly, more females were androgynous than males.

Of course, these are research results; not all males lack expressiveness and not all females are expressive. Other factors must also be taken into consideration such as socialization. For instance, both men and women raised in emotionally expressive families feel stronger emotions even if only the women display the emotions. Also, women and men are socialized into different gender communication cultures. Games that girls favour when they are young include playing house and school, and games which include sensitivity and cooperation between players. Boys' games, such as baseball, soccer, and war, have more clear-cut rules and rely less on talk and cooperation. Girls are taught to use talk expressively to deal with feelings, personal ideas, and problems and to build relationships. On the other hand, boys tend to use talk instrumentally to solve problems, take stands on issues, and give advice.

Etiquette

Etiquette, or the rules around what is socially appropriate or inappropriate, affects emotional expression. Many social situations have rules or norms that serve as guides to behaviour. Several of these norms also influence what constitutes appropriate emotional expression. First, many formal or public settings have social rules for emotional expression. While it may be appropriate to loudly laugh and scream in your dorm room, at a sporting event, or at a bar, few people would do the same in a funeral home or church (or other places of worship where this behaviour is frowned upon). Many workplaces also have rules that frown upon employees who are loud and boisterous when serious work is supposed to be taking place. Second, the social situation itself may dictate the type of emotional expression. People talking quietly about a recent disaster or sharing sad news would not be impressed by your latest imitation of the prime minister. This type of joking behaviour goes against the solemnity of the current topic. On the flip side, if everyone is laughing and joking, you will be seen as "bringing everyone down" if you appear glum or moody. Finally, etiquette may govern the intensity of emotional expression. When given a substantial raise by your boss, you are likely not going to literally jump up and down with joy in front of her. You will probably graciously thank your boss (then run into the washroom to jump up and down!).

Roles

The roles that people have in society also influence emotional expression. In many roles, you have to control your emotional expression. Teachers and many other professionals are expected to maintain rational behaviour and to control their emotions, particularly negative ones like anger. In other roles, such as salespeople, receptionists, and dentists, we wear a mask of pleasantry, even joviality. In other words, the roles we undertake dictate, to some extent, how much emotion we express and even what emotions we can express.

***

Skills for Recognizing and Sharing Emotions

Since emotions range in how easily we can recognize them, we need to learn some skills to better understand the emotions of others. A second set of skills that we need to learn is to better understand our own emotions and to learn effective ways to share how we feel with others. This final and critical section will cover both areas including a special section on recognizing and dealing with difficult emotions.

Skills for Dealing with Others' Emotions

Have you ever had the experience where you completely misunderstood another person and what he or she was trying to tell you? Instead of building communication bridges, you widen the gap of misunderstanding. Here we offer some tips to help you become more skilled in understanding how others feel and how you can more appropriately respond to their emotional states. Part of being an other-oriented communicator is to try to understand and respond to how others are feeling.

Recognize Individual Differences in How Emotions Are Experienced

It can be difficult to understand another person's feelings, because the same event may have made you feel differently. This is of paramount importance for you to realize; we all respond differently even to the same event including catastrophes, losses, and even the death of loved ones. Often we make an assumption that because we are sad or happy about an event, others will also feel similarly. While one person may be sad at the loss of a parent, another person can be relieved at the death of a parent. While the event is the same, the circumstances may be very different. Some events may evoke the same emotional response, such as a beautiful ballet or a nostalgic movie, but do not assume that others will react as you do.

Be Aware That Non-verbal Expression of Emotion Is Contagious

Have you ever noticed that when you watch a funny movie, you are more likely to laugh out loud if other people around you are laughing? That when you are around people who are sad or remorseful, you are more likely to feel and express sadness? There's a reason this happens. Non-verbal emotional expressions are contagious. People often display the same emotions that a communication partner is displaying. Emotional contagion theory suggests that people tend to "catch" the emotions of others. Interpersonal interactions with others can affect your non-verbal expression of emotions. The ancient Roman orator Cicero knew this when he gave advice to public speakers. He said, if you want your audience to experience joy, you must be a joyful speaker. Or, if you want to communicate fear, then you should express fear when you speak. Knowing that you tend to catch or imitate the emotions of others can help you interpret your own non-verbal messages and those of others; you may be imitating the emotional expression of others around you.

Use Perception Checking

…When you are unclear how another person is feeling, you can ask the person or tentatively interpret the other person's emotions. For example, if you arrive home from classes and see that your partner is "looking angry," you can check this out in a very non-threatening way by saying something like, "you look like you have had a rough day and something is troubling you. Want to talk about it?" Notice that this statement allows the other person to report back specifically how he or she is feeling without you "putting words into his or her mouth." Another way is to state what you think the person is feeling, but do so in a way that allows the other person to correct you. For example, using the above situation, you could say, "you look like you're having a bad day and something may have made you angry." By using the word *may,* the statement and hence your interpretation are not carved in stone. Perception checking opens the door for communication while minimizing the chances of the other person becoming defensive.

Use Humour

When others are feeling sadness, anger, frustration, fatigue, and other negative emotions, your use of humour can brighten a dismal day and encourage sharing. For example, a statement such as "Who let the bear in and where did my friend go?" might lighten your friend's mood and encourage talk. However, do not trivialize how another person feels with such comments or make fun of someone who is feeling low. Humour is best used when you know a person well.

Suggestions for Expressing and Managing Your Own Emotions

At home and work, we experience a broad range of feelings. Part of being an effective interpersonal communicator is to manage and communicate how you feel appropriately. Have you ever lost your temper and regretted your words later? Or did you not tell someone how you really felt only to lose the friendship or damage the relationship? If you have said yes to these questions, then you are already on your way to becoming a better "emotions manager." You have recognized that self-expression is not always an easy task, especially when you are feeling strong emotions. The following suggestions will assist you to become an even better "emotions manager" by providing you with some guidelines for expression.

Recognize Your Feelings

Sometimes, our lives get so busy and things get so hectic that we do not stop long enough to ask ourselves, "How do I feel?" When you do not take the time to gauge your emotions, they can take you by surprise. You can monitor your feelings by paying attention to the physiological signs that we discussed earlier. Your physiological state can be a clear indicator of how you are feeling. For example, your professor has requested a meeting with you after class in her office. If your hands are sweaty, your heart is beating wildly, and your mouth is dry prior to talking to your professor you may discover that you are nervous. Also, you can use your non-verbal language as a gauge of how you are feeling and how intense the emotion you are experiencing is. Before talking to your professor, are you pacing the hallway, clenching and unclenching your fists? Also, pay attention to what you are thinking. What are the thoughts that are causing this nervousness? For example, do you think you failed the last test or are in some other trouble? Maybe she wishes to speak to you about a possible summer job.

Take Ownership for Your Feelings

Often, we blame others for how we feel as if they were personally responsible for our emotional state. Have you ever said things like, "You make me so mad / happy / frustrated"? (Or fill in whatever feeling you like.) In reality, you make yourself feel the way you do; it is your perception and cognitions that often lead to your emotional state. A good example is "road rage," a term coined to refer to incidents where a driver (or drivers) engages in behaviour dangerous to others. We have all read about incidents where one driver has even stopped the other and hurt or killed the other person! In many "road rage" incidents, the victim may be unaware of his or her transgression. In other words, the driver made himself or herself angry and, as a result, behaved in dangerous, rude, or even illegal ways. We own our feelings and need to express them in that way. Instead of saying "You make me so mad," change this to "I feel mad when. . ." These "I messages" clearly state who owns the feelings: you. If you own the feelings, then you can change them by re-examining the precipitating factors or event. The Building Your Skills exercise below will assist you with a review of active listening by using "I messages." ... By changing your perception of an event, you can also modify your feelings. If you remember that not all drivers are out to get you, then you will likely not feel angry when someone cuts you off or turns into your path. If a co-worker continually requests help, change your perception of frustration to one a little more soothing. This co-worker requests your help because you are good at what you do and admires your skill. ... If you own your emotions, then you can change them.

Think, Before You Speak

While this tip seems obvious, this suggestion is not always followed, especially when we are under the influence of powerful emotions such as anger, frustration, or sadness. We launch out with a tirade about how we feel without really thinking about our feelings or even labelling them correctly. ... Instead of using simple terms like *mad, happy, great,* and *terrible,* expand your thoughts and describe your feelings in more detail. You can even use descriptions about how your body feels, such as "I'm shaking like a leaf," or "I feel all tied up in knots." These statements are more accurate and do not leave the person you are speaking to wondering what you really are feeling in a situation. Also, use phrases so that you describe how you are feeling in more detail. Feelings do not only happen one at a time. You can be feeling many emotions simultaneously. You may not just be mad at your partner. You may also be disappointed or embarrassed. If your roommate gets drunk at a party and shares a confidence loudly to everyone, you may feel angry and disappointed at the betrayal. You might also feel embarrassed to watch a friend act so foolishly. These are the feelings that you want to describe, not just the anger.

Know When to Feel, Talk, or Act

Sometimes we need to get in touch with how we feel before expressing ourselves, or acting on those feelings. When something happens to you, you may have many feelings that you need to sort out. For example, if your girlfriend breaks up with you, you can experience a lot of feelings—anger, sadness, confusion, disbelief—and you need time to sort these feelings out. Talking about your feelings can help you understand them and it may be appropriate to confide in a friend or family member to help you sort through your feelings. If you are experiencing a trauma or cannot understand your feelings, professional counselling can be a valuable way to talk about your experiences. Often, people act too quickly, even rashly, without thinking about their feelings or even talking about them with another. People who rebound into other relationships, for example, have not worked through their feelings and are often headed toward further relationship disaster.

Frustration

Frustration occurs when an individual is blocked from doing something he or she wants to do; behaviour toward a *goal* is thwarted. For example, if you are headed for an important appointment and have to drive behind a very slow driver, you may experience frustration, thinking you may be late. The experience of frustration may be the antecedent to conflict. For example, people who feel frustrated when driving may act out their frustration by tailgating or honking their horn, which may create conflict with the other driver. According to some research, frustration can lead to anger and subsequent aggression. The original **frustration-aggression hypothesis** proposed that frustration led to a tendency toward aggression. In other words, aggression was preceded by frustration. Later theories have included the cognitive component of appraisal. People think about the event and, based on their appraisal of it, decide whether or not the event is frustrating. If they appraise it as extremely frustrating, they may become angry and aggressive. In other words, how you perceive the event and the extent to which it arouses negative feelings influence how much aggression you will display, if any. For example, if the appointment is not that important to you or is perhaps distasteful (such as having a root canal), you may experience less frustration.

Anger

Anger is a common experience during a conflict. We all know that feeling—anger. It can build slowly or suddenly ignite, and it can make it hard to maintain control of oneself. **Anger** is a feeling of extreme hostility, indignation, or exasperation. Anger is stimulated when appraisal indicates that others are responsible for the achievement of an individual's goal. If you feel that someone is getting in the way of [your] achieving something, you may become angry. Anger creates stress and brings about a number of physiological changes that were discussed earlier. Internally, the heart rate increases, blood pressure increases, galvanic skin responses change, and breathing becomes shallower and quicker. But we cannot see these changes and need the help of other indicators that we can see when standing at a distance.

Recent research has shed some light on two types of maladaptive anger, termed "anger-in and anger-out." According to Martin and Wan, people prone to anger-in responses suffer frequent, ruminative angry feelings. These feelings do not go away and colour future judgments and appraisals. Those who experience anger-out lash out at others, doing such things as slamming doors, striking out at others, and being verbally abusive and threatening. Both types of anger contribute to the development of cardiovascular disease.

Non-verbal Signals of Anger

Outwardly, there may be several physical non-verbal indicators of anger that you can see if you are close enough. If the person is breathing more rapidly, you may notice it if the individual is wearing tighter-fitting clothing around the chest. While most people do not lose control when they are angry, it is good to know levels of anger and when to identify clues that someone's angry behaviour is escalating. One

78

noticeable indicator of anger is enlargement of the pupils, which creates the look known as "wide-eyed with rage."

According to Ouellette, a trainer in managing aggressive behaviour, there are three areas of non-verbal behaviour that can reveal anger. Gestures, including facial colour, can give many clues about anger. A person's face may redden if the person is light-skinned. However, when a person becomes extremely angry (rage), the face may drain of all colour—a sign of possible physical attack. Opening and closing fists and baring teeth are two other important gestures to examine.

Second, he recommends that the person's eyes be closely monitored. Eyes that dart from side to side or up and down may indicate that the person feels trapped. "Target glances" occur when a person looks at a target person before attack. For example, the person may look at your chin before trying to hit it. If the person is going to attempt to flee, he or she may glance at possible exits.

The third area that can reveal anger is the use of space. A person may try to close the distance when angry. People who are more aggressive try to intimidate by controlling personal space such as moving closer to the individual they are trying to control or manipulate. Have you ever had the experience with someone who is angry when they move closer to you and jab you in the shoulder with a finger? How do you feel? Do you feel angry yourself? Do you feel defensive?

It is also important that we learn to recognize the signs of our own anger. By recognizing when we are becoming angry, we can work on controlling our anger so that we don't do something that we may regret later. Being in control of such strong emotions will decrease the chances of doing or saying something that may have personal and/or professional repercussions....

Verbal Aggression

When some people are very angry, they may also become verbally aggressive. Why are some people verbally aggressive? There may be any of several reasons. ... [R]ecent research emphasizing what is called the "communibiological approach to communication" suggests that we are each born with certain traits or characteristics. It's just the nature of some people to be verbally aggressive. Being verbally aggressive is also closely linked to the concept of seeking power in a relationship. Verbally aggressive people often use hurtful language as a way of gaining or maintaining power over others. They may learn that they can get what they want by bullying others. As long as they continue to get what they want and are reinforced for their heavy-handed verbal aggressiveness, they will continue to do it. Still other people are verbally aggressive as a way of expressing bottled-up emotions and frustrations. And finally, verbal aggressiveness is contagious. When one person is verbally aggressive, the other person is likely to reciprocate.

What should you do if you are a victim of verbal aggressiveness? The simple and obvious answer is to avoid relationships with people who are verbally aggressive. The verbally aggressive person may need more power and confirmation of his or her own worth; trying to find constructive strategies to let the aggressor know he or she is valued may help. But if long-held patterns of being verbally aggressive are present, don't expect quick or dramatic changes in the aggressive person by just offering him or her compliments. Verbally aggressive comments by others are often triggered by anger just as the non-verbal elements are triggered....

Sadness

While sadness may not be the first emotion that crosses your mind as being a part of conflict, during or after a heated argument many people display sadness. Sadness covers a range of feelings from slight gloominess to overwhelming grief. All of us experience sadness and it can be a difficult emotion to manage. Sadness is a normal emotion and does not mean that something is wrong with us. Events that provoke sadness are often ones where we experience a loss: a friend, a romantic partner, a cherished possession, death of someone close to us. We can even become sad when we think about how things should have been or how things used to be. And how many of us have a "good" cry during a movie? Do not confuse normal sadness with depression. Depression is characterized by overwhelming feelings of gloom, despondency, and dejection. While you may feel depressed, only if there are several other long-term symptoms, such as diminished interest in everyday activities and pleasures, significant weight gain or loss, profound changes in sleeping habits (sleeping too much or insomnia), or loss of energy, would you be classified as experiencing depression. If these feelings and symptoms become extreme, you should get help immediately. If you notice these symptoms in someone you know well, you may want to encourage this person to also gain assistance.

Other than these obvious signs, what are the non-verbal indicators of sadness? A person who is sad may "droop" with sloping shoulders and appear to be "hunched into himself or herself." The mouth is downturned, and the chin may wobble as if the person were about to cry. A sad person may have difficulty with eye contact, and any talk about the problem may evoke an outpour of crying. The person may breathe irregularly as he or she tries to maintain control and keep emotions in check. One research study that focused on women found that sadness was an indicator in depression and was the dominant mood and emotion of the subjects. Other symptoms of depression include low mood, feelings of helplessness and hopelessness, negative attitudes about the self, and an inability to experience happiness or joy.

Managing Difficult Emotions When You Experience Them

Many of the earlier suggestions about managing your own emotions will also assist in helping you deal with these difficult emotions. However, emotions that are experienced frequently and interfere with you functioning effectively can be extremely debilitating. **Debilitating emotions** are intense and last a long time. For example, if I am angry at a co-worker because she is always late and I have to do extra work until she comes in, I can handle that anger appropriately through confrontation. I can say, "Sheila, you are consistently late and I end up doing your work. If it happens again, I will go to the boss. I will no longer pick up your slack." But what if I become enraged or let it bubble up inside me over a long period of time? This becomes a debilitating emotion. There have been many cases of such rage in the workplace leading a disgruntled worker to come back and shoot his co-workers. So how can you manage these debilitating emotions so that you do not become depressed, enraged, or so frustrated that you cannot cope? Here we offer several suggestions to assist you in managing powerful emotions such as anger.

Be Aware That You Are Becoming Angry and Emotionally Volatile

One characteristic of people who "lose it" is that they let their emotions get the best of them. Before they know it, they are saying and doing things that they later regret [an emotional Hi-Jack]. Unbridled and uncensored emotional outbursts rarely enhance the quality of an interpersonal relationship. An emotional purge may make you feel better, but your partner is likely to reciprocate, which will only escalate the conflict spiral. Before that happens, become aware of what is happening to you. As we described earlier, your body will start to react to your emotions with an increased heart rate. Be mindful of such changes. Be sensitive to what is happening to you physically.

***

UNDERSTANDING PERSONALITY TYPES:
A FIRST STEP TO HUMAN RELATIONS MASTERY

Excerpts from Chapter 1 of Anthony Falikowski's (2002) *Mastering Human Relations*, 2nd Edition, Toronto, Pearson Education.

***

Since the turn of the twentieth century, many different theories of personality have emerged. Two important ones have been the psychoanalytic and humanistic explanations. People such as Sigmund Freud (psychoanalytic) and Abraham Maslow (humanistic) have offered their own accounts of human personality functioning. One account that has received widespread attention is an offshoot of Carl Jung's analytical theory of personality types. A mother-daughter team of Katharine Briggs and Isabel Briggs Myers has taken the original insights of Jung, added to them, and developed for practical use the **Myers-Briggs Type Indicator (MBTI®),** an instrument used to help people identify their personality preferences. This instrument has been used by millions of people throughout the world for human resource development, team building and problem solving, as well as for personal counseling, therapy and education. The MBTI is a restricted psychological assessment tool that can only be used by trained and qualified personnel…

For our purposes here, I have created my own personality self-diagnostic that is different from the MBTI in terms of wording and format, but is theoretically consistent with its ideas and assumptions. It can help you to start thinking about your personality preferences using concepts and insights discussed by Jung, Myers and Briggs. While my informal self-diagnostic obviously will not be as reliable and valid as the highly researched MBTI, it can nonetheless help you form an initial hypothesis about your **psychological type,** the way you perceive, make decisions and orient toward the world. Most people who have completed both the MBTI and my self-diagnostic have tended to arrive at similar results. My self-diagnostic can therefore serve as a valuable tool for preliminary self-reflection. For those who are seriously interested in verifying their personality type, I would strongly suggest taking the MBTI with a qualified counsellor at your college or university. Ideally, your instructor would be in a position to have it administered to you in class. If that's not possible, you may wish to complete Gordon Lawrence's (1993) "Exercise: Thinking about Mental Habits" in *People Types and Tiger Stripes,* a source reference for my own work here. In any event, let us now establish our initial working hypothesis by completing Self-Diagnostic 1.1, Pinpointing My Personality Preferences.

Self -Diagnostic 1.1 Pinpointing My Personality Preferences

You can use this self-diagnostic tool to begin understanding yourself better. You're actually far too complex to "figure out" in one paper-and-pencil measure. Nonetheless, your results on this self-diagnostic can serve as a departure point for further self-exploration. See your results as a working hypothesis of who you are.

Instructions: Below are pairs of statements listed under lettered columns. Compare the statements in each pair and circle the letter beside the one that most accurately describes your preferences, behaviours or mental habits. Be sure to circle one—and ONLY one—letter in each pair. Some decisions may be difficult, especially when you like both statements. Simply pick the one for which you have the slightest preference. As well, choose the answer that feels right for you. Don't answer as you or others think you "should." Simply imagine yourself to be in a comfortable spot and answer the questions in a relaxed frame of mind. It's important to be accurate and honest. This is not your work-self or student-self answering; it is your "real" self.

Circle the statement of each pair below that describes you most accurately, E or I.

E		I	
E	I like fast living.	I	I like quiet time and space to contemplate my affairs.
E	I like the world outside.	I	I like the inner world
E	I like people and things.	I	I like ideas, thoughts and meanings.
E	I like to be talkative and outgoing.	I	I like to be quiet and reserved.
E	I like to be sociable with many.	I	I like to be introspective with few.
E	I like to be energized by activity.	I	I like to be energized by depth and intimacy.
E	I like to seek out new experiences.	I	I tend to avoid new experiences.
__	TOTAL	__	TOTAL

Add the number of both E and I statements circled. Place the letter with the highest total in the appropriate space below.

When it comes to E or I preferences, I tend to select ___ more.

Circle the statement of each pair below that describes you most accurately, S or N.

S		N	
S	I tend to be practical.	N	I tend to be idealistic.
S	I like the concrete.	N	I like the abstract.
S	I choose to use my eyes and ears and other senses to find out what's happening.	N	I choose to use my imagination to come up with new possibilities and novel ways of doing things.
S	I tend to be physically competitive.	N	I tend to be intellectually competitive.
S	I prefer to be results oriented.	N	I prefer to be idea oriented.
S	I like to look at the facts.	N	I like symbols, concepts and meanings.
S	I enjoy using skills I've already learned.	N	I enjoy using new skills more than practicing old ones.
__	TOTAL	__	TOTAL

Add the number of both S and N statements circled. Place the letter with the highest total in the appropriate space below.

When it comes to S or N preferences, I tend to select ___ more.

Circle the statement of each pair below that describes you most accurately, T or F.

T		F	
T	I like to make decisions based on logic.	F	I like to make decisions based on feelings and values even if illogical.
T	I tend to notice ineffective reasoning.	F	I tend to notice when people need support.
T	I prefer truthfulness over tact.	F	I prefer tactfulness over truth.
T	I decide more with my head.	F	I decide more with my heart.
T	I tend to focus on objective and universal principles.	F	I tend to focus on subjective and personal motives.
T	I like to deal with people firmly, when required.	F	I like to deal with people compassionately, when required.
T	I give more attention to ideas or things.	F	I give more attention to human relationships.
__	TOTAL	__	TOTAL

Add the number of both T and F statements circled. Place the letter with the highest total in the appropriate space below.

When it comes to T or F preferences, I tend to select ___ more.

Circle the statement of each pair below that describes you most accurately, J or P.

J		**P**	
J	I like closure, a sense of being finished.	P	I like to hang loose and stay open to new things.
J	I prefer advance notice.	P	I prefer spontaneous challenges.
J	I am task oriented.	P	I am process oriented.
J	I like to plan and decide.	P	I like to adapt and change.
J	I sometimes jump to conclusions prematurely.	P	I tend to postpone decisions and procrastinate.
J	I like to make things come out as they should.	P	I like to deal with unexpected and unplanned happenings.
J	I like to finish one thing before starting another.	P	I like to do several things at the same time, though I have trouble finishing them.
___	TOTAL	___	TOTAL

Add the number of both J and P statements circled. Place the letter with the highest total in the appropriate space below.

When it comes to J or P preferences, I tend to select ___ more.

Summary of Results

Under each set of paired statements you indicated your preference. Now place the letters of your four preferences below. The four letters taken together represent your personality type according to this self-diagnostic (e.g., ENTJ or ISFP)

_____   _____   _____   _____   (My personality type preferences)

E or I   S or N   T or F   J or P

Explanation of Results

The self-diagnostic you just completed is an informal assessment tool based on the personality theory initially put forward by Carl Gustav Jung, later refined and developed by Katharine Briggs and Isabel Briggs Myers. According to Jung, Myers and Briggs, people's behaviour is not completely random. Personality types reflect patterns in the ways people perceive and make judgments about the world. You may be extraverted or introverted (E or I), sensing or iNtuiting (S or N), thinking or feeling (T or F), and judging or perceiving (J or P). Your results, then, serve as a summary statement about your perceptual and decision-making mental processes. The rest of this chapter explains these preferences, thereby debriefing your results. For now, you may wish to glance below at the summary description of your own type as well as the other possibilities. Each type has its preferred energy source, its preferred way of gathering information and making judgments about it, as well as its particular orientation to the external world.

Summary Chart of Your Personality Preferences

Personality Type	Energy Source	Information Gathered	Decides with	Orientation to Outer World
ENTJ	External	Intuitively	Head	Judging
ENTP	External	Intuitively	Head	Perceiving
ENFJ	External	Intuitively	Heart	Judging
ENFP	External	Intuitively	Heart	Perceiving
ESFJ	External	Sensorily	Heart	Judging
ESFP	External	Sensorily	Heart	Perceiving
ESTJ	External	Sensorily	Head	Judging
ESTP	External	Sensorily	Head	Perceiving

INTP	Internal	Intuitively	Head	Perceiving
INTJ	Internal	Intuitively	Head	Judging
INFP	Internal	Intuitively	Heart	Perceiving
INFJ	Internal	Intuitively	Heart	Judging
ISFP	Internal	Sensorily	Heart	Perceiving
ISFJ	Internal	Sensorily	Heart	Judging
ISTP	Internal	Sensorily	Head	Perceiving
ISTJ	Internal	Sensorily	Head	Judging

1.3 Personality Types:

Recognizable Patterns of Diversity

According to Carl Jung, **human diversity** is not a completely random matter. At a psychological level, differences we see in people can be understood in terms of recognizable patterns. These patterns can be observed in the way people use their minds, particularly in the way they perceive the world and make judgments about it. **Perceptual mental processes** determine what we see or attend to in a situation. The **judgment function** influences how we make decisions about what we perceive. Jung also believed that differences in people can be understood in terms of **psychological attitude.** Attitude, in this context, refers to the energizing sources in life. Some individuals tend to focus their lives externally, while others tend to be more focused on the inner world of ideas.

As I mentioned earlier, Katharine Briggs and Isabel Briggs Myers made some minor modifications to Jung's work and elaborated upon it. They added to Jung's conception of type the idea of **external orientation**, the psychological stance adopted toward people, situations and events in the outer world. In what follows, you will find more detailed explanations of the orientations, attitudes, functions and mental processes that combine to establish type and type differences. The explanations will help you to understand better the results of Self-Diagnostic 1.1. They will also help you to appreciate for later purposes the usefulness and practical applications of psychological type for personal growth and interpersonal communication. See the four psychological preference scales in Table 1.1, which depict how the 16 personality types can be formed.

Table 1.1

The Four Psychological Preference Scales

Extraversion	or	Introversion
Sensing	or	iNtuition
Thinking	or	Feeling
Judging	or	Perceiving

Combining Preferences Leads to 16 Possible Personality Types

ISTJ	ISTP	ESTP	ESTJ
ISFJ	ISFP	ESFP	ESFJ
INFJ	INFP	ENFP	ENFJ
INTJ	INTP	ENTP	ENTJ

1.4   Energy Source: Extraversion Versus Introversion

Do You Have an Introverted or Extraverted Attitude?

Introvert to extravert: "Pardon me for speaking while you were interrupting."

Extravert to introvert: "Do you have any other speeds besides slow and stop?"

Probably by this time in your life you've referred to someone you know as being either introverted or extraverted. You likely have some intuitive notion of what these terms mean; however, you may not know that their technical psychological definition originates with the work of Carl Jung. According to Jung's analytical psychology, people differ with respect to the attitudes they adopt toward life. These attitudes are not something good or bad. Rather, think of them as approaches to life or psychological postures. Attitudes are characterized by what people find energizing. For instance, when you walk into a room full of people, do you feel excited? Or, is it more likely you feel drained?

***

Your response here reveals much about your attitude. Some people like to mingle and interact with many (**extraverts**), while others prefer to speak with one or two people at a time (**introverts**). (By the way, the correct spelling of extravert is "extrovert." However, Carl Jung's misspelling of the term has now become the convention for type theorists. It continues to be a source of irritation for spelling-bee champions!

Introverts—Life's Private "I"s

Attitudinal differences between introverts and extraverts are apparent when you look at the focus of their attention. Extraverts are more likely to focus their perceptions and judgments outwardly. The external world is their preoccupation. Introverts, by contrast, prefer to deal with the inner world of ideas; they are energized by concepts and inner reflections. This kind of individual (maybe you) would rather listen than talk. Intense and loud discussions are likely to be draining experiences. In order to "recharge," the introvert needs to be alone. Private time is important. "Alone, but not lonely" is a phrase that the introvert understands well.

If you are an introvert, chances are pretty good that sometime in your life you've felt underestimated. While I'm sure this happens to virtually everybody, this experience is more likely with introverts. The reason is that extraverts outnumber introverts by about three to one. Given the private nature of introverts, along with their smaller number, it's not surprising that many of the values and preferences of the extravert tend to dominate North American culture. Of course, many introverts learn to play the extraverted game of life very well. They become excellent at public relations and quite efficient in dealing with external matters. The problem is that they often feel drained, not energized, by becoming good at what they least prefer. (To appreciate why, do Application Exercise 1.1, Working in Your Wrong Hand.

Extraverts—Life's Party Types

As you might guess, the extravert loves what the introvert least prefers. Extraverted types tend to be energized by people and action, their orientation being outward. They generally enjoy being sociable, expressive and involved in external matters. Extraverts get their essential stimulation from the environment. As strong as the introvert's needs may be for privacy, so strong may be the extravert's need for social relationships. In contrast to the introvert, whose thoughts and reflections give depth to life, the extravert prefers breadth. (Do you complain about courses that are too superficial—an introvert's comment—or ones that are too narrowly focused and hence boring—an extravert's comment?)

Table 1.2

Key Descriptors—Sources of Energy

Introverts (I)	Extraverts (E)
Focus on inner world	Focus on outer world
Depth	Breadth
Private	Social
Reserved	Outgoing

| Think before acting | Act before thinking |
| Reflective | Active |

Where does your preference fall?

Introversion   *Extraversion*

| High | Moderate | Low | Low | Moderate | High |

Take note: We all display introverted and extraverted tendencies, but usually prefer one over the other.

By natural inclination, extraverts tend to act before thinking, whereas introverts reflect and then (maybe) act. Extraverts tend to think out loud. Introverts think to themselves. I suppose Alice in Wonderland exposed her extraverted preferences when she said at one point that she couldn't tell what she was thinking until she heard what she said. Like the proverbial extravert, she was "thinking out loud."

At this point, it is very important for you to note that we all display introverted and extraverted tendencies at different times; it's just that one is usually preferred and better developed. Nobody is entirely introverted or extraverted. We all show signs of both, but are energized by one. Table 1.2 shows common preferred tendencies for introverts and extroverts.

1.5   Information Gathering: Sensing Versus Intuition

What Do You Pay Attention to When You Gather Information?

Not all people experience and gather information about the world in the same way. How we take in information is determined by the psychological functions of sensing and intuition. We all use both functions in our lives, but again, we typically display a preference for one, and feel more confident about it.

Application Exercise

1.1   Working in Your Wrong Hand

This exercise, or some variation of it, is often used in workshops designed to help people appreciate the difficulties that arise when trying to operate with opposite or lesser preferred psychological functions.
Instructions: Write your name, address and telephone number on a piece of paper with your "wrong" hand. If you're right-handed, use your left hand. If you're left-handed, use your right hand.

For discussion: After finishing this task, evaluate your work. Is it better or worse than what you could have done with your preferred hand? How did you feel working with your "wrong" hand? What would be the effect on you if you were forced to operate all day long using your less-preferred hand? What generalizations could you possibly make about people's behaviour using this experiential exercise?

Introverts: Recall a time when you were required to function as an extravert. Where were you? What did you have to do? How did you feel? What did you think? How did you experience this situation?

Extraverts: Recall a time when you were required to function as an introvert. Where were you? What did you have to do? How did you feel? What did you think? How did you experience this situation?

Sensors – The Realists

Sensors, or sensing type individuals, can be fairly described as life's realists. I like to think of them as no-nonsense, "meat and potatoes" people. Sensing types pay a great deal of attention to information that is received through sensory channels. For them, seeing is believing.

Sensing types tend to focus on the here and now. They enjoy and experience what is currently happening, and focus less on what might or could be. Their present orientation causes them to concentrate on the facts and details of situations, people and events. Their greatest trust is placed in firsthand experience.

A noticeable characteristic of sensing types is their preference for set procedures and established routines. Deviations and unexpected changes to usual ways of doing things may not be welcomed. Sensing types also enjoy looking at things in terms of their specific parts and pieces. They like things to be definite and measurable. Anything fuzzy and open-ended is not terribly appreciated. You can also notice that sensors have a sequential approach to life. They prefer to start at the beginning of things and methodically complete them, one step at a time. Sensors are at their best when allowed to work at things "hands on." The next time you meet a no-nonsense, concrete realist who's particularly interested in the facts and practical details, you're probably facing a sensor.

Intuitives—The Innovators

Intuitives are unlike sensors insofar as they prefer to process information by way a "sixth sense." They may downplay sensory-based information and opt for intuitive hunches. In contrast to sensing types who prefer a routine, intuitives like exploring alternatives and change. Variety is the spice of life. This need for variety and change may make intuitives appear fickle or impractical, but this need is probably more reflective of their future orientation. Intuitives are possibility thinkers and always anticipate what might be or what could be. Intuitives therefore crave opportunities to be inventive because doing things in accepted routine ways is boring or limiting. Intuitives also don't seem to mind jumping in anywhere when tasks must be done. For them, "intuitive leaps" are commonly made of "sequential steps." In this vein, intuitives like to look for patterns, relationships and overall designs rather than concentrate on pieces and parts to make up the whole. The whole is the first object of attention.

Table 1.3 summarizes some of the key information gathering preferences of sensors and intuitives.

Table 1.3

Key Descriptors—Information Gathering

Sensors (S)	Intuitives (N)
Perspire	Inspire
Focus on present	Focus on future
Like routine	Choose variety
Enjoy	Anticipate
Conserve	Change
Stress facts	Stress innovations
Take sequential approach	Take random approach
Look for details	Look for patterns
Are practical	Are imaginative
Follow directions	Pursue hunches

Where does your preference fall?

Sensing   *Intuitive*

High	Moderate	Low	Low	Moderate	High

Take note: We all use sensing and intuitive processes, but usually prefer one over the other.

1.6   Decision Making: Thinking Versus Feeling

Do You Prefer to Decide with Your Head or Your Heart?

The thinking-feeling dimension of personality explains how we make decisions about what we see. Remember that our perceptions are obtained through sensing-intuiting channels. Thinking-feeling processes establish our personal style of making judgments on what is seen or perceived. As with attitudes and perceptual functions, people differ in ways explainable by a bipolar scale. Though we all use both thinking and feeling as a basis of decision making at different times in our lives, we generally prefer one over the other. The results of your self-diagnostic should begin to give you insights as to whether you're a thinking type or feeling type.

Thinkers—Life's Logicians

People with thinking preferences take a logical approach to life. Careful consideration is usually given to reasons, which justify actions. **Thinkers** tend to consider the consequences of actions in an unbiased, impersonal way. Decisions are taken objectively and based on truth or probabilistic calculations. Thinking types desire to make firm decisions based on detached and impartial judgments. Thinkers thus tend to have an intellectual orientation to life. They can appear at times to be very "cerebral." They place great confidence in their mental and cognitive processes. When values or emotions play a part in their decision making, they are usually used to support logical conclusions. Given this, thinkers frequently choose to be truthful rather than tactful. They are sometimes less sensitive to people and more likely to be aware of rational considerations. They choose their heads over their hearts in most instances. Thinkers often consider it a greater compliment to be regarded as fair than as likeable or compassionate.

Feelers—Life's Lovers

People with feeling preferences, or life's "lovers," tend to make decisions based on their emotions and personal values. When logic and reason come in to play, they are typically employed to support values-oriented conclusions. We find, then, that **feelers** are more "people-people," and that they're less likely to be regarded as detached and aloof, which is sometimes the case with objective-minded thinkers. Feeling types pick heart over head, preferring tact over truth. When hard decisions must be made, they are more likely to be compassionate than firm. They are not likely to stick to impersonal principles and rules at any cost. On this score, feeling types can be described as humane and personally involved. It's not that there's something wrong with the desire to be just and objectively fair, but for the feeler, subjective considerations and personal values take on a greater importance.

Feelers and thinkers usually make decisions according to their type's preferences, some of which are listed in Table 1.4.

Table 1.4

Key Descriptors—Way of Making Decisions

Thinkers (T)	Feelers (F)
Objective	Subjective
Impersonal	Personal
Rational	Emotional
Head	Heart
Truthful	Tactful
Logical	Values-oriented
Firm	Compassionate
Just	Humane
Critical	Appreciative

Where does your preference fall?

Thinking   *Feeling*

| High | Moderate | Low | Low | Moderate | High |

Take note: We all display thinking and feeling processes, but prefer one over the other.

1.6   Orientation to the Outer World: Judging Versus Perceiving

What's Your Preferred Way of Approaching External Reality?

By now you have learned something about what energizes you, what you pay attention to when gathering information, and how you go about making decisions. However, it is also insightful for you to consider your psychological orientation to people, places and events in the external world. What is your preferred **lifestyle orientation?**

By the use of this term, I'm not referring to your tastes in fashion or to your material possessions. Rather, the phrase refers to the psychological stance you assume vis-à-vis the world. Some of us tend to be judging types, while others are perceiving types. Be careful not to confuse judging with judgmental or perceiving with perceptive. No character evaluations are intended. It's just that people differ in their approaches to life. Neither approach is better or worse than the other. The judging-perceiving distinction points to how we relate to external reality. Some of us are decision makers; others are more comfortable as information gatherers.

Judgers—Life's Organizers

If you love making lists of things to do or if you like to use the expression "A place for everything and everything in its place," I would venture to guess that you are a judging type of person. **Judgers** create for themselves highly structured environments. Most activities are planned. For them, there may be a time and place for fun as well as an appropriate way to have it. For example, have you ever been to a party where there wasn't a moment of free time and where everything was organized and planned? If so, you simply couldn't do what you wanted since the party organizer had decided in advance what should be done and when.

Not only are judging types well-organized and highly structured in their approach to life, they are also decisive. Judgers need closure and therefore enjoy making decisions about what ought or ought not to be done in a given situation. Once plans or schedules are established, strong judgers like to follow them closely. This decisiveness gives judgers a sense of control and order. Once the target is fixed and the course is set, judgers enjoy taking action to achieve their goal.

If you are a judging type, you use either thinking (T) or feeling (F) as a preferred way of dealing with the external world. Your life may be organized in terms of impersonal considerations (e.g., time schedules and budgets) or in terms of interpersonal dealings (e.g., values and feelings). You can be decisive either with your head or your heart. Both are rational (i.e., reasonable) ways of making decisions. The judging type prefers one over the other.

Perceivers—Mellow Fellows and Females

People who display a strong preference for perceiving live noticeably different lifestyles compared to their judging cousins. In contrast to judgers who love to plan, schedule, organize and list, **perceivers** prefer to live spontaneously. Last minute changes to schedules, for example, may not be seen as problems, but rather as opportunities for new possibilities. Change is less of an enemy and more of a friend, because the perceiving person possesses the natural inclination to remain open to the unforeseen.

If you're a strong perceptive type, chances are pretty good that you feel uncomfortable when forced to come to quick conclusions. If you're typical of this type, then you prefer to adopt a tentative approach to life. Your conclusions will sound less like categorical judgments and more like testable hypotheses. You may feel a constant urge to learn more or gather additional information before making any final conclusions. In fact, the act of gathering information is probably a great source of pleasure for you. (Do you find researching a paper is more fun than writing it?)

Perceivers are distinguished by the tolerance and adaptability that they display. They are less likely to use worlds like "should" and "ought" when it comes to other people's lives. "Live and let live" is a saying that the perceiving person might use as a personal guideline. In short, perceptives tend to go with the flow of life and just let things happen.

If you are a perceiver, either sensing or intuition is your preferred way of dealing with the external world. An ESFP, for instance, relies most heavily on sensing, while, by contrast, an ESFJ is most reliant on feeling. Remember, sensing and intuition are perceiving functions, whereas thinking and feeling are decision-making processes. The last letter of your type (i.e., J or P) indicates whether you prefer perceptual processes (S or N) or decision-making processes (T or F) in your dealings with the external world. "J" points to T or F preferences. "P" points to S or N preferences.

Judgers and perceivers approach external reality quite differently, as can be seen from the descriptors listed in Table 1.5.

Table 1.5

Key Descriptors—Orientation to the Outer World

Judging (J)	**Perceiving (P)**
Structured	Flexible
Scheduled	Spontaneous
Ordered	Adaptive
Planned	Responsive to a variety of situations
Decisive	Wait and see attitude
Deliberate	Tendency to keep collecting new information
Definite	Tentative
Fixed	Flexible
Enjoy finishing	Enjoy starting

Where does your preference fall?

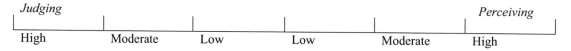

Judging					Perceiving
High	Moderate	Low	Low	Moderate	High

Take note: We all display judging and perceiving processes, but prefer one over the other.

Type Classifications

In total there are 16 personality types, which are grouped into four categories. Find the four-letter combination that summarizes your personality preferences. What type are you?

Sensing-Thinking Types	**Sensing-Feeling Types**
ISTJ	ISFJ
ISTP	ISFP
ESTP	ESFP
ESTJ	ESFJ

Intuitive-Feeling Types	**Intuitive-Thinking Types**
INFJ	INTJ
INFP	INTP
ENFP	ENTP
ENFJ	ENTJ

My preferences indicate that I am probably a(n) _____ type.

Table 1.6

Summary of Type Characteristics

Sensing-Thinking People	Sensing-Feeling People
Focus on facts and details	Open to impulse and spontaneous acts
Speak and write directly to the point	Do what feels good
Adapt easily to established procedures and guidelines	Sensitive to others' feelings
Concerned with efficiency and utility	Decisions made according to personal likes and dislikes
Goal or task oriented	Prefer to learn through human interaction and personal experience
Emphasize accuracy	Enjoy activities involving emotional expression
Approach tasks sequentially	Persuasive through personal interaction
Focus on the present	Keen observers of human nature
	Interested in people
Intuitive-Feeling People	**Intuitive-Thinking People**
Open to the unconventional	Need time to plan and consider consequences of an action
See facts and details as part of the larger picture	Like to organize and synthesize information
Express themselves in new and unusual ways	Focus on impersonal considerations
Adapt to new circumstances	Decisions based on evidence and logical thinking
Process oriented	Prefer to learn vicariously through books and symbolic forms
Highly interested in beauty, symmetry and form	Enjoy logical thinking activities
Enjoy exploratory activities	Persuasive intellectually
Focus on the future	Store huge amounts of knowledge and information
	Interested in ideas, theories and concepts

Application Exercise 1.2

Classroom Chemistry

No two college or university classes are alike. However, to explain why this is the case is a challenge. Instructors are sometimes amazed how a single lesson plan and delivery method can work wonderfully well in one section of a course and bomb in another. As a student, you may also wonder about the quiet and impersonal nature of your introductory psychology class, especially when you compare it to the noisy and emotionally charged nature of the psychological counselling class taught by the same instructor. Course content and class size might have some influence on atmosphere, but then again, the differences may have something to do with the psychological makeup of the students. The different makeup of each course section could affect the "chemistry of the classroom."

Instructions: On the blackboard or flip chart, draw a type table similar to the one illustrated below. You could also draw the table on a transparency sheet for overhead projection. Decide whether you wish to keep a permanent record for yourself.

ISTJ	ISFJ	INFJ	INTJ
ISTP	ISFP	INFP	INTP
ESTP	ESFP	ENFP	ENTP

ESTJ	ESFJ	ENFJ	ENTJ

Invite students to put their names (or check marks) in the appropriate boxes as indicated by their psychological type. No student should be forced to do this and no reasons for refusal need to be given. Respect everyone's privacy. In case there is some insecurity about making any self-revelations, remember, no type is any better or worse than any other. After completing the type table, answer the following questions. (This may be done in small groups or all together as a class.)

Introversion Versus Extraversion

1. How many introverts are in the class?
2. How many extraverts are in the class?

Letter of higher frequency _____ (I or E)

Discussion: Given what you know about introverted and extraverted preferences, what predictions about the class would seem reasonable? For example, will large or small group discussions flow more easily? Will class participation come readily? How could the introverted-extraverted chemistry of the classroom contribute to everyone's benefit? How could it pose challenges?

Sensing Versus Intuition

1. How many sensing types are in the class?
2. How many intuitive types are in the class?

Letter of higher frequency _____ (S or N)

Discussion: Given what you know about sensing and intuiting preferences, what predictions about the class would be reasonable? Will the class be conducted in a routine way or will members opt for variety? Will people be more likely to perform in a step-by-step fashion or will they be more likely to jump in wherever they feel comfortable?

Thinking Versus Feeling

1. How many thinking types are in the class?
2. How many feeling types are in the class?

Letter of higher frequency _____ (T or F)

Discussion: Given what you know about thinking and feeling preferences, what predictions about the class would seem reasonable? For example, will the group tend to be concerned with personal values or objective and emotionally detached considerations?

Judging Versus Perceiving

1. How many judging types are in the class?
2. How many perceiving types are in the class?

Letter of higher frequency _____ (J or P)

Discussion: Given what you know about judging and perceiving preferences, what predictions about the class would seem reasonable? For example, will it be necessary for most students to function according to a strict timetable or will it be relatively easy to deviate from the lesson plans?

What are the four dominant preferences of your class? Is there anyone who is the "pure" classroom type—the one whose personality captures all the dominant preferences of the class?

‾‾‾‾	‾‾‾‾	‾‾‾‾	‾‾‾‾
I or E	S or N	T or F	J or P

What are the class frequencies of

STs   Sensing-Thinking Types   _____?

SFs   Sensing-Feeling Types   _____?

NFs   Intuitive-Feeling Types   _____?

NTs   Intuitive-Thinking Types   _____?

Discussion: Given the chemistry of your class, what might be its strengths? What challenges might you anticipate? Who is likely to fit in most easily? What can be done to make others feel comfortable?

Application Exercise 1.3

TV Types Have Different Stripes

Now that you understand the basics of psychological type, it's time to apply your knowledge. Of course, there's nothing wrong in having a little bit of fun at the same time!

Instructions: Form small groups. Select a secretary and spokesperson for your group. Discuss the psychological profiles of the TV personalities and characters listed below. Place each name in the appropriate box labelled according to psychological preferences. If you need help, refer to the Summary of Type Characteristics above. For a variation of this activity, change any of the TV characters or personalities to suit the viewing tastes of the class.

Caution: Your group may choose to focus on particular features of the TV character or personality not emphasized by other groups. If your group's placements are different from those of other groups, use these differences as a basis for class discussion. In the end, the placement is less important than the rationale behind it.

TV Personalities/Characters

Frasier Crane	Chandler Bing	Dharma
Tony Soprano	Regis Philbin	Oprah Winfrey
Carrie Bradshaw	Mike Bullard	Ally McBeal
Elizabeth Corday	Homer Simpson	Dawson Leery

ST	SF
NF	NT

***

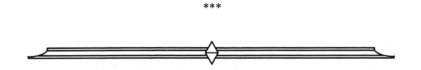

PSYCH SMART COMMUNICATIONS

Excerpts from Chapter 2 of Anthony Falikowski's (2002) *Mastering Human Relations*, 2nd Edition, Toronto, Pearson Education.

How To Communicate Effectively with Different Personality Types

***

Preferred Types of Communication

Corresponding to each psychological type are different **styles of communication.** Extraverts, for example, tend to communicate differently from introverts, while intuitives structure their messages somewhat differently from sensors. However, these differences do not suggest that extraverts cannot communicate with introverts or that intuitives and sensors are destined to a lifetime of miscommunication. As mentioned in the preceding chapter, outnumbered introverts may adapt to the majority world of the extravert very well. They may become good at "extraverted" communication, maybe even better than some extraverts. Sensors can also encode messages to suit intuitives and vice versa. In principle, any type can communicate according to opposite type preferences. However, being asked to use communication styles contrary to your own can be psychologically draining. The optimistic point is that everybody can learn to communicate effectively with all psychological types, even if we find some forms of communication less natural and more taxing than others.

***

2.6   Helpful Hints for Improving Communication

Tips for Introverts (Communicating with Extraverts)

- **Look alive** Some extraverts are frustrated by the speed at which introverts tend to respond. Try to be quicker in your responses and more spontaneous. Display a more lively, upbeat attitude.

- **Be expressive** For extraverts, you are part of the external world. Since they feed off your energy, make an attempt to show interest, emotion and involvement. Keep in mind that there's nothing wrong with enthusiasm. Just because you don't always show your feelings doesn't mean you don't have them.

- **Initiate contact** Rather than waiting for people to start conversations with you, you could start conversations yourself. Don't always leave it up to extraverts to get things going socially.

- **Provide feedback** Save others the guesswork of trying to figure out what you're silently thinking. Publicly state your agreements and disagreements. Providing information on where you stand on particular issues. After all, "Nobody can appreciate your music if they can't hear the tune you're playing."
- **Change your nonverbal communication** If you're strongly introverted, you probably look very serious to others. Try to look more relaxed and try to smile more. Assume inviting physical postures. Appear open. Don't withdraw.

- **Practise "non-productive" conversation** Learn to appreciate the value of social interaction for its own sake. Chit-chatting can be fun. The quality of ideas exchanged needn't always be a priority. Spending time in "idle conversation" has worth. It builds morale and positive relations.

Tips for Extraverts (Communicating with Introverts)

- **Respect privacy** If you're highly extraverted, you may not mind living your life as an open book to others. You may think that you have nothing to hide, feeling comfortable with a lot of self-disclosure. Understand that introverts generally have a greater need for privacy. Try, therefore, not to invade their private psychological territory. Don't ask them embarrassing questions or put introverts on the psychological hot seat.

- **Take time to listen** Introverts tend to be less spontaneous than extraverts. Their response time is also slower. Make an effort to allow introverts time to reflect before acting or responding to you. Do not make surprise demands on introverts for quick or immediate responses. Such demands are not usually welcome.

- **Foster trust** Make sure you guard as secret what you've been told by introverts in confidence. The sphere of private information is probably larger for the introvert than it is for you, the extravert. Be sure not to make public what others consider private.

- **Don't overpower** Introverts may sometimes perceive your enthusiasm and energy as frivolous. Your excitement may not be appreciated. You may wish to think about toning down your efforts, in order not to overwhelm others. They may not be impressed by your strident nature or extravagant expressions.

- **Don't judge** Be careful not to evaluate the more methodical and quieter introvert as less able and more dull. Preferences of one type should not be used as a standard of evaluation for other types. All preferences have their advantages.

2.6 Helpful Hints for Improving Communications

Tips for Sensors (Communicating with Intuitives)

- **Don't overgeneralize or state absolutes** Personal experience may give sensing realists confidence in their opinions and conclusions, but it does not guarantee necessary truth. You can be quite certain and confident but still be wrong. Understand that factual information is always incomplete and that your concrete experience is the experience of one. Not everybody experiences life the same way you do. Furthermore, experience cannot guarantee that something has been learned. "Experience is a great teacher; unfortunately not everybody understands the lesson."

- **Allow time for considering possibilities** Sensors prefer realism. The result is that you focus more on what "is" and less on what "could be." It's important not to limit your options with a limited imagination. Show greater tolerance toward idealistic thinking and intuitives who may have what you consider to be an unrealistic future orientation. Possibility thinking has real(istic) advantages.

- **Broaden your perspective** Try to display greater tolerance for broader-based conceptual thinking. Overreliance on facts and figures may get in the way of being productive or achieving longer-term goals. Preoccupation with details could lead intuitives to perceive you as petty.

- **Look for meanings and relationships** When communicating with intuitives, understand that they are less concerned with what the facts *are* and more concerned with what they *mean*. Expressing factual information outside any meaningful context will be less effective with intuitives. For intuitives, facts need to be interpreted and related to something. Allow time for this interpretation. Put your communication in a more global context.

- **Find new ways of expressing information** Intuitives appreciate novelty, unusual modes of expression and challenges. Straightforward, matter-of-fact presentations could be experienced as boring and uninteresting. Try to perk up your communication with some delightful differences. Instead of merely informing intuitives, you could try to "inspire" them. Dispirited communications are not appreciated.

Tips for Intuitives (Communicating with Sensors)

- **Focus on the here and now** You will make much more sense to the sensor if you adopt a present time orientation. Talk about future scenarios and long-term possibilities may be regarded as "intellectual masturbation" by hard-core realists concerned about today's problems. Such talk may be pleasurable for you, but for the sensor, it is probably unproductive.

- **Base your opinions and suggestions on factual information** You can gain the confidence of sensors by keeping both feet on the ground. Try to relate your opinions and suggestions to facts, figures, surveys and empirical evidence. Your gut-level intuitions may carry little persuasive weight for the sensing realist.

- **Be more direct in your communication** If you wish to communicate more effectively with practical, matter-of-fact kinds of people, try to speak more directly. Metaphors and analogies may sound poetic to you, but they may serve as obstructions to individuals who prefer to be economical in their language. Why say in many words what can be said in few? Why say indirectly what can be said directly? Be a "word economist." Save words and enjoy the dividends!

- **Appear more level-headed and businesslike** Your natural enthusiasm, idealism, genius and inspiration as an intuitive can sometimes be perceived as "flaky" by the sensor. For the sensor, your enthusiasm should be based on substance, your idealism tempered by practicality, your genius founded on hard work, and your inspiration led by discipline. Without a realistic basis to support your insightful and long-term propositions, you could be seen as flighty. It's hard to put confidence in people whose heads seem to be in the clouds.

- **Respect traditional ways of doing things** Remember that the old ways of doing things are not always the wrong ways. For many, past procedures, rules and regulations offer stability and direction. They are not regarded as outdated or boring. Appreciate the sensor's preference for established, systematic approaches. Routine may make you restless, but it is reassuring to many sensors.

*** *

2.6 Helpful Hints for Improving Communications

Tips for Thinkers (Communicating with Feelers)

- **Make communications personally relevant and meaningful** If you're a thinking-type person, you should consider making your ideas more personally relevant and meaningful to the receivers of your messages. A theory or idea may be exciting to you and others sharing your preferences, but it can be boring, useless and irrelevant for people of the opposite type.

- **Be more appreciative of others' comments** Thinking-type individuals are likely to consider their rationality and objectivity as virtues, and in many ways they are. The problem with cool objectivity, however, is that it can be perceived as callousness. Having an intellectual evaluation and analysis for just about everything could get the thinking type labelled a terminal critic or someone who argues simply for the sake of argument, regardless of the issue or effects on people's emotions. Before attacking points made by others, take time to understand and appreciate what they mean. Paraphrase others' comments. Explore what they think and feel. Then, go on to express your point of view. Take time to really hear what is said.

- **Expand your communication messages** As a thinking-type person you may take great pride in the clarity, precision and conciseness of your communications with others. However, a terse manner of expression is sometimes perceived as unfriendly and cold. If talking to you is like talking to a computer, you may wish to consider expanding your monosyllabic responses when answering others' questions. Perhaps you could elaborate on what you mean.

- **Make room for the nonrational and paradoxical** A helpful suggestion for you, the thinker, is to believe less that "life is a problem to be solved." See it more as a "mystery to be lived." Accept the proposition that not everything in life has a rational explanation or logical justification. Logic may be limited by whatever is mystical, ironic or paradoxical in life. Religious beliefs, for instance, may not be based on logic, but on faith. Such beliefs may lie beyond the domain of rational thought. Don't take rationality as the sole standard of truth.

Tips for Feelers (Communicating with Thinkers)

- **Get to the point** While other feelers like yourself may appreciate time-consuming communication, thinkers will probably not. Try to incorporate brevity in your messages to thinkers. Attempting to make friendly small talk could be perceived as a waste of time.

- **Be more objective** Try to reduce your naturally subjective orientation when communicating with thinkers. Your personal values and feelings may not be appreciated or regarded as very important to the subject at hand. The thinker is more impersonal and objective than you are. If you would have others listen and be persuaded, you must speak their language.

- **See both sides** There is absolutely nothing wrong with appreciating others. However, if personal likes and feelings get in the way of seeing flaws and difficulties, then problems can arise. Practise evaluating the pros and cons of different ideas, situations and alternatives.

- **Focus on content** If you're a high-level feeling type, process is probably more important to you than content. Chances are that you like experiential exercises and activities because of the personal involvement required. Remember that such process-oriented activities are less preferred by thinking types. In fact, some thinking types may greatly dislike "touchy-feely" communications. Be careful not to irritate or offend, especially in the case of introverted thinkers. Your personal approach may be perceived as a violation of privacy and inappropriate to the content being discussed.

***

2.6 Helpful Hints for Improving Communications

Tips for Judgers (Communicating with Perceivers)

- **Open up to the unexpected** Disruptions to your schedule need not necessarily be upsetting. Begin to see them as occasions to "stop and smell the roses." Some interruptions may even provide you with information and insights that can be used to reconsider your plans. Don't make other people who cause unexpected changes feel unwanted.

- **Build flexibility into your lifestyle** When organizing yourself, make sure you allow for "downtime." Make unforeseen circumstances foreseeable. In other words, expect the unexpected. Being psychologically prepared can help to reduce stress and frustration. Stressed and frustrated people are not usually pleasant to communicate with. Do everyone, including yourself, a favour, and "go with the flow."

- **Don't jump to conclusions** As a judger, your preference is to close matters as soon as possible. Note that your desire for closure may cause you to make decisions prematurely. Evaluations you make of people, situations and events may therefore be unjustified or ill-informed. If your stated conclusions are to be sound, they should be based on carefully considered information.

- **Listen to the other side** Counter-evidence to your own thinking may be uncomfortable to accept. Be careful not to repress or deny that which contradicts your personal beliefs, values, principles or ideas. Effective communication necessitates that you listen well, respect the viewpoints of others, and respond intelligently and sensitively to ideas contrary to your own.

- **Harness your need for control** Most J-types love to feel in control of situations. Plans, schedules, time frames and strategies of action provide a sense of personal power. While this may be good, caution yourself not to become overpowering. If you are controlled psychologically by your *need* to control, then you may become offensive to others. Most people do not like to feel dominated by others. If you wish to improve your communications as a judger, you may plan to relinquish some control and thereby "empower" others. Try this action as an experiment and witness how others begin to respond to you. If things get done and done well, but not according to your plans and schedules, what does it matter? Try not to communicate judgmentally with those having other styles of doing things.

Tips for Perceivers (Communicating with Judgers)

- **Be less vague** As a perceiver, you probably like to keep your options open. Perhaps you tend to make your decisions at the very last moment. Understand that for judgers, this tendency of yours is a bit like "holding out." The constant weighing of possibilities can represent for judgers vagueness or lack of preparation on your part. They may not be able to determine where you stand on particular issues. They have a greater need for quick confirmation. Tell judgers explicitly what considerations you are taking into account and what issues you need to resolve before coming to your final conclusions. If you can clearly articulate reasons for your indecision or inaction, then at least you provide the organized J-type with an explanation for what's holding you up. This information will likely be appreciated.

- **Be more decisive** This tip is related to the one before. As a perceiver, you have a natural tendency to gather as much information as you can. Make sure that this information-gathering process does not get in the way of making necessary and timely decisions. Tentativeness about making decisions may be perceived as insecurity or incompetence. It will be difficult for you to persuade others and to sell your ideas if you cannot gain their confidence.

- **Watch your use of *"yeah, but"*** Since you are keenly aware of contingencies, possibilities and alternatives, you can no doubt frequently offer "yeah, but" objections, as I call them, to almost any proposal or suggestion. Don't let your "yeah, but" get in the way of productive dialogue. Ensure that your concerns are real. Always protesting on the basis of highly improbable scenarios, for example, will lead others to take your comments less seriously.

- **Ensure your communications are on time** J-types like to operate according to schedule. While delivering a memo a day late may mean little for you, it may mean a lot for the person who requested the memo. It is helpful, therefore, if you plan ahead for your pondering and procrastination. Having things well thought out in advance and allowing yourself lots of time for a consideration of possibilities will enable you to be more prepared and decisive. For example, at meetings you won't need to scramble and squirm at the last moment about where you stand on particular issues or policies. Appearing unclear and unprepared is not in your best interest, especially if you wish to be heard and respected for your point of view.

***

THE SELF IN COMMUNICATION

Excerpts from Devito, J. (2001). *The Interpersonal Communication Book, 9th Ed.* Toronto: Addison Wesley Longman, Inc., pp. 60-65.

***

Self-Concept

You no doubt have an image of who you are; this is your **self-concept.** It consists of your feelings and thoughts about your strengths and weaknesses, your abilities and limitations. Your self-concept develops from at least four sources: (1) the image of you that others have and that they reveal to you, (2) the comparisons you make between yourself and others, (3) the teachings of your culture, and (4) the way you interpret and evaluate your own thoughts and behaviors (Figure 4.1).

Others' Images of You

If you wished to see the way your hair looked, you would likely look in a mirror. But what would you do if you wanted to see how friendly or how assertive you are? According to Charles Horton Cooley's (1992) concept of the *looking-glass self,* you would look at the image of yourself that others reveal to you through the way they treat you and react to you (Hensley 1996).

This diagram depicts the four sources of self-concept, the four contributors to how you see yourself: other's images of you, social comparisons, cultural teachings, and your own observations, interpretations, and evaluations. As you read about self-concept, consider the influence of each factor throughout your life. Which factor influenced you most as a pre-teen? Which influences you the most now? Which will influence you the most 25 or 30 years from now?

***

Figure 4.1 The Sources of Self-Concept

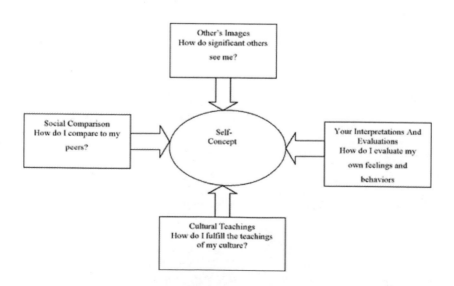

Social Comparisons

Another way you develop your self-concept is by comparing yourself with others. When you want to gain insight into who you are and how effective or competent you are, you probably look to your peers. For example, after an examination you probably want to know how you performed relative to the other students in your class. If you play on a baseball team, it's important to know your batting average in comparison with others on the team. You gain an additional perspective when you see your score in comparison with the scores of your peers.

Cultural Teachings

Through your parents, teachers, and the media, your culture instills in you a variety of beliefs, values, and attitudes—about success (how you define it and how you should achieve it); about your religion, race, or nationality; about the ethical principles you should follow in business and in your personal life. These teachings provide benchmarks against which you can measure yourself. Your success in, for example, achieving what your culture defines as success will contribute to a positive self-concept. Your failure to achieve what your culture teaches (for example, not being married by the time you're 30) will contribute to a negative self-concept.

When you demonstrate the qualities that your culture (or your organization) teaches, you'll see yourself as a cultural success and will be rewarded by other members of the culture (or organization). Seeing yourself as culturally successful and getting rewarded by others will contribute positively to your self-concept. When you fail to demonstrate such qualities, you're more likely to see yourself as a cultural failure and to be punished by other members of the culture, contributing to a more negative self-concept.

Your Own Interpretations and Evaluations

Much in the way others form images of you based on what you do, you also react to your own behavior; you interpret and evaluate it. These interpretations and evaluations help to form your self-concept. For example, let us say you believe that lying is wrong. If you lie, you will evaluate this behavior in terms of your internalized beliefs about lying. You will thus react negatively to your own behavior. You may, for example, experience guilt if your behavior contradicts your beliefs. In contrast, let's say you pulled someone out of a burning building at great personal risk. You would probably evaluate this behavior positively; you would feel good about this behavior and, as a result, about your self.

***

Self-Awareness

Your **self-awareness** represents the extent to which you know yourself. Understanding how your self-concept develops is one way to increase your self-awareness: the more you understand about why you view yourself as you do, the more you will understand who you are. Additional insight is gained by looking at self-awareness through the Johari model of the self, or your four selves (Luft 1984).

***

Your Four Selves

Self-awareness is neatly explained by the model of the four selves, the **Johari window.** This model, presented in Figure 4.2, has four basic areas, or quadrants, each of which represents a somewhat different self. The Johari model emphasizes that the several aspects of the self are not separate pieces but are interactive parts of a whole. Each part is dependent on each other part. Like that of interpersonal communication, this model of the self is a transactional one.

Figure 4.2 The Johari Window

	Known to Self	Not Known to Self
Known to Others	**OPEN SELF**	**BLIND SELF**
Not Known to Others	**HIDDEN SELF**	**UNKNOWN SELF**

Visualize this model as representing your self. The entire model is of constant size, but each section can vary, from very small to very large. As one section becomes smaller, one or more of the others grow larger. Similarly, as one section grows, one or more of the others must get smaller. For example, if you reveal a secret and thereby enlarge your open self, this shrinks your hidden self. Further, this disclosure may in turn lead to a decrease in the size of your blind self (if your disclosure influences other people to reveal what they know about you but that you have not known). How would you draw your Johari window to show yourself when interacting with your parents? With your friends? With your college instructors? The name Johari, by the way, comes from the first names of the two people who developed the model, Joseph Luft and Harry Ingham.

The Open Self The *open self* represents all the information, behaviors, attitudes, feelings, desires, motivations, and ideas that you and others know. The type of information included here might range from your name, skin color, and sex to your age, political and religious affiliations, and financial situation. Your open self will vary in size, depending on the situation you're in and the person with whom you're interacting. Some people, for example, make you feel comfortable and supported; to them, you open yourself wide, but to others you may prefer to leave most of yourself closed.

Communication depends on the degree to which you open yourself to others and to yourself (Luft 1969). If you don't allow other people to know you (thus keeping your open self small), communication between you and others becomes difficult, if not impossible. You can communicate meaningfully only to the extent that you know others and yourself. To improve communication, work first on enlarging the open self.

The Blind Self The *blind self* represents all the things about yourself that others know but of which you're ignorant. These may vary from the relatively insignificant habit of saying "You know," rubbing your nose when you get angry, or having a peculiar body odor, to things as significant as defense mechanisms, fight strategies, or repressed experiences.

Some people have a very large blind self; they seem totally oblivious of their faults and sometimes (though not as often) their virtues. Others seem overly eager to have a small blind self. They seek therapy at every turn and join every self-help group. Some believe they know everything there is to know about themselves, that they have reduced the blind self to zero. Most of us lie between these extremes.

Communication and interpersonal relations are generally enhanced as the blind self becomes smaller. But be careful of trying to help someone else "discover" his or her blind self. This could cause serious problems. Such a revelation might trigger a breakdown in defenses; it might force people to admit their own jealousy or prejudice when they're not psychologically ready to deal with such information. Such revelations are best dealt with cautiously or under the guidance of trained professionals.

The Hidden Self The *hidden self* contains all that you know of yourself and of others that you keep secret. In any interaction, this area includes everything you don't want to reveal, whether it's relevant or irrelevant to the conversation. At the extremes, we have the overdisclosers and the underdisclosers. The overdisclosers tell all. They keep nothing hidden about themselves or others. They tell you their marital difficulties, their children's problems, their financial status, and just about everything else. The underdisclosers tell nothing. They talk about you but not about themselves.

The problem with these extremes is that individuals don't distinguish between those who should and those who shouldn't be privy to such information. They also don't distinguish among the types of information they should or should not disclose. The vast majority of people, however, keep certain things hidden and disclose others; they make disclosures to some people and not to others. They're *selective* disclosers.

The Unknown Self The *unknown self* represents truths about yourself that neither you nor others know. The existence of this self is inferred from a number of sources. Sometimes it's revealed through temporary changes brought about by drugs or through special experimental conditions, such as hypnosis or sensory deprivation. Sometimes this area is revealed by certain projective tests or dreams. Mostly, however, it's revealed by the fact that you're constantly learning things about yourself that you didn't know before (things that were previously in the unknown self)—for example, that you become defensive when someone asks you a question or voices disagreement, or that you compliment others in the hope of being complimented back. Although you cannot easily manipulate this area, recognize that it does exist and that there are things about yourself and about others that you don't know and may never know.

Increasing Self-Awareness

You can increase your self-awareness in a number of ways: ask yourself about yourself, listen to others, actively seek information about yourself, see your different selves, and increase your open self.

Ask Yourself About Yourself One way to ask yourself about yourself is to take an informal "Who am I?" test (Bugental and Zelen 1950). Head a piece of paper "Who Am I?" and write 10, 15, or 20 times "I am…" Then complete each of the sentences. Try not to give only positive or socially acceptable responses; just respond with what comes to mind first. Take another piece of paper and divide it into two columns. Head one column "Strengths" and the other column "Weakness." Fill in each column as quickly as possible. Using these first two tests as a base, take a third piece of paper, head it "Self-Improvement Goals," and complete the statement "I want to improve my…" as many times as you can in five minutes. Since you're constantly changing, these self-perceptions and goals also change and so must be updated frequently.

Your cultural background will significantly influence your responses to this simple "Who Am I?" test. In one study, for example, participants from Malaysia (a collectivist culture) and from Australia and Great Britain (individualist cultures) completed this test. Malaysians produced significantly more group self-descriptions and fewer idiocentric self-descriptions than did the Australian or British members (Bochner 1994; also see Radford, Mann, Ohta, and Nakane 1993). If you completed the "Who Am I?" test, can you identify responses that were influenced by your individualist or collectivist orientation? Did other cultural factors influence your statements?

Listen to Others You can learn a lot about yourself by seeing yourself as others do. Conveniently, others are constantly giving you the very feedback you need to increase self-awareness. In every interpersonal interaction, people comment on you in some way—on what you do, what you say, how you look. Sometimes these comments are explicit; most often they're discoverable in the way in which others look at you, in what they talk about, in their interest in what you say. Pay close attention to this kind of information (verbal and nonverbal) and use it to increase your own self-awareness.

Actively Seek Information About Yourself Actively seek out information to reduce your blind self. You need not be so obvious as to say, "Tell me about myself" or "What do you think of me?" But you can use everyday situations to gain self-information: "Do you think I was assertive enough when asking for the raise?" Or "Would I be thought too forward if I invited myself for dinner?" Do not, of course, seek this information constantly; your friends would quickly find others with whom to interact. But you can make use of some situations—perhaps those in which you're particularly unsure of what to do or how you appear—to reduce your blind self and increase self-awareness.

See Your Different Selves Each of your friends and relatives views you differently; to each you're a somewhat different person. Yet you are really all of these selves. Practice seeing yourself as do the people with whom you interact. For starters, visualize how you're seen by your mother, your father, your teachers, your best friend, the stranger you sat next to on the bus, your employer, your neighbor's child. Because you're a composite of all these views, it's important that you periodically see yourself through the eyes of others. The experience will give you new and valuable perspectives on yourself.

Increase Your Open Self When you increase your open self and reveal yourself to others, you also reveal yourself to yourself. At the very least, you bring into clearer focus what you may have buried within. As you discuss yourself, you may see connections that you had previously missed, and with the aid of feedback from others you may gain still more insight. Also, by increasing the open self you increase the likelihood that a meaningful and intimate dialogue will develop; through such interactions you best get to know yourself. Do however, consider the risks involved in such self-disclosures.

Self-Esteem

How much do you like yourself? How valuable a person do you think you are? How competent do you think you are? The answers to these questions reflect your **self-esteem,** the value you place on yourself. People who have high self-esteem, for example, are going to communicate this throughout their verbal and nonverbal messages. The ways they phrase their ideas and questions or the way they hold their head and maintain eye contact are likely to differ greatly from the way the person with low self-esteem would communicate. Similarly, people with different views of themselves will develop and maintain relationships with friends, lovers, and family differently. As you read this unit, think about your own relationships and how the way you see yourself influences them.

Self-esteem is very important because success breeds success. When you feel good about yourself—about who you are and what you're capable of doing—you will perform better. When you think like a success, you're more likely to act like a success. When you think you're a failure you're more likely to act like a failure. Increasing self-esteem will, therefore, help you to function more effectively in school, in interpersonal relationships, and in careers. Here are a few suggestions for increasing self-esteem.

Attack Your Self-Destructive Beliefs

Self-destructive beliefs are those that damage your self-esteem and prevent you from building meaningful and productive relationships. They may be about yourself ("I'm not creative"; "I'm boring"), your world ("The world is an unhappy place"; "People are out to get me"), and your relationships ("All the good people are already in relationships"; "If I ever fall in love, I know I'll be hurt"). Identifying these beliefs will help you to examine them critically and to see that they're illogical and self-defeating.

Recognizing that you may have internalized self-destructive beliefs is a first step toward eliminating them. A second step involves recognizing that these beliefs are unrealistic and self-defeating. Psychotherapist Albert Ellis (1988, Ellis and Harper 1975) and other cognitive therapists (for example, Beck 1988) would argue that you can accomplish this by understanding why these beliefs are unrealistic and substituting more realistic ones. For example, following Ellis, you might try replacing an unrealistic desire to please everyone in everything you do with a more realistic belief that it would be nice if others were pleased with you but it certainly is not essential. A third step is giving yourself permission to fail, to be less than perfect, to be normal.

Do recognize that it's the unrealistic nature of these "drivers" that creates problems. Drivers are unrealistic beliefs that may motivate you to act in ways that are self-defeating (Butler 1981). Certainly, trying hard and being strong are not unhealthy when they're realistic. It's only when they become absolute—when you try to be everything to everyone—that they become impossible to achieve and create problems.

Engage in Self-Affirmation

Remind yourself of your success (Aronson, Cohen, and Nail 1998, Aronson, Wilson, and Akert 1999). There are enough people around who will remind you of your failures. Focus, too, on your good acts, your good deeds. Focus on your positive qualities, your strengths, your virtues. Focus on the good relationships you have with friends and relatives.

The way you talk to yourself about yourself influences what you think of yourself. If you talk positively about yourself, you will come to feel more positive about yourself. If you tell yourself that you're a success, that others like you, that you will succeed on the next test, and that you will be welcomed when asking for a date, you will soon come to feel positive about yourself. …

Seek Out Nourishing People

Psychologist Carl Rogers (1961) drew a distinction between *noxious* and *nourishing* people. Noxious people criticize and find fault with just about everything. Not surprisingly, these people are difficult to be around. More important, however, is that with time you may come to believe that their criticism and fault-finding are justified. When that happens, your self-esteem is likely to diminish.

Nourishing people, on the other hand, are positive. They're optimists. They reward you, they stroke you, they make you feel good about yourself. Here too, with time, you'll come to believe these compliments and positive statements and as a result are likely to raise your self-esteem.

Work on Projects That Will Result in Success

Some people want to fail, or so it seems. Often, they select projects that will result in failure. Perhaps the projects are too large or too difficult. In any event, they're impossible. Instead, select projects that will result in success. Each success helps build self-esteem. Each success makes the next success a little easier.

When a project does fail, recognize that this doesn't mean that you're a failure. Everyone fails somewhere along the line. Failure is something that happens; it's not something inside you. Further your failing once does not mean that you will fail the next time. So put failure in perspective. Don't make it an excuse for not trying again.

***

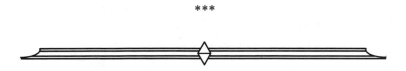

PSYCHO-LOGICAL DEFENSIVENESS

Excerpts from Chapter 3 of Anthony Falikowski's (2002) *Mastering Human Relations*, 2nd Edition, Toronto, Pearson Education.

***

3.2   Unconscious and Irrational Defensiveness

Defensiveness is something we should all try to reduce in our psychological and interpersonal lives. For our immediate purposes, it can be defined simply as the psyche's unconscious effort to protect the self from disquieting **anxiety,** either through **diversionary and intimidation tactics** or by **distortions of reality.** As you'll soon see, defensiveness takes on many forms, but whatever the form, you can probably already appreciate how irritating it can be to be around people who unwittingly try to reduce anxiety by twisting things, by constantly attacking others, or by rationalizing their actions. Such people tend to be insecure and abrasive. For reasons we don't always understand, they seem to take things too personally. Being around defensive people can lead to conversations that are very one-sided and uninteresting, making interactions with them emotionally draining. As the title of this section suggests, being defensive can be offensive to others. It is important, therefore, that you learn more about defensiveness so that you can reduce it in yourself. You probably don't want your own defensiveness to get in the way of positive and fruitful relationships; nor do you want it to prevent you from achieving your goals…

In advance of our discussion of … psychological defensiveness, it is only fitting to make brief reference to the work of Sigmund Freud. His pioneering work in **psychoanalysis,** developed and furthered by daughter Anna, has helped us to understand the unconscious dimensions of life and how we often twist reality in order to feel better about ourselves. According to Freud, not all psychological experience takes place at a **conscious** level. Some things are found at the **preconscious** level and others are deeply buried in the **unconscious.** What is conscious is what we are currently experiencing with respect to our feelings, thoughts and sensations. What is preconscious is that which we can call up at will. For instance, if now asked, you could no doubt give someone your birthdate or telephone number—things that were probably not occupying your conscious mind just a moment ago. However, what is unconscious is currently unavailable to self-awareness. The fact that there are things happening in the unconscious mind is important to remember. Frequently, in response to underlying fears and anxiety-provoking situations, we unwittingly resort to the use of psychic defences that allow us to cope. These defences reduce unpleasant feelings or shield them from conscious awareness.

Unfortunately, an over-reliance on unconscious defensiveness as a **coping mechanism** can lead to gross distortions of reality. A failure to appreciate the role played by unconscious defensiveness in your life can also prevent you from functioning in healthy, autonomous ways. Buried fears and anxieties may dictate your actions and thoughts in ways you don't recognize. By learning more about defensiveness and by reducing it in ourselves, we can free ourselves from unconscious debilitating forces and we can learn to perceive situations and other people with less anxiety-based distortion.

A Glossary of Freudian Terms

Levels of Consciousness

Conscious: Includes thoughts, feelings, sensations and experiences that we are aware of at any moment in time.

Preconscious: Lies just below the level of conscious awareness. Contents of preconscious can be called into conscious awareness with a minimum of effort.

Unconscious: Comprises drives and instincts outside the realm of conscious experience. Access to it can be gained indirectly by free association, dream analysis and other psychotherapeutic techniques.

Structure of Personality

Id: Refers to the biological components of personality (e.g., sex drive). It operates on the pleasure principle and is irrational and impulsive. The id makes up the largest part of the psyche; it is most influential in determining behaviour.

Superego: Houses our moral conscience and ego ideals. It is instrumental in making value judgments and helping us to distinguish between right and wrong. It operates on the perfection principle.

Ego: The rational part of personality. It operates on the reality principle. It serves to balance all parts of the personality to minimize anxiety.

Figure 3.1

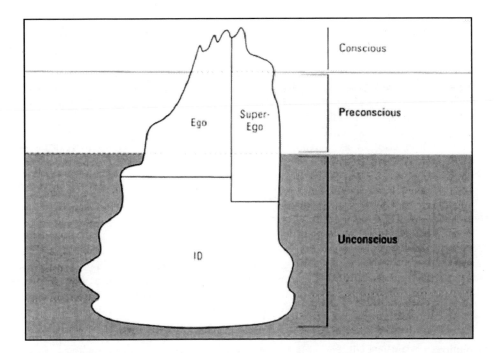

Psychological Defence Mechanisms

Since anxiety is inherently unpleasant, human beings have developed strategies to reduce its intensity. One strategy requires us to confront or run away from the threats that face us. We thereby eliminate difficulties, lower the chance of their future occurrence, or decrease the prospects of additional anxiety in the future.

A second strategy for coping with anxiety is to employ **psychological defence mechanisms.** They include repression, rationalization, projection, reaction, formation, displacement, identification, regression, fantasy formation, intellectualization / isolation, denial and sublimation.

As mentioned before, defence mechanisms operate on an unconscious level. This explains why defensive people are usually unaware of their defensiveness. Also recall that defence mechanisms distort the reality of the anxiety-provoking situations that give rise to the mechanisms in the first place. When we use defence mechanisms, then, we unconsciously seek to protect ourselves against any real or perceived threat by falsifying the nature of the threat. Freud calls that part of the psyche that uses psychological defence mechanisms the **ego.**

You should note that everybody uses defence mechanisms. If we didn't, we could all be overwhelmed by anxiety. The danger for us comes from an overreliance on the mechanisms. If we become too dependent on them, they could cause gross distortions of reality and we could begin to lose touch with what's really going on...

3.3   Repression

Repression is the primary ego defence that makes all other psychological defensiveness possible. It is the central mechanism used by the ego to prevent anxiety-provoking thoughts from entering the conscious level of awareness. These thoughts may originate in our biological instincts or from painful events experienced during our lifetime. Unacceptable sexual desires, for instance, may be repressed to the unconscious, as could childhood traumas. It is important to emphasize that "repressed" people are not aware of their own anxiety-provoking conflicts in the psyche, nor do they consciously remember the emotionally traumatic past events now buried in the unconscious recesses of the mind. As Freud (1915: 147) put it, "The essence of repression lies simply in turning something away and keeping it at a distance from the consciousness."

Despite its very real potential for harm, the use of repression helps us cope with everyday problems. Let's suppose, for example, that a friend said something spiteful to us. We might conveniently forget what was said to maintain the relationship...

Repression can also act as a temporary coping mechanism in response to conflict and pain stemming from our individual histories. Unpleasant things may have happened to us that are too horrible to bear consciously. Distancing ourselves psychologically for a time may help us to survive, even if we are emotionally wounded...

Obstacles

On the negative side, repressed memories, conflicts, thoughts, feelings and impulses do not just disappear when repressed. They remain active in the unconscious. Psychic energy is continually spent to prevent their emergence into conscious awareness. This strain drains much of the ego's resources and, therefore, less energy is available for more constructive, self-enhancing and creative behaviours (Hjelle and Ziegler, 1992). After all, "It's hard to expand your horizons when you're busy defending your borders."

As well as draining your creative energies, repression has the negative effect of precluding any possible resolutions to conflicts still buried in the unconscious. If you don't know what's disturbing you, it's difficult to make the appropriate adjustments in your life. Affected by anxiety, the true source of which is not understood, repressed people tend toward rigidity, lack of spontaneity and an inability to meet the challenges of life head-on. They may consequently seem awfully "stiff" or overly reserved to those communicating with them.

Even more seriously, highly repressed people may develop other unhealthy psychological and physical symptoms. Phobias (e.g., fear of snakes) are derivative of repressed feelings as are hysterical reactions. Psychosomatic illnesses (e.g., asthma and arthritis) may also be linked to repressed anxiety (Frager and Fadiman, 1997). Psychosexual disorders (impotence and frigidity) probably have a basis in repression as well.

In his treatment of patients, Freud discovered that repressed impulses find outlets in dreams, slips of the tongue and in other manifestations of what he described as the "psychopathology of everyday life" (Hjelle and Ziegler, 1992). You might wish to engage in some dream analysis yourself to uncover any personal repressions. What are your nighttime fantasies or daydreams all about? What could the themes indicate? Also, try to catch yourself in the act of "changing the subject," "pretending that your didn't understand" or making it appear that you "didn't hear what someone said." That which was changed, not understood or not heard may give you some insights into yourself and the workings of your mind. You may be able to uncover some fears and anxieties that you never consciously knew you had.

3.3   Rationalization

A defence mechanism that many people rely on heavily is **rationalization.** In this case, the ego enlists the powers of reason to attempt to cope with disquieting anxiety. To protect the self, unacceptable thoughts, actions, mistakes, poor judgments and failures must somehow be explained away. What the ego self does in its own defence is provide "reasonable" but dishonest explanations and justifications to support behaviours recognized at an unconscious level as wrong or undesirable. To recognize and admit our failures, wrongdoings or unacceptable cravings consciously could be too painful to bear. Instead, the ego disguises our true motives, distorts the reality of situations and makes things look more morally acceptable than they are. This self-deception helps us to cope with immediate anxiety; however, it is not productive to the extent that it shields us from recognizing the real reasons behind our behaviours, attitudes, thoughts and feelings.

Two "fruitful" examples of rationalization are "sour grapes" and "sweet lemons." Using the sour grapes rationalization, we try to minimize something to which we've aspired but failed. Simply, we wanted something, but after discovering the impossibility of getting it, we undercut its value. Aesop's fable serves us well here. Remember the fox who wanted to eat the grapes? When the fox discovered they couldn't be reached, he decided that they were probably sour anyway. It's emotionally easier to cope with the fact that something *undesirable* is out of reach than something much sought after. Failing to get what we want produces frustration and anxiety.

Using the sweet lemon rationalization, people glorify things that were not considered very attractive or desirable in the first place. For example, people may be forced to do unwanted tasks only to react later by praising the benefits of doing them. In truth, there may be little to be gained, but believing there is a benefit allows people to cope with unpleasant situations…

Obstacles

One negative result of rationalization is impaired judgment. If we see life as a collection of sweet lemons and sour grapes, we may end up with a basket of rotten fruit. Describing objects of our desire as less desirable or making undesirable objects sound more desirable may help us to feel better temporarily, but it certainly won't enable us to see clearly, impartially and objectively. As rationalizing people, our judgments are more reflections of our wants and frustrations than accurate evaluations of objects and events in the external world. Impaired judgment, like impaired driving, is dangerous and may get you into a lot of trouble. This idea takes us to the ethical problems associated with rationalization.

If we rely on rationalization whenever we violate social norms or personal standards of conduct, then we cease to function as moral people. Rationalizing helps us to justify unjustifiable acts in our own minds. It helps us to get off the hook of moral responsibility for all wrongdoing. Heavy reliance on rationalization spares us from guilt and self-blame. From the vantage point of others, however, refusing to accept responsibility for our wrongdoing can be perceived as immature, if not immoral. No doubt, appearing childish and unethical is not in your personal self-interest. These qualities are not likely to endear you to others. It is important, therefore, that you minimize rationalization in your efforts to reduce anxiety in your life and improve your interpersonal effectiveness.

3.3   Projection

Projection is the unconscious act of attributing to others one's own feelings, thoughts and intentions. Through the process of projection, undesirable aspects of one's own personality can be displaced from within onto the external environment of people, animals or objects. By externalizing what is in fact internal, people can deal with anxiety-provoking thoughts and intentions without having to admit or be aware of the fact that these disturbing thoughts are their own (Frager and Fadiman, 1997). Projection offers temporary relief from anxiety as it allows people to blame someone or something else for their own personal shortcomings (Hjelle and Ziegler, 1992). Projection thus seems to come in handy whenever the ego or self-esteem is threatened.

The danger with projection is that it may become too intense and habitual. If this occurs, then gross distortions of reality can result. People could even become psychologically ill or disturbed. They might, for example, become paranoid and attribute aggressive thoughts to others that originate within themselves… The next time you criticize anyone about anything, it could be insightful for you to ask, "To what extent is my criticism an accurate reflection of reality?" or "What does my criticism of another tell me about myself?"

Obstacles

The use of projection could have negative social consequences for people relying on it too frequently. If you unconsciously attribute to others your own hostile, aggressive urges and impulses, you may develop unwarranted suspicions. You won't be very trusting as an individual. This will surely make it difficult to establish close relationships (Barocas, Reichman and Schwebel, 1990)…

Excessive projection could also make you fall prey to social prejudice and scapegoating. Ethnic and racial groups provide convenient targets for the attribution of your own negative personal characteristics to others (Adorno, Frenkel-Brunswick, Levinson and Sanford, 1950, cites in Hjelle and Ziegler, 1992). For instance, people who feel inferior may project their inferiority onto selected racial, ethnic or religious groups. Ambitious types may blame the "system" or some stereotyped elitist group for their difficulties in achieving success. Projection deflects attention away from ourselves and helps us to feel better about our personal shortcomings. Unfortunately, these better feelings come at the expense of others.

***

3.3   Reaction Formation

Reaction formation is used by the ego to control the expression of forbidden impulses. This mechanism works in two ways. First, unacceptable impulses are repressed in the unconscious. Second, opposites to the impulses are expressed on a conscious level (Hjelle and Ziegler, 1992). For example, people who are threatened by their own sexual urges or libidinal impulses may become crusaders against pornography and liberal laws on sexual conduct. Others who are highly anxious about their violent tendencies may become pacifists or animal rights advocates. In a letter to Jules Masserman, a famous psychologist who did work on alcoholism in cats, an antivivisectionist's moral crusade "covers up" the person's apparent violent tendencies. Notice in the following letter the lack of love and compassion for the drunkard and the personal assault on Masserman.

I read [a magazine article... on your work on alcoholism].... I am surprised that anyone who is as well educated as you must be to hold the position that you do would stoop to such a depth as to torture helpless little cats in the pursuit of a cure for alcoholics....

A drunkard does not want to be cured—a drunkard is just a weak-minded idiot who belongs in the gutter and should be left there. Instead of torturing helpless little cats why not torture drunks or better still exert your would-be noble effort toward getting a bill passed to exterminate the drunks....

My greatest wish is that you have brought home to you a torture that will be a thousand fold greater than what you have, and are doing to the little animals.... If you are an example of what a noted psychiartist [sic] should be I'm glad I am just an ordinary human being without letters after my name. I'd rather be myself with a clear conscience, knowing that I have not hurt any living creature...No punishment is too great for you and I hope I live to read about your mangled body and long suffering before you finally die—and I'll laugh long and loud. (Masserman, 1961: 35)

Of course, not all advocates of peace or animal rights display reaction formation defensiveness. Many have genuine, legitimate ethical disagreements with war and the destruction of animals. The clue in determining the difference between true feelings and defensiveness is found in the degree to which the feelings are emphasized (Hergenhahn, 1993). Reaction formations have a tendency to be more intense and extravagant in their expression... Unconsciously, there is the fear that the unacceptable urge or impulse will break through if repeated attacks on it, or denials of it, do not continue.

Obstacles

There are negative social consequences to using reaction formation. Relationships may be crippled by the defensive person's rigidity. Reaction formation contributes to building an "all or nothing" attitude toward life that makes the defensive person unyielding and inflexible. Little compromise may be possible with those whose strong feelings about something are merely a cover-up for unconscious fears and anxieties. Reasoning with unconsciously defensive people may sometimes seem next to impossible. Try, for example, to debate rationally the issue of pornography with a person whose moral zeal is based on personal guilt and insecurity. Not much will be accomplished.

3.3   Displacement

Like other defence mechanisms, **displacement** is an unconscious process. It too has much to do with our primitive, instinctual impulses. Whenever we feel the urge to meet the demands of the **id** (a term used by Freud to designate the part of the personality directed at biological need satisfaction), we invest **psychic energy** in need-satisfying objects. When objects that would directly satisfy the impulses of the id are not available, or when they include some threat or unpleasantness, we may shift our impulses onto other objects. This substitution is called displacement (Engler, 1999). Sigmund Freud used the term **cathexis** to describe the investment of psychic energy in objects that satisfy needs (Hergenhahn, 1998). If need-satisfying objects are not available, an intense longing may manifest itself in the form of thoughts, images and fantasies. Such thoughts persist until needs are satisfied. When needs are finally satisfied, psychic energy dissipates to become available for other cathexes.

***

... [T]he human psyche has developed a moral superego that functions to inhibit primitive urges, instincts and desires. This inhibition requires energy to be spent on preventing unacceptable cathexes. Energy that is used to prevent unacceptable cathexes is called **anticathexis** (Hergenhahn, 1998). If an unacceptable cathexis were allowed to emerge, the superego would ensure that anxiety would result. To reduce anxiety, the ego and the **superego** (a term used by Freud to capture the notion of moral conscience) combine their efforts to create an anticathexis that is sufficiently strong to inhibit the primitive cathexes of the id. Note that the original needs of the id do not vanish. Rather, the original cathexis is displaced onto other safer objects and activities....

In general terms, we can say displacement occurs whenever an instinctual impulse is redirected from a more threatening activity, person or object to a less threatening one (Hjelle and Ziegler, 1992). As a student angered by the comments of one of your instructors, you might swear at a roommate or sibling. If you are upset because your parents won't let you have the car this weekend, you might kick your pet in frustration...

A less common form of displacement involves "turning against the self" (Hjelle and Ziegler, 1992). In this case, hostile impulses toward other people are redirected at one's own person. The result can be things like depression and self-deprecation. If other innocent and less threatening objects are unavailable for displacement, the self can become its own target.

Figure 3.3

An Example of Displacement

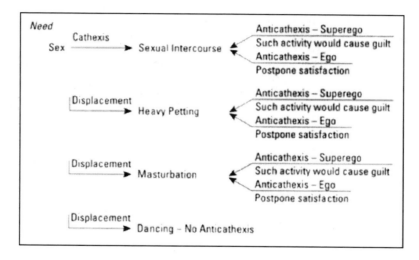

Obstacles

Social and interpersonal manifestations of displacement can be rather unpleasant. First of all, innocent people are attacked, criticized, abused and hurt. They suffer merely by virtue of their relatively non-threatening natures. Unjustified psychological assault can thus be destructive to interpersonal relationships. Second, people unconsciously relying on displacement tend to exhibit hypersensitivity to minor annoyances (Hjelle and Ziegler, 1992). For example, people criticized by over-demanding bosses may react violently to the slightest provocation from a spouse or friend. Target objects of hostility are simply substitutes for the boss who cannot be attacked... If some "little comment" you innocently made once was met with undue anger or hostility, perhaps you witnessed displacement... You benefit from knowing this by increasing your compassion for those experiencing psychological pain. You needn't take their aggressive outbursts personally....

3.3   Identification

Identification is a psychological defence mechanism unconsciously used to decrease anxiety by increasing feelings of self-worth. It involves taking on the characteristics of someone admired or considered successful (Hergenhahn, 1998). An obvious example of identification is the hero worship exhibited by school-age boys and girls (Barocas, Reichman and Schwebel, 1990). Typical heroes are rock stars and athletes. Young people are very motivated to learn everything they can about their heroes. They join fan clubs, purchase tapes and CDs, buy sports cards and memorize statistics and facts about those whom they idolize. Identification is clearly present when they adopt their favourite hero's hairstyle and dress or when they begin to imitate the hero's behavioural traits and speech patterns. Sometimes people identify with sports celebrities by "feeling part of the team" (e.g., the Vancouver Canucks) and basking in the sunshine of its glorious victories. Being on the side of the winner is one way to feel good about yourself and to convince yourself you're not a "loser." The fact that you don't actually play on the team or work for the organization may be unimportant details in the minds of those identifying themselves in such a way. The fact that team colours and sweaters are being worn is more significant for purposes of identification. Through identification, people temporarily gain security and postpone the inevitable confrontation with the problem of forming an individual identity.

Identification doesn't disappear in adulthood. Older individuals may still identify with athletic teams, but more commonly with service clubs, professional organizations, successful individuals and political leaders. As with youngsters, adults unconsciously attempt to bolster feelings of self-worth through identification and thereby protect themselves from anxieties related to the self...

It is important to remember that the purpose of identification is to reduce anxiety. By assuming the characteristics of models who appear to us to be highly successful we can come to believe that we also possess their attributes (Engler, 1999)....

Apart from helping us to cope with anxiety, identification also has an important role to play in the formation of personality. When, as children, we identified with our parents and caretakers, we came to accept their values. This identification enables us to limit or eliminate punishments that would otherwise come from expressing contrary and conflicting values. Therefore, this acceptance and internalization of parental values not only reduces the fear of retribution, but also helps to form the superego. Later on in life we develop our superego further by internalizing society's values and norms.

Obstacles

Ironically, overuse of identification can contribute to problems of personal identity. If you're always trying to be like someone else, then you're not spending much time being yourself. This can lead to inauthenticity. You can't really know yourself or express who you are if you're always trying to imitate others. Emulating your heroes may give rise to playing roles and behaving in unnatural ways. It could also lead to certain pretences. Your attraction to others and emulation of them may erroneously lead you to conclude that you share their qualities and personal characteristics. Being a hard-core fan of somebody does not make you that somebody, just as hanging around intelligent people doesn't make you smart.

Another potential problem related to identification is ostracism or separation from others. If you choose to be loyal to certain groups, you may have to reject others. They may have different values, norms and patterns of behaviour. Furthermore, strong identification with any group or person may make you a target for opponents of that person or group. If you wish to be a neo-Nazi skinhead, for example, don't be surprised if you're shunned by mainstream society. You may be stereotyped as much as you stereotype those outside your identified group.

***

3.3   Regression

Like other defence mechanisms, **regression** is used to defend against the conscious experience of anxiety. We use it to revert to an earlier, more childlike stage of development. This "going back" enables us to alleviate anxiety by retreating to a previous period in life that was experienced as being more secure and pleasant. At this earlier stage, there were fewer responsibilities and more parental/caretaker attention. Security came from being cared for and having one's gratification assured (Barocas, Reichman and Schwebel, 1990). Calvin Hall (1954: 95-96) offers us a list of regression examples below.

Even healthy, well-adjusted people make regressions from time to time in order to reduce anxiety, or, as they say, to blow off steam. They smoke, get drunk, eat too much, lose their tempers, bite their nails, pick their noses, break laws, talk baby talk, destroy property, masturbate, read mystery stories, go to the movies, engage in unusual sexual practices, chew gum and tobacco, dress up as children, drive fast and recklessly, believe in good and evil spirits, take naps, fight and kill one another, bet on the horses, daydream, rebel against or submit to authority, gamble, preen before the mirror, act out their impulses, pick on scapegoats, and do a thousand and one other childish things. Some of these regressions are so commonplace that they are taken to be signs of maturity. Actually they are all forms of regression used by adults.

As with any defence mechanism, regression only temporarily relieves the experience of anxiety. It leaves the root cause unaddressed (Hjelle and Ziegler, 1992). Hence, anxiety-producing conflicts and situations are not truly resolved by regression, only obscured from conscious awareness...

Obstacles

Regression obviously interferes with human communication. Someone reduced to babbling will not send coherent messages. Also, if highly anxious individuals display regressive symptoms by throwing tantrums, then it will be difficult to conduct level-headed conversations. Furthermore, if regressed people are preoccupied with the need to be cared for, they will appear very narcissistic or selfish to others. It is difficult to develop intimate relationships with those who only wish to take from others in order to satisfy their own security needs. Some people are simply put off by the immaturity of regressive behaviour. People displaying this behaviour may be avoided.

3.3   Fantasy Formation

Fantasy formation is a defence that involves "gratifying frustrated desires by thinking about imaginary achievements and satisfactions" (Weiten, Lloyd and Lashley, 1999). Through fantasy formation, we become what we're not, we have what we don't own, we accomplish what we've never done and we visit places to which we've never been. Fantasy formation provides yet another way of helping us to cope with anxiety. Let's suppose you just failed a test; dreaming about the day you graduate may help you to deal with the temporary setback. Or, think of somebody you particularly dislike; expressing your hostile feelings in fantasy is much better than physically or verbally assaulting the target of your aggression. In short, creative use of fantasy can sometimes be the key to dealing effectively with negative emotions and periodic frustrations.

Most obvious examples of fantasy are found with children. Often powerless to control others, they create imaginary playmates or animals who obey them (Barocas, Reichman and Schwebel, 1990). If threatened by guilt, they may conjure up monsters in their minds. Such fantasizing prepares children for reality and for the need to relieve pain.

Obstacles

Extended use of fantasy formation can transport people psychologically away from real problems and real situations. Presented with the threat of anxiety, some people may use fantasy as a way of retreating from relationships of all kinds (Barocas, Reichman and Schwebel, 1990). In this case, problems and people are not directly faced. Avoidance and illusion are used to sweep the dirt of anxiety under the carpet of conscious awareness. Personal and interpersonal problems go unnoticed.

People relying heavily on fantasy formation as a defence mechanism may be difficult to communicate with. Their perceptions of reality may be highly unrealistic. Living in a future dream of success, they may overlook their current failures. Imagining how things could be, they may be blind to how things actually are. Pragmatic discussions, for example, ones that are based on facts and reality, may be difficult to hold with those living in a fantasy world.

3.3   Intellectualization/Isolation

Intellectualization (or **isolation**) is a way of suppressing unpleasant emotions by engaging in detached analyses of threatening problems (Weiten, Lloyd and Lashley, 1999). This defence mechanism enables us unconsciously to "isolate" anxiety, separating parts of a situation from the rest of the psyche. Through this act of partitioning, little or no emotional reaction to the situation or event is consciously experienced (Frager and Fadiman, 1997). By isolating problems and conflicts from the rest of the personality, events can be recounted without feeling. The emotional detachment makes it seem like the situation or event involves a third party. By withdrawing more and more into the world of ideas, intellectualizing people need less and less to deal with the reality of their own feelings (Frager and Fadiman, 1997). Of course, there is nothing wrong in analyzing situations or intellectualizing them. This problem occurs only when isolation is being used unconsciously to protect the ego from acknowledging anxiety-provoking aspects of situations, events or interpersonal relationships. Thinking, in itself, is not necessarily a diversion from emotional experience.

The quotation below provides an illustration of intellectualization. In it, a person named Alan presents many great ideas about threatening matters (e.g., sex) but does not possess the feelings that normally accompany them. Let's see how.

> Alan offers a perfect example. At eighteen, one of his chief delights is to discuss philosophic ideas on love, politics, and death. But he thinks very little about his daily life. His lofty views on love in no way prevent him from being childish and callous with women. He wittily criticizes the middle-class marriage for its imperfections and hypocrisies. But he cannot move past the most obvious clichés in his own relationships.
>
>   (Barocas, Reichman and Schwebel, 1983: 118)

***

Obstacles

Intellectualization can cause problems for effective interpersonal communication. For example, if people are not in touch with their real feelings, they will not be able to share them with others. Also, if individuals persist in analyzing and intellectualizing their lives, intimacy may suffer. Conversations may begin to sound more like theoretical debates. This need not be frustrating in itself; however, sensitive receivers of "intellectualized" defensive messages may become frustrated because they cannot make personal contact with the defensive people involved or appreciate what they are truly experiencing. Intellectualizing can create psychological distance.

3.3   Denial

The defence mechanism of **denial** blocks from the ego threatening events or facts found in external social reality (Atwater, 1999). Not accepting the fact that your ex-fiancée is having a sexual relationship with your best friend would be a case of denial. Here, threatening thoughts would surface in your conscious mind, but you would refuse to believe them. There would be a conscious effort to suppress what you'd experienced as unpleasant.

***

As a defence mechanism, denial does offer certain adaptive advantages. In certain situations it can effectively reduce stress (Atwater, 1999). It can also enable people to live through difficult times and unbearable situations. For example, two psychiatrists at the Massachusetts General Hospital found that "major deniers" of heart trouble had better survival rates than those people who only partially or minimally denied.

Obstacles

Over-reliance on denial may indicate that mature problem-solving methods of dealing with life have not been learned and that some degree of maladjustment may be present (Barocas, Reichman and Schwebel, 1983). For instance, alcoholics who deny they drink too much are not doing themselves any favours. Physical symptoms can arise and social relationships can begin to suffer. People who eat too much and then deny it by blaming their weight on metabolism are probably not doing much in the long run to improve their self-esteem. In short, some painful realities have to be faced before they can be overcome. Not facing up to them probably doesn't help others and in most cases probably doesn't help you.

***

Defence Mechanisms in Summary

In summary to this section, it should be repeated that psychological defence mechanisms help us to reduce disquieting anxiety by distorting our perceptions of reality. They protect the psyche from internal imbalances and external tensions.

The defences avoid reality (repression), exclude reality (denial), redefine reality (rationalization), or reverse reality (reaction formation). They place inner feelings on the outer world (projection), partition reality (isolation), or withdraw from reality (regression). (Frager and Fadiman, 1984: 29)

Defence mechanisms not only help us to deal with unacceptable anxiety-provoking instinctual impulses, they also help us to master a variety of life conflicts. For instance, they can help us to contain ourselves emotionally when confronted with sudden life crises (e.g., a serious illness). They can help us to fashion changes in our self-image when required (e.g., after a demotion). Defences enable us to cope with unresolvable conflicts with significant others as well as to survive major conflicts of conscience stemming from our (mis) treatment of other people (Vaillant, 1977).

The danger of defensiveness arises when reality distortions become too great and too frequent. They diminish strength and rob energy from more creative and productive psychological functioning. As isolated responses to temporarily weakened egos, defence mechanisms have their uses. However, if they are unconsciously adopted as general strategies to deal with life, they are potentially unproductive and detrimental to personal well-being. They certainly can get in the way of effective interpersonal relations. See Table 3.3 for typical defences used in various kinds of anxiety-provoking situations.

Table 3.3

Typical Defensive Response Patterns

Anxiety-Provoking Stimulus	**Commonly Used Defences**
Prohibited sexual urges or behaviour	Sublimation, repression, rationalization and projection
Feelings of inferiority	Fantasy, identification and regression
Guilt	Rationalization and projection
Failure	Intellectualization/isolation, projection and rationalization
Hostility	Sublimation, displacement, reaction formation, repression and fantasy
Disappointment	Intellectualization, fantasy and rationalization
Personal limitations	Denial, fantasy and regression

Source: Adapted from Coleman and Hammen (1974)

Aim: The purpose of this activity is to help you deal more effectively with defensiveness in yourself and others.

Instructions: Get into small groups. Next to each defence mechanism listed, provide an example to illustrate its workings. The example can be real or hypothetical. Choose what feels comfortable. For each example, brainstorm ways you could deal with the defensiveness. First, see yourself as the one being defensive in the example. Second, see yourself as the one witnessing the defensiveness in another. What could you do to help yourself? What could you do to help another person?

Defence Mechanism	Example/ Illustration	Effective Handling (Yourself and Others)
1. Repression		
2. Rationalization		
3. Projection		
4. Reaction formation		
5. Displacement		
6. Identification		
7. Regression		
8. Fantasy formation		
9. Intellectualization/ Isolation		
10. Denial		
11. Sublimation		

***

BETTER RELATIONSHIPS THROUGH TRANSACTIONAL ANALYSIS

Excerpts from Chapter 4 of Anthony Falikowski's (2002) *Mastering Human Relations*, 2nd Edition, Toronto, Pearson Education.

***

4.5 Types of Transactions

Now that we are familiar with all three ego states, we can move on and examine communication patterns that involve them. Berne writes that when people verbally communicate with each other, **transactions** take place.

> The unit of social intercourse is called a transaction. If two or more people encounter each other… sooner or later one of them will speak, or give some other indication of acknowledging the presence of others. This is called the transactional stimulus. Another person will then say or do something which is in some way related to the stimulus, and that is called the transactional response. (Berne, cited in Harris, 1969: 33).

It is important to note that transactional stimuli and transactional responses arise from ego states. Our job and the task of transactional analysts is to appraise "which ego state implemented the transactional stimulus and which executed the transactional response" (Berne, 1964: 29). There are several types of transactions, depending on how ego states interact and what was really intended by the messages transmitted. Here we'll look at complementary transactions, crossed transactions and ulterior transactions.

Complementary Transactions

There are two types of **complementary transactions.** In the first type, the receiver of a message responds to it from the same ego state the sender used in transmitting the message. For example, the sender sends a Parent message and the receiver responds in the Parent mode. Complementary transactions of this sort can also take place at the level of Adult and Child. See Figure 4.6 below.

A second type of complementary transaction is based on unequal relationships. For instance, the transaction could be from Parent to Child or vice versa. It might also be from Child to Adult or Adult to Child. In all unequal complementary transactions, the lines of communication are still parallel. Whether transactions are equal or unequal, the first rule of T.A. is that when source stimulus and receiver response occur in a parallel fashion, transactions are complementary and can go on indefinitely (Harris, 1969). For an illustration of unequal complementary transactions, see Figure 4.7.

Figure 4.6
Type 1 Complementary Transactions

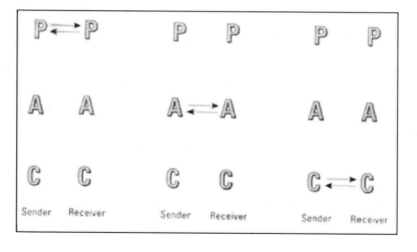

Figure 4.7
Type 2 Unequal Complementary Transactions

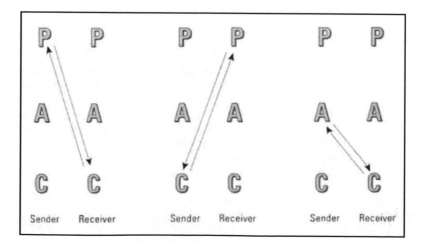

118

In his book *I'm OK—You're OK,* Harris provides an example of a complementary transaction occurring between two women complaining to each other about how their bus is going to arrive late at its destination. This transaction occurs in a parallel fashion at the Parent ego state level. A paraphrase of Harris's example is found below.

Elvira: *While glancing at her watch, mumbling to herself and catching the eye of the female passenger next to her, she sighs wearily.*
Lilith: *Sighs back in response; adjusts herself and looks at her watch.*
Elvira: *We're going to be late again.*
Lilith: *It always happens.*
Elvira: *Have you ever seen this bus arrive on time?*
Lilith: *Never have.*
Elvira: *Just like I was saying to my husband yesterday—you just don't get quality service like you used to.*
Lilith: *You're absolutely right. I don't know what's wrong with people today.*
Elvira: *They still like to take your money, though, don't they?*

In the example above, both passengers engage in a judgmental exchange about service. They seem to enjoy complaining to each other. Communicating Parent to Parent, they could go on forever. Harris (1969: 94-95) says:

> When we blame and find fault, we replay the early blaming and fault-finding which is recorded in the Parent, and this makes us feel OK, because the Parent is OK, and we are coming on Parent. Finding someone to agree with you, and play the game, produces a feeling well-nigh omnipotent.
>   *Source:* Reprinted by permission of Harper Collins Publishers.

Crossed Transactions

In **crossed transactions,** the lines of communication are not parallel. Rather, they cross or intersect each other at some point. Instead of promoting further communication, crossed transactions disrupt it. Thus, a second rule of T.A. "… is that communication is broken off when a crossed transaction occurs" (Berne, 1964: 30). Crossed transactions come in two types. A Type 1 crossed transaction is illustrated in Figure 4.8.

In a Type 1 crossed transaction the message stimulus is Adult-to-Adult. In the example below, an appropriate response to the question regarding the whereabouts of the book would have been something like "No, I don't" or "The last time I saw it, it was on your desk in class." Instead, what we have is a receiver who flares up and responds in a Child-to-Parent fashion. As Figure 4.8 shows, the two vectors of communication cross. Communication is thereby broken off. If communication is to resume, either the sender must become Parental to complement the receiver's Child or the receiver's Adult ego state must be activated as a complement to the sender's Adult.

In a Type 2 crossed transaction, an Adult-to-Adult stimulus message is answered with a Parent-to-Child response. Let's modify the example about the textbook to illustrate the point. See Figure 4.9.

In both Type 1 and Type 2 crossed transactions, communication about the book stops. Either a digression must be made about who got blamed for what or talk must resume about who's acting like a child. The location of the book becomes a dead issue. See Figure 4.10 for additional illustrations of crossed transactions.

Figure 4.8
Type 1 Crossed Transaction

Figure 4.9
Type 2 Crossed Transaction

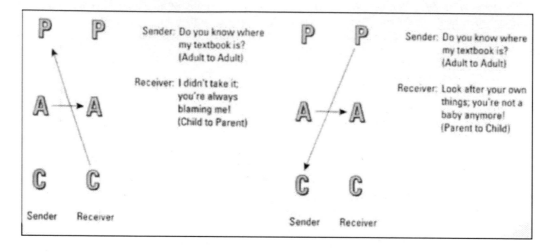

Figure 4.10
More Crossed Transactions

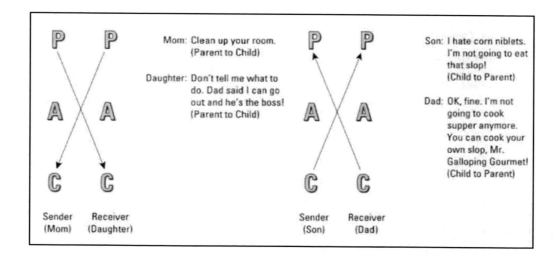

120

Figure 4.11
Ulterior
Angular
Transactions

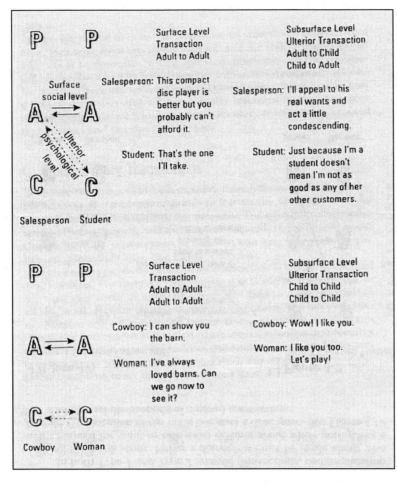

Ulterior Transactions

Ulterior transactions are complementary transactions that include **hidden messages** intended to serve **ulterior motives** (Weiten, Lloyd and Lashley, 1991). Ulterior transactions are more than two ego states simultaneously (Berne, 1964). When observing ulterior transactions we discover surface level and subsurface level messages being communicated at the same time. At the obvious surface level, there is the manifest content of the message. Below the surface occurs the latent, but more meaningful exchange (Weiten, Lloyd and Lashley, 1991). In ulterior transactions, Adult-to-Adult surface communication patterns, for example, may be adopted for the sake of appearances. Underneath appearances, however, another totally different sort of communication may be taking place.

Ulterior transactions may be angular or duplex. Angular ulterior transactions involve three ego states. Berne (1964) uses the example of a salesman to illustrate this point. See Figure 4.11 for an adaptation. Duplex ulterior transactions involve four ego states (Berne, 1964). We commonly find them in flirtation games. Again, in this instance, there is the obvious message at the social level of communication as well as the latent message at the subsurface psychological level...

We see that at the social level an Adult conversation about barns is taking place. At the psychological level we find a Child conversation involving innocent foreplay. It would appear that the more interesting interaction is taking place at the hidden or subsurface level.

4.6   Strokes

Whatever the nature of people's communication transactions (complementary, crossed, ulterior), the basic motivation behind the social interaction is the need for **strokes** (Dusay and Dusay, 1979: 377). All three ego states require stroking for optimal development. The Parent might need strokes for being a good listener, caretaker, advice giver or character model. The Child may crave stroking for displaying creativity and curiosity or for being fun-loving and spontaneous. The Adult might need strokes for being a good thinker and decision maker (Gilliland, James and Bowman, 1989).

The idea that we all have a basic need for strokes comes from research in infant development. Studies indicate that touch is important. For instance, it stimulates an infant's chemistry for mental and physical growth (see Spitz, 1945: 53-74). "Infants who are neglected, ignored, or for any reason do not experience enough touch, suffer mental and physical deteriorization even to the point of death" (James and Jongeward, 1978). Their spinal cords tend to shrivel and deteriorate. This condition is known as **marasmus** (see Freed and Freed, 1973). If you ever have a chance to visit a neonatal ward in a hospital, take note of the nurses, parents and volunteers who are instructed to physically "stroke" premature infants for about 15 to 20 minutes daily. This stroking helps them to thrive. Without stroking, premature infants develop more slowly and, with extreme neglect, may not survive.

Transactional analysts claim that the need for strokes does not end with infancy. As ego states develop, the Parent, Adult and Child in us all require stroking for healthy growth and development. A gentle and caring touch continues to be a positive stroke for us throughout our lifespan. As we emerge from infancy, however, we begin to experience strokes often on a more subtle and symbolic level (Gilliland, James and Bowman, 1989). Whenever we enter the awareness of another person and express the message verbally or nonverbally that "I know you're there and I recognize you," we provide a life-sustaining stoke (Gilliland, James and Bowman, 1989). While this stroke could be a nonverbal touch, it could also be a wish or letter. It could come in the form of a thank-you, an effort to remember a name, or it might be delivered as a specific verbal reinforcer (Harris and Harris, 1985). Listening in an attentive fashion is perhaps one of the finest strokes you can give to another person (James and Jongeward, 1971). We all like to be listened to and taken seriously. It's annoying to speak with people who aren't paying attention, who are preoccupied or who look right through us. Such things **discount** the importance of what we're saying. They can also discount us personally.

Strokes come in different forms and are delivered under varying sets of circumstances. Some strokes come as freebies, some are earned and still others are requested (Freed and Freed, 1973). The freebies are the best.

***

In contrast to warm fuzzies, which are pleasant, some strokes can be unpleasant. These are referred to as **cold pricklies** (Steiner, 1977). Such strokes, though negative, at least make us feel alive. If we can't get the warm fuzzies we need, we'll do what it takes to get cold pricklies. As Freed and Freed said, "Any stroke is better than no stroke" (1973: 12). This point can be illustrated by the individual who'd rather be hated than not be noticed at all. The overlooked child may act up to get parental attention, even if punishment follows.

***

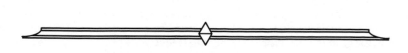

122

INTERACTIONAL RITUALS

Excerpts from Chapter 6, of Knapp, M. L. & Vangelisti, A. L. (1996). *Interpersonal Communication and Human Relationships,* Third Edition. Needham Heights, MA: Allyn & Bacon.

***

Dear Dr. Vangelisti,

I have a question. I'd like to ask about "breaking the ice" when meeting a woman for the first time. I don't want her to think I'm too straightforward but on the other hand shyness is just as bad if not worse. What I usually do is talk openly and tell her a lot about myself. I also try to get her to tell me about herself. My problem is that although at first, my relationships tend to drop off after only about a week. This drives me crazy and I spend most of my time wondering what I do to offend these women. Can you give me any ideas about what I might be doing wrong?
Eager to Please

The first few seconds of talk with another person can be extremely important in setting the tone for further conversation and contact. This chapter discusses some of the factors that may facilitate or inhibit communication during this time. The extent to which we violate or adhere to certain interaction rules and how we choose to formulate our greetings, address terms, relational openings, and small talk should provide a basis for explaining why some contacts appear to be "'Winners" and some seem to be "losers."

Relational life wavers between order and disorder, certainty and uncertainty, permanence and change. Rituals help to balance these competing forces by providing order and formality in regions of relational life that may be easily threatened by disorder and informality. -ARTHUR P. BOCHNER

Sometimes we simply don't know what to say, when to say it, or how to say it. At other times the social situation seems almost to demand a certain kind of communication. It's as if both communicators are following a script written by someone else - a script each of them has performed before. And, although it often seems that we could make better use of our time than perform these rituals, we continue to "'go through the motions." Interaction rituals may be short or long, performed by many or few, elaborate or plain, but they are an important part of the process of establishing, sustaining, and terminating relationships.

Communication Rules

Interaction rituals are created and sustained by the existence of communication rules. A *communication rule* is a followable prescription that indicates what communication behavior (or range of communication behavior) is obligatory, preferred, or prohibited in certain social situations. It is a probability statement about the expectations for the situation - what is the likelihood that X must be said or that Y must not be said? Some of these rules are limited to a single person -"When Harry starts to yell at me, I will stop talking to him." Other rules apply to the behavior of both partners in a relationship - "If we have a fight, we won't go to bed while we're still angry at each other." There are also rules that pertain to specific groups of people - When fathers want to show affection for their sons, they shouldn't kiss them on the lips. Then there are those rules that apply to most people in the society - when someone greets you, you should return the greeting. From these examples, we can see that the influence of communication rules is not limited to initial interactions. On the contrary, as we will see in Chapter 8, people involved in long-term relationships develop and negotiate rules that are unique to those relationships. Argyle and Henderson have also found that there are some rules that cut across most relationship types. For instance, in Britain, Italy, Hong Kong, and Japan, people said that the following applied to most relationships: (1) partners should respect each other's privacy; (2) partners should look one another in the eye during conversation; (3) partners should not discuss with others what is said in confidence; (4) partners should not criticize one another in public; (5) partners should seek to repay debts, favors, and, compliments - no matter how small; and (6) partners should (or should not) engage in sexual activity with their partner.

Regardless of how specific or general a rule is, when an individual, couple, group, or society follows a rule most of the time, it is considered a *communicative* norm - the most typical behavior relative to the rule. People may acknowledge the existence of a rule but fail to follow it, so it doesn't become a norm. And sometimes people seem to be engaging in similar or normative behavior, but it is not rule-governed behavior - i.e., they may depart from the norm without any positive or negative sanctions. Rules may also develop about who can make the rules. A husband may agree that he spends too much money but disagree that his wife should tell him to stop spending so much.

We begin learning about communication rules as children. Some of these rules give direction concerning what we say - for example, we learn "Mama" is not a form of address appropriate for all human beings, or we learn what is acceptable to say and what is not ("Don't say that ... its not nice.") Other rules pertain to the structuring of conversations - we're taught not to talk when another person is talking or not to start a conversation cold without some rapport building. We learn the implicit and explicit rules for getting the floor so we can talk, giving up the floor so the other will know it is his or her turn, maintaining our turn so another can't get in, and helping someone else to maintain his or her turn as we inject occasional comments without interrupting the conversational flow. We also learn rules that help us to manage certain conversational episodes. We know to be discrete when someone tells us a secret, to act concerned when someone is hurting, and to try to stay relatively calm and rational when having an argument in public. Researchers remind us that the application of any rule to a situation or a relationship varies - most of us know romantic partners who have no qualms about fighting in public - and that these variations serve to define the nature of our relationships.

Rules develop in a variety of ways. Sometimes we talk openly about the rule-related issue and negotiate a rule acceptable to both parties. More often, though, rules are established in much more subtle ways. Metacommunication may be the process that tells others how to behave relative to particular communicative responses. As a result of these "unspoken," processes used to establish agreed-upon rules of interaction, it is not uncommon for two people not to be able to state the specific rules that guide their behavior.

Common sense tells us that learning and obeying these rules is crucially linked to the way others evaluate us. Allgeier, for instance, found that an individual's ratings of interpersonal attraction and adjustment increased as that person more closely approached an equal share of the talk time in a conversation. Berger and his colleagues documented the fact that when people violate the norms of small talk (not reciprocating appropriate information, not giving the right number of compliments, or not following an impersonal-to-personal sequence of information giving), communicators were judged to be less attractive and too unpredictable.

***

Violating Communicative Rules

Norms are brought vividly to our attention when they are violated. Davis provides some excellent examples:

> In our society, a person can achieve the status of mental patient either by casually telling a mere acquaintance what would generally be considered his most intimate aspects or by arduously telling his friend what would generally be considered his least intimate aspects. Thus, he could get himself committed to a mental hospital either by matter-of-factly describing to an acquaintance his disgusting anatomical details ("I have a terrible case of hemorrhoids. Let me show them to you") or by agonizingly confessing to his friend, after months of hinting that he would like to reveal to him his essential secret, something he has never told anyone before, that, more than anything else in the world, he hates the color blue ("it's everywhere! I cant stand it! I see it wherever I go!").

A further illustration of what happens when conversational rules are violated is found in an assignment ethnomethodologist Harold Garfinkel gave his undergraduate students. Students were instructed to engage an acquaintance or a friend in ordinary conversation and without indicating that anything was out of the ordinary, insist that the other person clarify the sense of his or her commonplace remarks. The following dialogues represent typical student experiences.

Case One

"Hi, Ray. How is your girlfriend feeling?"
"What do you mean, how is she feeling? Do you mean physical or mental?"
"I mean how is she feeling? What's the matter with you?" (He looked peeved.)
"Nothing. Just explain a little clearer what do you mean?"
"Skip it. How are your Med School applications coming?"
"What do you mean, how are they?"
"You know what I mean."
"I really don't."
"What's the matter with you? Are you sick?"

Case Two

On Friday night my husband and I were watching television. My husband remarked that he was tired. I asked, "How are you tired? Physically, mentally, or just bored?"
"I don't know, I guess physically, mainly."
"You mean that your muscles ache, or your bones?"
"I guess so. Don't be too technical."
(After more watching)
"All these old movies have the same kind of old iron bedstead in them."
"What do you mean? Do you mean all old movies, or some of them, or just the ones you have seen?"
"What's the matter with you? You know what I mean."
"I wish you would be more specific."
"You know what I mean! Drop Dead!"

The foregoing conversations highlight how much we take for granted as we converse with others - how much we "let pass." We assume that any important ambiguities in a person's discourse will be cleared up later. If we violate that rule too often (as illustrated in the cases presented), the other communicator will no doubt observe our violation and sanction us accordingly.

Like any rules, communicative rules require adherence. When the rule is broken, some type of sanctioning usually takes place - rejection, frustration, puzzled or disapproving looks, avoidance, reprimands, or simply a facial expression which visually says "You're weird!" While this is usual, it is not always the case. In many of our interactions, there is a norm for politeness that discourages us from letting others know that their behavior is strange or inappropriate. Even if someone is talking too much or disclosing information that is too personal, we will sometimes listen attentively to avoid being rude. There are also times, however, when we choose not to sanction rule violations because of a characteristic or behavior demonstrated by the rule violator.

One way to break communicative rules successfully, incurring little punishment, is to be perceived as a person who was not aware of the expectations for the situation, or one who was aware but was incapable of doing anything about them. A person may be seen as irresponsible or naive ("He didn't know an better"). For example:

Grandma: How does my favorite boy like the nice warm sweater Grandma knitted for him?
Child. It's yucky.

Or he or she may be perceived as handicapped ("She couldn't help it") or as boxed in ("He had no alternative"). A person may also get away with rule violations if seen as "just having fun" ("She didn't mean it").

Sometimes one rule can be violated, but other contiguous rules are not violated, so that one's total behavior is considered balanced. A high school teacher may talk about sex in the classroom, but do so in an educational manner. As long as the violation does not violate the relationship, there should be less concern on the part of the message receiver(s).

Rule violations can also be offset by apologies, but a more strategic method of defusing negative reactions is to acknowledge that the rule is about to be broken—a 25-year-old male says to a 45-year-old female stranger: "I know I probably shouldn't ask—and you don't have to answer if you don't want to—but how old are you?" Disclaimers of this type were the subject of study by Hewitt and Stokes. They categorized the following types of disclaimers:

1. **Hedging.** This disclaimer conveys: what follows is tentative and I'm willing to accept other views. "I'm no expert, of course, but..."; "I haven't thought this through very well but..." or "Let me play the devil's advocate here."

2. **Credentialing.** This conveys: I know you'll react unfavorably to what I'm about to say, but I'll try to establish special credentials that will soften that reaction. "Don't get me wrong, I like your work, but..." or, "I'm not prejudiced; some of my best friends are..."

3. **Sin Licenses.** This conveys: I know you'll react negatively, but that's the way it has to be. "What I'm going to do is contrary to the letter of the law but not its spirit..."

4. **Cognitive.** This conveys: I realize you may think I'm losing touch with facts or reality, so I'll acknowledge the fact, thereby showing I am in control. "I know this sounds crazy, but...."

5. **Appeal for Suspended Judgment.** This conveys: I know you're going to be tempted to react unfavorably, but wait until you hear the whole story. "I don't want to make you angry by saying this, but..." or "Hear me out before you explode..."

If the rule violation is perceived as an isolated instance, it has a greater chance of being accepted, particularly if the significant others (interaction partners and others involved in the situation) can find some unusual, but plausible explanation for the actions. For example, a person may break down and cry in front of a casual acquaintance who knows that that individual's brother just died of cancer.

A rule can be violated and unpleasant reactions circumvented by choosing the rule very carefully. If the violated rule is not deeply internalized or ego-related to the relevant, or significant, other(s) or it is not bound by severe sanctions (violations are expected), punishment will be minimal. Asking a total stranger on the street for a cigarette or forgetting the name of someone you were just introduced to would probably fall into this category. Notice how many times the slightest pause in re-greeting a person you've been introduced to will cause them to help you by quickly restating their name. In some situations, people realize the rules are not widely known so that violators are given a greater range of behavior before the rule is considered violated. For example, there seem to be few widely accepted rules for interactions involving one's former spouse. And people who are overtly solicitous with a handicapped person may, at first, be gently encouraged to interact in more conventional ways rather than reprimanded. Argyle found people reacting very negatively to violations that prohibited conversation from even taking place. These people considered the following to be totally disruptive: speaking an unknown language; being overly aggressive or disinterested; responding to an idea by changing the topic. The same people reacted less negatively to violations of rules that would be considered non-essential for conversation to take place. The following were considered only mildly disruptive to conversations: lying on the floor; sitting too close; sitting too far away.

We also know that some people get away with rule violations because it is done with class or style - the violations are not perceived as too gross or too crude. Those who proffer sexual invitations in the initiating or early experimenting stages of a relationship are no doubt acutely aware of this need for sophistication. We would suspect that as the intensity of the conversation and the use of loaded language increases, there is a corresponding increase in the possibility that one or both participants will feel that a rule has been violated.

126

Shimanoff notes three other reasons why rule violations may not be negatively sanctioned: (1) the violator may be of a higher status and it may therefore be in the best interests of the other person to overlook the violation; (2) the violation may be viewed as a violation for the purpose of emphasis of humor; and (3) the act of giving a negative evaluation to someone may, itself, violate a rule of politeness so it is not proffered.

In some situations, people do not care about negative reactions to rule violations. The violation may be used to disorient, frustrate, or elicit defensiveness in the other as a means to gain power over them. On other occasions, rule violations are used to get an early reading of the other person. At such times the person may feel he or she has an adequate number of friends and thus choose to channel the energy into developing relationships with only those who react well in a difficult situation - for example, a rule violation. Also, the person may be extremely fearful of investing time and energy in a close relationship that may end up being hurtful. At such times, rigidity, rejection, and/or responses in line with the norm for the given situation by the recipient may not provide the necessary motivation to develop a closer relationship. Attempts by the recipient to counter the original rule violation with an even stronger violation may also work against attraction in situations of this type. These outcomes pertain to rules or conventions developed by a pair to fulfill their specific needs and desires. These rules can be easily changed (if both participants so desire) and sanctions are normally applied only by the other party, although in some cases "'outside executioners" are shipped in.

Most communicative rules are considered informal, nothing like Robert's Rules of Order. This informal nature may cause wide variations in adherence. Some people feel almost an obligation to break a rule once it is brought to their attention; others will adhere tenaciously for fear of not being correct. Most of us lie between such extremes. We recognize and can appreciate the fact that communicative rules add predictability, order, and structure to our world. We also recognize that they can be changed - that violations are not necessarily tantamount to social incompetency; we recognize that rules often make life easier - keeping us from having to make an interminable number of interpersonal decisions during each encounter; we understand how helpful a knowledge of communicative rules can be when facing new social situations - giving us guidelines for achieving certain communicative goals like acceptance, influence, understanding, and acknowledgment; and we realize the role communicative rules play in the satisfaction of interpersonal needs-affection, ego support (or the lack of damage to it), inclusion, control., avoiding conflict, maintaining order, insuring interaction (or the absence of it), and so on.

With this understanding of the backbone of interaction rituals, communicative rules, the rest of the chapter will explore four common, but important rituals - greetings, forms of address, relationship openings, and small talk.

The Rhetoric of Hello

On the surface, interpersonal greetings seem to be a rather quick, simple, and routinized way of initiating communication. Generally we don't give much thought to what happens during those first few seconds of interaction unless something unusual happens - receiving a warm smile and a "hi" from an unknown passerby or receiving a fully documented medical report when we query, "How are you?" For some time, scholars have regarded greetings and other similarly routinized social sequences (e.g., ordering food at a restaurant) as conversational scripts or sequences of actions that we carry out automatically, with very little thought. More recently, however, an important qualification has been added to this description of scripts. Although they are routine and regular, conversational scripts are not static (unchanging). Instead they are flexible and adaptive. In the case of greetings, this means that we adjust what we say to the person we are greeting - depending on our relationship with the person, the mood he or she is in, and how the person responds to us.

It is also important to remember that just because we normally don't pay much attention to greetings doesn't mean that they are simple or unimportant. In a very real sense when we say hello (verbally and/or nonverbally), we have implicitly agreed to interfere with another's life. It could be argued, then, that this seemingly insignificant intrusion into another's life brings with it an added responsibility for the other's welfare. Perhaps this is one reason why city dwellers are sometimes described as cold when they do not respond to the well-meaning salutations of strangers; the city dwellers are expressing a need not to get involved. Consider how you feel when a person you know passes you and fails to acknowledge your existence. Conversely, consider how difficult it is for you to intentionally ignore a greeting from an acquaintance. The act of initiating communication is the first step in becoming a part of another person's life. Even passing greetings between strangers provide a form of social recognition, affirmation of a fellow human being's existence, and mutual access to one another.

For our purposes, the most important feature of the greeting ritual is what it tells us about the relationship between the interacting parties.

Greetings and Relationships

Since the manner in which a greeting is performed will help structure the dialogue to follow, it is not surprising that greetings convey information about the relationship. This information may appear in a variety of verbal and nonverbal behaviors. Strangers, for instance, might be more apt to engage in handshaking, formal forms of address (Mr.), and formal expressions like "Good morning"; "Nice to meet you"; or "Pardon me, but…" Intimates may greet each other with an embrace or a kiss, avoid handshaking, use shortened verbalizations like "Hey!" or some specialized nonverbal gesture unique to themselves. One form of these specialized greetings has been labeled the "friendly insult greeting" - e.g., "Hi, dummy!" or "You rotten son-of-a-bitch, how ya doin?" The "insult" is not intended to be taken literally at all, but the metamessage is that "we have such a close relationship, I am confident that you will understand that I mean the opposite of what I'm saying." Of course, there are times when it is not clear to the person being greeted that this is the case, so such greetings may be risky with all but the best of friends.

Status relationships may be noted in the ritual that requires a subordinate in the army to maintain a salute until it is returned by the greeted officer. Greetings by subordinates in executive suites may be proffered from a greater distance. Without belaboring the point, it should be clear that one of the things we say, when we say hello, is what the nature of our relationship is, so the forthcoming dialogue can follow suit. While our choice of words and behaviors in these situations depends, in part, on our efforts to be socially appropriate (polite) and conversationally efficient, the nature of our relationship with the person we are greeting can override the usual norms for both politeness and efficiency. For instance, researchers have noted that intimates disregard some of the steps that people usually go through when they greet each other on the telephone. While politeness norms suggest that people should identify themselves at the beginning of a phone conversation, frequently friends, family members, and lovers skip over this step. Because they tend to recognize each other's voices and speak to each other frequently, intimates don't always need to identify themselves or the purpose of their call.

When people have been parted for a period of time, it is often necessary to dramatize relationship features. An overly enthusiastic greeting may communicate that the absence has not changed what was previously a good relationship. Hence, the amount of time separating our greetings with a particular person may affect the expansiveness of the greeting. Goffman has proposed an *attenuation rule* which argues that the expansiveness of the greeting will gradually subside with each subsequent greeting, especially when an individual is forced to greet a person numerous times during the day - which is the case in many offices. One of our colleagues, Robert E. Smith, felt it was also the case at the professional conventions of communication scholars which he attends - as his composition testifies:

Convention Book of Days

I
Heeeeyyyy! Jim!
Good to see you!
Looking fantastic
When did you get in?
Flight down went OK
How are things at the university?
Congratulations
That's great about Susan
Jimmy, first string, Wow
Barby, first clarinet, Great
Research going well?
Maybe dinner tomorrow
Heeeeyyyy! Bill ...

II
Hi, Jim
Enjoying the convention?
Good paper last meeting
Cup of coffee, all right?

III
Hi, Jim

IV
(Buzz off, Jim)

This attenuation rule may also be applicable to the various stages of a relationship. For example, we would expect greetings in the early stages of a relationship to be more inflated or exaggerated than greetings between intimates. Relationships that are coming apart may also reflect a return to the more visibly formalized and stereotyped greetings. The very nature of the relationship between close friends, relatives, or married couples speaks so powerfully that the expansiveness of greeting behavior is allowed to subside and is instead expressed in many subtle and spontaneous ways. Kendon and Ferber have observed the following greeting sequence:

1. Sighting, Orientation, and Initiation of the Approach.

2. Distant Salutation. This is the "official ratification" that a greeting sequence has been initiated and who the participants are. A wave, smile, or call may be used for recognition. Several types of head movements were noted. One, the "head dip," has also been observed in other situations as a marker to transitions between activities or shifts in psychological orientation. This movement was not observed if the greeter did not continue the approach.

3. Approach. As the greeters continued to move toward each other, gazing probably helped signal that channels were cleared for talking. An aversion of this gaze, however, was seen just prior to the close salutation stage. Grooming behavior and one or both arms positioned in front of the body were also observed at this point. When the participants were within ten feet of each other, mutual gazing, smiling, and a positioning of the head not seen in the sequence thus far were seen. The palms of the hands were sometimes turned toward the other person.

4. Close Salutation. As the participants negotiated a standing position ritualistic comments like Hi, Bob! How ya doin ? were heard. And, if the situation called for body contact (handshakes, embraces), it would occur at this time.

While it would be literally impossible to catalogue each specific verbal and nonverbal greeting behavior for each type of person in every situation and every kind of relationship, a general taxonomy has been developed.

Nonverbally, greetings are frequently initiated by a vertical or sideways motion of the head accompanied by eye contact. Kendon notes that a head toss probably invites further interaction - as does a tilting of the head back and/or raising of the eyebrows. But nods or a lowering of the head while making some other greeting gesture (e.g., wave) is likely to be just a greeting-in-passing. One of the functions of eye contact is signaling that the channels of communication are open. Should you not wish to pursue a conversation with a person, the avoidance of eye contact is imperative since a prolonged mutual glance almost obligates you to extend the encounter. Other eye-related greeting behaviors include winks or what is known as an *eyebrow flash,* a distinct up-and-down movement of the eyebrows which is barely detectable. Some observations from other cultures suggest that the eyebrow flash may be a universal behavior attendant to greetings. The hands may also be very active in the greeting process. Salutes, waves, handshakes, handslaps, and various emblematic gestures such as the peace sign, raised fist, or thumbs up may be seen. The hands may also be engaged in grooming attendant to the greeting-running fingers through one's hair. Touching, in the form of embraces, kisses, or hitting on the arm is also common. The mouth may take the form of a smile or an oval shape which suggests a possible readiness for subsequent talk.

Sometimes we find ourselves in close contact with strangers and wish to signal that we do not want to greet them. Observations of people in such circumstances in a bar, shopping center, and on a college campus found the following nonverbal behaviors occurring in most of the situations: lip compression; lip bite; tongue-show;

tongue-in-cheek; downward, lateral, and maximal lateral gaze avoidance; hand-to-face, hand-to-hand, hand-to-body, and hand-behind-head automanipulations; and postures involving flexion and adduction of upper limbs. These behaviors which signaled "stay away" or "greeting will not be well received" abruptly ceased after the strangers left the scene. Verbally, greetings may be classified along the following lines:

1. Verbal salutes - "Good morning."
2. Direct references to the other person by name, nickname, or personal pronoun "Hi, babe!" or "Jeremiah!"
3. Questions of personal inquiry - "What's new with you?" or "How ya doin?"
4. Verbalizations expressing a desire to continue a past relationship - "Long time no see" or "Nice seeing you again."
5. Compliments - "You're sure looking good."
6. References to here-and-now surroundings - "May I get you another drink?" or "Can you tell me who did that painting?"
7. References to people or things, outside the immediate interaction setting "How do you like this weather we're having?"
8. References to the other's behavior - "I noticed you were sitting all alone over here."
9. References to oneself - "Boy, have I had a rough day!" or "Hi, I'm Mark Knapp."
10. Apologies - "Excuse me, but…"
11. Unexpected, humorous, or whimsical phrases designed to break the ice - "How's your sex life?" or "This is the best drink I've had since breakfast."
12. Immediate topic initiation which usually excludes any preliminary comments - "The reason I wanted to talk to you..."
13. Single words or vocalizations that are essentially content-free - "Well!" or muted grunting sound.

The preceding list of behaviors is representative, but not necessarily exhaustive. Any given greeting may fall into several of the categories discussed. A legitimate question at this point might be: So what? So what if we go to all the trouble to dissect greeting behavior? In answer, the major advantage of this classification system is that it may eventually help us to understand more precisely what particular form greetings take at various stages of development and deterioration in human relationships. Once we are able to identify typical and regular patterns associated with specific stages and in specific situations, we have taken a giant step toward explaining the success or failure experienced later in the encounter. For instance, if you greet a close friend with behaviors typically found in interactions with strangers, a greater quantity of subsequent messages about the relationship itself may be required to make up for this unexpected behavior.

Forms of Address

Like greetings, the way we address another person may be brief, but it can say volumes about the relationship we have with that person. We are able to communicate our relative status to the other person, how well we are acquainted with him or her, whether we are angry or affectionate toward him or her, and whether the situation is a formal or informal one - all by the way we choose to address that person. Fortunately, most of us have a variety of names and titles that provide several options as forms of address - Colonel Maxwell Q. Black, Colonel Black, Sir, Max, Maxie, "Ol' Stonedface." If a person offers a limited number of mutations of his or her name, others will often invent their own variations. This does not mean, of course, that we don't have trouble deciding how to address people. When we have difficulty determining our relative status or degree of intimacy to another, choices are frustrating - the familiar student dilemma: Dr., Professor, Mr., Mrs., Ms., Miss, Herbert or Mary Ellen? And what are the in-laws to be known as: Mr. and Mrs., Mom and Dad, Jim and Mavis, or should it wait until they can be Grandma and Grandpa? As a rule, the more intimate we feel toward someone, the more we will be inclined to use less formal forms of address. The manifestations of this rule, and the exceptions to it, will be discussed in conjunction with the following continuum of formality for forms of address: (1) formal-impersonal; (2) ambiguous formality; (3) informal; and (4) intimate-affectionate.

Formal-Impersonal

The formal forms of address are generally used with strangers, new acquaintances, and those we perceive to have greater status than we do. In each case, the social distance between the communicators is high. Brown has identified what he feels is a universal norm underlying forms of address: Higher-status persons address subordinates with a form that people of equal status use when they are well acquainted or intimate (Bill or Willie); subordinates, on the other hand, must address the higher- status person with a form that people of equal status use when they are strangers or new acquaintances (Mr. Jennings). This norm which incorporates indices of status and affection seems to have parallels in other behavior as well. For instance, Henley argues that people are most likely to initiate touching behavior with those of a status lower than their own - just as they do with people toward whom they feel affectionate. Similarly, we've observed Ph.D.'s calling the janitor they may see once or twice a week for thirty seconds by his nickname - "Hi, Mac." Researchers have argued that shorter names (like Mac) tend to be associated with approachability, whereas longer names (like Katherine or Alexander) tend to be linked to success and/ or morality. Although this is clearly not always the case, it may be part of the reason why people of a lower status are often addressed by their nicknames. Also, as we will note later, the use of nicknames is generally associated with people who feel more intimate with each other. Some observers of the current social scene have noted that women are more often called by their affectionate nickname (Billie, Georgie, Lilly) than men, who are more often known by an informal nickname (Bill or Bob, but not Billy or Bobby). In view of the parallels between affection and superiority presented thus far, such a finding (if it were true) would certainly have value for analyzing traditional perceptions of women in contemporary U.S. society.

The formal forms of address are most often used when we perceive the other person's age, title, authority, eminence, or seniority as greatly above our own and when we feel this discrepancy needs to be manifested in the way we address the person. Formal forms of address will also manifest themselves when we fear the other person or when we want to build the addressee's ego through ingratiation strategies.

Ambiguous Formality

In the process of our life growth, our growth in school, or in our careers, we will periodically reach points where the perception of ourselves, relative to another in a particular situation, is vague. In short, we just don't know how to address someone. It might be a situation in which we feel a particular person doesn't warrant deference any longer because status differences have grown fuzzy - calling parents by their first names rather than "Mom" or "Dad," or calling a dissertation advisor by his or her first name. Imagine the dilemma for the Nixon cadre during and after the Watergate coverup - Mr. President? Mr. Nixon? Dick? Sir? Ahhh ... ? It might also be a situation in which a person asks us to call him or her by his or her first name and we are reluctant to do so. There are any number of reasons why we will feel uncertainty or ambiguity about what to call someone. As a result, we may end up using any of the following strategies: (1) The most formal of the ambiguous forms of address includes Sir, Miss, Ma`am, Ms., etc. (2) The playful in-between is exemplified by "Doc" for a Ph.D. (3) The least formal response to the ambiguous situation is what Little and Gelles call the *Hey you form of address.* A good example is the extended and amplified "Ahhhhh…" (with upraised finger) in place of a name or title.

Informal

The informal forms of address are usually derived from a person's first name - Jim is an informal form of James. In status-differentiated encounters the higher status individual will usually ask the subordinate to call him or her by a less formal name. Many times, people try to speed up a relationship by deliberately using another person's first name when the situation calls for a more formal appellation. When you encounter a car salesperson and become offended by the salesperson's casual and frequent use of your first name, it may be because you perceive a needed formality for your relationship (strangers) and for the situation (business deals), not to mention the feeling that his or her usage immediately limits you to either subordinate or peer status at best.

Intimate-Affectionate

This represents the least formal of the forms used to address others. Ordinarily, this form is reserved for close friends or intimates. Even within this category, however, there seem to be subcategories of formality: (1) A further alteration of one's given name seems to be the most formal - Jimmy or Trish. Sometimes names do not have natural intimate forms so others will invent them - Marko for Mark. The usual manner of inventing these alterations is to add an ie or y to make an "ee" sound. However, most adult males regard this as too symbolic of childhood names; many exceptions do exist, however - Bobby Kennedy, Teddy Roosevelt, Jimmy Carter. A variation on given-name alteration is to use a person's middle name when it is not known to others and knowledge of it is symbolic of interpersonal closeness. (2) Nicknames that have been given because they are somehow associated with one's appearance, role, or activities represent the next lower level of formality - "Stretch," "Fireplug," "Chief," "Goose," or "Hands." Sometimes a name that starts out as a nickname becomes so commonly used in so many different relationships that it no longer has the uniqueness necessary to qualify as an intimate form of address - "Dr. J" for basketball player Julius Erving. (3) Even more personal are those names that are considered traditional terms of endearment. These generally encompass terms designating the person as either sacred ("Angel"), an innocent small animal ("Chickadee") or child ("Babe," "Honey Child"), or a pleasant taste experience ("Sugar," "Honey"). (4) The most intimate forms of address seem to be those that have no apparent explanation, are often nonsensical, and are likely to be embarrassing if used in the presence of others - "Poopsie," "Booper," or "Snookums."

Although we would predict more personal forms of address between intimates, variations will appear, depending on how long intimacy has been established and what conditions exist in the environment for communicating. For instance, we are likely to find that longtime intimates may cease to use any mode of address. In addition, they may occasionally use the more formal forms, perhaps to emphasize closeness or just to be playful - "Thelma Z. Peters, I love you very much." Furthermore, the presence of others may cause an individual to address a close friend in a very formal manner - in a graduate student's oral examination, you might hear close friends addressing each other as Dr. and Professor. Obviously, the audience is not the friend and the friend understands. Formality may also change as the situation and roles change - Professor Ruggirello in the classroom becomes "Frank" in the touch football game.

As we mentioned earlier, the same form of address can be used to express anger or affection. Depending on the vocal inflection, the phrase "Look here, Baby Doll" could be demeaning and hateful or tender and loving. Naturally, the use of the intimate form greatly assists a demeaning vocal inflection in eliciting a defensive response. At other times anger or serious intent can be shown by simply increasing the degree of formality (and vocal volume). The following, familiar message construction seen in parent-child episodes illustrates this:

Most Intimate   Herbie, no.

                      Herb, don't.

                      Herbert, don't do that…please.

                      Herbert Wilson - I've told you a hundred times not to do that!

Most Formal   Herbert Wilson Knapp - I want you to stop that this instant!

Relationship "Openers"

How do you begin a relationship? Earlier in this chapter we noted that there are rules that help guide our communication choices. In most communication situations, we can recognize behaviors that are socially appropriate and others that are socially inappropriate. For instance, when greeting a superior, we tend to use more formal address terms than we would when greeting a peer. While rules such as these seem as if they should provide us with a prescription for how to begin relationships, they rarely do. In fact, often when we would like to initiate a relationship with someone, it is much easier for us to think of inappropriate behaviors than it is to think of appropriate ones. As a result, some people spend a great deal of time planning and rehearsing how to begin their first conversation with a man (woman). The classic example of this involves what many refer to as the "'opening line."

Many prescriptions for good and bad opening lines are offered by the media and friends and acquaintances. However, many do not identify important contingencies such as the relationship between the communicators and the setting, the nonverbal cues used by communicators, and the ability of each communicator to elicit disclosure from the other. Those prescriptions that fail to recognize the importance of such factors tend to take on the characteristics of interpersonal burlesque. One book which says it will "lead you out of the singles jungle and into a happy marriage", is advertised by the following paragraph:

From its initial, exclusive publication - at $95 a copy - to its rise to the top of the bestseller lists, this is the book that has helped women across the country escape the rut of a going-nowhere relationship - and start marrying the men of their choice. From the first date to getting to know a man, from dealing with your competition to steering romance into marriage, HOW TO MARRY THE MAN OF YOUR CHOICE will guide you directly to the altar - regardless of your looks, your past, your age!

Another book, which sports "50 Great Opening Lines," is advertised this way:

The techniques in THE PICKING UP GIRLS KIT work for all men. You don't have to be brave, rich or good looking. Just walk up to the woman you have your eye on, use one of the simple techniques described in your kit, and you will pick her up. There is simply no way she can refuse you. WE GUARANTEE IT.

From the never-fail fifty, we selected our favorite ten. You be the judge.

1. Do you have an aspirin?
2. Hi.
3. How long do you cook a leg of lamb?
4. Excuse me, I'm from out of town and I was wondering what people do around here at night.
5. What kind of dog is that? He's great-looking.
6. Wow! What a beautiful day.
7. Please pass the ketchup.
8. Didn't I meet you in Istanbul?
9. Who's your dentist?
10. Don't tell me a beautiful girl like you doesn't have a date tonight.

Another author who felt it necessary to justify his classification of "Hello" as a good opening line comments: "This is a fantastic opening line. I wish I could take credit for it. Probably millions of relationships between men and women have begun on this basis. If you feel more comfortable with "Hi" the results will be equally good. This same author identifies the following as bad opening gambits between men and women:

1. Haven't I met you someplace before?
2. You are a beautiful person.
3. Let's go to bed.
4. I love you. Do you believe in love at first sight?
5. Do you think it will rain?
6. You look like a movie star.
7. Are you alone?
8. You look lonely.
9. Why are you here?
10. Where have I seen you before?

None but the most foolhardy would "guarantee success" with any message without some knowledge of who said it, to whom it was said, how it was said (vocal tone), whether, or how often, it had been said before, where it was said, what messages preceded it or would follow it. The assumptions underlying these prescriptions from the popular press are, however, important. Recipes for cookbook communication designed to initiate encounters are based on the belief that: (1) enough people have experienced difficulty in initiating communication to seek simple, guaranteed prescriptions, and (2) a number of people in this culture attach a great deal of importance to these initial behaviors, recognizing their role in facilitating or inhibiting the communication that follows.

In an attempt to survey people who might actually use these opening lines and to categorize them according to different locations, psychologist Chris Kleinke asked several hundred college students in California and Massachusetts to write down all the opening lines they could think of that men might use with women at beaches, supermarkets, and bars. After selecting the 100 most frequently cited openers, Kleinke asked 600 more students from the same two states to rate each line from "terrible" to "excellent." Both men and women respondents seemed to prefer the "direct" and "innocuous," lines over the "cute/ flip." ones. But most men underestimated how much women were put off by the cute/ flip approach. Some of the top-rated lines included:

In General Situations:
"I feel a little embarrassed, but I'd like to meet you." (direct)
At the Beach:
"The water is beautiful today, isn't it?" (innocuous)
At the Supermarket:
"Can you help me decide here? I'm a terrible shopper." (direct)
At the Bar:
"What do you think of the band?"' (innocuous)
The bottom-rated lines included:
In General Situations:
"Is that really your hair?"
"Your place or mine?"
"You remind me of a woman I used to date."
At the Beach:
 "Let me see your strap rnarks."
At the Supermarket:
"Do you really eat that junk?"
At the Bar:
"Bet I can outdrink you."

In another study, Murray found that the almost 3,000 opening lines he observed fell into three categories: questions (e.g., How're you?), advertisements/ declarations (e.g., "My name is Heather,") and compliments (e.g., "I like your suit").

He also found that the use of sexual propositions and all three types of opening lines increased drastically from 10:00 p.m. to 11:00 p.m. and continued to increase at a slower rate until 1:00 am. Since his study was conducted in singles bars, this pattern is not surprising. As Murray himself notes, patterns of alcohol consumption, increased desperation (as closing time neared), and increases in perceived attraction (as desperation increased) probably account for this phenomenon.

One final study of note asked adults as well as elementary, high school, and college students how they would initiate a friendly contact with a stranger of the same sex. The two most popular approaches reported were: (1) to ask the stranger to participate in an activity with you - e.g., children might ask the person to play with them during recess; and (2) to ask the person questions in order to find out more about him or her.

One consistency that runs throughout all of these studies is that "good" opening lines rarely reveal the candid thoughts of the speaker. Even the most direct lines (e.g., "I'd sure like to meet you") typically don't focus on relational or sexual issues. Douglas explains this by noting that although we might like to be more direct and efficient (e.g., "Do you find me physically attractive?"), we must balance our conversational efficiency with social appropriateness. Certainly, it would be easier to reduce our uncertainty about potential relational partners by being more direct. However, since relational development is based on the wants and needs of *both* people, we must consider how the other person is going to respond to our direct inquiries.

In many cases, the response to an opening line is observable because the line is delivered and received in a face-to-face context. However, there are a number of different channels available to those seeking a romantic relationship, including personal ads, video dating services, match makers, and computer networks. These alternative channels probably restrict some forms of communication (e.g., the ability to observe potential partners' nonverbal behavior) and allow for more freedom with regard to others (e.g., direct questions and impression management). Although the communication that occurs between people who use these channels may differ from face-to-face interaction, it provides an idea of what some people think they want in a relational partner as well as what they believe others want. For instance, in studies of personal ads placed by heterosexual and homosexual men and women, several trends emerged: (1) heterosexual men wanted what heterosexual women offered - physical attractiveness; (2) heterosexual women sought what heterosexual men offered - financial security; (3) homosexual men emphasized physical attractiveness in their ads even more than did heterosexual men; and (4) homosexual women tended to de-emphasize physical attractiveness as something to be sought or offered.

134

While using a "bad" opening line may be a sure-fire way to discourage a relationship, using a "good" opening line doesn't ensure relationship development. Bell and Daly have found that people believe they use a number of other communication strategies to get people to like and appreciate them. These *affinity-seeking* strategies include behaviors that: (1) demonstrate one's *control and visibility* (e.g., being dynamic and interesting), (2) encourage *mutual trust* (e.g., consistently fulfilling commitments), (3) display politeness (e.g., adhering to conversational rules), (4) demonstrate concern and caring (e.g., listening to and supporting the other), (5) involve the other (e.g., including the other in activities), (6) show self-involvement (e.g., including oneself in the other's activities), and (7) focus on commonalities (e.g., pointing out similarities). People who were reported as using many of these affinity-seeking strategies were also rated as being more likable, socially successful, and satisfied with their lives. In addition, individuals' choice of affinity-seeking strategies depended on the context. People did not believe they used the same strategies in task-oriented situations as they did in social situations. Furthermore, status differences influenced strategy choice. These findings underline both the complexity and the mutuality of our initial interactions. When two people converse, both of them determine whether the conversation is successful and satisfying and both determine whether to continue the relationship. It is impossible to plan a conversation in its entirety (choosing the appropriate greeting, form of address, and affinity-seeking strategy) because we don't know how the other person will respond to us. Communication rules provide us with a guideline, but it is a very general and necessarily flexible guideline.

After achieving contact and making our initial approach to conversation, the most common type of communication typically follows.

Small (?) Talk

What we commonly know as small talk has been discussed by other authors using terms like: grooming talk, phatic communion, social cosmetics, and cliché conversation. For some, this activity seems to be unimportant, even repugnant. Powell correctly identified small talk as superficial, conventional, and perhaps the lowest level of communication about oneself. Indeed, small talk is characterized by breadth, not depth. We might expect to find a fair range of topics discussed, but very little motivation to reveal seldom-seen parts of one's inner self. Powell added, however, that small talk "represents the weakest response to the human dilemma." This opinion appears to be a gross miscalculation of the role of small talk in everyday life. The human condition is dependent on our ability to draw from a vast repertoire of topics, strategies, and feelings, in order to communicate at various levels of intimacy. Small talk represents a form of communication that is critical to developing relationships and thereby represents at times the strongest or most important response to "the human dilemma." In some contexts, such as the workplace, small talk is associated with trust. In other situations small talk is almost the demanded form of communication - cocktail parties, family gatherings, first encounters. Without the ability to engage another in small talk in these situations, the human condition would surely suffer.

Personal careers may also suffer. Management Information Services (MIS) managers, according to one survey, had a high need to advance professionally and a low need to interact with others on a purely social level. As a result, one trade publication urged these managers to deliberately plan informal chitchat sessions with their non-data-processing colleagues or jeopardize their chances for promotion. Although the specifics of exactly how to conduct these informal small-talk sessions were not presented, it is likely to be an important issue. Those people who castigate small talk are probably expressing a displeasure with the way in which it was conducted, not with the act of small talk per se. Like greetings, the act of engaging in small talk may be as important as the content of the exchange. Notice how engaging in small talk in the following example serves an important function in relationship building, even though the participants do not speak the same language:

> ... a U.S. businessman who, while traveling to Europe for the first time, finds himself seated across from a Frenchman at lunch. Neither speaks the other's language, but each smiles a greeting. As the wine is served, the Frenchman raises his glass and gesturing to the American says, "Bon appetit!" The American does not understand and replies, "Ginzberg." No other words are exchanged at lunch. That evening at dinner, the two again sit at the same table and again the Frenchman greets the American with the wine, saying, "Bon appetit!" to which the American replies, "Ginzberg." The waiter notices this peculiar exchange and, after dinner, calls the American aside to explain that "the Frenchman is not giving his name - he is wishing you good appetite; he is saying that he

hopes you enjoy your meal." The following day the American seeks out the Frenchman at lunch, wishing to correct his error. At the first opportunity the American raises his glass and says, "Bon appetit!" to which the Frenchman proudly replies, "Ginzberg."

Even when communicators speak the same language, listening may not be the intent and the exchange of noises assumes precedence over substance.

The prevention of silence is, itself, an important conversational goal fulfilled by small talk. For some, it is difficult to accept the fact that there are communicative exchanges that shouldn't be taken too literally: Trivial conversation at parties doesn't mean everybody there (except us) was somehow devoid of intelligent things to say; and people who can't remember the topic of the sermon immediately upon leaving church may still have had a deeply religious experience. In many instances the literal translation of the words spoken is less important than the fact that words have been spoken. When a new student walks into a professor's office and sees him or her surrounded by papers, furiously pounding at the computer, and asks, "Are you busy?", the professor doesn't usually turn around and say, "No, I'm relaxing." The student's words were intended to be translated, "Hello! There's somebody here to see you. I want to talk to you. I realize I'm interrupting you. You may not want to talk to me or you may not have time so I'll ask a question that will give you the opportunity to ease out of this encounter by saying you're busy. I hope you appreciate the way I handled this interruption - so much so that you won't use the excuse I've given you." So, like this example of an opening line, small talk is often an end in itself. But small talk is also a means to an end - that is, it serves several important interpersonal functions.

Functions of Small Talk

Small talk is a way of maintaining a sense of community or fellowship with other human beings. It helps us cement our bond of humanness. Desmond Morris calls it a "friendly mutual aid system" akin to the grooming and licking rituals of nonhuman primates which provide feelings of comfort, security, and acceptance. Hayakawa calls it "the language of social cohesion." Keeping the lines of communication open with members of your own species and enjoying the togetherness of talking often take precedence over subject matter.

In the jargon of Schutzs interpersonal needs, we could say small talk is most effective in satisfying inclusion needs, since it is designed so that each party can (or must) contribute. Perhaps this is one reason that we find so little disagreement or conflict in small talk; supportiveness and affirmation are indispensable for maintaining effectively a sense of community with our fellow humans.

Small talk also serves as a proving ground for both new and established relationships. Small talk in this sense, then, becomes an "audition for friendship." We noted earlier how potential friends and acquaintances are visually filtered; during small talk we apply a verbal filter. Only after we are satisfied with the communication at the superficial level of small talk do we venture into ""big talk" - communication characterized by greater focus and depth of personal disclosures. Sometimes we mistakenly associate seriousness exclusively with big talk. However, it is easy to think of many serious conversations (task-oriented business discussions or courtship games) that still offer only surface information about the participants. Other times, we make the mistake of assuming that big talk is more important than small talk for maintaining relationships. But Duck and his colleagues have found that intimates really spend a relatively small portion of their everyday conversation engaged in self-disclosure discussions. While intimacy is usually a precursor to self-disclosure, self-disclosure doesn't always characterize intimate relationships. For instance, one of the necessary magic tricks for the person seeking instant intimacy is to give the illusion of serious self-revelation which can be shrugged off as superficial small talk, should the request for instant intimacy be denied; the other person has not truly become a confidant. In established relationships small talk may be dispensed with more quickly and easily, but it is a necessary prelude to more intimate dialogue. The frustration of this Playboy reader aptly illustrates the process:

Because of a job transfer, my girlfriend and I live in different states; we see each other only on holidays and special trips. Every time we meet, we go through a ritual period of adjustment that wastes precious time and often causes discord. She insists that we fill each other in on the changes we have undergone. I would just as soon spend our time on the simple joys of being together and let the changes in our personalities surface

136

gradually, but she sees this soul unveiling as vital to our relationship. We do love each other. How do we resolve our difficulties? - E. A., Omaha, Nebraska.

It appears that the reader's girlfriend is hoping some initial small talk will assure her that surface changes have not occurred during their absence from each other and that this will allow them to escalate to their past-relationship-level talk once again.

Small talk provides a safe procedure for indicating who we are and how another can come to know us better. We're playing for time, trying to display our best features. If one of our many selves doesn't seem to work, we can always shift gears and bring out another self. For instance, one researcher found that women used the telephone strategically to influence the way their male dating partners perceived them. These women made decisions about how often to call their dating partners, when to return calls, and what to talk about so that the men they were dating would not see them as overly aggressive. Small talk allows us to further reduce uncertainties about the other without revealing too much too soon. It can also allow others to focus more specifically on who we are. The fewer the uncertainties, the greater the chances of accurate predictions about the person - and the greater the chances of moving from small talk to big talk.

Another function of small talk is to serve as an interpersonal pacifier. It is a nonthreatening, time-killing activity devoid of the pressures involved in more analytical or introspective processes. In short, it can be a release, an escape valve, or a diversion from other kinds of talk which require more conscious programming.

And finally, small talk provides a means for uncovering integrating topics, or, more simply, openings for more penetrating conversations and relationships. We now turn our attention to the nature of these topics, which is the information derived and exchanged during small talk.

Name, Rank, and Serial Number

When strangers meet for the first time, the first few minutes will usually be devoted to an exchange of demographic or biographical information - name, occupation, marital status, hometown. They are attempting to obtain a sociological profile of the other person in the hope that certain similarities will be uncovered and form a common ground for conversational pursuit. The exchange of biographical information is more involved when the environmental cues do not provide much information about who a partner might be. In other situations, the environment allows participants to make more inferences with more certainty. For example, if you meet a person in a University building carrying books, you might not feel the need to ask if the person was a student, where the person goes to school, what general age range the person represents, and so forth. In some cases, the environmental forces will be so compelling that strangers will begin exchanging attitudes and opinions before seeking demographic data-two delegates who meet at a political gathering. During the early information exchange - a period Berger calls the *entry phase* - a norm often seems to be operating which says: If I provide you with some information about myself, you will reciprocate by giving me an equal amount of information about yourself. Or, in simpler terms, "I'll tell you my hometown if you tell me yours."

The reason biographical information is so predominant in a new relationship is that it is something each party is sure to know about himself or herself, and it is generally nonthreatening because it is nonarguable. Sure, we could start an argument over somebody's hometown, but we generally reserve that for later.

Other topics commonly encountered in initial small talk may be derived from the situation or surroundings. "I'm building a house and I was wondering what kind of insulation you selected for this room?" The weather seems to be a topic everyone knows, is a part of every situation, and is generally nonthreatening. The topic of weather will probably occur more often in certain areas of the country and at certain times during the year. Some sections of the country seem to have local guidelines for small talk topics. In Lafayette, Indiana, for instance, it is not unusual to talk about the dearth of good restaurants in the area, the quality of the local newspaper, and the fact that it's a "'good place to raise kids." Another currently popular ploy is to talk about how much you hate small talk and how people really aren't open with each other. Of course, talking *about* openness meets all the necessary criteria for small talk and is very different from actually *being* open by disclosing more intimate aspects of your personality. Finally, Beinstein's research shows how the topics for small talk will often reflect the environment, the time allowed for interaction, the distance between the participants, and the ostensible purpose for the meeting. She obtained data on topics discussed in twenty-eight barber shops, thirty beauty shops, and thirty pharmacies in Philadelphia during the summer. It is no surprise that vacations were a frequent topic in all the shops, nor that beauticians talked with their customers mainly about fashions, nor that pharmacists talked with their customers mainly about health problems. The only surprise is that barbers talked about vacations more than sports.

Once we have sufficiently stocked our biographical warehouse, we can begin to focus on those aspects that seem to be productive avenues for further conversation (increase the depth) or pursue additional areas that seem logically related (increase the breadth). Upon learning that a couple is not married and just living together, you may choose to slowly tap the conditions and value system that led to that decision or you may seek another different, but related area-"Yeah, a lot of things are changing nowadays. My sister got married with the understanding that she would not have any kids." More often than not, breadth is our choice with strangers and acquaintances; when depth is pursued, however, it is usually a brief foray unless the communicators already have a close relationship or unless special circumstances indicate that the other person needs and wants to uncover a particular inner area.

His own small talk, at any rate, was bigger than most people's large. "I believe it was Hegel who defined love as the ideality of the relativity of the reality of an infinitesimal portion of the absolute totality of the Infinite Being" he would chat at dinner. Peter De Vries

Thus, through small talk we eventually obtain knowledge about the other person - hobbies, interests, likes, dislikes, tastes, future plans, other acquaintances and friends. Gradually, small talk will move past the highly superficial, biographical level, and information will be gained about attitudes, opinions, goals, and specific ways of behaving - how the person handles mistakes, conflict, play, and support for others. It is only when we begin to tap those things that a person does not reveal to just anybody - topics which are held in the middle layers of Altman and Taylor 's Social Penetration Model - that we have moved from small talk to big talk.

Berger points out the usefulness of this harvesting of biographical information in predicting possible attitudes a person might hold - similar backgrounds may suggest similar attitudes. It seems we work backward too, predicting possible biographical information from perceived attitudes. If we disagree or agree with someone, we sometimes try to relate that back to some previously uncovered aspect of background similarity or dissimilarity. It is likely, however, that when we're surprised (background dissimilarities turn into attitude agreements or background similarities turn into attitude disagreements) we will be less inclined to recall our earlier store of information and attribute the situation, instead, to the current phase of the relationship.

Small talk also aids friends who have been separated to pick up their relationship again. When friends are separated, uncertainty increases and once again they have to start the feeling - out process. Since biographical data are the least apt to change, friends often start their small talk by asking what's been happening, what they've been doing since they last saw each other, etc. By telling friends what happened during a separation, we help them to "catch up" with our past and provide them with knowledge that may facilitate their interaction with us in the future. Most of us engage in this type of small talk on a more limited basis with roommates, family, and lovers when we talk with them about what happened in our day. "Debriefing" a relational partner about the events of our day seems to have an important function in our relationships. Researchers have found that spouses who spent more time talking together about the events of their day tended to be more relationally satisfied.

In an attempt to summarize some of the material discussed thus far, let's look at a study conducted by Berger and his colleagues. Over 200 adult residents of a Chicago suburb were asked to imagine they were observing a two-hour conversation between people meeting for the first time. These "observers" sorted 150 pre-selected statements into eight fifteen-minute segments. They were also asked to place those statements that they felt would not occur in a two-hour conversation of this type into a separate category. Generally, the results confirm what we've been saying thus far: Demographic and superficial information about oneself tends to be disclosed to new acquaintances first; personal, sexual, and family problems are consistently placed in later time slots. Some noteworthy exceptions do exist - one's salary and age, although seemingly superficial information, are not disclosed early. In such cases, we might assume that speakers may not want listeners to infer deeper personality aspects from this biographical information. Table 6.1 presents a sampling of these results:

TABLE 6.1   Perceptions of When Information Might Be Revealed Between Strangers In a Two-Hour Conversation

Zero to Fifteen Minutes:
1. I'm a volunteer at a local hospital.
2. I'm from New York.
3. My son is a freshman at Penn State.
4. I have a dog, three cats, and a parakeet.

Fifteen to Thirty Minutes:
1. My wife is a good cook.
2. I've been skiing only once.
3. I like hunting for antiques.
4. I really enjoy playing tennis.
5. The Chicago Bears are a lousy football team.

Thirty to Forty-Five Minutes:
1. I've never really had a vacation.
2. I wish I knew more about politics.
3. Most of my clothes are blue or green.
4. One of my favorite authors is Norman Mailer
5. I wear contact lenses.

Forty-Five to Sixty Minutes:
1. I am thirty-five years old.
2. It bothers me to see young women cursing and swearing.
3. My parents were much more politically conservative than I am.
4. I make it a point to see the doctor, dentist, and optometrist once a year.
5. I want to give my children all of the things I never had as a child.

Sixty to Seventy-Five Minutes:
1. I don't like people who smile all the time.
2. People who don't finish what they start always annoy me.
3. I don't believe in evolution.
4. I dislike my job so much I would like to quit tomorrow and move to a farm.
5. Any American who is a Communist should be deported from the country.

Seventy-Five to Ninety Minutes:
1. I don't believe that there is an afterlife, but I'm really not sure.
2. I hate lying in bed at night, listening to the clock tick.
3. I wish my church was more relevant to my life.
4. I believe in mercy-killing when there is absolutely no hope of survival.
5. My mother-in-law really dislikes me.

Ninety to One Hundred Five Minutes:
1. I have a violent temper.
2. I find it difficult to respond rationally when I am criticized.
3. I suspect people's motives when they compliment me.
4. I think we got married much too young.
5. There are times when I feel I have wasted my life.

One Hundred Five to One Hundred Twenty Minutes:
1. Sometimes I'm afraid I won't be able to control myself.
2. I wish my husband would feel free to cry as an emotional release.
3. I don't really like myself very much.
4. I often wonder why people don't like me.
5. My husband and I stay together for the sake of the children.

Statements Perceived as Not Occurring In a Two-Hour Conversation Between Previously Unacquainted Persons:
1. I had my first sexual experience when I was twenty-one.
2. I make $13,000 a year.
3. I'm suspicious of my husbands constant need to work late.

4. I have considered committing suicide on more than one occasion.
5. We got married earlier than we'd planned because I was pregnant.

Whether you agree or disagree, with the particular order of the preceding statements is irrelevant as long as you recognize that we all organize our revelations to others in some way. Some people may not mind mentioning their salary early in the conversation and even the people in this study - given additional information about the other person, e.g., an investment counselor for people in lower income brackets - may have revealed the salary information. The point is that *whatever* information you perceive to be more personal about yourself will most likely be revealed to another person only after the exchange of more superficial information. Naturally, there are exceptions. Bartenders, strangers on public transportation, and people who deliberately express a desire to listen to another person's troubles will experience a great deal more "unloading" of personal information during the early phases of the encounter. In many of these cases, there is no intent to build a relationship that would last beyond the needed catharsis. Relationships can and do develop under such circumstances, but they must, at some point, go back and exchange more superficial information.

Earlier, you will recall we suggested that while small talk disgruntles many people, it is not the small talk per se that bothers them, it is the way in which small talk is usually conducted. The following are a few of the many possible sources of this irritation: (1) You might engage in a great deal of demographic information exchange with no opportunity or motivation to pursue any of the possible commonalities. Sometimes fraternity or sorority rush parties impose these conditions. Just as you finish providing a biographical overview, it is time to switch partners and go through the same routine again. (2) You may encounter a person who is locked into one specific subject - and he or she doesn't even want to talk about that subject in much depth. Hence, breadth is cut off and the chances of finding integrating topics are decreased. If a person's lone topic happens to be themselves, small talk may seem especially boring. However, dissatisfaction may not accrue if that person's lone subject is also one you enjoy talking to death. (3) You may feel that there is an inequality of information exchange. You end up giving all the information and the other person does not reciprocate. Unless you are performing a counseling function, extremely high or low amounts of talking may not be perceived favorably during initial interaction. People who talked *80* percent of the time were judged to be domineering, outgoing, selfish, inconsiderate, inattentive, impolite, cold, and disliked by their interaction partner. People who talked 50 percent of the time were evaluated as likable, warm, attentive, and polite. Those who talked only 20 percent of the time were viewed as submissive, introverted, unselfish, and unintelligent. Rightly or wrongly, our perception of how much help the other person is giving us in continuing the dialogue is closely related to our perception of whether the other wants to continue the conversation and the relationship. With new acquaintances and strangers, small talk allows us to avoid the anxiety caused by long silences. While this is confusing and/or irritating to the information giver, it may be that the receiver just doesn't understand the important role of questions in small talk. (4) You may also meet a person who violates the pleasantness norm in small talk, and brings the conversation dangerously close to conflict before the relationship can withstand the strain.

In summary, we have a form of public dialogue that serves a number of crucial personal and social functions, is omnipresent, is quantitatively superior to almost any other form of talk, and according to Malinowski, is pan-cultural - and we choose to call it small talk! The covert question underlying all small talk is: Do you want our encounter and our relationship to continue? Should both parties agree to sustain their association, they will make some rather specific plans regarding when and where. Should either or both participants feel less enthusiastic about pursuing the relationship, the where and when of the next meeting will probably be left vague - "I'll probably run into you sometime." This vagueness serves the purpose of leaving the door open but does not commit either party to inviting the other in immediately. Obviously, additional encounters are used to help verify knowledge previously obtained or inferred and provide a mechanism to learn new things. Additional encounters are necessary in order to look for consistency or disparity across situations, between what was said and what was observed, between what the person says and what others say....

***

IMPROVING COMMUNICATION:
HOW TO SEND MESSAGES

Excerpts from: Hanna, S. L. (2000). *Person to Person: Positive Relationships Don't Just Happen*, Third Edition. Toronto: Prentice Hall Inc., Chapter 5.

***

STYLES OF VERBALIZING

Pretend you are the listener in the following conversations and assess each one in terms of your reactions:

1. People in this neighborhood just don't care about their property. They let their houses run down, and their yards are a disaster. You'd think they'd never heard of a lawn mower! Anyone who owns property should keep it up or just move...

2. I've noticed in the last few months that the houses in the neighborhood look shabbier than they used to. And I haven't seen anyone mow a yard for at least a week. I'm frustrated by it because I take pride in my property and believe that it's considerate to keep my house in good condition.

Essentially, the same message was delivered. Yet, if you are like most people, your reaction to each would have been different. In the first one, the speaker used the **closed style of verbalizing [C.O.N.T.R.O.L. talk]**. This means that the comments were definite and left little opportunity for a reasonable response. The closed style, because of its absoluteness, finality, forcefulness, and all-inclusive/exclusive language, stifles positive exchange. A student once commented about a friend, "I cannot win his kind of conversation, so I just keep my mouth shut." The closed style fosters a negative communication climate. Opinions stated as inflexible truths invariably close the door to healthy communication.

In the second example the **open style of verbalizing [D.I.A.L.O.G.U.E. talk]** is used, and discussion is encouraged. A point of view is stated in a flexible manner. Because the expressed ideas sound open, they invite a reasonable, positive response. Open communicators are refreshing! Others appreciate their receptiveness and want to converse with them. Rather than offending or turning others off, open communicators attract people and are more likely to develop and maintain healthy relationships. The old adage "It's not what you say, but how you say it" has a great deal of merit.

Changing from Closed to Open Communication

Awareness of the closed style and recognition of its use is the first step toward becoming an open communicator. Following are descriptions of three types of closed communication and ways to change to the open style.

1. Dogmatic [Allness] – "definitely definite," rigid, absolute, and inflexible. When verbalizing, a dogmatic communicator sounds like the final authority. A key measure of dogmatism is closed mindedness (Vogt, 1997), and in verbalization this comes across as *expression of opinion as fact or truth*. Here are some dogmatic statements:

"The weather is lousy" or "It's a beautiful day today."
"Valentino's has the best pizza in the world" or "Valentino's has the worst pizza in the world."

"He has been a very poor president" or "He has been an excellent president."
"Religion is necessary for a happy life," or "It isn't necessary to be religious to be happy."

How a comment is stated, not its content, makes it dogmatic. Each example expresses an opinion; yet it comes across as the "way it is."

Using "I" statements. The basic technique of open style communication is to rid yourself of dogmatic comments by the use of "I" statements. Because you are speaking for yourself, "I" statements are also regarded as assertive language and are self-empowering. "I" statements are less inflammatory, put responsibility on the speaker, and are much more likely to be heard (McKay, Fanning, & Paleg, 1994). In sign language, "I" statements are also effectively utilized.

"I" statements can be divided into two categories. The first group consists of phrases known as actual "I" statements. The word "I" is said first or begins a phrase used elsewhere in the sentence (see Table 7-1*). A common error is to use "I know" for "I think" such as "I know students do better in smaller classes." The speaker does not *know* this, and "I know" is not considered an "I" statement. When a fact is being stated, then "know" is correct. The second category is made up of phrases that give an "I" meaning. These, too, demonstrate that the speaker's opinions do not necessarily take precedence over others (see Table 7-2*).

Following are rewordings of the dogmatic statements.

"I like (or don't like) the weather."
"As far as I'm concerned, Valentino's has the best (or worst) pizza in the world."
"I think he has been a poor (or excellent) president."
"In my opinion, religion is necessary (or not necessary) for a happy life."

Remember that "I" statements are not necessary in all verbalizations. When you express facts, they certainly aren't. My dad, who died at the age of 77, expressed many of his opinions in a dogmatic way. I suggested that others would react much more positively to him if he used "I" statements. He "leaped" into this in his usual enthusiastic fashion, and it was as if the three words "in my opinion" gave him freedom to say anything. In his zeal, he used the phrase frequently. One day he came into the house and said, "It's raining outside," and then, looking directly at me, added, "In my opinion." I hurriedly explained that when expressing a fact, "I" statements aren't necessary!...

To become an open communicator, listen for your dogmatic statements and concentrate on using "I" statements. A world of difference exists, *in my opinion,* between saying, "College just doesn't prepare you for the real world," and "I think that college experiences rarely reflect what goes on in the world." Remember that you affirm yourself when you express opinions in an open style.

TABLE 7-1 ACTUAL "I" STATEMENTS

I think	*I like*	*I want*
I believe	*I consider*	*I feel*
I feel that	*I prefer*	*I am or was*

Note: An opposite could be made of each by inserting don't or another appropriate word.

TABLE 7-2 PHRASES CONVEYING "I" MEANING

In my opinion	*In my way of thinking*
As far as I'm concerned	*It seems to me*
My thoughts are	*To me it appears*

2. *Commando (Heavy C.O.N.T.R.O.L. talk)* – forcing, pressuring. This category includes words and phrases such as "should," "have to," "must," "ought," and "need to" that leave little, if any, opportunity for alternatives. Note the authoritarian, commanding nature of these statements:

"You should get a job."　　"They must learn to work before they play."
"She has to listen better."　"You had better take my advice."

Consider how you react to forcing words, especially when they are preceded by the word "you." Defensively? In a study, adolescents rated accusatory "you" statements as more aversive and likely to evoke stronger antagonistic response inclinations than assertive "I" statements. Using "you" with angry messages increased hostile responses and provoked resistance and rebellion …

Being tentative and flexible. When the "commando" type has been used, first check to see whether the statement is also dogmatic. If so, create an "I" statement and then replace the forcing part with a flexible and tentative phrase. See Table 7-3 for examples. Following are changes in the above commando statements.

"I think it would be a good idea for you to get a job."
"As far as I'm concerned, getting work done before play is important."
"I believe she would benefit from listening better."
"It seems to me that my advice could be helpful to you."

The forcing words "should," "must," "has to," and "had better" were replaced with tentative phrases, and "I" statements were used. The same point is made in a less demanding way.

TABLE 7-3 SOME TENTATIVE PHRASES

| *It would be a good idea if* | *It seems important that* | *He or she, they, or you might be wise to* |
| *You might want to consider* | *It could be helpful if* | *He or she, they, or you could benefit from* |

3. *Grandiose [Sweeping Judgments or Generalities]* – exaggerated, all-inclusive or all-exclusive, and often dramatic. The use of this type can lead to inaccuracy or a distortion of the facts. Following are examples of grandiose words and statements in which they are expressed: everyone-no one, everybody-nobody, all-none, always-never, everything-nothing-anything, only, every:

"All kids today are disrespectful."　　"I never know what's going on."
"He doesn't do anything except lie around."　"I don't have anything to wear."

… Note that grandiose statements are almost always (not always) dogmatic.

A statement that contains grandiose words is usually inaccurate. How often is "always" correct? Be careful you don't answer that with "never." At times, "always" is accurate! Not only can the literal meanings be incorrect, but the words are often emotionally laden and tend to harm rather than enlighten (Satir, 1976). Years ago I suggested the possible elimination of the words "always" and "never" from the language until Ed, a good friend, reminded me of their accuracy in certain statements. He noted that the Pope is always Catholic and never Jewish! I quickly agreed! In most cases, grandiose words are used only for their dramatic effect. Yet, because they usually create an inaccurate statement, the point can be lost. I have often cautioned parents not to say to a child, "Your room is always a mess" or "You never clean your room." Why? The child can clean once in a 5-year period and prove that you are wrong… Try inwardly responding with the suggestions in parentheses when you hear these types of statements:

"All men are that way." (All? Really?)
"You never do anything right." (Surely once in a while the person does!)

143

"All he does is eat.'" (That's all he does? Amazing!)
"I'm always late." (Not even once on time?)

Depending on your relationship with the grandiose speaker, you may be able to verbalize these questions....

Adding or replacing with qualifiers. To correct the "grandiose" type, an "I" statement may be needed to get rid of dogmatism. Then replace or modify the grandiose word with a qualifier (see Table 7-4). For example, if "always" or "never" has been used, check for accuracy. Is the word correct? If not, select a qualifier that does not change the meaning to any extent. In the statement "She's never on time," what word could be used to qualify "never"? Some possibilities are "rarely" or "hardly ever" as replacements or adding "almost" in front of "never" as a modifier. Be careful that you don't change the meaning to any great extent. For example, if you are rewording "Everyone is so rude," the meaning would be significantly changed if you replaced "everyone" (the grandiose word) with "someone." Instead, use "many people" or add "almost" to "everyone." Some possible open statements are "I've noticed that she is rarely on time" and "It seems to me that most people are rude."

Using qualifiers makes statements accurate and less hurtful. A young man said that his father repeatedly told him, "You'll never amount to anything." "Never" and "anything," felt like arrows accentuating the attack on his self-esteem. Qualifiers decrease the sting of a critical remark. Again, compare the statements that follow with the ones given in the description of the grandiose type.

"In my opinion, many kids today are disrespectful."   "I feel as if I rarely know what's going on."

"It seems to me that he spends a lot of time lying around not doing much."   "I don't have many things to wear."

These reworded statements are accurate, less dramatic, and open. Note that each is an "I" statement.

TABLE 7-4 WORDS USEFUL AS QUALIFIERS

almost	often	several	sometimes
rarely	hardly ever	quite a few	usually
infrequently	some	few	generally
frequently	many	seldom	probably
nearly	most	possibly	in general

All three types of the closed style set up obstacles to honest interactions. Either they stop communication or, if exchange does take place, disagreement or combativeness is apt to occur. Statements that contain all three types aren't unusual.

***

BECOMING A POSITIVE LISTENER

Excerpts from: Hanna, S. L. (2000). *Person to Person: Positive Relationships Don't Just Happen*, Third Edition. Toronto: Prentice Hall Inc., Chapter 6.

"Listening is an active process of attending, receiving, and interpreting auditory stimuli and then providing feedback. Listening well includes observing and interpreting nonverbal behaviors and reacting to a speaker. Listening goes beyond hearing because it involves interpretation and responding."

***

Open and Attentive Body Position

Do you appear to be listening? The way you position yourself in relation to the speaker makes a difference. Establishing a comfortable distance apart is basic ... Being on the same level sets the tone for the interchange because if one stands and the other sits, the person seated can feel at a disadvantage. Facing the speaker is essential. Turning your body away carries a message of disinterest and lessens your involvement, while facing the speaker squarely and leaning slightly forward demonstrates attentiveness.

Adopting an open, attentive posture indicates interest, openness, and involvement. Sitting with legs and arms crossed, slouching, or leaning away from the speaker is likely to give negative impressions... A relaxed position of openness and attentiveness is ideal.

Positive Eye Contact

Maintaining eye contact in North American society is a must. In fact, conversation usually doesn't even start until eye contact is made ... Poor eye contact may be interpreted as a lack of confidence or as indicative of dishonesty or lying. Knowledge of various cultures is important, as a student from the Middle East commented that direct eye contact is discouraged in his society. In other societies looking down rather than at the speaker is respectful.

... [R]ealize that eye contact is almost never a direct meeting between sets of eyes. You don't have to look squarely into a speaker's eyes; you can focus anywhere on the face, including the nose, mouth, or ear... in glances lasting from 1 to 7 seconds.

Facial Expression

To a great extent, feedback is delivered by changes in facial expression. A "poker face" is helpful in a card game; it is generally useless, and often demeaning, in the listening process. A positive listener reacts to what is being said by registering any thinking and feeling responses...

Head and Body Movements

... A nod can motivate and energize a speaker. "Nodders" are worth their weight in gold! Even a side-to-side nod indicating confusion or disagreement can be helpful if the objective is to arrive at shared meaning ... Since it is possible to nod too much, be sure to use the movement moderately and when appropriate...

Touching

Depending on your relationship with the speaker, listening can be improved by an appropriate touch. One day a student came in to talk about a personal conflict and was having difficulty expressing herself. I reached over and touched her hand, and the words poured out. The touch had evidently reassured her so she could speak freely. The arm is generally considered to be a neutral or non-vulnerable area... being appropriate is important ...

Verbal Responses

Listening is usually a nonverbal activity; however, verbal responses are also included in positive listening. These can vary from a simple "Oh" or "Hmm" to "I see" or "That sounds interesting." You can, however, use too many responses ... "Really," "I know," or "I understand" stated after each comment is distracting and annoying. A question that encourages the speaker to continue is an excellent response. Some possibilities are: "How do you feel about that?" … "What happened next?" If you are an attentive listener, your question will not move the conversation away from the point … Open questions requiring more than a simple yes or no answer are preferred because they are encouraging and move the conversation forward….

Verbal responses can involve more than short reactions or questions. [To provide understanding feedback] **paraphrasing is restating** in your own words what you think the speaker said. Here is an example of paraphrasing.

SPEAKER: My kids have been driving me crazy.
LISTENER: It sounds like you are really bothered by them.

When you paraphrase, you don't add to the message; instead, you repeat the meaning you received. This shows that you received the message and want to be sure the meaning is shared. You can use such lead-ins as, "It sounds like," "You mean that," "What I hear you saying is," or "Let me make sure I understand what you mean." Paraphrasing may seem clumsy at first; yet once you find and practice a few phrases that sound natural, using them will become easier.

The benefits of paraphrasing are worth the initial discomfort. First, people appreciate that they were heard. Paraphrasing can stop anger from escalating and cool a crisis situation, decrease misinterpretation because errors can be corrected immediately …

Gaining a clear understanding of the speaker's emotions is also helpful. Jason tells Nancy that he is "down in the dumps." She says, "It sounds as if you are really depressed." Jason can then think about her impression. He may respond, "I'm not really that unhappy," or he can say, "Yes, I am really down." When the listener provides an idea of the feeling that is sensed, the speaker receives valuable information…

***

Elimination of Negative Listening Behaviors

Knowing what to do is essential; knowing *what not to do* is equally important. The opposites or extremes of the behaviors just described are obvious negatives. In addition, an inappropriate facial expression can be unsettling. For example, have you ever tried to describe a serious incident to a listener who is slightly grinning?

Interrupting, unfortunately, is common and is one of the surest signs that a person isn't truly listening. Individuals who enjoy talking have more difficulty with this bothersome behavior. One study found that male and masculine-oriented individuals of either sex interrupted most often (Campbell, Klein & Olson, 1992) …

Certain listening gestures and sounds can bother the speaker and create a negative communication climate. Several are identified by Ernst (1973).

Cheek puffing and corners of mouth going down
"Basket hands" (fingertips touch then open and close)
Eye rolling
Foot or leg bouncing up and down at high speed

Shoulder shrugging to indicate an
I-don't-care attitude

Drumming the feet or
fingers …

***

Reading Twelve

Conflict

Excerpts from Falikowski, A. (2002). *Mastering Human Relations*, Third Edition. Toronto: Pearson Education, Chapter 6.

***

[In Chapter 6]... we looked at a number of psycho-logical defence mechanisms people often employ when conflicts and strong disagreements lead to anxiety and other unpleasant emotions. We learned how people do things such as twist reality, divert attention or intimidate others when involved in disputes or confrontations of egos. In this chapter, what we'll do is look more carefully at the nature of conflict itself. We'll see how theorists have conceptualized conflict, how people adopt different psychological orientations toward it, and how there are different methods and styles of conflict resolution. By understanding such things, we'll be better able to manage conflict and to deal with it in our personal and professional lives, as well as in our informal interactions with friends, relatives and neighbours.

6.1 The Nature of Conflict

Though commonplace, conflict is not something that permits precise and easy definition. *The New Webster's Encyclopedic Dictionary of the English Language* defines it as "a fighting or struggle for mastery." It is also defined as "combat, a striving to oppose or overcome; active opposition; contention; strife." As a verb, to conflict means "to meet in opposition or hostility; to contend; to strive or struggle; to be in opposition; to be contrary; to be incompatible or at variance...

6.2 Types of Conflict

Psychological

Perhaps the best place to start our explorations is with the individual. Some conflict that occurs in life happens internally. We call this **psychological conflict.** This type of conflict could be going on within you right now with nobody else around even noticing. For example, you may be having erotic fantasies about someone in the class, but be experiencing guilt because such fantasies violate your religious values and beliefs. In this case, your biological sexual instincts may be at odds with your moral standards.... in Freudian psychoanalytic terms, the "id is in conflict with the superego"... For Freud, life itself is a continuing saga of conflict. The conscious rational ego must balance the opposing parts of the psyche and reconcile primitive biological urges with the demands presented by civilized society. According to Freud, our personalities are always in conflict to some degree.

Social

As you can no doubt readily appreciate, some conflictual experience in life occurs between or among people, not strictly within them. You and your siblings may, for example, be strong rivals, always fighting over things like who gets the telephone next or who gets the bigger bedroom in the new house. This *me against you* type of conflict involving two different individuals can be described as **interpersonal conflict.**

Approach–Avoidance

Whether conflict is social or psychological in nature, some people have found it useful to think of it in terms of desirable and undesirable characteristics or approach-avoidance features. In this light, conflict can be described as approach-approach, avoidance-avoidance or approach-avoidance. See Figure 6.2 for an illustration.

Let's consider **approach-approach conflict** first. Suppose you want to go out on a date with a special somebody, for example, but you also want to go skiing with other friends at the same time. We'll assume that taking your date skiing is not possible. In this case, two desirable things are wanted, but only one option can be chosen.

When we face two equally unattractive alternatives, we face **avoidance-avoidance conflict.** You may not wish to study for an exam or mow your lawn. Nonetheless, you are asked by your parents to do one or the other (some choice, eh!), or you won't be allowed to use the family car.

Figure 6.2
Types of Conflict

Approach—Approach "I want this" but "I also want that"
Avoidance—Avoidance "I don't want this" and "I don't want that"
Approach—Avoidance "I want this" but "I don't want what this entails"

A third kind is **approach-avoidance conflict,** which you may experience, for example, if you wish to change college or university programs. The problem is that you're insecure about setting off on a whole new course (no pun intended). Obviously, there are attractive and unattractive aspects to either choice. If you stay in your current program, you will continue to be dissatisfied, though confident. If you move on, you'll be energized and enthusiastic, though insecure. In some respects, "you're damned if you do and damned if you don't."

***

Functional Versus Dysfunctional Conflict

Because conflict is often associated with disruptions and unpleasant feelings, many people try to avoid it as much as possible. Common experience tells us that conflict can frequently be counterproductive. This kind of **dysfunctional conflict** hinders group performance and upsets personal psychological functioning. If you're "torn apart" by conflict, you may not be able to concentrate on your studies or do your job at work. If there is great animosity between individuals in an organizational department, differences between them may become irreconcilable. Productive teamwork and cooperative efforts may become next to impossible to achieve.

By contrast, writers and researchers have noted that there also exists **functional conflict** (Robbins, 1998). Some companies, such as IBM, see such conflict from an **interactionist perspective.** At IBM, conflict is encouraged, "… on the grounds that a harmonious, peaceful, tranquil, and cooperative group is prone to becoming static, apathetic, and nonresponsive to the needs for innovation" (ibid.: 446). From this view, a small and optimum level of conflict can help to keep groups viable, self-critical and creative. To determine whether a (social) conflict is functional or dysfunctional, it is helpful to look at group performance. If the conflict serves to achieve group objectives in the end, then it is functional. If it gets in the way and undermines group performance, then it is dysfunctional.

6.3 Benefits of Conflict

By making a distinction between functional and dysfunctional conflict, the idea is captured that not all conflict is necessarily bad. Optimistically speaking, conflict needn't be destructive at all in some cases. When handled properly, it can be an occasion for growth and development. Conflict, like argument, should be seen as an opportunity, not an obstacle. On this note, David Johnson (1999) has listed the benefits of conflict, when skillfully managed. They are paraphrased as follows.

1. Conflicts enable us to become aware of problems within relationships.
2. Conflicts serve as a catalyst for positive change. Maybe we need to experiment and do things a little differently (for our good and the good of others).
3. Conflicts are energizing and can motivate us to deal with immediate problems.
4. Conflicts add spice to life. They stimulate interest and curiosity.
5. Conflicts can be cathartic. A good argument may relieve minor tension associated with interacting with other people. (Isn't it enjoyable to make up after a good "fight"?)
6. Conflicts can cause decisions to be made more carefully and thoughtfully.
7. Conflicts promote self-knowledge. For example, they heighten awareness concerning what angers us; what frightens us, and what is important to us.
8. Conflicts are potentially energizing and fun, if not taken too seriously. Competitive games and sports can be enjoyable when conflict is involved.
9. Conflicts can improve relationships in the long term. People learn that relationships can hold up under stress. Conflicts can clear the air of unexpressed resentments.

6.4 Psychological Orientations to Conflict

Whether or not people see value in conflict will largely depend on their psychological orientations toward it. Clayton Lafferty and Ronald Phillips (1990) at Human Synergistics in Plymouth, Michigan, have identified 12 individual styles of approaching conflict, which they group into three basic orientations. Before we examine each one in turn, however, let us first spell out what is meant by the notion of **orientation** itself.

For our purposes here, it will be helpful to conceptualize a **conflict orientation** as something psychological. When faced with conflict, we all display certain **predispositions**. Some of us are inclined to approach people with whom we disagree, while others are more inclined to withdraw or attack those who choose to dispute with us. The notion of psychological orientation also involves one's **beliefs** and **perceptions.** There are those who see opportunity and challenge in conflict, whereas others believe that it is something essentially destructive and undesirable. Furthermore, when faced with conflict, some of us wish to resolve differences and get on with things. By contrast, others apparently have a real need to win or come out on top. In other words, people have different **motivations** in their dealings with conflict. **Intentions** vary as do corresponding **behaviours.** A psychological orientation to conflict can be defined, then, by our perceptions, motivations and predispositions, as well as by our beliefs and intentions. See Figure 6.3 for an illustration of psychological orientations to conflict.

Figure 6.3
Psychological Orientations to Conflict

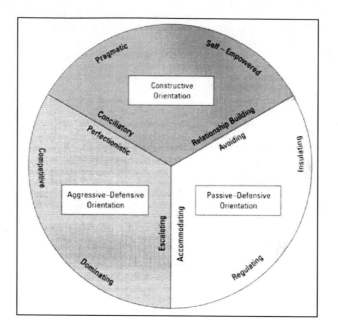

It's worth noting at this point that no one's psychological orientation to conflict is carved in stone. It is possible to change from one orientation to another. For example, if you've fallen into some bad habits where conflict is concerned—say, stomping away in anger—you can learn new behavioural patterns and effect necessary attitude adjustments to more productively handle conflict in the future.

Constructive Orientation

Since we've already had a chance to consider the potential benefits of conflict and because we're on the topic of handling conflict productively, perhaps it's best to start with the **constructive orientation to conflict** resolution. From this vantage point, conflict is regarded as something normal and commonplace. It is viewed as useful for achieving longer-term interests. People with a constructive orientation are **realistic,** using their analytical abilities to clarify and discuss issues. Adopting the **pragmatic approach** means that feelings are expressed in honest and direct ways. The pragmatism also means that those adopting this orientation dissociate their self-worth from any results arising from the dispute. Not getting one's own way is not a blow to self-esteem or a slight against one's ego.

Another important characteristic about people choosing a constructive orientation is that they are **self-empowered.** This means they are **"internally centered,"** so to speak. They recognize that their power comes from inside themselves and not from associations with others, wealth or expertise. Self-empowered individuals respect their opponents in conflictual situations, refusing to become hostile and defensive toward them. They tend to address differences with sensitivity and patience.

Constructively oriented people are **conciliatory.** They assume that people are basically well-intentioned and that they prefer to work through differences in a **fair** and **reasonable** fashion. Instead of being offended by caustic behaviour, these individuals look for the underlying needs and desires motivating it. An insult, for instance, would not be taken at face value, but appreciated in terms of what's going on inside the person who issued it. By standing back from the unpleasantness often associated with conflict, constructive people maintain an **objective perspective.** They make efforts to diffuse passions and facilitate negotiations by refusing to be diverted by irrelevant side issues. Finally, constructively oriented people

150

place great value on loyalty to the relationship. For them, few issues are important enough to break the bonds of a friendship.

Passive-Defensive Orientation

A less than constructive psychological approach to conflict is the **passive-defensive orientation.** Rather than seeing conflict as normal and possibility-generating, people with this orientation view conflict as threatening. They avoid getting involved and make efforts to" calm troubled waters." The belief is held that conflict is unnecessary and destructive.

People with a passive-defensive orientation are **accommodating.** With an aim to maintain a climate of perpetual harmony, they have a tendency to passively acquiesce and do what others expect. They are upset by conflict and believe that little good comes from it. For accommodating individuals, self-worth is measured by others' acceptance and approval.

Passive-defensive individuals try to **insulate** themselves from controversies and disputes. Conflict is regarded as a power struggle in which they are powerless to defend their own interests. Insulating persons often feel frightened and helpless and, as a result, try to remain unnoticed and inconsequential. Passive-defensive people are always "hiding out," so to speak. This fact points to the notion that passive-defensives are **avoiders,** frequently withdrawing from conflict or denying that it exists. Since conflict is seen as unnecessary and destructive, they flee from it whenever possible. Others are allowed to handle disputes. The passive-defender **regulates** things by staying in the background, trying to shame antagonists into more cooperative behaviour. Seldom, then, will you find passive-defensive individuals balking at authority. Instead, you're more likely to find them behaving as loyal, law-abiding employees or citizens, seeking out dependent relationships with those more powerful than they are.

To increase the probability of constructive conflict outcomes, passive-defensive individuals need to do the following:

- Recognize that conflicts can be useful
- State their interests clearly and forcefully
- Stand up for themselves and for what's important
- Recognize that power can be given away
- Stop believing that others will necessarily protect their interests
- Accept that conflict does indeed exist, if others say it does

Aggressive-Defensive Orientation

In stark contrast to the passive-defensive orientation that minimizes conflict, the **aggressive-defensive orientation** intensifies or **escalates** it. Aggressive-defensive individuals believe that competence—particularly intellectual prowess—is the key to their acceptance by others. We see in escalators a desire to **aggrandize** themselves at their opponent's expense. The primary strategy here is to camouflage their own inadequacies by highlighting those of others. You can tell when you're around escalating, aggressive-defensive types, for they tend to create a highly adversarial climate of attack and counterattack.

Another variation of this orientation is found in the **dominator.** Dominators seek the high ground of **power** and **authority.** They attempt to dictate the terms of their relationships. High-level dominators take every opportunity to attack the power of opponents either directly or by indirect means. Dominating aggressive types live by the ethic "Might makes right," using force to manipulate others.

From the vantage point of the aggressive-defensive orientation, conflict is about **competition.** Conflict becomes a context in which people either gain or lose status. When involved in any conflictual situation, the primary motivation is to gain recognition and the admiration of others. Winning is important for it is associated with self-worth. According to the competitive aggressive-defensive type, there is no such thing as a win/win solution.

Finally, some individuals express their aggressive-defensive orientation through **perfectionism.** They set unrealistic standards and demand the impossible from others. No outcome is ever accepted as good enough, while the belief is held that an ideal solution to conflict is indeed possible. By explicitly or implicitly communicating that others have failed or fallen short, a position of (dishonest) superiority can be maintained. Because perfectionistic individuals make unrealistic demands on themselves too, they never feel good enough and, hence, suffer from low self-esteem. In their minds, it is better to have others feel inadequate than to feel inadequate oneself.

Things aggressive-defensive people can do to achieve more constructive resolutions to conflict include the following:

- Don't confuse force with power. "…[T]he more force used to assert your interests, the less power you have to sustain them."
- Separate your personal worth from the outcome of a conflict.
- Apply standards of fair conduct.
- Explore differences rather than force win/lose settlements.
- Be willing to accept less than perfect solutions.
- Respect the interests of others.
- Learn to accept feelings as facts.

Application Exercise 6.1
My Personal Experience of Conflict

Your task in this exercise is to bring to mind a memorable conflict that you've experienced sometime in your life. This is a conflict you're willing to comment on and share with others in the class. (You needn't get too personal or too detailed!) Answer the following questions:

1. What was the conflict about?
2. How did you feel? What were your thoughts? What did you do? How did you act?
3. What type of conflict were you involved in? Was it functional or dysfunctional, psychological or interpersonal, approach-avoidance or something else?
4. Were there any benefits arising from the conflict? If so, explain. Was the conflict destructive? Why?
5. What sort of psychological orientation did you assume in the conflictual situation? If others were involved, what attitudinal stance did they adopt? How did these orientations facilitate or hinder conflict resolution?

6.6   Conflict Management Styles

In view of the fact that people display different psychological orientations to conflict and differing behavioural tendencies—to approach, attack or withdraw from others who are involved—it is perhaps not surprising that different conflict management styles have been identified (see Lafferty and Phillips, 1990; David Johnson, 1999; Stephen Robbins, 1998; and M.A. Rahim, 1983). To identify your own personal conflict management style, do Self-Diagnostic 6.1.

Self-Diagnostic 6.1 can help you to begin identifying your dominant and back-up **conflict management styles.** Here, we'll look at each of your preferred styles as well as others to promote further self-understanding. We'll examine the basic features of each style, the ego states energized by each style, the types of situations created by the different conflict resolution approaches, the advantages and disadvantages of each style, and suggestions about when each style could best be used.

Writers and researchers in the field of human relations have identified at least five different conflict management styles (Lussier, 1995; Johnson, 1999):

1. Forcing (or competing)
2. Avoiding (or withdrawing)
3. Accommodating (or smoothing)
4. Compromising
5. Collaborating (or problem confronting)

Each of these styles takes into account the two major concerns people have when they get into conflict: **goals** and **relationships.** When you experience interpersonal conflict, you typically have a goal that is at odds with another person's goal. Your goal may or may not be highly important to you. As well, when you are in conflict, you're usually required to take into account relationship considerations. Either the relationship in the conflict situation is, or is not, important to you. Looking at the importance of goals in light of the importance of relationships allows us to identify the five conflict management styles listed. Johnson (1999) has associated, in a playful and creative way, different animals with each one….

Self Diagnostic 6.1:   What's My Conflict Management Style?

Instructions: Listed below are 15 statements. Each statement provides a possible strategy for dealing with conflict. Give each statement a numerical value (i.e., 1=always, 2=Very often, 3=Sometimes, 4=Not very often, 5=Rarely, if ever) depending on how often you rely on it. Don't answer as you think you should; answer as you actually behave.

_____ a. I argue my case with peers, colleagues and coworkers to demonstrate the merits of the position I take.
_____ b. I try to reach compromises through negotiation.
_____ c. I attempt to meet the expectations of others.
_____ d. I seek to investigate issues with others in order to find solutions that are mutually acceptable.
_____ e. I am firm in resolve when it comes to defending my side of an issue.
_____ f. I try to avoid being singled out, keeping conflict with others to myself.
_____ g. I uphold my solutions to problems.
_____ h. I compromise in order to reach solutions.
_____ i. I trade important information with others so that problems can be solved together.
_____ j. I avoid discussing my differences with others.
_____ k. I try to accommodate the wishes of my peers and colleagues.
_____ l. I seek to bring everyone's concerns out into the open in order to resolve disputes in the best possible way.
_____ m. I put forward middle positions in efforts to break deadlocks.
_____ n. I accept the recommendations of colleagues, peers and coworkers.
_____ o. I avoid hard feelings by keeping my disagreements with others to myself.

Scoring: The 15 statements you just read are listed below under five categories. Each category contains the letters of three statements. Record the number you placed next to each lettered statement. Calculate the total under each category.

				TOTALS
Forcing Shark	a. _____	e. _____	g. _____	_____
Collaborating Owl	d. _____	i. _____	l. _____	_____
Avoiding Turtle	f. _____	j. _____	o. _____	_____
Accommodating Teddy Bear	c. _____	k. _____	n. _____	_____
Compromising Fox	b. _____	h. _____	m. _____	_____

Results: My dominant style is _____ (lowest score) and my back-up style is _____ (Second lowest score).

Interpretation of Results: Read the section of the text entitled "The Conflict-Management Menagerie," [below].

Source: Based on the work of David Johnson (1984), Stephen Robbins (1993) and M.A. Rahim (1983).

According to Johnson, the particular conflict strategy you should use in any given situation depends on how important goals and relationships are to you. For him, each conflict management style has its proper place. It's probably not well-advised to behave in the same fashion in every conflict you encounter. Johnson says. "To be truly skilled in conflict management, you need to be competent in all five strategies and be able to vary your behaviour according to the person and the situation. You do not want to be an overspecialized dinosaur who can deal with conflict in only one way" (Johnson, 1990: 248). An important point to note here is that you have choice. Conflict resolution styles are not inborn or innate, but learned. If you have learned only one and rely too heavily on it, it's probably best that you familiarize yourself with the others and practise them when appropriate. Although Self-Diagnostic 6.1 has helped you to identify your two most preferred styles, nothing prevents you from using others.

The Conflict Management Menagerie

The [Forcing or] Competing Shark

Sharks are highly goal-oriented people who use a **forcing** (or **competing**) conflict management style where conflicts are concerned. Relationships take on a much lower priority for them. Sharks do not hesitate to use aggressive behaviour to resolve conflicts. They try to achieve their goals at all costs. Unconcerned with the feelings and needs of others, they are uncooperative, autocratic or authoritarian. They can also be very threatening and intimidating. They seek to force resolutions onto problems. Sharks have a need to win and for them this means that others must lose; in other words, Sharks create win-lose situations in their dealings with conflict. They do so by employing the Critical Parent and Adapted Child ego states...

One advantage of this conflict style is that better decisions can be made (assuming the Shark is right) as compared with less effective, compromised decisions. A deterrent to using this style is that it may breed resentment and hostility toward the person (leader) using it. The forcing style is appropriate to use when:

- The conflict involves personal differences that are difficult to change.
- Fostering intimate or supportive relationships is not critical.
- Others are likely to take advantage of noncompetitive behaviour.
- Conflict resolution is urgent, in emergency situations, or when decisive action is vital.
- Unpopular decisions need to be implemented.

The Avoiding Turtle

Turtles adopt an **avoiding** (or **withdrawing**) conflict management style, choosing to ignore conflicts rather than resolve them. Metaphorically speaking, they withdraw into their shells. Turtles' need to avoid or delay confrontation usually leaves them uncooperative and unassertive. Since they stay away from contentious issues, they give up their personal goals and relationships; they do this while displaying the passive behaviour of the Adapted Child or Nurturing Parent ego state. By leaving conflicts alone, they create lose-lose situations.

One advantage of Turtle avoidance is that it may help to maintain relationships that would be hurt by efforts at conflict resolution (Lussier, 1995). On the downside, conflicts remain unresolved. Furthermore, Turtles overusing this style may find that people are walking all over them...Turtle avoidance can appropriately be used when:

- The personal stakes are not high or the issue is trivial.
- Confrontation will hurt a working relationship.
- There's little chance of satisfying your wants.
- Disruption outweighs the benefits of conflict resolution.
- Gathering information is more important than an immediate decision.
- Others can more effectively resolve the conflict.
- Time constraints demand a delay.

The Accommodating Teddy Bear

Teddy Bears use an **accommodating** (or **smoothing**) conflict management style, placing a great deal of importance on human relationships. However, their own goals are of little importance. The Teddy Bear tries to resolve conflicts by giving in to others. Anyone using this style of conflict resolution operates passively in the Adapted Child or the Nurturing Parent ego state. The general approach is unassertive and cooperative. The result of this approach is a win-lose situation. The Teddy Bear loses, but the other party involved in the conflict wins.

As with the other conflict management styles already discussed, there are advantages and disadvantages associated with this one. On the upside, accommodating helps to maintain relationships. On the downside, giving in to another in conflict may not be productive… Overreliance on accommodation may lead others to take advantage of Teddy Bears, which is certainly not in their personal best interest.

Lussier (1995) and Thomas (1977) offer us suggestions as to when accommodating is the best conflict style to use:

- When maintaining a relationship far outweighs the importance of all other considerations.
- When suggestions and changes are not important to the accommodator.
- When trying to minimize losses in situations where you are outmatched and losing.
- When time is limited.
- When harmony and stability are valued.

The Compromising Fox

Foxes use a **compromising** conflict management style because they are concerned with both goals and relationships. They try to resolve interpersonal conflicts through concessions. They are willing to forfeit some of their goals while persuading the other person in conflict to give up part of his. Conflicts are resolved by both sides getting something. Foxes will accept sacrifice in order to achieve agreement.

This process of compromise elicits both assertive and cooperative Adult ego-state behaviours. Win-lose or lose-lose situations may be created by the compromises found. When both parties give up what they want and get what they don't want, a lose-lose compromise results. In this case, nobody is really satisfied with the resolution. When each party gets some of what's wanted and loses some, you could say a win-lose situation results.

Compromise, as a conflict resolution strategy, is beneficial because relationships are maintained and conflicts are removed relatively quickly. The problem is that compromise sometimes creates less than ideal outcomes. Game playing may also result. Understanding that things will have to be given up, people may make exaggerated and unrealistic demands, hoping to get what they really want. Use compromise when:

- Important and complex issues leave no clear and simple solutions.
- All conflicting people are equal in power and have strong interests in different solutions.
- There are time constraints.

The Collaborating Owl

Owls adopt a **collaborating** (or **problem confronting**) conflict management system and they value both their goals and relationships. Owls view conflicts as problems to be solved. Collaborators try to resolve disputes by finding solutions agreeable to all parties. They use their Adult ego state to find win-win situations. They believe that a conflict is not settled until people get what they want and all tensions and negative feelings have been extinguished. The disadvantage is that solving every conflict consumes a great deal of time and effort. Collaboration is useful when:

- Maintaining relationships is important.
- Time is not a concern.
- Peer conflict is involved.
- Trying to gain commitment through consensus building.
- Learning and trying to merge differing perspectives.

For a summary statement of conflict management styles, associated ego states, resulting situations, and occasions when indicated, see Table 6.1.

Table 6.1

Conflict Management Styles

Conflict Management style	Associated Ego States	Resulting Situations	When Indicated	Pros and Cons
Competing Shark	Critical Parent Adapted Child	Win-Lose	High Goal-Low Relationship Concerns	Pro: Better Decisions Con: Resentment and Hostility
Avoiding Turtle	Adapted Child Nurturing Parent	Lose-Lose	Low Goal-Low Relationship Concerns	Pro: Relationship Maintenance Con: Unresolved Conflict
Accommodating Teddy Bear	Nurturing Parent Adapted Child	Win-Lose	Low Goal-High Relationship Concerns	Pro: Preserves Relationship Con: Exploitation of Accommodator
Compromising Fox	Adult Ego State	Win-Lose Lose-Lose	Moderate Goal-Moderate Relationship Concerns	Pro: Conflict Resolution, Relationships Maintained Con: Less-than-ideal Outcomes, Game Playing
Collaborating Owl	Adult Ego State	Win-Win	High Goal-High Relationship Concerns	Pro: Best Resolutions Con: Required Time and Effort

Application Exercise 6.2

Pick the Most Appropriate Conflict Resolution Style

Your task in this exercise is to analyze the following case study in light of what you've learned on the subject of conflict and conflict management. What sort of conflict or conflicts are we dealing with? Explain, given the facts, which conflict management style is the best one to use. What led you to your conclusion?

> *Mr. Wonderful is the teacher of your general education elective in philosophy offered by the computer studies department. Try as he might, his class is not going very well by mid-term. Mr. Wonderful has noticed that several students in the class always sit close to each other and disrupt proceedings by their rude behaviour and sarcastic questions intended not to clarify matters, but to embarrass the instructor and others. On top of this, students in the elective class don't get along well together. They come from various streams of study within the computer studies department. Some students are fresh out of high school, while others are direct entry, meaning that they already possess either a diploma or degree at the time of course enrollment. Still others are "mature students" who qualified for admission to computer studies by virtue of their age and experience. Often, you can hear arguments among the students who group themselves according to stream. In fact, physical fights have even broken out in the hallways. Mr. Wonderful wishes the conflict would end, that a civilized environment for learning could be reestablished and that everybody would get back to their schoolwork.*
>
> In your own words, describe the conflict situation. What should Mr. Wonderful do? What conflict management style would be reflected by these suggested actions? Why do you favour this style in this case?

***

Application Exercise 6.3

Type Tips for Conflict Resolutions

By this point in your efforts to master human relations you have become quite familiar with matters of psychological type, temperament and the notion of differing cognitive and behavioural preferences. This familiarity can help you to appreciate better the psychology of conflict as well as accommodate differing preferences in an effort to resolve interpersonal disputes. In *Type Talk at Work,* Otto Kroeger and Janet Thuesen say that "any conflict-resolution model that does not consider personality differences is doomed to fail" (Kroeger and Thuesen, 1993: 128). This claim may be somewhat overstated; nonetheless, personality is clearly one important variable to be taken into account when trying to resolve any interpersonal conflict. In fact, sometimes personality differences are the causes of conflicts. What the thinker may interpret as simply making a case, for instance, the feeler may understand as provoking an argument.

To prevent any defensiveness here, I'd like to emphatically state that no one type has a monopoly on starting conflicts, nor does any one type excel at dealing with them. Conflict can unfortunately bring the worst out in all of us. For example, TJs (thinking-judging types) tend to become overly rigid, while extraverts can become excessively loud and needlessly aggressive (Kroeger and Thuesen, 1993). In their work, Kroeger and Theusen have identified five steps to conflict resolution. This strategy is type sensitive. The five steps are listed below. Following the steps, I've paraphrased their recommendations for all types involved in conflict resolution.

Five Steps to Conflict Resolution

1. Define the issues involved.
2. Try to put the issues into a typological framework, ideally pinpointing them to a letter preference.
3. Examine the probable cause of the conflict, in typological terms if possible.
4. Ask each party involved to identify with the other's point of view.
5. Seek compromises or contracts that can move the conflict toward resolution.

A type-sensitive strategy for resolving conflicts requires that

- **extraverts** stop to look and listen. Care must be taken to appreciate the other person's point of view.
- **introverts** express themselves. They must be heard by extraverts, who sometimes won't let them get a word in edgewise.
- **sensors** get beyond the facts. Facts are sometimes misleading or perceived differently by different people. Look to extenuating circumstances. Other issues besides the facts may need to be taken into account.
- **intuitives** address the issues; they do not cloud the issues with vague generalities. They must try to deal with the specifics that contribute to the conflict at hand.
- **thinkers** allow for the possibility of expressing emotion. They must understand that expressing emotion and dealing with it is integral to successful conflict resolution.
- **feelers** be direct and confrontative. They must say what's on their minds. They shouldn't apologize for their feelings. Rather, they should just state them. Frankness will be appreciated.
- **judgers** recognize that they're not always right. They must stop seeing life and situations in purely black-and-white terms. They must accept the fact that judgers can be wrong.
- **perceivers** must learn to take a stand. They cannot forever remain flexible and undecided. Sooner or later decisions must be made and actions must be taken.

Personal "Shoulds" for Conflict Resolution

In the spaces provided below, list the four letters of your psychological type. Next to each letter, indicate what you should do or consider when faced with conflict, given the type-sensitive suggestions listed earlier.

My psychological type is

_____ (E or I)

_____ (S or N)

_____ (T or F)

_____ (J or P)

When in conflict with others, I should

(What should I do about my E or I attitude?)

_____

_____

(What should I notice about my S or N perceptions?)

_____

_____

(What should I realize about my T or F decision-making tendencies?)

_____

_____

(How should I deal with my J or P orientation to the external world?)

_____

_____

6.7   Win-Win Conflict Resolutions

The ideal resolution to conflict is **win-win.** In this case, everybody benefits and nobody loses. Of course, unequal power relationships, time constraints and other concerns sometimes make win-win resolutions to conflicts difficult to manage. But when conflicting parties are peers or colleagues with essentially equal power, and when they have a desire to achieve mutually beneficial outcomes, the collaborating or problem confronting style of conflict management is to be preferred; this style makes win-win outcomes most probable.

David Johnson (1999) has done an excellent job of explaining the steps involved in using the win-win confronting/collaborating style of conflict resolution. The step-by-step discussion that follows draws heavily from his work.

Seven Steps to Constructive Conflict Resolution Using the Collaborative Style

1.   Confront the opposing party.
2.   Define the conflict together.
3.   Communicate personal positions and feelings.
4.   Express cooperative intentions.
5.   Understand the conflict from the other party's viewpoint.
6.   Be motivated to resolve the conflict and to negotiate in good faith.
7.   Reach an agreement.

Step 1:   Confront the Opposing Party

If you're going to resolve any conflict constructively using the collaborative strategy, the first thing you have to do is to let the other person(s) know that a conflict exists. If the other party doesn't know that you're bothered or upset about something, then from that person's perspective, there is no conflict and nothing is wrong. When you properly confront another person, what you must do is express your view of the conflictual situation and relate your feelings about it, while inviting the other party to do the same.

Of course, whether you choose to confront depends on the quality of relationship, the importance you place on it, and how the person is likely to respond to the confrontation. As a general rule, the stronger or more solid the relationship, the more forceful the confrontation may be. As Johnson (1999) points out, however, if the other party in the conflict displays high anxiety and a low motivation for change, or if the confrontation will not be used as an invitation for self-examination, then confrontation should be avoided. "Whether you decide to open your mouth or button your lips depends on the other person and the situation" (Johnson, 1990: 239).

Step 2:   Define the Conflict Together

After you have confronted the other person, your second task is to define the conflict in a mutually agreeable fashion. Both of you must agree on what the problem, in fact, is. This must be done fairly and objectively and in a way that doesn't make anyone feel defensive.

Whey you try to arrive at a common definition of the problem, make efforts to avoid insults, veiled statements and negative value judgments. Personal attacks and prejudgments on the issues are not likely to take you very far down the road of constructive conflict resolution. Furthermore, when defining the conflict, try to be as clear and specific as possible. Leaving things vague or implicit may lead to misunderstandings and crossed communications. As part of defining the conflict situation, accurately describe your feelings and, for purposes of verification, reflect back to the other person her feelings as you experience and understand them. Try as well to control your passions as you describe your own actions and the actions of the other person that contribute to the conflict as you see it.

Step 3: Communicate Personal Positions and Feelings

During the process of conflict resolution, positions taken on issues may change, as may feelings on them. It is important, therefore, to keep the lines of communication open. If you're going to disagree with another person's position, you must know what that position is. The same is true if you wish to suggest changes to that position or if you wish to criticize it. If you don't understand how the other person's thoughts, feelings, wants and goals differ from your own, then the chances of reconciling your differences are jeopardized. Similarly, if the other person doesn't properly appreciate where you stand, or how your stand has changed, finding satisfactory solutions to the conflict will be much more difficult.

While exploring your positions in a conflict situation, seek to uncover precisely what your differences are. Also look for commonalities and points of agreement. Identify which behaviours, on both sides of the conflict, parties find objectionable. Explore possible solutions to the expressed conflict that would prove satisfying to all parties concerned. Think about the things both you and the other person need to do to resolve the conflict.

Step 4: Express Your Cooperative Intentions

If you're going to adopt a constructive orientation to conflict resolution in dealings with people whom you value, then you don't want differences to terminate or somehow undermine your relationships with them. It's a good idea, therefore, to make it clear to others that you don't wish to threaten friendships and ongoing associations. Make it known that you want to work together to reach a settlement that is agreeable to all. Show optimism and confidence that the conflict can eventually be resolved with the net effect of strengthening the bonds you have already established.

Step 5: Understand the Conflict from the Other Party's Viewpoint

Problems with conflict resolution sometimes arise because people remain "**cognitively egocentric**"; that is, they tend to see problems and conflicts only from their own psychological standpoint. They have difficulties "de-centring" from their own point of view to see things more objectively, from different angles and from other perspectives. I suspect that the more emotionally invested a person is in his own position, the more difficult it is for that individual to appreciate things from alternative vantage points. Certainly, if you wish to constructively resolve conflicts, you cannot ignore, fail to recognize or discount the perspectives of others. Such actions would violate the spirit of mutually respectful win-win negotiations.

Step 6: Be Motivated to Negotiate in Good Faith

It is important in win-win negotiations not to use dishonesty, deception or misrepresentation. Trying to fool people into believing they have gotten what they wanted, when you know this isn't true, is bargaining in **bad faith.** Healthy and long-lasting relationships cannot be based on lies, half-truths and broken promises. It is important, therefore, to be motivated by **honorable intentions.** Also, ask yourself if you really want to perpetuate the conflict. What would you gain by ending the conflict? What would the other person gain? What would you and the other person lose if you prolonged the dispute? Are the losses worth it? Are you both motivated, then, to come out as winners? Understand that people's motivations to terminate conflicts can change. If you can increase the gains for resolving conflict or show how the costs of continuing the conflict are likely to increase, you might be able to motivate conflicting parties to make quicker changes that would lead to a settlement of the conflict.

Step 7: Reach an Agreement

Once you have defined and confronted the problem, communicated personal positions and associated feelings; expressed cooperative intentions, understood the problem from alternative vantage points, negotiated in good faith, and shown your resolve to reach a solution, then it is time to finalize an agreement. A win-win agreement requires that everyone be satisfied and that they be committed to abide by the agreement. A successful resolution specifies clearly the shared position adopted. It also specifies how people will act differently in the future and how cooperation will be restored if someone backslides and acts inappropriately. It is also advantageous if conflicting parties can agree to meet later on in order to discuss how cooperation can be strengthened.

***

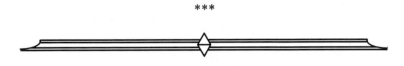

GENDERED VERBAL COMMUNICATION

Excerpts from Chapter 5 of Julia Wood's (2005), *Gendered Lives: Communication, Gender, and Culture, 5th Edition.* Belmont, CA: Wadsworth Publishing Company.

The tongue has the power of life and death.
PROVERBS 18.21

Consider these five sentences:

I now pronounce you man and wife.

Bob baby-sat his son while his wife attended a meeting.

Leave it to the French girl to make a Wimbledon fashion statement . . . Tatiana
Golovin had the hottest pants" (Cassidy, 2004, p. 3B)

Freshmen find it difficult to adjust to college life.

What do these sentences reflect about Western culture's views of women and men? The first sentence designates man an individual, whereas wife is defined only by her relationship to the man. In the second sentence, the word baby-sat implies that the father was performing a special service, one for which we usually pay. Have you ever heard someone say that a mother baby-sat her children? The third sentence defines an accomplished tennis player as a child (girl) and focuses on her sexy outfit, diverting attention from her athletic skill. Unless the fourth sentence refers to first-year students at an all-male school, the word freshmen erases first-year female students.

In this chapter and the one that follows, we examine relationships between communication and gender…In addition, we will consider how individuals embody or refuse to embody cultural expectations about gender-that is, how individual women's and men's communication reflects or challenges cultural prescriptions for femininity and masculinity.

Verbal Communication Expresses Cultural Views Of Gender

Language is one of our most complex symbol systems. The language we learn and use both reflects and reinforces cultural views and values, including those about gender.

Male Generic Language Excludes Women

One way that language erases women is through the use of male generic language, which purports to include both women and men yet refers specifically only to men. Examples of male generic language are nouns such as businessman, chairman, mailman, and mankind, and pronouns such as he used to refer to both women and men. Some people think that there is no problem with male generic language and that using inclusive language, such as he or she, is just about political correctness.

Research makes it clear that inclusive language is about something far more substantial than political correctness. In a classic study of the effects of male generics (Schneider & Hacker, 1973),

162

children were asked to select photographs for a textbook with chapters entitled "Urban Man" and "Man in Politics" or "Urban Life" and "Political Behavior?' The children almost always chose pictures of men when the titles included male generic language. When the titles did not refer only to men, the children chose more photographs that portrayed both sexes. The language of the titles shaped what they thought was appropriate to include in the chapters....Later research confirmed the finding that male generic language leads many people to assume only males are included (Beal, 1994; Gastil, 1990; Hamilton, 1991; Switzer, 1990).

***

Language Defines Men and Women Differently

Women are frequently defined by appearance or by relationships with others, whereas men are more typically defined by activities, accomplishments, or positions. For instance, coverage of women's sports frequently focuses more on women athletes' appearance than on their athletic skills. Stories about female athletes often emphasize wardrobes ("Venus is sporting a cool new outfit"), bodies ("She's gotten back in shape and is looking good on the field"), and hairstyles ("She's wearing a shorter cut with highlights"), whereas stories about male athletes focus on their athletic abilities ("He sunk two dream shots").

In the opening of this chapter, you read a reporter's description of Tatiana Golovin's hot pants. The same reporter noted that Maria Sharapova's "asymmetrical hemline was slit to the hip, adding a little sauce" (Cassidy, 2004, p. eB). An even more dramatic example of focusing on a woman athlete's appearance more than her skill is Frank Deford's article about Anna Kournikova, which was published in the June 2000 issue of Sports Illustrated. In addition to calling her "sports' hottest pinup girl" (p. 98), Deford referred to her as "the Jezebel of sweat" (p. 98) and stated that "on the court she is like a trim sloop, skimming across the surface" (p. 99). Kournikova is physically stunning, and she herself accents that. However, in focusing more on her sex appeal than on her skill on the courts, Deford defined her as more woman than tennis player. Can you imagine such descriptions of male athletes featured in Sports Illustrated?

***

Language also reflects social views of women as passive and men as active when engaged in sexual activity. Have you noticed that people say, "He laid her," "He balled her' "He screwed her' "She got laid' and "He made love to her"? Each of these phrases suggests that, in sexual activity, men are active, whereas women are passive. Perhaps because men are expected to be sexual initiators, inappropriate sexual initiative by men is sometimes described in language that makes it seem acceptable. For instance, why did no one challenge Arnold Schwarzenegger's use of "playful" and "rowdy" to describe the multiple incidents of sexual harassment revealed during his campaign for the governorship of California? And why did Fox news commentator Greta Van Susteren refer to Kobe Bryant's rape trial as a "sex scandal" (Morgan, 2003/2004, p. 95)? A sex scandal is about spouse-swapping or other unconventional but consensual sexual activity. Rape is not a sex scandal!

Our language also reflects society's view of women as defined by their relationships with others rather than as independent agents. When covering female newsmakers, news reports are more likely to include personal information, such as marital status and information about children, than when covering male newsmakers (Carter, 1998). On prime-time television, even professional women are often depicted primarily in interpersonal contexts, and their appearance is highlighted (Lott, 1989; Merritt, 2000).

In the West, a woman who doesn't marry and thus isn't defined in relation to a man has historically been viewed as a failure. For years, unmarried American women were called spinsters or old maids (contrast this with the nonpejorative term bachelor for men). Today, we seldom hear unmarried women described that way in this country. In Japan, however, unmarried women are called leftover, underdog, and parasite single (Onishi, 1998; Retherford, Ogawa, & Matsukura, 2001).

***

Language Shapes Awareness

Naming is important. We give names to things that matter to us. We don't bother to name what doesn't matter (Coates, 1997; Spender, 1984a, 1984b). The power of naming is clear with sexual harassment and date rape. For most of history, sexual harassment occurred frequently but was unnamed (Wood 1992b, 1993f). Because it wasn't named, sexual harassment was not visible or salient, making it difficult to recognize, think about, discipline, or stop. If sexual harassment was discussed at all, it was described as making advances, getting out of line, or being pushy. None of these phrases conveys the abusiveness of sexual harassment. Only when the term sexual harassment was coined did the general public recognize it as unwanted behavior that ties sexuality to security and advancement. And only with this awareness were efforts to redress sexual harassment devised.

Similarly, for many years women who were raped by their dates had no socially recognized way to name what had happened to them. Until we coined the term date rape, women had to deal with their experiences without the language to define and help them think about grievous violations that often had lifelong repercussions (Wriggins, 1998). Naming creates awareness.

***

Language Organizes Perceptions of Gender

We use language to organize experience and perceptions. Two ways in which language organizes perceptions of gender are stereotyping men and women and encouraging polarized perceptions of sex and gender.

A stereotype is a generalization about an entire class of phenomena based on some knowledge of some members of the class. For example, if most women you know aren't interested in sports, you might stereotype women as uninterested in sports. This stereotype could keep you from noticing that many women engage in sports and enjoy attending athletic events. Relying on stereotypes can lead us to overlook important qualities of individuals and to perceive them only in terms of what we consider common to a general category.

Many people stereotype women as emotional and weak and men as rational and strong. Stereotypes such as these can distort our perceptions. For instance, women's arguments are sometimes dismissed as emotional when in fact they involve evidence and reasoning (Mapstone, 1998). The stereotype of women as emotional can lead people to judge women's ideas in terms of the stereotype, not the reality. A man who has an emotional outburst may be perceived as forcefully stating his ideas, because he is seen through the stereotype of men as rational.

The English language may also encourage polarized thinking, which is conceiving of things as absolute opposites. Something is right or wrong, good or bad, appropriate or inappropriate. Our vocabulary emphasizes all-or-none terms and thus all-or-none thinking. English includes few words that indicate degrees and increments.

Polarized language and thinking are particularly evident in how we think about gender: People are divided into two sexes, male and female, which are translated into two genders, masculine and feminine. In reality, of course, most of us have a number of qualities, some of which our society designates as feminine and some as masculine. Our culture's binary labels for sexual identity encourage us not to notice how much variation there is among women and among men (Lorber, 2001). Because our language encourages polarized thinking, men who don't conform to social views of masculinity and women who don't conform to social views of femininity are often judged negatively. Research indicates that women who use the assertive speech associated with masculinity are frequently perceived as arrogant and rude, whereas men who employ the emotional language associated with femininity are often perceived to be "wimps" or gay (Rasmussen & Moley, 1986).

***

Language Evaluates Gender

Language reflects cultural values and is a powerful influence on our perceptions. Despite progress in reducing sexism, language continues to devalue females and femininity by trivializing, deprecating, and diminishing women and anything associated with femininity.

Women are often described in trivializing terms. Numerous terms label women as immature or juvenile (baby doll, girlie, little darling) or equate them with food (dish, feast for the eyes, good enough to eat, sugar, sweet thing, cookie, cupcake, hot tomato) and animals (catty, chick, pig dog, cow, bitch).

Diminutive suffixes designate women as reduced forms of the standard (male) form of the word: suffragette, majorette. Calling women girls (a term that technically refers to a female who has not gone through puberty) defines them as children, not adults. Women who are sexually active may be called derogatory names such as slut or worse, whereas men who are equally sexually active are described with complimentary language such as stud.

Language Allows Self-Reflection

Because we are symbol users, we name not only the phenomena around us but also ourselves. For instance, one alternative to traditional sex-typing is androgyny…Androgynous people possess qualities the culture defines as masculine and feminine instead of only those assigned to one sex. Androgynous women and men are, for example, both assertive and sensitive, both ambitious and compassionate (Bern, 1993). Many women and men decide not to limit themselves only to those qualities society associates with one gender.

Larry May (1998b) has a different idea for defining new versions of gender. He suggests that men should define themselves as taking a "progressive male stand-point" that encourages men to adopt some traditionally masculine qualities, such as ambition and competitiveness, but to reject other traditionally masculine qualities, such as domination and violence. May's vision of ideal masculinity calls on men to "accept responsibility for the men they are and to strive toward the men they can become" (p. 151). Because May's research focuses on men, he has not defined a parallel progressive female standpoint. You might want to think about which traditionally feminine qualities would and would not fit within a progressive female standpoint.

Gendered Interaction: Masculine And Feminine Styles Of Verbal Communication

In addition to expressing cultural views of gender, language reflects our own gendered identities. In the pages that follow, we'll explore masculine and feminine styles of speech and some of the confusion that results from differences between them. Keep in mind that we're looking at gendered styles of communicating, not necessarily sex-based styles. In other words, although most girls learn feminine style, some boys also do, and although most boys learn masculine style, some girls also do. We want to understand how each style evolves, what it involves, and how to interpret verbal communication in ways that honor the standpoints of those using it.

Gendered Speech Communities

Philosopher Suzanne Langer (1953, 1979) asserted that culture, or collective life, is possible only to the extent that a group of people share a symbol system and the meanings encapsulated in it. Langer's attention to the ways in which language sustains cultural life is consistent with the symbolic interactionist and cultural theories that we discussed in Chapter 2. William Labov (1972) extended Langer's ideas by defining a speech community as a group of people who share norms about communication. By this, he meant that a speech community exists when people share understandings about goals of communication, strategies for enacting those goals, and ways of interpreting communication.

It's obvious that we have entered a different speech community when we travel in countries whose languages differ from our own. Distinct speech communities are less apparent when they rely on the same language but use it in different ways and attach different meanings to it. Yet, there are speech communities defined by race-ethnicity, economic class, and gender. As we noted in Chapter 2, our standpoint influences what we know and how we act. Standpoint theory also implies that distinct communication styles evolve out of different standpoints.

Studies of gender and communication convincingly show that most girls and women and boys and men are socialized into distinct speech communities (Campbell, 1973; Coates, 1986, 1997; Coates & Cameron, 1989; Johnson, 2000). To understand these different communities, we will first consider how we are socialized into feminine and masculine speech communities. After this, we will explore divergence in feminine and masculine speech communities. Please note the importance of the word typically and other words that indicate we are discussing general differences, not absolute ones. Not all women learn and use a feminine style of communication, and not all men learn or choose to adopt a masculine style of communication.

The Lessons of Children's Play

Initial insight into the importance of children's play in shaping patterns of communication came from a classic study by Daniel Maltz and Ruth Borker (1982). As they watched young children engaged in recreation, the researchers were struck by two observations: Young children almost always play in sex-segregated groups, and girls and boys tend to play different kinds of games. Maltz and Borker found that boys' games (football, baseball) and girls' games (school, house, jump rope) cultivate distinct ways to communicate.

More recent research on children's play confirms Maltz and Borker's original findings. Sex-segregated groups remain the norm for children in the United States (Clark, 1998; Goodwin, 1990; Gray & Feldman, 1997; Kovacs, Parker, & Hoffman, 1996; Maccoby, 1998; McGuffey & Rich, 2004; Moller & Serbin, 1996). Even children as young as 2 or 3 years old (about the time that gender constancy develops) show a preference for same-sex playmates (Martin, 1991, 1994, 1997; Ruble & Martin, 1998).

Boys' games. Boys' games usually involve fairly large groups nine individuals for each baseball team, for instance. Most boys' games are competitive, have clear goals, involve physically rough play, and are organized by rules and roles that specify who does what and how to play (Alexander & Hines, 1994; Pollack, 2000).

Because the games boys typically play are structured by goals, rules, and roles, there is little need to discuss how to play, although there may be talk about strategies to reach goals. In playing games, boys learn to communicate to accomplish goals, compete for and maintain status, exert control over others, get attention, and stand out (Messner, 1997a). Specifically, boys' games cultivate four communication rules:

1. Use communication to assert your ideas, opinions, and identity.
2. Use talk to achieve something, such as solving problems or developing strategies.
3. Use communication to attract and maintain others' attention.
4. Use communication to compete for the "talk stage?' Make yourself stand out; take attention away from others, and get others to pay attention to you.

These communication rules are consistent with other aspects of masculine socialization that we have discussed. For instance, notice the emphasis on individuality and competition. Also, we see that these rules accent achievement doing something, accomplishing a goal. Boys learn they must do things to be valued members of the team. Finally, we see the undercurrent of masculinity's emphasis on invulnerability: If your goal is to control and to be better than others, you cannot let them know too much about yourself and your weaknesses.

Girls' games. Turning now to games girls have traditionally played, we find that quite different patterns exist, and they lead to distinct ways of communicating. Girls tend to play in pairs or in very small groups rather than large ones (Benenson, Del Bianco, Philippoussis, & Apostoleris, 1997). Also, games such as house and school do not have preset, clear-cut goals and roles. There is no touchdown in playing house, and the roles of daddy and mommy aren't fixed like the roles of guard and forward. Because traditional girls' games are not highly structured by external goals and roles, players have to talk among themselves to decide what to do and what roles to play.

When playing, young girls spend more time talking than doing anything else- a pattern that is not true of young boys (Goodwin, 1990; Maccoby, 1998). Playing house, for instance, typically begins with a discussion about who is going to be the daddy and who the mommy. The lack of stipulated goals for the games is also important because it tends to cultivate girls' skill in interpersonal processes. The games generally played by girls teach four basic rules for communication:

1. Use communication to create and maintain relationships. The process of communication, not its content, is the heart of relationships.
2. Use communication to establish egalitarian relations with others. Don't outdo, criticize, or put down others. If you have to criticize, be gentle.
3. Use communication to include others-bring them into conversations, respond to their ideas.
4. Use communication to show sensitivity to others and relationships.

The typically small size of girls' playgroups fosters cooperative discussion and an open-ended process of talking to organize activity, whereas the larger groups in which boys usually play encourage competition and external rules to structure activity (Campbell, 1993). In a study of preschoolers, boys gave orders and attempted to control others, whereas girls were more likely to make requests and cooperate with others (Weiss & Sachs, 1991). In another investigation, 9- to 14-year-old African American girls typically used inclusive and nondirective language, whereas African American boys tended to issue commands and compete for status in their groups (Goodwin, 1990).   -

The conclusion from much research is that girls tend to engage in more affiliative, cooperative play, whereas boys tend to engage in more instrumental and competitive play (Fabes, 1994; Harris, 1998; Leaper, 1991, 1994, 1996). The lessons of children's play are carried forward. The basic rules of communication that many adult women and men employ are refined and elaborated versions of those learned in childhood games (Clark, 1998; Mulac, 1998).

Erin offered this comment in 2005 when she was a student in my class. She's right that young girls today often play competitive sports and that doing so allows them to learn and use the rules of masculine speech communities. This is consistent with standpoint theory's premise that members of subordinated groups are motivated to learn the standpoint of dominant groups. However, Erin is not entirely correct in saying that children's games are no longer sex segregated. How many boys play house and school? It is much more acceptable and much more common for girls to play traditional boy games than vice versa.

Gendered Communication Practices

We will consider features of feminine and masculine speech that have been identified by researchers. We'll also explore some of the complications that arise when people of different genders operate by different rules in conversations with each other.

Feminine speech. People who are socialized in feminine speech communities -most women and some men - tend to regard communication as a primary way to establish and maintain relationships with others. They engage in conversation to share themselves and to learn about others (Johnson, 1996). For feminine people, talk is the essence of relationships. Consistent with this primary goal, feminine people use language to foster connections, support, closeness, and understanding.

Establishing equality between people is important in feminine communication. To achieve symmetry, communicators often match experiences to indicate "You're not alone in how you feel." Typical ways to communicate equality would be saying, "I've felt just like that" or "Something like that happened to me, too, and I felt like you do." Growing out of the quest for equality is a participatory mode of interacting in which communicators respond to and build on each other's ideas in the process of conversing

167

(Hall & Langellier, 1988). Rather than a rigid "You tell your ideas, then I'll tell mine" sequence, feminine speech more characteristically follows an interactive pattern in which different voices inter- weave to create conversations.

Also characteristic of feminine speech is support for others. To demonstrate support, communicators often express understanding and sympathy with a friend's situation or feelings. "Oh, you must feel terrible" communicates that we under- stand and support how another feels. Related to these first two features is attention to the relationship level of communication (Eisenberg, 2002; MacGeorge, Gfflihan, Samter, & Clark, 2003). You will recall that the relationship level of talk focuses on feelings and on the relationship between communicators rather than on the content of messages. Conversations between feminine people tend to be characterized by many questions that probe for greater understanding of feelings and perceptions surrounding the subject of talk (Alexander & Wood, 2000; Dunn, 1999). "How did you feel when it occurred?" "How does this fit into the overall relationship?" are probes that help a listener understand a speaker's perspective.

A fourth feature of feminine speech style is conversational "maintenance work" (Fishman, 1978; Taylor, 2002). This involves efforts to sustain conversation by inviting others to speak and by prompting them to elaborate their ideas. Questions are often used to include others: "How was your day?" "Did anything interesting happen on your trip?" "Do you have anything to add?" Communication of this sort maintains interaction and opens the conversational door to others.

`A fifth quality of feminine speech is responsiveness. A feminine person might make eye contact, nod, or say "Tell me more" or "That's interesting?' Responsive- ness reflects learned tendencies to care about others and to make them feel valued and included (Chatham-Carpenter & DeFrancisco, 1998). It affirms the other person and encourages elaboration by showing interest in what was said.

A sixth quality of feminine talk is personal, concrete style (Campbell, 1973; Hall & Langellier, 1988). Typical of feminine talk are details, personal disclosures, anecdotes, and concrete reasoning. These features cultivate a personal tone, and they facilitate feelings of closeness by connecting communicators' lives.

A final feature of feminine speech is tentativeness. This may be expressed in a number of forms. Sometimes people use verbal hedges, such as "I kind of feel you may be overreacting." In other situations, they qualify statements by saying, "I'm probably not the best judge of this, but . ." Another way to keep talk provisional is to tag a question onto a statement in a way that invites another to respond: "Mr. and Mrs. Smith was a pretty good movie, wasn't it?" Tentative communication leaves the door open for others to respond and express their opinions.

There has been controversy about tentativeness associated with feminine speech. Robin Lakoff (1975), who first reported that women use more hedges, qualifiers, and tag questions than men, claimed that these indicate uncertainty and lack of confidence. Calling women's speech "powerless' Lakoff argued that it reflects women's low self- esteem and socialization into subordinate roles. It's important to note that Lakoff's judgment that feminine speech is powerless was based on the assumption that masculine speech is the standard. If we use feminine speech as the standard, the use of hedges, qualifiers, and tag questions may reflect not powerlessness but the desire to keep conversations open and to include others (Mills, 1999; Wood & Lenze, 1991b). You should realize, however, that people outside feminine speech communities may use masculine standards, as Lakoff did, to interpret tentative speech.

Masculine speech. Masculine speech communities tend to regard talk as a way to accomplish concrete goals, exert control, preserve independence, entertain, and enhance status. Conversation is often seen as an arena for proving oneself and negotiating prestige.

The first feature of masculine speech is the effort to establish status and control. Masculine speakers do this by asserting their ideas and authority, telling jokes and stories, or challenging others. Equally typical is the tendency to avoid disclosing personal information that might

168

make a man appear weak and vulnerable (Lewis & McCarthy, 1988; Saurer & Eisler, 1990). One way to exhibit knowledge and control is to give advice. For example, a person might say, " the way you should handle that is... " or "Don't let your boss get to you." On the relationship level of meaning, people socialized in feminine interpret advice as the speaker saying she or he is superior smarter, more experienced, etc.-to the other person.

A second prominent feature of masculine speech is instrumentality the use of speech to accomplish instrumental objectives. In conversation, this is often expressed through problem-solving efforts to get information, discover facts, and suggest solutions. Conversations between women and men are often derailed by the lack of agreement on the meaning of this informational, instrumental focus. To many women, it feels as if men don't care about their feelings. When a man focuses on the content level of meaning after a woman has disclosed a problem, she may feel that he is disregarding her emotions. He, on the other hand, thinks he is supporting her in the way that he has learned to show support by suggesting how to solve the problem.

A third feature of masculine communication is conversational command. Despite jokes about women's talkativeness, research indicates that, in most contexts, men tend to talk more often and at greater length than women. This tendency, although not present in infancy, is evident in preschoolers (Austin, Salehi, & Leffler, 1987). Compared with girls and women, boys and men talk more frequently and for longer periods of time both in face-to-face conversation, on Usenet, and in e-mail discussion groups (Aries, 1987; Crowston & Kammeres, 1998). Further, masculine speakers may reroute conversations by using what another says as a jumping off point for their own topics, or they may interrupt. Although both sexes interrupt, most research suggests that men do it more frequently (Johnson, 2000; Mulac, Wiemann, Widenmann, & Gibson, 1988; West & Zimmerman, 1983).

Not only do men interrupt more than women, they may do so for different reasons. Research indicates that men are more likely to interrupt to control conversation by challenging other speakers or wresting the talk stage from them, whereas women interrupt to indicate interest and respond to others (Anderson & Leaper, 1998; Aries, 1987; Mulac et al., 1988; Stewart, Stewart, Friedley, & Cooper, 1996). A different explanation is that men generally interrupt more than women because interruptions are considered normal and good-natured within the norms of masculine speech communities (Wood, 1998). Whereas interruptions that reroute conversation might be viewed as impolite and intrusive in feminine speech communities, the outgoing, give and take character of masculine speech may render interruptions just part of normal conversation.

Fourth, masculine speech tends to be direct and assertive. Compared with women's language, men's is typically more forceful and authoritative (Murphy & Zorn, 1996; Wood, Christiansen, Hebi, & Rothgerber, 1997). Tentative forms of speech, such as hedges and disclaimers, are used less frequently by men than by women. When another person does not understand or follow masculine rules of communication, however, speech that is absolute and directive may seem to close off conversation and leave no room for others to speak.

Fifth, masculine speech tends to be more abstract than feminine speech. Men frequently speak in general terms that are removed from concrete experiences and distanced from personal feelings (Johnson, 2000). The abstract style typical of many men's speech reflects the public and impersonal contexts in which they often operate and the less personal emphasis in their speech communities. Within public environments, norms for speaking call for theoretical, conceptual, and general thought and communication. Yet, within more personal relationships abstract talk sometimes creates barriers to intimacy.

Finally, masculine speech tends to be less emotionally responsive than feminine speech, especially on the relationship level of meaning. Men, more than women, give what are called minimal response cues (Parlee, 1979), which are verbalizations such as "yeah" or "umhmm." People socialized into feminine speech communities may perceive minimal response cues as indicating lack of involvement (Fishman, 1978; Stewart et al., 1996). Men's conversation also often lacks self-disclosure as well as expressed sympathy and understanding (Eisenberg, 2002; Lynch & Kilmartin, 1999). Within the rules of masculine speech communities, sympathy is a sign of condescension, and the revealing of personal problems is seen as making one vulnerable. Yet, within feminine speech communities sympathy and disclosure are understood as demonstrations of equality and support. This creates potential for misunderstanding between women and men.

Gender-Based Misinterpretations in Communication

In this final section, we explore what happens in conversations between people from different gender speech communities. We'll consider five communication misunderstandings that can arise.

Showing support. Martha tells George that she is worried about her friend Betsy. George gives a minimal response cue, saying only, "Oh." To Martha, this suggests he isn't interested, because women make and expect more of what Deborah Tannen (1986) calls "listening noises" to signal interest. Yet, if George operates according to norms of masculine speech communities, he is probably thinking that, if Martha wants to tell him something, she will. Masculine rules of speech assume people use talk to assert themselves.

Even without much encouragement, Martha continues by describing the ten- sion in Betsy's marriage and her own desire to help. She says, "I feel so bad for Betsy, and I want to help her, but I don't know what to do." George then says, "It's her problem, not yours. Just butt out." At this, Martha explodes: "Who asked for your advice?" George is now completely confused. He thought Martha wanted advice, so he gave it. She is hurt that George didn't tune into her feelings. Both are frustrated.

The problem is not so much what George and Martha say and don't say. Rather, it's how they interpret each other's communication actually, how they misinterpret it, because they fail to understand that they are operating by different rules of communication. George is respecting Martha's independence by not pushing her to talk. When he thinks she wants advice, he offers it in an effort to help. Martha, on the other hand, wants comfort and a connection with George- that's her primary purpose in talking with him. To her, George's advice seems to dismiss her feelings. He doesn't offer sympathy, because masculine rules for communication define this as condescending. Yet, the feminine speech community in which Martha was socialized taught her that giving sympathy is a way to show support.

"Troubles talk." Talk about troubles, or personal problems, is a kind of interaction in which hurt feelings may result from the contrast between masculine and feminine styles of communicating. Naomi might tell her partner, Greg, that she is feeling down because she didn't get a job she wanted. In an effort to be supportive, Greg might respond by saying, "You shouldn't feel bad. Lots of people don't get jobs they want." To Naomi, this seems to dismiss her feelings-to belittle them by saying lots of people experience her situation. Yet within masculine speech communities, you show respect by assuming that others don't need sympathy.

Now, let's turn the tables and see what happens when Greg feels troubled. When he meets Naomi, Greg is unusually quiet because he feels down about not getting a job offer. Sensing that something is wrong, Naomi tries to show interest by asking, "Are you okay? What's bothering you?" Greg feels she is imposing and trying to get him to show a vulnerability he prefers to keep to himself. Naomi probes further to show she cares. As a result, he feels intruded on and withdraws further. Then Naomi feels shut out.

But perhaps Greg does decide to tell Naomi why he feels down. After hearing about his rejection letter, Naomi says, "I know how you feel. I felt so low when I didn't get that position at Datanet." She is matching experiences to show Greg that she understands his feelings and that he's not alone (Basow & Rubenfeld, 2003). According to the communication rules that Greg learned in a masculine speech community, however, Naomi's comment about her own experience is an effort to steal the center stage from him and focus on herself.

The point of the story. Another instance in which feminine and masculine communication rules often clash is in relating experiences. Masculine speech tends to follow a linear pattern, in which major points in a story are presented sequentially to get to the climax. Talk tends to be straight forward without a great many details. The rules of feminine speech, however, call for more detailed, less linear storytelling. Whereas a man is likely to provide rather bare information about what happened, a woman is more likely to embed the information within a larger context of the people involved and other things going on (Wood, 1998, 2000). Women include details, not because they -- are important at the content level of meaning but because they matter at the relationship level of meaning. Recounting details is meant to increase involvement between people and to invite a conversational partner to be fully engaged in the situation being described.

Because feminine and masculine rules about details differ, men often find feminine accounts wandering and tedious. Conversely, the masculine style of story- telling may strike women as leaving out all the interesting details. Many a discussion between women and men has ended either with his exasperated demand, "Can't you get to the point?" or with her frustrated question, "Why don't you tell me how you were feeling and what else was going on?" She wants more details than his rules call for; he is interested in fewer details than she has learned to supply.

Relationship talk. "Can we talk about us?" is the opening of innumerable conversations that end in misunderstanding and hurt. In general, men are interested in discussing relationships only if there are particular problems to be addressed. In contrast, women generally find it pleasurable to talk about important relation- ships even-or perhaps especially-when there are no problems (Acitelli, 1988).

The difference here grows out of the fact that masculine speech communities view communication as a means to doing things and solving problems, whereas feminine speech communities regard the process of communicating as a primary way to create and sustain relationships. No wonder many men duck when their partners want to "discuss the relationship' and women often feel a relationship is in trouble when their partners don't want to talk about it.

Public speaking. Differences in feminine and masculine communication pat- terns also surface in public contexts. Historically, men have dominated politics. Thus, it's not surprising that the assertive, dominant, confident masculine style is the standard for public speaking. This male generic standard for public speaking means that feminine speakers are judged by a standard that neither reflects nor respects their communication goals and values (Campbell & Jerry, 1988). Women who are effective in politics tend to manage a fine balance in which they are sufficiently feminine to be perceived as acting appropriately for women and sufficiently masculine to be perceived as acting appropriately for politicians. Women who are considered effective public speakers, such as former Texas governor Ann Richards, manage to combine the traditionally feminine and masculine communication styles (Dow & Torn, 1993).

These are only five of many situations in which differences between feminine and masculine communication styles may lead to misunderstandings. Many people find they can improve their relationships by understanding and using both feminine and masculine communication styles. When partners understand how to interpret each other's rules, they are less likely to misread motives. In addition, when they learn to speak the other's language, they become more gratifying conversational partners, and they enhance the quality of their relationships.

***

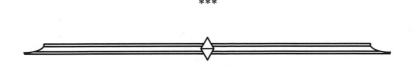

READING FOURTEEN

INTERPERSONAL ATTRACTION: FROM FIRST IMPRESSION TO CLOSE RELATIONSHIPS

Excerpts from Chapter 9 of Aronson, E., Wilson, T., Akert, R., Fehr, B. (2007) *Social Psychology, 3rd Canadian Edition.* Toronto, Pearson Education.

***

"Then I met Nina." These four little words changed a man's life. A few years ago, Bradley Bird, a Canadian newspaper writer in his early forties, was on a trip, covering a series of sad dark events-the experiences of Chechen refugees and conflict in Kosovo and Kurdish Turkey. As he wearily boarded a bus in Georgia (near Russia), bracing himself for the 20-hour ride to northeast Turkey for one last story, a woman took the seat beside him. She was a tall, attractive, raven-haired woman in her thirties. As the bus headed into the night, the woman turned to him and asked his name. Bradley recalls, "I looked at her seriously for the first time and was pleased to see a face as lovely as I'd ever beheld, with dark mysterious eyes, a perfect nose, and full red lips" (Bird, 2001). The woman's name was Nina. To Bradley's surprise, he found himself asking her if there was a man in her life. She answered "no." He surprised himself still more by saying, 'You need me, and I need you." Because she said she spoke only a little English, he repeated it to make sure she understood. She smiled, and they gazed into each other's eyes. It was midnight and the driver turned off the interior lights. Her arm brushed against his in the darkness. "The sensation was incredible," Bradley exclaims, 'electric, and I couldn't stop myself; I gave her arm a gentle squeeze." Nina reciprocated.

At first they tried to hide their feelings from the other passengers but, 12 hours into the ride, they were unable to contain their joy. Bradley informed the driver that his plans had changed and he would now stay on the bus an additional 13 hours so he could have more time with Nina. The driver and passengers began to celebrate with them. An older, heavy man brought out a bottle of vodka to mark the occasion. Bradley reports that by then he and Nina were inseparable and began to make plans for her to come to Canada. He begged to accompany her to Sophia, Bulgaria, where she was going to visit her sister, but she refused. So, he got off the bus in Istanbul and, instead of flying home as scheduled, waited there for three weeks, hoping to catch Nina on her way back to Georgia. During that time he tried to reach her at her sister's, but the phone number she had given him didn't work. Reluctantly, he returned home and mailed her the documents she would need to get a visa. It was May.

Nina wrote back, assuring Bradley of her desire to be with him. She also told him he would have to return to Turkey and plead her case to the Canadian embassy there. By this time, it was August, and Bradley had accepted a teaching position. What to do now? The answer was clear. Bradley promptly quit his job and spent the next few months trying to reach Nina to make arrangements for them to meet in Turkey. The phone lines were always busy or not working. In December, he decided he simply had to take action. He booked a flight to Turkey and two tickets to return to Canada. He managed to track down Nina's sister in Bulgaria and asked her to let Nina know that he was coming. 'Oh, Bradley," she said, "Nina is back with her husband. Her daughter insisted on it." With those words, Bradley's dream of a life with Nina was shattered. But Bradley Bird isn't bitter. In his words: "I will always be grateful to Nina for giving me 33 of the happiest hours of my adult life" (Bird, 2001).

As Bradley Bird's experience illustrates, the need to love and be loved is one of the most fundamental human needs. Despite all of the warning signs -the fact that he had just met this woman and knew nothing about her, and had been given the wrong phone number for her sister in Bulgaria - Bradley just couldn't help himself. He fell in love with the mysterious Nina, and it changed his life. This man in his forties, who had experienced other relationships (he was once married), describes the bus ride with Nina as the happiest 33 hours of his adult life!

What, exactly, is love, and why are we so motivated to seek it? Or perhaps the question should be why are we so motivated to seek it even when it comes at a high cost? Research conducted by Susan Boon and Karen Pasveer (1999) at the University of Calgary suggests that people are well aware of the risks associated with relationships. One of their participants, a 26-year-old woman, wrote:

> Some of my friends who aren't in relationships are dying to get into one. I don't understand why because most of the time it's a more hurtful than it is an enjoyable experience. I told them, "Enjoy being single because it's more fun and I think it's a lot less hassle." Getting into a relationship ... falling for somebody, and you're bound to set yourself up for a lot of hurt ... and misery."

Despite the hurt and misery, most people are highly motivated to find love. Why? This is one of the basic questions to be addressed in this chapter.

We will discuss the antecedents of attraction, from the initial liking of two people meeting for the first time to the love that develops in close relationships.

***

Major Antecedents of Attraction

When social psychologist Ellen Berscheid asked people of various ages what made them happy, at or near the top of their lists were making and maintaining friendships and having positive, warm relationships (Berscheid, 1985; Berscheid & Peplau, 1983; Berscheid & Reis, 1998). The absence of meaningful relationships with other people makes people feel lonely, worthless, hopeless, helpless, powerless, and alienated (Baumeister & Leary, 1995; Hartup & Stevens, 1997; Peplau & Penman, 1982, Stroebe & Stroebe, 1996). We start this chapter with research on what attracts people to one another in the first place.

The Person Next Door: The Propinquity Effect

One of the simplest determinants of interpersonal attraction is proximity-sometimes called propinquity. The people who, by chance, you see and interact with most often are most likely to become your friends and lovers (Berscheid & Reis, 1998; Fehr, 1996; Moreland & Beach, 1992; Newcomb, 1961; Segal, 1974). This includes people in your city, your neighbourhood, and on your street. Now, this might seem obvious. However, the striking thing about proximity and attraction, or the propinquity effect as social psychologists call it, is that it works on a micro level.

Consider a classic study conducted in a housing complex for married students at the Massachusetts Institute for Technology. Leon Festinger, Stanley Schachter, and Kurt Back (1950) tracked friendship formation among the couples in the various apartment buildings. For example, one section of the complex, Westgate West, was composed of 17 two-storey buildings, each having 10 apartments. The residents had been assigned to their apartments at random as vacancies opened up, and nearly all of them were strangers when they moved in. The researchers asked the residents to name their three closest friends in the housing project. Just as the propinquity effect would predict, 65 percent of the residents mentioned people who lived in the same building, even though the other buildings were not far away. Even more striking was the pattern of friendships within a building...The researchers found that 41 percent of the next-door neighbours indicated that they were close friends, 22 percent of those who lived two doors apart did so, and only 10 percent of those who lived on opposite ends of the hall did so.

Festinger and colleagues (1950) demonstrated that attraction and propinquity rely not only on actual physical distance but also on the more psychological, functional distance. Functional distance is defined as certain aspects of architectural design that make it likely that some people will come into contact with each other more often than with others…Couples living at the foot of the stairs, and in one case near the mailboxes, saw a great deal of upstairs residents…

The propinquity effect works because of familiarity, or the mere exposure effect - the more exposure we have to a stimulus, the more apt we are to like it. We see certain people a lot, and the more familiar they become, the more friendship blooms. Of course, if the person in question is an obnoxious jerk, then, not surprisingly, the more exposure you have to him or her, the greater your dislike (Swap, 1977). However, in the absence of such negative qualities, familiarity breeds attraction and liking (Bornstein, 1989; Bornstein & D'Agostino, 1992; Griffin & Sparks, 1990; Moreland & Zajonc, 1982; Zajonc, 1968).

A good example of the propinquity and mere exposure effects is your classroom. All semester long, you see the same people. Does this increase your liking for them? Richard Moreland and Scott Beach (1992) tested this hypothesis by planting female research confederates in a large university classroom. The women did not interact with the professor or the other students; they simply walked in and sat quietly in the first row, where everyone could see them. The confederates differed in how many classes they attended, from 15 meetings down to the control condition of zero. At the end of the semester, the students in the class were shown slides of the women, whom they rated on several measures of liking and attractiveness… mere exposure had a definite effect on liking. Even though they had never interacted, the students liked the woman more, the more often they had seen her in class.

Before leaving this topic, we should note that familiarity can occur without physical exposure. These days strangers can get to know each other through electronic mail and computer chat rooms. Computer-mediated communication offers a twist on the propinquity effect; the fact that someone is thousands of kilometres away no longer means you can't encounter him or her. Are computer-based relationships the same as ones formed in everyday life? Do computer relationships survive when they move from the computer screen to face-to-face interactions? Researchers are beginning to explore these questions …

For example, recent laboratory experiments have shown that people report being more comfortable revealing their "true" self to a partner over the Internet compared to a face-to-face interaction (Bargh, McKenna, & Fitzsimons, 2002; McKenna, Green, & Gleason, 2002). Interestingly, McKenna et a!. (2002) found that participants also tended to report more liking for an Internet partner than a partner they met in person - even when, unbeknownst to the participants, it was actually the same person! Perhaps most importantly, research is showing that relationships formed over the Internet resemble those developed face-to-face in terms of quality and depth (Bargh & McKenna, 2004). In addition, a recent two year follow up of romantic relationships originally formed over the Internet found that breakup rates were similar to those generally reported for relationships formed in person (McKenna et al., 2002)…

Similarity

While propinquity does affect friendship choices, it is also the case that we don't become good friends with everyone who is near us in physical space. The "fuel" is similarity - the match between our interests, background, attitudes, and values and those of the other person. Are we more attracted to people who are like us (the concept of similarity), or are we more attracted to people who are our opposites (the concept of complementarity)? Folk wisdom may suggest that "opposites attract," but research evidence proves that it is similarity, not complementarity, that draws people together (Berscheid & Reis, 1998).

Dozens of tightly controlled experiments have shown, for example, that, if all you know about a person whom you've never met is his or her opinions on several issues, the more similar those opinions are to yours, the more you will like him or her (Byrne, 1997; Byrne & Nelson, 1965; McPherson, Smith-Lovin, & Cook, 2001). And what happens when you do meet? In a classic study, Theodore Newcomb (1961) randomly assigned male students at the University of Michigan to be roomates in a particular dormitory at the start of the school year. Would similarity predict friendship formation? The answer was yes. Men became friends with those who were demographically similar (e.g., shared a rural background), as well as with those who were similar in attitudes and values (e.g., were also engineering majors or also held liberal political views).

Since Newcomb conducted this research, dozens of studies have demonstrated that similarity in terms of attitudes and values is an important predictor of attraction in both friendships and romantic relationships (Fehr, 1996). Similarity in other domains matters as well. For example, we are more likely to be attracted to someone who enjoys the same kinds of leisure activities that we do (Werner & Parmelee, 1979); in fact, according to a study conducted at the University of Waterloo, for some people, similarity in terms of activity preferences is a stronger predictor of attraction than is similarity of attitudes (Jamieson, Lydon, & Zanna, 1987). We also are attracted to people who are similar to us in terms of interpersonal style and communication skills (Burleson & Samter, 1996).

Why is similarity so important in attraction? There are several possibilities. First, we tend to think that people who are similar to us will be inclined to like us. Given this reasonable assumption, we take the first steps and initiate a relationship (Berscheid, 1985; Condon & Crano, 1988). Second, people who are similar provide us with important social validation for our characteristics and beliefs - that is, they provide us with the feeling that we are right (Byrne & Clore, 1970)...In addition to feeling validated, recent research suggests that we are more likely to feel understood by those who are similar to us. Murray, Holmes, Bellavia, Griffin, and Dolderman (2002) found that students in dating relationships and married couples living in the Kitchener-Waterloo area overestimated the degree of similarity between themselves and their partner. The greater the similarity they perceived, the more understood they felt by their partner. Feelings of understanding, in turn, predicted relationship satisfaction...

***

Reciprocal Liking

Most of us like to be liked. Not surprisingly, reciprocal liking liking someone who likes us in return - is one of the prime determinants of interpersonal attraction. Liking is so powerful it can even make up for the absence of similarity. In one experiment, for example, when a young woman expressed interest in male research participants simply by maintaining eye contact, leaning toward them, and listening attentively, the men expressed great liking for her despite the fact that they knew she disagreed with them on important issues (Gold, Ryckman, & Mosley, 1984). Whether the clues are nonverbal or verbal, perhaps the most crucial determinant of whether we will like someone is the extent I) which we believe that person likes us (Berscheid & Walster [Hatfield], 1978; Condon & rano, 1988; Kenny, 1994; Kubitscheck & Hallinan, 1998; Secord & Backman, 1964).

Interestingly, reciprocal liking can come about because of a self-fulfilling prophecy (see Chapter 3), as demonstrated in an experiment by Rebecca Curtis and Kim Miller (1986). University students who did not know one another took part in the study in pairs. The researchers led some students to believe that they were liked by the student with whom they would be paired. Other students were led to believe that they were disliked by their partner for the study. The pairs of students were then given an opportunity to have a conversation. Just as predicted, those individuals who thought they were liked behaved in more likeable ways with their partner; they disclosed more about themselves, disagreed less about the topic under discussion, and generally behaved in a warmer, more pleasant manner than did those individuals who thought they were disliked. As a result, their partners ended up liking them-more so than did the partners of students who believed they were disliked...

***

The Effects of Physical Attractiveness on Liking

Propinquity, similarity, and reciprocal liking are not the only determinants of who we will come to like. We also are affected by people's looks their physical attractiveness. How important is physical appearance to our first impressions of people? A classic study by Walster (Hatfield) and her colleagues revealed a surprising answer (Walster [Hatfield] et al., 1966). These researchers matched 752 incoming students at the University of Minnesota for a blind date at a dance during orientation week. The students had previously taken a battery of personality and aptitude tests; however, the researchers paired them up at random. On the night of the dance, the couples spent a few hours together dancing and chatting. They then evaluated their date and indicated whether they would like to date that person again. Of the many possible characteristics that could have determined whether they liked each other such as their partner's intelligence, independence, sensitivity, or sincerity-the overriding determinant was physical attractiveness. What's more, there was no great difference between men and women on this score.

The powerful role that physical appearance plays in attraction is not limited to heterosexual relationships. Paul Sergios and James Cody (1985) conducted a replication of the blind date study described above, with gay men as the research participants. The gay men responded just as the heterosexual men and women had in the earlier study: the physical attractiveness of their dates was the strongest predictor of their liking for them.

The findings of Waister (Hatfield) and colleagues' 1966 study, and subsequent replications, raise a perplexing issue. When people are asked about the qualities they desire in a dating partner or a mate, physical attractiveness is not at the top of the list (Buss & Barnes, 1986). Yet when it comes to people's actual behaviour what people do, rather than what they say, appearance seems to be the only thing that matters, at least in situations where strangers are forming their first impressions of each other. Are people unaware of the importance they place on looks, or are they simply unwilling to admit that they so highly value such a superficial characteristic?

To find out, Hadjistavropoulos and Genest (1994) designed a clever study. They presented female students at the University of Saskatchewan with photographs of men varying in physical attractiveness, along with descriptions of their (supposed) personality traits. Participants were asked to rate the men in terms of their desirability as a dating partner. The researchers found that attractive men received higher ratings than did unattractive men. Moreover, attractiveness was the best predictor of desirability more so than personality information. So far this sounds just like the other studies we have been describing. But here's the interesting twist: some of the participants were connected to an impressive-looking apparatus that they were told was a highly accurate lie detector. The researchers reasoned that if people aren't aware of the emphasis they place on looks, lie detector participants should give the same responses as participants who were not connected to a lie detector. If, on the other hand, people are aware that they base their evaluations of people on looks but feel they shouldn't admit it, then those who are attached to a lie detector should be more likely to "confess" to this than those who are not. And that is exactly what happened. The findings suggest that we are aware of the value we place on looks but, as long as we can get away with it, we won't admit it.

Before leaving this topic we should note that while both sexes value attractiveness in a potential sexual partner (Regan & Berscheid, 1995, 1997; Graziano et al., 1993), there is a tendency for men, more so than for women, to place greater emphasis on looks particularly when choosing a long-term mate (Buss, 1989; Buss & Barnes, 1986; Feingold, 1990). Later, when we discuss evolutionary theories of love, we will consider some reasons for this gender difference.

What Is Attractive?

Is physical attractiveness in the "eye of the beholder," or do we share some of the same notions of what is beautiful and handsome? From early child- hood on, the media tell us what is beautiful, and they tell us that this specific definition of beauty is associated with goodness. For example, illustrators of most traditional children's books, as well as the people who draw the characters in Disney movies, have taught us that the heroines-as well as the princes who woo and win them-all look alike. They all have regular features - small, pert noses; big eyes; shapely lips; blemish-free complexions and slim, athletic bodies: pretty much like Barbie and Ken dolls.

Bombarded as we are with media depictions of attractiveness, it is not surprising to learn that we share a set of criteria for defining beauty (Fink & Penton-Voak, 2002; Tselon, 1995). Look at the six photographs below of models and actors who are considered attractive in Western cultures. Can you describe the facial characteristics that have earned them this label? Michael Cunningham (1986) designed a creative study to deter- mine these standards of beauty. He asked male university students to rate the attractive- ness of 50 photographs of women, taken from a college yearbook and from an international beauty pageant program. Cunningham then carefully measured the relative size of the facial features in each photograph. He found that high attractiveness ratings were given to faces with large eyes, a small nose, a small chin, prominent cheekbones and narrow cheeks, high eyebrows, large pupils, and a big smile. Cunningham and his colleagues also examined women's ratings of male beauty in the same manner. They found that higher attractiveness ratings of men were associated with large eyes, prominent cheekbones, a large chin, and a big smile (Cunningham, Barbee, & Pike, 1990).

There is some overlap in the men's and women's ratings. Both sexes admire large eyes in the opposite sex; these are considered to be a "baby face" feature, for newborn mammals have very large eyes for the size of their faces. Baby face features are thought to be attractive because they elicit feelings of warmth and nurturance in perceivers-take, for example, our response to babies, kittens, and puppies (e.g., Berry, 1995; McArthur & Berry, 1987; Zebrowitz, 1997; Zebrowitz & Montepare, 1992). Both sexes also admire prominent cheekbones in the opposite sex, an adult feature that is found only in the faces of those who are sexually mature. Note that the female face that is considered beautiful has more baby face features (small nose, small chin) than the handsome male face, suggesting that beauty in the female, more so than in the male, is associated with childlike qualities.

Cultural Standards Of Beauty

Are people's perceptions of what is beautiful or handsome similar across cultures? According to a recent review of this literature by University of Toronto social psychologist Karen Dion (Dion, K.K., 2002), the answer is a surprising yes (see also Cunningham et al., 1995; Jones & Hill, 1993; McArthur & Berry, 1987; Perrett, May, & Yoshikawa, 1994; Rhodes et al., 2001). Researchers have asked participants from various countries, ethnicities, and racial groups to rate the physical attractiveness of photographed faces of people who also represent various countries, ethnicities, and racial groups. The participants' ratings agree to a remarkable extent. One review of this literature found, for example, that correlations between participants' ratings ranged from .66 to .93 (Langlois & Roggman, 1990), which are very strong correlations (see Chapter 2). A meta analysis of many studies conducted by Judith Langlois and colleagues (2000) also found evidence for cross-cultural agreement in what constitutes a beautiful or handsome face. While there is variation in people's judgments, across large groups a consensus emerges. Perceivers think that some faces are just better looking than others, regardless of cultural background (Berscheid & Reis, 1998).

How can we explain these results? Judith Langlois and Lori Roggman have suggested that humans came to find certain dimensions as attractive during the course of our evolution (Langlois & Roggman, 1990; Langlois, Roggman, & Musselman, 1994). They hypothesized that attractive faces for both sexes are those whose features are the arithmetic mean or average for the species, not the extremes. These researchers have used computer technology to merge up to 32 photographs of faces into a single face that is the exact mathematical average of the facial features of the original people's photographs. The photographs on the next page show the result of the merging of two photographs of women. Interestingly, in studies conducted by Langlois and her colleagues, research participants judge the composite photograph (the arithmetic average of all the faces) as more attractive than the individual photographs that make up the composite. This is the case for both male and female photographs. The facial composites produce what the researchers call a typical or "familiar" face. Individual variation in facial features is melted away in the composite; what is left is a good-looking human being, whose face has a familiar and highly pleasing aspect to it.

Do these results mean that "average" faces are the most attractive? Not necessarily. Langlois and her colleagues found that the "average" composite face was perceived as more attractive than all of the faces that made it up. However, that does not mean that these composite "average" faces had all of the physical qualities that people cross culturally agree are highly attractive. To explore this issue, D. I. Perrett and colleagues (1994) created two types of composite faces. One composite was made up of 60 individual photographs and was called the "average attractive" composite. The other composite was composed of the 15 photos from the original 60 that had received the highest ratings of attractiveness on a pretest. This composite was called the "high attractive" composite. The researchers made these two kinds of composites using photographs of White and Japanese women and men. They then asked research participants in Great Britain and Japan to rate all of the composite faces for attractiveness. They found, first, that the 'highly attractive" composites were rated as being significantly more attractive than the "average attractive" composites. Second, the Japanese and British participants showed the same pattern when judging the faces, reinforcing the idea that similar perceptions of facial attractiveness exist cross-culturally.

You may be wondering what these "highly attractive" composite faces look like. Their facial shapes, whether Japanese or Caucasian, matched the profile of attractiveness for women and men identified by Michael Cunningham and colleagues, which were discussed earlier (Cunningham, 1986; Cunningham, Barbee, & Pike, 1995). For example, the Japanese and Caucasian "highly attractive" female composites had higher cheekbones, a thinner jaw, and larger eyes relative to the size of the face than the "average attractive" composites did. Thus, the "average" composite face is attractive to us because it has lost some of the atypical or unfamiliar variation that makes up individual faces. However, the most attractive composite face is one that started out above average and only became more so as variation was smoothed over.

The Power Of Familiarity

The crucial variable that explains interpersonal attraction may actually be familiarity (Berscheid & Reis, 1998). We've seen that averaging the attractiveness of many faces together produces one face that looks typical, familiar, and physically attractive (see also Halberstadt & Rhodes, 2000). Recent research has found evidence for an even more startling effect for familiarity: When research participants rated the attractiveness of faces, they preferred the faces that most resembled their own! The researchers then compute -morphed a picture of each participant's face-without the participant's knowledge into that of a person of the opposite sex. When they presented this photo to participants, they gave the photo of their opposite-sex "clone" even higher ratings of attractiveness (Little & Perrett, 2002).

Familiarity also underlies the other concepts we've been discussing: propinquity - that is, people we see frequently become familiar through mere exposure, similarity that is, people who are similar to us will also seem familiar to us, and reciprocal liking that is, people who like each other get to know and become familiar with each other. All of these attraction variables may be expressions of our "underlying preference for the familiar and safe over the unfamiliar and potentially dangerous" (Berscheid & Reis, 1998, p. 210).

Assumptions About Attractive People

Most people assume that physical attractiveness is highly correlated with other desirable traits. The results of many studies indicate that beauty constitutes a powerful stereotype - what Karen Dion, Ellen Berscheid, and Elaine Walster (Hatfield) (1972) have called the "what is beautiful is good" stereotype (Ashmore, Solomon, & Longo, 1996; Brigham, 1980; Hatfield & Sprecher, 1986a). Most research on the "what is beautiful is good" stereotype has been conducted with young people, usually university students. An exception is a study by Perlini, Bertolissi, and Lind (1999), who showed photographs of attractive and unattractive younger and older women to first-year university students and to senior citizens living in Sault Ste. Marie, Ontario. The researchers found that participants attributed more positive qualities to attractive women regardless of their age. There was, however, one exception. Older men attributed more positive qualities to attractive young women than to attractive older women. Thus, it appears that the "what is beautiful is good" stereotype applies to older people as well. The exception is older men, for whom e stereotype seems to be "what is beautiful and younger is good," at least with regard to their perceptions of women.

Luckily for those of us who do not look like supermodels, the stereotype is relatively narrow, affecting people's judgments about an individual only in specific areas. Meta-analyses conducted by Eagly, Ashmore, Makhijani, and Longo (1991) and by Alan Feingold (1992a) have revealed that physical attractiveness has the largest effect on both men's and women's attributions when they are making judgments about social competence. The beautiful are thought to be more sociable, extroverted, and popular than the less attractive. They are also seen as more sexual, more happy and more assertive.

Interestingly, the stereotype that the beautiful are particularly gifted in the area of social competence has some research support; highly attractive people do develop good social interaction skills and report having more satisfying interactions with others than do the less attractive (Berscheid & Reis, 1998; Feingold, 1992b; Reis, Nezlek, & Wheeler, 980; Reis et al., 1982). An analysis of national survey data gathered by the Institute for social Research at York University also revealed that attractiveness and income are positively correlated at least for men (Roszell, Kennedy, & Grabb, 1989). Thus, there pears to be a kernel of truth in the "what is beautiful is good" stereotype. The reason is at beautiful people, from a young age, receive a great deal of social attention that helps in develop good social skills-which, in turn, may lead to other positive outcomes, such as interpersonal and occupational success. You probably recognize the self-fulfilling prophecy at work here, a concept we discussed in Chapter 3. The way we treat people affects how they behave and, ultimately, how they perceive themselves.

Can a "regular" person be made to act like a "beautiful" one through the self-fulfilling prophecy? Mark Snyder, Elizabeth Decker Tanke, and Ellen Berscheid (1977) decided to find out. They gave male university students a packet of information about other research participant, including her photograph. The photograph was of either an attractive woman or an unattractive woman. The purpose of the photograph was to invoke the men's stereotype that "what is beautiful is good" - that the woman would be more warm, likeable, poised, and fun to talk to if she was physically attractive than if she as unattractive. The men then had a telephone conversation with a woman, whom they were told was the woman in the photograph; they actually spoke with a different woman. The important question is: did the men's beliefs create reality? Yes the men who thought they were talking to an attractive woman responded to her in a warmer, more sociable manner than did the men who thought they were talking to an unattractive woman. Not only that, but the men's behaviour influenced how the women themselves responded. When observers later listened to a tape recording of the women's half of the conversation, they rated the women whose male partners thought they were physically attractive as more attractive, confident, animated, and warmer than the women whose male partners thought they were unattractive. In short, if a man thought he was talking to an attractive woman, he spoke to her in a way that brought out her best and most sparkling qualities.

This study was later replicated with the roles switched. Andersen and Bern (1981) showed female participants a photograph of either an attractive or an unattractive man; the women then had a phone conversation with him. The men on the other end of the line were unaware of the women's belief about them. Just as in the Snyder, Tanke, and Berscheid (1977) study, the women acted on their stereotype of beauty, and the unknowing men responded accordingly.

Cultural Differences

You might have wondered whether the "what is beautiful is good" stereotype operates across cultures. The answer appears to be yes. Ladd Wheeler and Youngmee Kim (1997) asked students in Seoul, South Korea, to rate a number of year- book photographs that varied in physical attractiveness. They found that the Korean male and female participants thought the more physically attractive people would also be more socially skilled, friendly, and well adjusted-the same group of traits that North American participants thought went with physical attractiveness (see Figure 9.4).

Korean and North American students differed, however, in some of the other traits they assigned to the beautiful; these differences highlight what is considered important and valuable in each culture (Markus, Kitayama, & Heiman, 1996; Triandis, 1995). For the North American students, who live in individualist cultures that value independence, individuality, and self-reliance, the "beautiful" stereotype included traits of personal strength (see Figure 9.4). These traits were not part of the Korean "beautiful" stereotype. Instead, for the Korean students, who live in a collectivist culture that values harmonious group relations, the "beautiful" stereotype included traits of integrity and concern for others-traits that were not part of the North American stereotype...

Attraction and the Misattribution of Arousal

Imagine that you go to see a scary movie with an extremely attractive date. As you are sitting there, you notice that your heart is thumping and you are a little short of breath. Is this because you are wildly attracted to your date, or because the movie is terrifying you? It is unlikely that you could say, "Fifty-seven percent of my arousal is due to the fact that my date is gorgeous, 32 percent is due to the scary movie, and 11 percent is due to indigestion from all the popcorn I ate." Because of this difficulty in pinpointing the precise causes of our arousal, we sometimes form mistaken emotions. You might think that most of your arousal is a sign of attraction to your date, when in fact a lot of it is due to the movie (or maybe even indigestion).

In recent years, many studies have demonstrated the occurrence of such misattribution of arousal, whereby people make mistaken inferences about what is causing them to feel the way they do (Ross & Olson, 1981; Savitsky et al., 1998; Schachter, 1977; Storms & Nisbett, 1970; Valins, 1966; Zillmann, 1978). Consider, for example, an intriguing field experiment by Donald Dutton and Arthur Aron (1974). Imagine you are one of the participants (all of whom were men). You are one of many people visiting the Capilano Canyon in scenic North Vancouver. Spanning the canyon is a narrow, 137-metre suspension bridge made of wooden planks attached to wire cables. You decide to walk across it.

When you get a little way across, the bridge starts to sway from side to side. You feel as though you are about to tumble over the edge and you reach for the handrails, but they are so low that it feels even more likely that you will topple over. Then you make the mistake of looking down. You see nothing but a sheer 70-metre drop to rocks and rapids below. You become more than a little aroused your heart is thumping, you breathe rapidly, and you begin to perspire. At this point, an attractive young woman approaches you and asks whether you could fill out a questionnaire for her, as part of a psychology project on the effects of scenic attractions on people's creativity. You decide to help her out. After you complete the questionnaire, the woman thanks you and says she would be happy to explain her study in more detail. She tears off a corner of the questionnaire, writes down her name and phone number. How attracted do you think you would be to this woman? Would you phone her and ask her out?

Think about this for a moment, and now imagine that the same woman approaches you under different circumstances. You decide to take a leisurely stroll farther up the Capilano River. You notice a wide sturdy bridge made of heavy cedar planks. The bridge has high handrails, even though it is situated only 3 metres above a shallow rivulet that runs into the main river. You are peaceably admiring the scenery when the woman asks you to fill out her questionnaire. How attracted do you feel toward her now? Dutton and Aron's prediction is clear: If you are on the high, scary bridge, you will be considerably aroused and will mistakenly think some of this arousal is the result of attraction to the beautiful woman. This is exactly what happened in the actual experiment. Half of the men (50 percent) who were approached on the high suspension bridge telephoned the woman later, whereas relatively few of the men (12.5 percent) who were approached on the low, sturdy bridge called her. (As you probably have guessed, the woman was a confederate someone hired by the researchers-and she approached only men who were not accompanied by a woman.)

In summary, we have discussed four major determinants of attraction: propinquity, similarity, reciprocal liking, and physical attractiveness. ...

Forming Close Relationships: What Is Love?

After getting to this point in the chapter, you should be in a pretty good position to make a favourable first impression the next time you meet someone. Suppose you want Claudia to like you. You should hang around her so you become familiar, emphasize your similarity to her, and find ways of showing that you like her. It also wouldn't hurt to look your best. But what if you want to do more than make a good impression? What if you want to have a close friendship or a romantic relationship?

***

Defining Love

In the opening of this chapter, we described Bradley Bird's falling-in-love experience. But what, exactly, is love? For centuries, philosophers, poets, and novelists have grappled with this question. More recently, social psychologists have attempted to provide a scientific answer. One of the first to attempt a scientific analysis of love was Zick Rubin (1970, 1973). He defined love as feelings of intimacy, attachment, and passion, and argued that love is a feeling distinct from liking. Subsequently, social psychologists attempted to dive deeper into the study of love and reached a conclusion that you may already have discovered. There probably isn't a single, simple definition of love because love comes in many forms.

Companionate Versus Passionate Love

If you have ever been in love, think back to how you felt about your sweetheart when you first got to know him or her. You probably felt a combination of giddiness, longing, joy, and anxiety-the kinds of feelings that Bradley Bird experienced when he met Nina. The ancient Greeks considered this strange bewildering set of feelings to be a form of madness, causing all sorts of irrational and obsessional acts. Though times have changed, most people are familiar with the tormenting exhilaration that comes with falling in love. Now think about how you feel toward your mother or your brother or a very close friend. You might also use the word love to describe how you feel about these important people in your life, but in this case the feelings are probably quite different from the feelings you have for your sweetheart.

Ellen Berscheid and Elaine Walster (Hatfield) (1974, 1978) attempted to capture this distinction when they proposed that there are two major kinds of love: companionate and passionate. Companionate love is defined as the feelings of intimacy and affection we feel toward someone with whom our lives are deeply intertwined. People can experience companionate love in nonsexual relationships, such as close friendships or familial relationships, or in sexual relationships, where they experience feelings of intimacy but not a great deal of heat and passion. Passionate love involves an intense longing for another person. When things are going well the other person loves us too we feel great fulfillment and ecstasy. When things are not going well, we feel great sadness and despair. This kind of love is characterized by obsessive thoughts about the loved one, as well as heightened physiological arousal wherein we actually feel shortness of breath and a thumping heart when we are in our loved one's presence (Regan, 1998; Regan & Berscheid, 1999).

Elaine Hatfield and Susan Sprecher (1986b) developed a questionnaire to measure passionate love. Passionate love, as measured by this scale, consists of strong uncontrollable thoughts, intense feelings, and overt acts toward the target of one's affection… Cross-cultural research comparing an individualistic culture (the United States) and a collectivistic culture (China) indicates that American couples tend to value passionate love more than Chinese couples do, and that Chinese couples tend to value companionate love more than American couples do (Gao, 1993; Jankowiak, 1995; Ting-Toomey & Chang, 1996). In comparison, the Taita of Kenya, Africa, value both equally; they conceptualize romantic love as a combination of companionate love and passionate love. The Taita consider this the best kind of love, and achieving it is a primary goal in the society (Bell, 1995)…

Triangular Theory Of Love

Other researchers are not satisfied with a simple dichotomy of two kinds of love. Robert Sternberg (1986, 1988, 1997; Sternberg & Beau, 1991), for example, presents a triangular theory of love, which depicts love as comprising three basic ingredients: intimacy, passion, and commitment. Intimacy refers to feelings of being close to and bonded with a partner. Passion refers to the "hot parts" of a relationship feelings of arousal and sexual attraction. Commitment consists of two decisions the short-term one to love your partner, and the long-term one to maintain that love and stay with your partner. These three ingredients-intimacy, passion, and commitment can be combined in varying degrees to form different kinds of love… Love can consist of one component alone or any combination of these three parts. For example, you may feel a great deal of passion or physical attraction (infatuation) but not know the person well enough to experience intimacy and not be ready to make any kind of commitment. As the relationship develops, it might blossom into romantic love, characterized by passion and intimacy, and maybe even consummate love-the blending of all three components. Note that Sternberg uses the term companionate love in the same way we explained earlier, to describe love that is characterized by intimacy and commitment but not passion (Aron & Westbay, 1996; Hassebrauck & Buhi, 1996; Lemieux & Hale, 1999).

"Ordinary" People's Definition Of Love

So far we have been discussing social psychologists' answers to the question: What is love? Beverley Fehr (1988, 1994;Fehr & Russell, 1991) has been interested in how ordinary people define love. This is an important issue because the way in which people define love can determine how they act in their close relationships (e.g., deciding whether they are truly "in love," or whether they are experiencing the kind of love that leads to commitment). In an initial set of studies, Fehr (1988) asked students at the University of British Columbia to define love: specifically, participants were asked to list the features or characteristics of the concept of love. The definitions of love that were generated included both companionate features (e.g., warmth, intimacy, caring) and passionate features (e.g., heart rate increases, sexual attraction, thinking about the other person all the time). In follow-up research, other participants were shown these features and asked to rate which were most prototypical, or important, in defining love. … contrary to the stereotype that university students would view love only in passionate terms, Fehr found that companionate love was seen as capturing the meaning of love, more so than passionate love. Moreover, participants reported that they relied on the level of companionate love, rather than the level of passionate love, when deciding whether a relationship was progressing or deteriorating.

These studies have been replicated by researchers on the east coast of Canada (Button & Collier, 1991) and on the west coast of the United States (Luby & Aron, 1990; Aron & Westbay, 1996). Participants in these studies have shown remarkable agreement on the features of love. The companionate features of love are especially likely to be mentioned, and also consistently receive the highest importance ratings. These findings suggest that, at least within North America, people tend to agree on the meaning of love (Fehr, 1993; 2001…Thus, ordinary people's view of love fits nicely with Berscheid and Hatfield's (Walster's) companionate/passionate distinction (Fehr, 2001). Love is seen as including both companionate and passionate aspects, although the companionate aspect is considered to be the essence of love.

Gender and Love

Who is all mushy and romantic when it comes to love? Who is practical and solid? If you are like many people, you will answer "women" to the first question and "men" to the second. But think back to our opening story of Bradley Bird and you may come up with a different answer - one that is more consistent with the results of social psychological research. Indeed, when social psychologists began to conduct research on this question, they found that men fall in love more quickly than women and are more likely to endorse romantic beliefs such as "True love lasts forever." Men are also more likely than women to report having experienced love at first sight-as Bradley Bird can attest. In contrast, women hold a more practical, friendship-based orientation to love (essentially, a companionate view of love). One of the first studies that discovered these gender differences was conducted by Kenneth Dion and Karen Dion (1973) at the University of Toronto. These differences in how women and men view love continue to be found, even among culturally diverse participants (Dion & Dion, 1993; Hendrick & Hendrick, 1986, 1992; Hendrick, Hendrick, & Adler, 1984; Rubin, Peplau, & Hill, 1981; Sprecher & Metts, 1989)...

On the other hand, researchers are beginning to realize that there also are similarities in women's and men's definitions and experience of love (Hendrick & Hendrick, 1995). In a recent set of studies conducted at the University of Winnipeg, Beverley Fehr and Ross Broughton (2001) obtained the classic finding - namely, that men gave higher ratings to romantic and passionate love than did women, and women's ratings of friendship love were higher than men's. However, some additional, interesting findings emerged. These researchers measured several kinds of companionate love (e.g., familial love, sisterly love, affection), rather than just friendship love, as is usually done. It turned out that men rated these other kinds of companionate love just as high as women did. Moreover, Fehr and Broughton found that even though men rated romantic passionate kinds of love higher than did women, both sexes gave these kinds of love the lowest ratings and the companionate kinds of love the highest ratings. The researchers concluded that women's and men's views of love are actually more similar than has been thought.

Culture and Love

While love is certainly a human emotion experienced everywhere on the planet, culture does play a role in how people label their experiences and in what they expect, and tolerate, in close relationships. For example, Japanese describe amae as an extremely positive emotional state in which one is a totally passive love object, indulged and taken care of by one's romantic partner, as in a mother-infant relationship. There is no equivalent word for amae in English or any other Western language; the closest in meaning is the word dependency, an emotional state that is considered by Western cultures to be unhealthy in adult relationships (Dion & Dion, 1993; Doi, 1988). The Chinese have an important relationship concept, gan qing, which differs from the Western view of romantic love. Gan qing is achieved by helping and working for another person; for example, a "romantic" act would be fixing someone's bicycle or helping them learn new material (Gao, 1996). Another way of conceptualizing love is expressed by the Korean concept of Jung. Much more than "love," jung is what ties two people together. Though couples in new relation- ships feel strong love for each other, they have not yet developed strong jung that takes time and many mutual experiences. Interestingly, jung can develop in negative relation- ships, too-for example, between business rivals who dislike each other. Jung may unknowingly grow between them over time, with the result that they will feel that a strange connection exists (Lim & Choi, 1996).

As you can see from these examples, how love is defined and experienced varies across cultures. Throughout this book we have noted that Western and Eastern cultures vary in important ways, with Western cultures emphasizing that the individual is autonomous, self-sufficient, and defined in terms of his or her personal qualities. Eastern cultures, in contrast, tend to be collectivistic, emphasizing the individual's loyalty to the group and defining him or her through membership in the group (Heine et al., 1999; Hofstede, 1984; Hui & Triandis, 1986; Markus, Kitayama, & Heinman, 1996; Triandis, 1995). According to Karen Dion and Kenneth Dion (1993, 1996, 2001), romantic love has less value in collectivist societies than in individualist societies. In individualist societies, romantic love is a heady, highly personal experience; one immerses oneself in the new partner and often virtually ignores friends and family for a while. The decision as to who to become involved with or marry is for the most part a personal one. In comparison, in collectivist cultures, the individual in love must take into account the wishes of family and other group members; in fact, marriages are often by arrangement, with the respective families matching up the bride and groom (Fiske et al., 1998; Levine et al., 1995).

Not surprisingly, research has found that Canadian university students have different attitudes about love, depending on their ethnocultural background: Asian (studies of Chinese, Korean, Vietnamese, Indian, Pakistani), Anglo-Celtic (studies of English, Irish, Scottish), or European (studies of Scandinavian, Spanish, German, Polish). In comparison to their peers, the Asian respondents were significantly more likely to identify with a companionate, friendship-based romantic love, a "style of love that would not disrupt a complex network of existing family relationships" (K. L. Dion & K. K. Dion, 1993, p. 465). In a similar study, college students in 11 countries around the world were asked: "If a man [woman] had all the qualities you desired, would you marry this person if you were not in love with him [her]?" These researchers found that marrying for love was most important to participants in such Western and Westernized countries (e.g., the United States, Brazil, England, and Australia) and of least importance to participants in less developed Eastern countries (e.g., India, Pakistan, and Thailand) (Levine et al., 1995).

The results of these studies indicate that the concept of romantic love is to some extent culturally specific (Dion & Dion, 1996; Gao & Gudykunst, 1995; Hatfield & Rapson, 1996, 2002; Hatfield & Sprecher, 1995; Sprecher, Aron et al., 1994). Love can vary in definition and behaviour in different societies. We all love, but we do not necessarily all love in the same way-or at least we don't describe it in the same way. As noted earlier, anthropologists found evidence of romantic (passionate) love in 147 of the 166 cultures sampled (Jankowiak, 1995; Jankowiak & Fischer, 1992); it was present even in societies "that do not accept [romantic love] or embrace it as a positive ideal" (Jankowiak, 1995, p. 4). Therefore, it may be that romantic love is nearly universal in the human species, but cultural rules alter how that emotional state is experienced, expressed, and remembered (Levinger, 1994). Robert Moore noted, in summarizing his research in the People's Republic of China, "Young Chinese do fall deeply in love and experience the same joys and sorrows of romance as young Westerners do. But they do so according to standards that require ... the individual [to] sacrifice personal interests for the sake of the family .... This means avoiding fleeting infatuations, casual sexual encounters, and a dating context [where] family concerns are forgotten" (1998, p. 280).

***

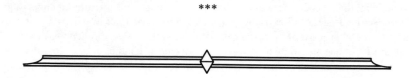

CONFLICT AND PROBLEM-SOLVING IN LONG TERM RELATIONSHIPS

A KEY POINT SUMMARY OF THREE READINGS

By Dalton Kehoe

Readings:

Talylor, Anita and Miller, Judi Beinstein. (1994) <u>Conflict and Gender.</u> New Jersey: Hampton
    Press Inc.
Gottman, J.M., (1994) <u>What Predicts Divorce?</u> New Jersey: Lawrence Erlbaum Associates
    Publishers.
Gottman, J.M., (1999) <u>The Marriage Clinic.</u> New York: W.W. Norton & Company, Chapters 8 and 9.

From Taylor and Beinstein, <u>Conflict and Gender</u>

- When, in 1988, Canary et al. asked undergraduate students to describe a "typical" conflict in a close relationship, women were more likely to report using personal criticism and showing anger, whereas men were more likely to report denying the existence or extent of the conflict. (p. 174), women reported using negative emotion such as crying, pouting, getting angry more frequently than men did. Men reported using more coercive strategies than did women.

- In Kelley et al.'s (1978) research, women portrayed themselves, as did their partners, as more emotional and critical of the male's insensitivity. In turn, men portrayed themselves, as did their partners, as logical, unemotional, showing open anger, and providing reasons for a delay. These results are consistent to sex-role stereotypes: men are "conflict avoidant" and women are "conflict confrontive." However, Kelley et al. also found non-stereotyped comments used more frequently than sex-typed comments by both women and men and concluded that women's and men's conflict behavior is largely interchangeable. (p. 175)

- Billingham and Sack (1987) found that **the more emotionally committed a couple was, the more they reported using reasoning and verbal aggression strategies**. Irrespective of emotional involvement, the women reported using more reasoning and more verbal aggression than did the men. Women also were perceived by the men as engaging in more physical violence than vice versa and were characterized as more direct in managing conflict with their male partners. (p. 175)

- Fitzpatrick and Winke (1979)--The greater their emotional involvement, the more likely the couples were to report using strategies of emotional appeal (e.g. promise to be more loving) and personal rejection (e.g. withhold affection, ignore). The less involved they were, the more likely they were to use strategies of manipulation (acting nice, being pleasant) and non-negotiation (refuse to discuss, repeating point of view).

- Women and men differ in how they deal with same sex friends--women reported using more personal rejection, emotional appeal, and empathic understanding (e.g. focus on mutual needs) strategies, whereas men relied more on non-negotiation strategies. The differences between women's and men's responses for same-sex relationships parallels differences for opposite-sex relationships that are high versus low in emotional involvement and may be related to theoretical distinctions between female connection and male autonomy that are often found in the literature. (Pp. 175-176)

- Baxter and Shepherd (1978)--**attachment to the partner rather than gender made a difference in women's and men's approval of different management styles**--the more emotional involvement they had, the more likely they were to report using direct strategies, which emphasized emotional connection between partners. Thus, it may be that the relationships for which women and men are reporting conflict behavior differ in attachment and that gender differences in conflict behavior are due to these differences. (p. 176)

- Bell, Chaftez, and Horn (1982) interviewed 30 married couples to identify decisions over which there was disagreement and strategies that had been used to resolve the conflict. Women and men mentioned similar strategies in the following descending order: influence, authority, control, and manipulation. In general, husbands tended to win the conflicts regardless of the strategies employed by them or their wives. Other resources such as educational level of the husband, labor force status of the wife, and family traditionalism were related to outcome.

- Weingarten and Douvan (1985)--Women viewed their goal to be an understanding of parties and their differences, whereas men saw their goal to be the development of an agreement. Men believed they should be neutral, whereas women believed they should facilitate balance between conflicting parties. (p. 186)

From Gottman, What Predicts Divorce?

- It seems that as marital conflict becomes more severe and problems remain unsolved, negative affect will become increasingly more pervasive in all the couples' interactions, and that they will be less likely to rebound from a conflict discussion. (p. 66)

- Three years after having taken part in a study of marital happiness, couples were tested again and **two findings became apparent determinants of marital happiness:**

  - Negative affect reciprocity (sharing negative feelings) was a strong predictor of change in relationship satisfaction, and

  - Physiological arousal was highly predictive of declines in levels of marital satisfaction. (p. 74)

- **[Emotionally] regulated couples (those who express more positive emotions regarding the marriage than negative) had happier marriages than non-regulated couples (who expressed more negative emotions about the marriage than positive).** (p. 94)

- Non-regulated couples had more dysfunctional marriages and reported less marital satisfaction. They are more likely to consider marital dissolution and more likely to actually separate. Consideration of dissolution and actual separation were arguably among the clearest behavioral signs of marital distress. (p. 106)

- Non-regulated wives were less likely to express positive emotions of interest/caring and joy/enthusiasm and more likely to express disgust/contempt. Both unregulated husbands and wives were found to be more likely to express the negative emotions of anger and whining. Unpleasant and unproductive interaction does not bode well for the ultimate stability of a marriage. (p. 106)

- Non-regulated wives showed evidence of greater sympathetic nervous system arousal in their cardiovascular responses during their problem-area interactions. They were also in poorer health generally than regulated wives, and much poorer health than both regulated and Non-regulated husbands.

- **The number of non-regulated couples that divorced was twice as large as the number of regulated couples.** (p. 108)

- **The negative interaction process cascade, which predicts marital dissolution, is as follows:**

  - Complaining and criticizing leads to

  - Contempt, which leads to

  - Defensiveness, which leads to

  - Listener Withdrawal from interaction (stonewalling).

  - **He calls these four corrosive marital behaviors are called "The Four Horsemen of the Apocalypse."** (p. 110)

- In addition to direct observation of the couple interacting and measurement of the bodily responses (e.g. galvanic skin response, changes in breathing and heart rate) as well as "before and after" analysis of changes in blood chemistry, Gottman also uses a set of inventories that index **distance and isolation** along firve dimensions:

  - **Loneliness** (e.g. Sometimes I feel so lonely it hurts),
  - **Parallel lives** (e.g. My partner and I live pretty separate lives),
  - **Severity of problems** (e.g. solvable to "gridlocked")
  - **Flooding by partner's negative affect** (e.g. Partner A feels that partner B's negative emotions arise unexpectedly and are overwhelming and disorganized to partner A),
  - **Works problems out alone, not with spouse** (e.g. It is better to avoid problems or to work them out alone than with the spouse).

  - Higher scores on all of these dimensions predict a negative marital cascade. (pp. 113-117)

From Gottman, The Marriage Clinic (Chapter 8 & 9)

- **Two pronged approach to probem-solving in marriage:**

  1. Functional problem-solving for resoluble problems

  2. Establishing a dialogue for perpetual problems (also called a "gridlocked problem")
  (Gottman, p. 218)

Conflict Discussions:

- Any issue can be gridlocked or a solvable one, it depends entirely on how long the issue has lasted and whether the partners wind up feeling attacked, hurt, or rejected whenever they discuss it.
- Perpetual or gridlocked problems are usually a result of either (1) fundamental differences in individual personalities that repeatedly create conflict, or (2) fundamental differences in lifestyle needs--needs are basic to sustaining an each individual's identity, to expressing who they are as a person. (p. 219).
- Any issue, no matter how specific or trivial is seems, can have huge symbolic meaning that is truly at the core of the person's sense of self.

- **The work on effective problem-solving in marriages includes the following four skills:**
  1. Softened start-up
  2. Repair and de-escalation

3. Accepting influence

4. Compromise

Basic to all skills is a fifth skill:

5. Physiological soothing (making the marriage a port in a storm)

- **Softened Start-up:** -- The person initiating the discussion does by themselves (pp. 224-225).

  - Purpose is to change the way that partners begin the conflict discussion, so that it is softened rather than harsh.
    - eg. Topic: You want your partner to express more affection toward you.
      Harsh start-up: You never touch me.

      Softened alternative: I loved it when you kissed me in the kitchen the other day. You are a natural-born kisser. Would you please do more of that?

  - Softened start-up must be the result of an internal dialogue in which what wins is friendship and sympathy and understanding of the other's current life situation.

    - Eg. You are having a bad day, doing the chores and taking care of the kids while your partner is having lunch with a friend--internal dialogue leads you to not even raise this as an issue, or to do it in a softened way: "I'm having a bad day, doing a lot more that my partner is doing. That really annoys me, but my partner is still pretty terrific. Cool out, enjoy the day as much as you can, and don't make a big deal out of this. I hope my partner is enjoying the day."

  - You *still raise issues*, but just in a way that minimizes their partner's defensiveness.

- **Repair and De-escalation:** (pp. 225-227).

  - Purpose is to formalize the repair process--repair is absolutely critical in the regulation of conflict and is a natural process.
  - Couples can make a list of repair attempts – techniques to make things better. They can post it on the fridge for easy access
  - When attempt to repair a problem they can check it and announce the repair attempt to their partner by number before their attempt, or they can just say it without using the number:
    - eg. "I'm trying # 6", or " I'm feeling sad because..."
  - The job of the receiver of a repair attempt is to try to *accept* the repair attempt which means that the receiver must find that part of the repair attempt that he or she can agree with right now and to view the partner's effort as an attempt to make things better.

- **Flooding and Self-soothing:** (pp.227-231)
  -
  - Purpose is to teach couples how to recognize when one of them feels flooded during a conflict and how to ritualize taking a break, during which they self-soothe.
  - Discuss the **diffuse physiological arousal (DPA)**--the physiological state of one's body affects the ability to listen, access to recently learned behaviors and ways of thinking , and the ability to creatively solve problems--leading to reliance on over-learned behavior patterns and ways of thinking (fight or flight routines)
  - DPA is an aversive state related to flooding, which begins the Distance and Isolation Cascade.

  - **Sex differences in the DPA** (p. 229)

- After conflict discussions men tend to remain vigilant and rehearse distressing-maintaining thoughts
- Women exercise their capacity for self-soothing and rehearse relationship-enhancing thoughts
- Chronic flooding in marriages is very bad for the physical health of both husbands and wives.

- **Pursuer-distancer pattern:** One partner (usually the woman) brings up an issues that she thinks is creating emotional distance in the relationship where the other partner (usually the husband) doesn't want to talk about it and may not even think there is a problem--the issue is brought up and pursued in a way that is very negative to the listener who ends up (1) running away and/or (2) escalating the conflict and rejecting all influence from the speaker. This tends to worsen over time until one or both become flooded.

- **Flooding Intervention A. Take a Break:** (p. 231)

  - Purpose is to introduce a "withdrawal ritual" into the marriage.
  - After learning about DPA, learn to take heart rate and take at least a 20 min. break and truly relax--no rehearsing distress-maintaining thoughts.
  - Schedule a time to get back together
  - This reduces heart rate and makes the next interaction on the conflict topic more positive--must return to the issue after the break.

- **Flooding Intervention B. Imagining and Self-soothing:** (p. 231-233)

  - Purpose is to give partners a reliable tool for self-soothing during times of flooding.
  - Take couple through imaging exercise using the following steps:
    Tell them "When you are feeling tense and find yourself going into DPA, use the repair attempt in which you tell your partner you want to take a short break to calm yourself down. Here's what to do during those times.

There are **five steps for soothing yourself**.

  1. Get control of your beathing--do six breaths a minute.
  2. Notice areas of tension in your body and intentionally contract and relax them.
  3. Let the region (of tension) become heavy, to feel as if you are weighted down and leaden.
  4. Imagine the region becoming comfortably warm--gets the blood flowing there and begins the deep relaxation.
  5. Think of a personal image that brings all four steps into focus and memory (e.g. imagine yourself in a field...).

  - Biofeedback machine is useful for providing a large beat-by-beat readout of heart rate and oxygen consumption--can set to alarm if gets too high--helps people to recognize when they need to do some self-soothing.

- **Accepting Influence:** (p. 233)

  - Purpose is to get both partners to yield a bit and find their common ground so that they can arrive at a compromise position on the issue.
  - Help partners find those parts of their partner's position that they can understand and with which they can agree--learning that sharing or relinquishing influence is an asset in the marriage.
  - Spouses work together to develop a common way of thinking about the issue and to start constructing a compromise that they can both live with. They will each be asking their partner these questions:

- How can we understand this issue? Can we develop a compromise view here?
- What are our common feelings or the most important feelings here?
- What common goals do we have here?
- What methods can we agree upon for accomplishing these goals?

- These questions for work **for solvable** problems only.

Establishing Dialogue With Perpetual (or Gridlocked) Problems

- **The Dreams-Within-Conflict Interviews:** (p. 234-236)

- In this part of therapy there is one major intervention with two parts:
  - First--breaking up the couple's logjam by uncovering the dreams that underlie each person's entrenchment in an uncompromising position.
  - Both involve metaphors, stories, hopes and dreams uncovered in a safe marital climate.
  - Second--the changing the influence patterns in the marriage so that both people can proceed to honor one another's dreams.

- **Recognizing Strengths:** (pp. 236-238)

- Purpose is to help partners become aware of the adaptation they have already made but not congratulated themselves for.

  - Partners have already accepted a great deal of what they can't change in their marriage. Have each person ask their partner these questions:
    - What adaptations has each of us already made in our marriage? Are there parts of one another's personalities that are not ideal but to which we have already made adjustments?
    - Are one person's feelings more important on this issue than the other's?
    - Is it possible to have some kind of trade-off, for example, across issues, with one person "winning" on one issue and the other person "winning" on another issue?
    - How can we further adapt to this?
    - Can we minimize the importance of the issue, emphasize common ground, laugh about this, accept one another's foibles?
    - Is it okay for this problem to never be fully resolved?
  - Even seemingly small and trivial issues can have great symbolic value.

- **Imagining Others' Dreams:** (pp. 238-247)
- Purpose is to help partners recognize the dream within the gridlocked position in *someone else's conflict.*

  - See if you can imagine and identify a dream within each position (of gridlocked issues in marriages as given on p. 238). Make up a story, or narrative, for each side of the gridlock. Imagine that this is your position and that it is very hard for you to yield on it. Think about how this dream relates to your own past life history--will eventually help you with your own gridlocked conflict.

- **Dreams Within Conflict:** (pp.247-250)

- Purpose is to uncover the unacknowledged dreams underlying fixed positions on conflict issues--not about airing resentments.

  - Couple discusses a gridlocked) marital issue but do not, under any circumstances, try to solve it. They look over checklist of dreams that people sometimes have that could underlie the position they have taken on this issue. Then they explain and share this with their partner. Husband speaks for 20 mins. and then they switch.
  - They ask each other these questions:
    - What do you believe about the issue?
    - What do you feel about it? Tell me all of your feelings about it.
    - What do you want to happen?

- What does it mean to you?
- How do you think your goals can be accomplished?
- When you look over the list of sample dreams, what symbolic meaning do you find for your position?

- Speaker's job: say honestly what this position means to him/her, what the dream might be behind this position, and to tell the story of what this dream means--where it comes from and what it symbolizes. Must be as clear as possible so partner understands.
- Listener's job: just listen the way a friend would listen. "Tell me the story of that." Listener suspends judgment and acts like someone who wants to hear the partner's story and the dream behind it--don't try to solve the problem.

[Gottman argues that you don't want to have the kind of marriage in which you win and are influential in the marriage but wind up crushing your partner's dream. You want the kind of marriage in which you are supporting one another's dreams. If your dreams connect, so much the better.]

- Implicit reframing in this exercise: Marital therapists have discovered that most marital conflict is defined by each spouse in terms of negative things they want the partner to stop doing. Change this way of thinking by getting spouses to describe what positive things they wish to see amplified in the marriage--focus solely on the positive.
- The gridlock could be resolved if each person were to understand what the partner's position meant symbolically--forget about the conflict and go for the hidden dream.

- **Honoring One Another's Dreams**: (pp. 250-251)

- Purpose is to help the couple find a way of honoring both people's life dreams within the gridlocked conflict. Honoring can mean many things, but it always means supporting and respecting.
  - Change the influence processes so that the couple moves toward honoring both people's life dreams.

- **Three steps to follow:**

  1. Define the minimal core areas that you cannot yield on.
  2. Define areas of greater flexibility that are not so "hot" emotionally.
  3. Come up with a temporary compromise and a plan.
      - E.g. She wants a cabin in a forest and it is very important for symbolic reasons. He feels that they cannot afford this and financial security is symbolically important for him.
  - Step 1: they define the minimal core areas--she wants at least a 3-room cabin on 2 acres of land, and he wants at least $30,000 as a start-up for long-term financial investment.
  - Step 2: they define their areas of flexibility--she says that time is an area of flexibility and wants the cabin in the next 3 yrs.
  - Step 3: they come up with the temporary compromise so that both dreams are realized. He says he can see saving half the extra money in the next 3 years for the cabin and some for the investment start-up fund. She will take on extra work to pay the mortgage, once they buy the cabin.

READING SIXTEEN

CULTURE AND INTERCULTURAL COMMUNICATION

Excerpts from: Devito, J. A. (2002). *Messages: Building Interpersonal Communication Skills*, 5th Edition, Boston, MA: Allyn & Bacon, Chapter Nine.

***

The word *culture,* you'll recall from Chapter 1, refers to the lifestyle of a group of people; their values, beliefs, artifacts, ways of behaving, and ways of communicating. Culture includes everything that members of a social group have produced and developed—their language, ways of thinking, art, laws, and religion— and that is transmitted from one generation to another through a process known as **enculturation.** You learn the values of your culture (that is, you become enculturated) through the teachings of your parents, peer groups, schools, religious institutions, government agencies, and media.

Acculturation refers to the processes by which a person's culture is modified through direct contact with or exposure to (say, through the mass media) another culture (Kim, 1988). For example, when immigrants settle in the United States (the host culture), their own culture becomes influenced by the host culture. Gradually the values, ways of behaving, and beliefs of the host culture become more and more a part of the immigrants' culture. At the same time, of course, the host culture changes too. Generally, however, the culture of the immigrants changes more. As Young Yun Kim (1988) puts it, "a reason for the essentially unidirectional change in the immigrant is the difference between the number of individuals in the new environment sharing the immigrant's original culture and the size of the host society."

The acceptance of the new culture depends on several factors (Kim, 1988). Immigrants who come from cultures similar to the host culture will become acculturated more easily. Similarly, those who are younger and better educated become acculturated more quickly than do older and less educated persons. Personality factors are also relevant. Persons who are risk takers and open-minded, for example, have a greater acculturation potential. Also, persons who are familiar with the host culture before immigration—whether through interpersonal contact or through mass media—will be acculturated more readily…

Intercultural communication is communication that takes place between persons of different cultures and is greatly influenced by both enculturation and acculturation processes. And **barriers to intercultural communication** often exist between persons who have different cultural beliefs, values, or ways of behaving.

...

Culture influences every aspect of your communication experience. And, of course, you receive messages through the filters imposed by a unique culture. Cultural filters, like filters on a camera, color the messages you receive. They influence what you receive and how you receive it. For example, some cultures rely heavily on television or newspapers for their news and trust them implicitly. Others rely on face-to-face interpersonal interactions, distrusting any of the mass communication systems. Some look to religious leaders as guides to behavior; others generally ignore them.

The term *intercultural* is used broadly to refer to all forms of communication among persons from different groups as well as to the more narrowly defined area of communication between different cultures….The model of intercultural communication…applies equally to communication between a smaller culture and the dominant or majority culture, communication between different smaller cultures, and communication between a variety of other groups. The following types of communication may all be considered "intercultural" and, more important, subject to the same barriers and gateways to effective communication identified in this chapter:

Communication between cultures—for example, between Chinese and Portuguese, or between French and Norwegian; races (sometimes called *interracial communication*): ethnic groups (sometimes called *interethnic communication*); people of different religious groups; nations (sometimes called *international communication*); smaller cultures existing within the larger culture; a smaller culture and the dominant culture; between gender.

...

Regardless of your own cultural background, you will surely come into close contact with people from a variety of other cultures—people who speak different languages, eat different foods, practice different religions, and approach work and relationships in very different ways. It doesn't matter whether you're longtime resident or a newly arrived immigrant: You are or soon will be living, going to school, working, and forming relationships with people who are from very different cultures. Your day-to-day experiences are sure to become increasingly intercultural.

Consider your own willingness to engage in intercultural communication by taking the self-test below...

TEST YOURSELF
How Open Are You Interculturally?

Instructions: Select a specific culture (national, racial, or religious) different from your own, and substitute this culture for the phrase *interculturally different person* in each item below. Indicate how open you would be to engage in each of the following communications, using this scale:

5 = very open and willing, 4 = open and willing, 3 = neutral, 2 = closed and unwilling, and 1 = very closed and unwilling.

____ 1. Talk with an interculturally different person while waiting alone for a bus.

____ 2. Talk with an interculturally different person in the presence of people who are culturally similar to you.

____ 3. Have a close (or "best") friendship with an interculturally different person.

____ 4. Have a long-term romantic relationship with an interculturally different person.

____ 5. Participate in a work team composed predominantly of interculturally different people.

____ 6. Listen openly and fairly in a conversation with an interculturally different person.

____ 7. Self-disclose to an interculturally different person to the same degree that you'd disclose to someone culturally similar to you.

____ 8. Listen to an interculturally different person disclosing his or her inner feelings in the same way as you would to someone culturally similar to you.

____ 9. Use the same conflict management strategies in an argument with an inter-culturally different person as in an argument with someone culturally similar to you.

____ 10. Take orders and direction from a supervisor who is interculturally different from you as you would from a supervisor culturally similar to you.

HOW DID YOU DO? This test was designed to raise questions rather than to provide answers. The items refer to various forms of interpersonal communication. High scores for any question or group of questions indicate considerable intercultural openness; low scores indicate a lack of intercultural openness.

WHAT WILL YOU DO? Use these numbers for purposes of thinking critically about your intercultural openness rather than to indicate any absolute level of openness or closeness. Did you select your "interculturally different" group on the basis of how positive or negative your attitudes were? What group would you be most open to interacting with? Least open? Are there specific types of interpersonal communication in which you're less likely to be interculturally open than others? For example, did you indicate a greater level of openness in item 1 than in item 10? Why is this so?

HOW CULTURES DIFFER

Cultures differ in terms of their (i) orientation (whether individualistic or collectivist), (2) context (whether high or low), and (3) masculinity—femininity; and each of these dimensions of difference has a significant impact on interpersonal communication (Hofstede, 1997; Hall & Hall, 1987; Gudykunst, 1991). Cultures also differ in their characteristic attitudes toward uncertainty, a topic discussed in Chapter 3.

Individualistic and Collectivist Cultures

...

The distinction between **individualistic** and **collectivist cultures** revolves around the extent to which the individual's goals or the group's goals are given greater importance. Individualistic and collectivist tendencies are not mutually exclusive; this is not an all-or-non orientation but rather one of emphasis. Thus, you may, for example, complete with other members of your basketball team for most baskets or most valuable player award. In a game, however, you will act in a way that will benefit the group. In actual practice both individualistic and collectivist tendencies will help you and your team each achieve your goals. Even so, at times these tendencies may conflict; for example, do you shoot for the basket and try to raise your own individual score, or do you pass the ball to another player who is better positioned to score the basket and thus benefit your team?

In an individualistic culture you're responsible for yourself and perhaps your immediate family; in a collectivist culture you're responsible for the entire group. In an individualistic culture success is measured by the extent to which you surpass other members of your group; you would take pride in standing out from the crowd. And your heroes—in the media, for example—are likely to be those who are unique and who stand apart. In a collectivist culture success is measured by your contribution to the achievements of the group as a whole; you would take pride in your similarity to other members of your group. Your heroes are more likely to be team players who do not stand out from the rest of the group's members.

In an individualistic culture you're responsible to your own conscience, and responsibility is largely an individual matter. In a collectivist culture you're responsible to the rules of the social group, and responsibility for an accomplishment or a failures is shared by all members. In individualistic cultures competition is promoted; in collectivist cultures cooperation is promoted.

...

Distinctions between in-group members and out-group members are extremely important in collectivist cultures. In individualistic cultures, which prize a person's individuality, these distinctions are likely to be less important.

High- and Low-Context Cultures

In a **high-context culture** much of the information in communication is in the context or in the person—for example, information shared through previous communications, through assumptions about each other; and through shared experiences. The information is not explicitly stated in the verbal message. In a **low-context culture** most information is explicitly stated in verbal messages, or, in formal transactions, in written (contract) form.

To appreciate the distinction between high and low context, consider giving directions ("Where's the voter registration center?") to someone who knows the neighborhood and to newcomer to your city. With someone who knows the neighborhood (a high-context situation), you can assume the person knows the local landmarks. So you can give directions such as "next to the laundromat on Main Street" or "the corner of Albany and Elm." With the newcomer (a low-context situation), you cannot assume the person shares any information with you. So you have to use directions that a stranger will understand; for example, "Make a left at the next stop sign" or "Go two blocks and then turn right."

High-context cultures are also collectivist cultures. These cultures (Japanese, Arabic, Latin American, Thai, Korean, Apache, and Mexican are examples) place great emphasis on personal relationships and oral agreements (Victor, 1992). Low-context cultures, on the other hand, are individualistic cultures. These cultures (German, Swedish, Norwegian, and American are examples) place less emphasis on personal relationships and more emphasis on explicit explanations and, for example, on written contracts in business transactions.

Members of high-context cultures spend lots of time getting to know each other before any important transactions take place. Because of this prior personal knowledge, a great deal of information is shared and therefore does not have to be explicitly stated. Members of low-context cultures spend less time getting to know each other and therefore do not have that shared knowledge. As a result everything has to be stated explicitly. High-context societies, for example, rely more on nonverbal cues in reducing uncertainty (Sanders, Wiseman, & Matz, 1991).

...

Another frequent difference and source of misunderstanding between high-and-low-context cultures is face saving (Hall & Hall, 1987). People in high-context cultures place a great deal more emphasis on face-saving. For example, they are more likely to avoid argument for fear of causing others to lose face, whereas people in low-context cultures (with their individualistic orientation) will use argument to win a point. Similarly, in high-context culture cultures criticism should take place only in private so the person can save face. Low-context cultures may not make this public-private distinction.

Members of high-context cultures are reluctant to say no for fear of offending and causing a person to lose face. So, for example, it's necessary to understand when a Japanese executive's yes means yes and when it means no. The difference is not in the words but in the way they are used. It's easy to see how a low-context individual may interpret this reluctance to be direct—to say no when you mean no—as a weakness or as an unwillingness to confront reality.

Members of high-context cultures also are reluctant to question the judgments of their superiors. So, for example, if a product were being manufactured with a defect, workers might be reluctant to communicate this back to management (Gross, Turner, & Cederholm, 1987).

...

TABLE 9.1 Some Individualistic and Collectivist Culture Differences

This table, base on the work of Hofstede (1997) and Hall and Hall (1987; Hall, 1983) and on interpretations by Gudykunst (1991) and Victor (1992), parallels the self-test presented earlier. As you read through the table, consider which statements you agree with, which you disagree with, and how these beliefs influence your communications. Can you identify additional differences between Individualistic and collectivist cultures?

INDIVIDUALISTIC (LOW-CONTEXT) CULTURES	COLLECTIVIST (HIGH-CONTEXT) CULTURES
Your goals are most important	The group's goals are most important
You're responsible for yourself and to your own conscience	You're responsible for the entire group and to the group's values and rules.
Success depends on your surpassing others; competition is emphasized	Success depends on your contribution to the group; cooperation is emphasized
Clear distinction is made between leaders and members	Little distinction is made between leaders and members; leadership is normally shared
Personal relationships are less important; for example, little time is spent getting to know each other in meetings	Personal relationships are extremely important; for example, much time is spent getting to know each other in meetings
Directness is valued; face-saving is seldom considered	Indirectness is valued; face-saving is a major consideration

IMPROVING INTERCULTURAL COMMUNICATION

Here are a variety of principles for increasing intercultural communication effectiveness—in conversation, on the job, in friendship and romantic relationships. These guidelines are based on the intercultural research of a wide variety of researchers (Barna, 1985; Ruben, 1985; Gudykunst, 1991, 1994; Hofstede, 1997). (Either before or after reading this section you may want to try your hand at intercultural communication with an exercise, "Random Paris," at .)

Reduce Your Ethnocentrism

Ethnocentrism, one of the biggest obstacles to intercultural communication, is the tendency to see others and their behaviors through your own cultural filters—even to see them as distortions of your own behaviors. It's the tendency to evaluate the values, beliefs, and behaviors of your own culture as more positive, logical, and natural than those of other cultures. To achieve effective interpersonal communication, you need to see your own and others' cultures as different but neither inferior nor superior—not a very easily accomplished task.

Ethnocentrism exists on a continuum. People are not either ethnocentric or non-ethnocentric; rather, most are somewhere between these extremes (Table 9.2 on the next page). Note also that your degree of ethnocentrism will depend on the group on which you're focusing. For example, if you're Greek American, you may have a low degree of ethnocentrism when dealing with Italian Americans but a high degree when dealing with Turkish Americans or Japanese Americans. Most important for our purposes is that your degree of ethnocentrism (and we're all ethnocentric to at least some degree) will influence your interpersonal (intercultural) communications.

Be Mindful

Being mindful rather than mindless (a distinction considered in Chapter 8) is generally helpful in intercultural communication situations. When you're in a mindless state, you often act on the basis of assumptions that would not pass intellectual scrutiny. For example, you know that cancer is not contagious, and yet many people will avoid touching cancer patients. You know that a person who cannot see does not necessarily have hearing problems, and yet many people use a louder voice when talking to persons without sight. In one study approximately one-third of the participating college students said that they would not go swimming in a pool used by mental patients and that they would wash their hands after touching a mental patient (Jones et al., 1984). When the discrepancies between behaviors and available evidence are pointed out and your mindful state is awakened, you quickly realize that such behaviors are not logical or realistic.

When you deal with people from other cultures, you're often in a mindless state and therefore may function nonrationally in many ways. Thus, suggestions for increasing intercultural communication effectiveness may appear logical (even obvious) to your mindful state but are probably frequently ignored in your mindless state. When your mindful state is awakened, as it is in textbook discussions such as this one, you may then turn to a more critical thinking mode and recognize, for example, that other people and other cultural systems may be different but not inferior or superior.

...

SKILLS TOOLBOX

7 Ways to Effective Intercultural Communication

The characteristics of conversational effectiveness (Chapter 8) are especially useful in the increasingly intercultural workplace. Exercise caution, of course, as there may be important cultural differences in the way these characteristics are expected to be used. Generally, however.

1. *Be open* to differences among people; especially to different values, beliefs, and attitudes, as well as ways of behaving. Recognize, too, that a person's willingness to self-disclose or to respond to disclosures is influenced both by the person's culture and by the culture of the organization. The lawyers on *Ally McBeal* are a lot more open with one another than lawyers are likely to be at real-life law firms.

2. *Empathize;* put yourself into the position of the person from another culture. Try to see the world from this different perspective. Let the person know that you feel as he or she is feeling. Use facial expressions, an attentive and interested body posture, and understanding and agreement responses to communicate your empathy.

3. *Communicate positiveness;* it helps put the other person at ease. Be aware, though, that the appropriateness of positive statements about the self will vary greatly with the culture. For example, some cultures expect speakers to use self-denigrating comments and to minimize their own contribution to, say, a team effort. Other cultures expect each person to acknowledge openly and without embarrassment his or her own contribution.

4. *Use immediacy* to unite yourself with others; communicate a sense of togetherness to counteract obvious intercultural differences. But realize that members of some cultures prefer to maintain greater interpersonal distance from others. The organizational culture will also influence the extent to which immediacy is expected.

5. *Engage in effective interaction management;* be especially sensitive to differences in turn-taking styles. Many Americans, especially those from large urban centers, have the habit of interrupting or of completing the other person's sentences. Some cultures consider this rude. In some organizations management is "permitted" to interrupt a worker's comments but not the other way around.

6. *Communicate expressiveness.* When differences among people are great, some persons feel uneasy and unsure of themselves. Counteract this by communicating genuine involvement in the interaction. Smile. Allow your facial muscles to express your interest and concern. At the same time, recognize that some cultures may frown on too much expressiveness.

7. *Be other-oriented;* focus your attention and the conversation on the other person. To show other-orientation use the techniques already considered, such as active listening, asking questions, and maintaining eye contact. Because some cultures may find these techniques too intrusive, look carefully for feedback that comments on the appropriateness of your other-oriented messages.

***

TABLE 9.2 The Ethnocentrism Continuum

Drawing from several researchers (Lukens, 1978; Gudykunst & Kim, 1984; Gudykunst, 1991), this table summarizes some interconnections between ethnocentrism and communication. In the table five degrees of ethnocentrism are identified; in reality, of course, there are as many degrees as there are people. Under "Communication Distance" are general terms that characterize the major communication attitude dominating that level of ethnocentrism. Under "Communications" are some ways people might behave given their particular degree of ethnocentrism. How would you have rated yourself on this scale five years ago? How would you rate yourself today?

DEGREES OF ETHNOCENTRISM	COMMUNICATION DISTANCE	COMMUNICATIONS
Low	Equality	Treats others as equals; evaluates other ways of doing things as equal to own ways
	Sensitivity	Wants to decrease distance between self and others
	Indifference	Lacks concern for others but is not hostile
	Avoidance	Avoids and limits interpersonal interactions with others; prefers to be with own kind
High	Disparagement	Engages in hostile behavior; belittles others; views own culture as superior to other cultures

Values Across Cultures

To explain the cultural value contrast more clearly, we developed the accompanying table, which compares specific contrasting values of American, Japanese, and Arab cultures. Reading across the table from left to right provides perspective on the values of each culture.

CULTURAL CONTRASTS IN VALUE

American		Japanese		Arabs	
1.	Freedom	1.	Belonging	1.	Family security
2.	Independence	2.	Group harmony	2.	Family harmony
3.	Self-reliance	3.	Collectiveness	3.	Parental guidance
4.	Equality	4.	Age/Seniority	4.	Age
5.	Individualism	5.	Group consensus	5.	Authority
6.	Competition	6.	Cooperation	6.	Compromise
7.	Efficiency	7.	Quality	7.	Devotion
8.	Time	8.	Patience	8.	Very patient
9.	Directness	9.	Indirectness	9.	Indirectness
10.	Openness	10.	Go-between	10.	Hospitality
11.	Aggressiveness	11.	Interpersonal	11.	Friendship
12.	Informality	12.	Hierarchy	12.	Formal/Admiration
13.	Future-orientation	13.	Continuation	13.	Past and present
14.	Risk-taking	14.	Conservative	14.	Religious belief
15.	Creativity	15.	Information	15.	Tradition
16.	Self-accomplishment	16.	Group achievement	16.	Social recognition
17.	Winning	17.	Success	17.	Reputation
18.	Money	18.	Relationship	18.	Friendship
19.	Material possessions	19.	Harmony with nature	19.	Belonging
20.	Privacy	20.	Networking	20.	Family network

In examining the table, we note that one of the top American values listed is freedom—freedom to choose your own destiny—whether it leads to success or failure. Japanese culture, on the other hand, finds a higher value in belonging. In this culture, you must belong to and support a group(s) to survive. Belonging to a group is more important to Japanese culture than individualism. Arab culture is less concerned with individualism or belonging to a group, concentrating instead on maintaining their own family security and relying on God for destiny. Individual identity is usually based on the background and position of each person's family.

The value American culture places on independence and individual freedom of choice naturally leads to the idea that everyone is equal regardless of age, social status, or authority. Japanese and Arab cultures, however, place more value on age and seniority. The Japanese individual will always give way to the feelings of the group, while Arabs respect authority and admire seniority and status.

In most business situations, Americans would come with a competitive attitude. The Japanese, conversely, value group cooperation in the pursuit of success. An Arab will make compromises in order to achieve a shared goal between two parties.

In American culture, the phrase "time is money" is commonly accepted as a framework for the desire to finish a task in the shortest amount of time with the greatest profit. If a process is considered inefficient, it "wastes" time and money, and possibly will be abandoned. The Japanese, however, value high quality over immediate gain, and they patiently wait for the best possible result. Arab culture also values quality more than immediacy, but the trust in the business relationship is the most important value.

Americans emphasize individual achievement and are results-oriented; therefore, they value directness and openness when dealing with others, enabling individuals to finish tasks more quickly. Because of these values of directness and equality, Americans tend to be informal when speaking and writing, often using first names. The Japanese prefer to follow an indirect, harmonious style when dealing with others. Go-betweens help to move the process along, and interpersonal harmony is considered more important than confrontation. However, Arabs prefer to negotiate directly in the spirit of hospitality and friendship until a compromise is reached.

American tend to be oriented toward the present and immediate gains, which explains why Americans value taking risks. To an American, accomplishing a task as quickly as possible brings the future closer. The Japanese, however, view time as a continuum, and are long-term oriented. As a result of their value of a long term, quality based relationship, the Japanese tend to be conservative and patient. The Arab culture believes that the present is a continuation of the past and that whatever happens in the future is due to fate and the will of God.

A principal value of American culture is individual achievement. When someone accomplishes something by him or herself, he or she expects and receives recognition for being a creative person, or the one who developed the best idea. The Japanese, because of their value of group achievement, seek information in order to help the entire group succeed. In Arab culture, the individual is not as important as preserving tradition. An Arab measures success by social recognition, status, honor, and reputation.

Source: From *Multicultural Management,* pp. 62-64, by Farid Elash-mawi and Philip R. Harris. Copyright © 1993 by Gulf Publishing Company. Used with permission. All rights reserved.

Face Fears

For example, you may fear for your self-esteem. You may become anxious about your ability to control the intercultural situation, or you may worry about your own level of discomfort. You may fear that you'll be taken advantage of by members of another culture. Depending on your own stereotypes, you may fear being lied to, financially duped, or made fun of. You may fear that members of this other group will react to you negatively. They may not like you, or they may disapprove of your attitudes or beliefs, or they may even reject you as a person. Conversely, you may fear negative reactions from members of your own group. They might, for example, disapprove of your socializing with the interculturally different.

These fears—coupled with the greater effort that intercultural communication takes and the ease with which you communicate with those who are culturally similar—can easily create sufficient anxiety to make some people give up.

Recognize Differences

When you assume that all people are similar and ignore the differences between yourself and the culturally different, your interculturally efforts are likely to fail. This is especially true in the area of values, attitudes, and beliefs. It's easy to see and accept different hairstyles, clothing, and foods. But when it comes to values and beliefs, it's easier to assume (mindlessly) that deep down we're all similar. We aren't. Henry may be a devout Baptist, Carol may be an atheist, and Jan may be a Muslim. Because of the differences in their religious views, these three individuals will see their lives as having very different meanings. When you assume similarities and ignore differences, you may implicitly communicate to others that you feel your ways are the right ways and theirs are the wrong ways. The result can be confusion and misunderstanding on both sides.

***

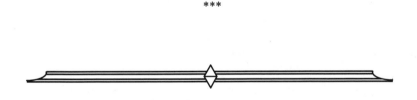

KEY REFERENCES

THE UNIVERSALS OF COMMUNICATION

The Interpersonal Communication book by J. Devito. (2001).

Albert, Rosita, and Nelson, Gayle L. (1993). Hispanic/Anglo American Differences in Attributions to Paralinguistic Behaviour. *International Journal of Intercultural Relations* 17 (Winter): 19-40.

Aune, R. Kelly, and Kikuchi, Toshiyuki. (1993). Effects of Language Intensity Similarity on Perceptions of Creditability, Relational Attributions and Persuations. *Journal of Language and Social Psychology* 12 (September): 224-238.

Bateson, Gregory (1972). *Steps to an Ecology of Mind.* New York: Ballantine.

Bavelas, Janet Beavin. (1990). Can One Not Communicate? Behaving and Communicating: A Reply to Motley. *Westin Journal of Speech Communication* 54 (Fall): 593-602

Beach, Wayne A. (1990). On (Not) Observing Behavior Interactionally. *Western Journal of Speech Communication* 54 (Fall): 603-612.

Buller, David B., and Aune, R. Kelly. (1992). The Effects of Speech Rate Similarity on Compliance: Application of Communication Accommodation Theory. *Western Journal of Communication* 56 (Winter): 37-53.

Buller, David B., LePoire, Beth A., Aune, R. Kelly, and Eloy, Sylvie. (1992). Social Perceptions as Mediators of the Effect of Speech Rate Similarity on Compliance. *Human Communication Research* 19 (December): 286-311.

Clement, Donald A., and Frandsen, Kenneth D.. (1976). On Conceptual and Empirical Treatments of Feedback in Human Communication. *Communication Monographs* 43: 11-28.

Giles, Howard, Mulac, Anthony, Bradac, James J., and Johnson, Patricia. (1987). Speech Accommodations Theory: The First Decade and Beyond. In *Communication Yearbook* 10, ed. Margaret L. McLaughlin. Thousand Oaks, CA: Sage, pp. 13-48.

Graham, E. E. (1994). Interpersonal Communication Motives Scale. In Communication Research Measures: A Sourcebook, ed. R. B. Rubin, P. Palmgreen, and H. Sypher. New York: Guilford, pp. 211-216.

Graham, E. E., Barbato, C. A., and Perse, E. M. (1993). The Interpersonal Communication Motives ` Models. *Communication Quarterly* 41: 172-186.

Holden, Janice M. (1991). The Most Frequent Personality Priority Pairings in Marriage and Marriage Counseling. *Individual Psychology Journal of Adlerian Theory, Research and Practice* 47 (September): 392-398.

Jaksa, James A., and Pritchard, Michael S. (1994). *Communication Ethics: Methods of Analysis*, (2nd ed.). Belmont, CA: Wadsworth.

Johannesen, Richard L. (1996). *Ethics in Human Communication.* 4th ed. Prospect Heights, IL: Waveland Press.

Main, Frank, and Oliver, Ronald. (1998). Complementary, Symmetrical, and Parallel Personality Priorities as Indicators of Marital Adjustment. *Individual PsychologyJournal of Adlerian Theory, Research and Practice* 44 (September): 324-332.

Malinowski, Bronislaw. (1923). The Problem of Meaning in Primitive Languages. In *The Meaning of Meaning*, ed. C. K. Ogden and I. A. Richards. New York: Harcourt Brace Jovanovich, pp. 296-336.

Martin, Matthew M., and Anderson, Carolyn M. (1995). Roommate Similarity: Are Roommates Who Are Similar in Their Communication Traits More Satisfied? *Communication Research Reports* 12 (Spring): 46-52.

McLaughlin, Margaret L. (1984). *Conversation: How Talk Is Organized*. Thousand Oaks, CA: Sage.

Motley, Michael T. (1990a). On Whether One Can(not) not Communicate: An Examination via Traditional Communication Postulates. *Western Journal of Speech Communication* 54 (Winter): 1-20.

Motley, Michael T. (1990b). Communication as Interaction: A Replay to Beach and Bavelas. *Western Journal of Speech Communication* 54 (Fall): 613-623.

Prosky, Phoebe S. (1992). Complimentary and Symmtrical Couples. *Family Therapy* 19:215-221.

Richards, I. A. (1951). Communication Between Men: The Meaning of Language. *In Cybernetics, Transactions of the Eighth Conference*, ed. Heinz von Foerster.

Rubin, Rebecca B., Fernandez-Collado, C., and Hernandez-Sampieri, R., (1992). A Cross Cultural Examination of Interpersonal Communication Motives in Mexico and the United States. *Interpersonal Journal of Intercultural Relations* 16:145-157.

Rubin, Rebecca B., and Graham, Elizabeth, E. (1988). Communication Correlates of College Success: An Exploration Investigation. *Communication Education* 37:14-27.

Rubin, Rebecca., Pearse, Elizabeth, and Barbato, Carole A. (1988). Conceptualization and Measurement of Interpersonal Communication Motives Scale. *Human Communication Research* 14:602-628.

Rubin, Rebecca B., and Martin M. M. (1994). Development of a Measure of Interpersonal Communication Competence. *Communication Research Reports* 11:33-44.

Schutz, Astrid. (1999). It Was Your Fault! Self-Serving Biases in Autobiographical Accounts of Conflict in Married Couples. *Journal of Social and Personal Relationships* 16:193-208.

Sptizberg, Brian H., and Cupach, William R. (1984). *Interpersonal Communication Competence*. Thousand Oaks, CA: Sage.

Watzlawick, Paul, Beavin, Janet Helmic, and Jackson, Don D. (1967). *Pragmatics of Human Communication: A Study of Interactional Patterns, Pathologies, and Paradoxes*. New York: W. W. Norton.

Weinstein, Eugene A., and Deutschberger, Paul. (1963). Some Dimensions of Altercasting. Sociometry 26:454-466.

Wertz, Dorothy C., Sorenson, James R., and Heeren, Timothy C. (1988). Can't Get No (Dis) Satisfaction: Professional Satisfaction with Professional-Client Encounters. *Work and Occupations* 15 (February): 36-54.

VERBAL MESSAGES

Messages: Building Interpersonal Communication Skills by J. DeVito. (2002).

Axtell, Roger. (1993, September). *Do's and Taboos Around the World* (3rd ed.). New York: Wiley.

Berger, Charles R., and Bradac, James J. (1982). *Language and Social Knowledge: Uncertainty in Interpersonal Relations.* London: Edward Arnold.

Berger, Charles R., and Calabrese, Richard J. (1975, Winter). Some Explorations in Initial Interaction and Beyond: Toward a Theory of Interpersonal Communication. *Human Communication Research,* 1 99-112.

Bosmajian, Haig. (1974). *The Language of Oppression.* Washington, DC: Public Affairs Press.

Coates, J., and Cameron, D. (1989). *Women, Men and Language: Studies in Language Linguistics.* London: Longman.

Gudykunst, W. B. (1994). *Bridging Differences: Effective Intergroup Communication* (2nd ed.). Thousand Oaks, CA: Sage.

Hecht, Michael L., Collier, Mary Jane, and Ribeau, Sidney. (1993). *African American Communication: Ethnic Identity and Cultural Interpretation.* Thousand Oaks, CA: Sage.

Hofstede, Geert. (1997). *Cultures and Organizations: Software of the Mind.* New York: McGraw-Hill.

Jandt, Fred E. (2000). *Intercultural Communication.* (3rd ed.). Thousand Oaks, CA: Sage.

Korzybski A. (1933). *Science and Sanity.* Lakeville, CT: The International Non-Aristotelian Library.

Kramarae, Cheris. (1974a). Folklinguistics. *Psychology Today,* 8, 82-85.

Kramarae, Cheris. (1974b). Stereotypes of Women's Speech: The Word from Cartoons. *Journal of Popular Culture,* 8, 624-630.

Kramarae, Cheris. (1977). Perceptions of Female and Male Speech. *Language and Speech,* 20, 151-161.

Kamarae, Cheris. (1981). *Women and Man Speaking.* Rowley, MA: Newbury House.

Larson, Charles U. (1998). *Persuasion: Reception and Responsibility* (8th ed.). Belmont, CA: Wadsworth.

Lever, Janet. (1995, August 22). The 1995 Advocate Survey of Sexuality and Relationships: The Women, Lesbian Sex Survey. *The Advocate,* 687/688, 22-30.

Lustig, Myron W., and Koester, Jolene. (1999). *Intercultural Competence: Interpersonal Communication Across Cultures* (3rd ed.). New York: HarperCollins.

Maggio, Rosalie. (1997). Talking About People: A Guide to Fair and Accurate Language. Phoenix, AZ: Oryx Press.

Penfield, Joyce (ed.). (1987). *Women and Language in Transition.* Albany: State University of New York Press.

Rich, Andrea L. (1974). *Interracial Communication*. New York: Harper and Row.

Schwartz, Marilyn, and the Task Force on Bias-Free Language of the Association of American University Presses. (1995). *Guidelines for Bias-Free Writing*. Bloomington: Indiana University Press.

Weinberg, Harry L. (1959). *Levels of Knowing and Existence*. New York: Harper and Row.

Wrighter, Carl. (1972). *I Can Sell You Anything*. New York: Ballentine.

NON VERBAL MESSAGES

Messages: Building Interpersonal Communication Skills by J.A DeVito. (2002).

Albas, Daniel C., McCluskey, Ken W., and Albas, Cheryl A. (1976, December).Perception of the Emotional Content of Speech: A Comparison of Two Canadian Groups. *Journal of Cross-Cultural Psychology*, 7, 481-490.

Argyle, Michael. (1988). *Bodily Communication* (2nd ed.). New York: Methune.

Argyle, M., and Ingham, R. (1972). Gaze, Mutual Gaze and Distance. *Semiotica*, 1, 32-49.

Axtell, Roger E. (1990). Do's and Taboos of Hosting International Visitors. New York: Wiley.

Bosmajian, Haig. (1974). *The Language of Oppression*. Washington, DC: Public Affairs Press.

Brody, Jane E. (1994, March 21). Notions of Beauty Transcends Culture, New Study Suggests. *The New York Times*, p. A14.

Burgoon, Judee K., Buller, David B., and Woodall, W. Gill. (1995). *Nonverbal Communication: The Unspoken Dialogue* (2nd ed.). New York: MaGraw-Hill.

Cappella, Joseph N. (1993, March-June). The facial Feedback Hypothesis in Human Interaction: Review and Speculation. *Journal of Language and Social Psychology*, 12, 13-29.

Coates, J., and Cameron, D. (1989). *Women, Men and Language: Studies in Language Linguistics*. London: Longman.

Devito, Joseph A., and Hecht, Michael L. (Eds.). (1990). *The Nonverbal Communication Reader*. Prospect Heights, Il: Waveland Press.

Ehrenhaus, Peter. (1988, March). Silence and Symbolic Expression. *Communication Monographs*, 55, 41-57.

Ekman, Paul. (1985b). *Telling Lies: Clues to Deceit in the Marketplace, Politics and Marriage*. New York: Norton.

Ekman, Paul, Friesen, Wallace V., and Ellsworth, Phoebe. (1972). *Emotion in the Human Face: Guidelines for Research and an Integration of Findings*. New York: Pergamon Press.

Goffman, Erving. (1967). *Interaction Ritual: Essays on Face-to-Face Behavior*. New York: Pantheon.

Graham, Jean Ann, and Argyle, Michael. (1975, December). The Effects of Different Patterns of Gaze Combined with Different Facial Expressions, on Impression Formation. *Journal of Movement Studies,* 1, 178-182.

Graham, Jean Ann, Bitti, Pio Ricci and Argyle, Michael. (1975, June). A Cross-Cultural Study of the Communication of Emotion by Facial and Gestural Cues. *Journal of Human Movement Studies,* 1, 68-77.

Hall, Edward T. (1959). *The Silent Language.* Garden City, NY: Doubleday.

Hall, Edward T. (1966). *The Hidden Dimension.* Garden City , NY: Doubleday.

Hall, Judith A. (1984). *Nonverbal Sex Differences.* Baltimore: John Hopkins University Press.

Hecht, Michael L., Collier, Mary Jane, and Ribeau, Sidney. (1993). African American Communication: Ethnic Identity and Cultural Interpretation. Thousand Oaks, CA: Sage.

Hess, Eckhard H. (1975). The Tell-Tale Eye. New York: Van Nostrand Reinhold.

Hess, Ursula, Kappas, Arvid, McHugo, Gregory J., Lanzetta, John T., et al. (1992, May). The Facilitative Effect of Facial Expression on the Self-Generation of Emotion.*International Journal of Psychophysiology,* 12, 251-265.

Jackson, Linda A., and Ervin, Kelly S. (1992, August). Height Stereotypes of Women and Men: The Liabilities of Shortness for Both Sexes. *Journal of Social Psychology*, 132, 433-445.

Jandt, Fred E. (2000). *Intercultural Communication.* (3rd ed.). Thousand Oaks, CA: Sage.

Jaworski, Adam. (1993). *The Power of Silence: Social and Pragmatic Perspectives.* Thousand Oaks, CA: Sage.

Johannesen, Richard L. (1974, Winter). The Functions of Silence: A Plea for Communication Research. *Western Speech,* 38, 25-35.

Jones, Stanley, and Yarbrough, A. Elaine. (1985). A Naturalistic Study of the Meanings of Touch. *Communication Monographs,* 52, 19-56.

Keyes, Ralph. (1980). *The Height of your Life.* New York: Warner Books.

Knapp, Mark L., and Hall, Judith. (1996). *Nonverbal Behavior in Human Interaction.* (3rd ed.). New York: Holt, Rinehart, and Winston.

Lanzetta, J. T., Cartwright-Smith, J., And Kleck, R. E. (1976). Effects of Nonverbal Dissimulations on Emotional Experience and Autonomic Arousal. *Journal of Personality and Social Psychology*, 33, 354-370.

Larsen, Randy J., Kasimatis, Margaret, and Frey, Kurt. (1992, September). Facilitating the Furrowed Brow: An Unobtrusive Test of the Facial Feedback Hypothesis Applied to Unpleasant Affect. *Cognition and Emotion*, 6, 321-338.

Leathers, Dale G. (1997). *Successful Nonverbal Communication: Principals and Applications* (2nd ed.). New York: Macmillan.

Lever, Janet. (1995, August 22). The 1995 Advocate Survey of Sexuality and Relationships: The Women, Lesbian Sex Survey. *The Advocate*, 687/688, 22-30.

Ma, Ringo. (1992, Summer). The Role of Unofficial Intermediaries in Interpersonal Conflicts in the Chinese Culture. *Communication Quarterly*, 40, 269-278.

MacLachlan, James. (1979). What People Really Think of Fast Talkers. *PsychologyToday*, 13, 113-117.

Maggio, Rosalie. (1997). Talking About People: A Guide to Fair and Accurate Language. Phoenix, AZ: Oryx Press.

Malandro, Loretta A., Barker, Larry, and Barker, Deborah Ann. (1989). *Nonverbal Communication* (2nd ed.). New York: Random House.

Marshall, Evan. (1983). *Eye Language: Understanding the Eloquent Eye*. New York: New Trend.

Matsumoto, David. (1991, Winter). Cultural Influences on Facial Expressions of Emotion. *Southern Communication Journal*, 56, 128-137.

Mir, Montserrat. (1993). *Direct Requests Can Also Be Polite*. Paper presented at the annual meeting of the International Conference on Pragmatics and Language Learning, Champaign, IL.

Molloy, John. (1977). The Women's Dress for Success Book. Chicago: Follett.

Montagu, Ashley. (1971). Touching: The Human Significance of the Skin. New York: Harper and Row.

Noble, Barbara Presley. (1994, August 14). The Gender Wars: Talking Peace. *The New York Times*, p. 21.

Penfield, Joyce (ed.). (1987). *Women and Language in Transition*. Albany: State University of New York Press.

Rich, Andrea L. (1974). *Interracial Communication*. New York: Harper and Row.

Rundquist, Suellen. (1992, November). Indirectness: A Gender Study of Flaunting Grice's Maxims. *Journal of Pragmatics*, 18, 431-449.

Schwartz, Marilyn, and the Task Force on Bias-Free Language of the Association of American University Presses. (1995). *Guidelines for Bias-Free Writing*. Bloomington: Indiana University Press.

Tannen, Deborah. (1994b). *Talking from 9 to 5*. New York: Morrow.

Tarnove, Elizabeth J. (1988). *Effects of Sexist Language on the Status and Self-Concept of Women*. Paper presented at the annual meeting of the Association for Education. In Journalism and Mass Communication, Portland, OR.

Trager, George L. (1958). Paralanguage: A First Approximation. *Studies in Linguistics*, 13, 1-12.

Trager, George L. (1961). The Typology of Paralanguage. *Anthropological Linguistics*, 3, 17-21.

SOCIAL COGNITION:
HOW WE THINK ABOUT THE SOCIAL WORLD

From Social Psychology, 3rd Canadian Edition by E. Aronson, T. Wilson, R. Akert, B. Fehr (2007).

Anderson, C. A. (1995). Implicit personality theories and empirical data: Biased assimilation, belief perseverance and change, and covariation detection sensitivity. *Social Cognition, 13*, 25-48.

Anderson, C. A. (1999). Attributional style, depression, and loneliness: A cross- cultural comparison of American and Chinese students. *Personality and Social Psychology Bulletin, 25*, 482-499.

Anderson, C. A., Lepper, M. R., & Ross, L. (1980). The perseverance of social theories: The role of explanation in the persistence of discredited information. *Journal of Personality and Social Psychology, 39*, 1037-1049.

Anderson, C. A., & Lindsay, J. J. (1998). The development, perseverance, and change of naive theories. *Social Cognition, 16*, 8-30.

Babad, E. (1993). Pygmalion-25 years after interpersonal expectations in the classroom. In P. D. Blank (Ed.), *Interpersonal expectations: Theory, research, and applications.* (pp. 125-153.) New York: Cambridge University Press.

Bargh, J. A., & Chartrand, T. L. (1999). The unbearable automaticity of being. American Psychologist, 54, 462-479.

Bargh, J. A., & Ferguson, M. J. (2000). Beyond behaviorism: On the automaticity of higher mental processes. *Psychological Bulletin, 126*, 925-945.

Bartlett, D. C. (1932). *Remembering*. Cambridge: Cambridge University Press.

Behrmann, M., Winocur, G., & Moscovitch, M. (1992). Dissociation between mental imagery and object recognition in a brain damaged patient. *Nature, 359, 636-637.*

Blank, P. D. (Ed.) (1993). *Interpersonal expectations: Theory, research, and applications.* New York: Cambridge University Press.

Branscombe, N. R., Owen, S., Garstka, T. A., & Coleman, J. (1996). Rape and accident counterfactuals: Who might have done otherwise and would it have changed the outcome? *Journal of Applied Social Psychology, 26*, 1042-1067.

Brattesani, K. A., Weinstein, R. S., & Marshall, H. H. (1984). Student perceptions of differential teacher treatment as moderators of teacher expectation effects. Journal of *Educational Psychology, 76*, 236-247.

Brophy, J. E. (1983). Research on the self-fulfilling prophecy and teacher expectations. *Journal of Educational Psychology, 75*, 631-661.

Buehler, R., Griffin, D. W., & Ross, M. (2002). Inside the planning fallacy: The causes and consequences of optimistic time preferences. In T. Gilovich, D. W. Griffin, & D. Kahneman (Eds.), *Heuristics and biases: The psychology of intuitive judgment* (pp. 250-270.) New York: Cambridge University Press.

Chaiken, S. (1987). The heuristic model of persuasion. In M. P Zanna, J. M. Olson, & C. P. Herman (Eds.), *Social influence: The Ontario Symposium.* (Vol. 5, pp. 3-39.) Hillsdale, NJ: Erlbaum.

Chen, M., & Bargh, J. A. (1997). Nonconscious behavioral confirmation processes: The self-fulfilling consequences of automatic stereotype activation. *Journal of Experimental Social Psychology, 33*, 541-560.

Chen, S., & Andersen, S. M. (1999). Relationships from the past in the present: Significant other representations and transference in interpersonal life. In M. P. Zanna (Ed.), *Advances in experimental social psychology.* (Vol. 31, pp. 123-190.) San Diego, CA: Academic Press.

Darley, J. M., & Akert, R. M. (1993). Biographical interpretation: The influence of later events in life on the meaning of and memory for earlier events. *Unpublished manuscript*, Princeton University.

Davies, M. F. (1997). Belief persistence after evidential discrediting: The impact of generated versus provided explanations on the likelihood of discredited outcomes. *Journal of Experimental Social Psychology, 33*, 561-578.

Davis, C. G., & Lehman, D. R. (1995). Counterfactual thinking and coping with traumatic life events. In N. J. Roese & J. M. Olson (Eds.), *What might have been: The social psychology of counterfactual thinking.* (pp. 353-374.) Mahwah, NJ: Eribaum.

Devine, P. G. (1989b). Stereotypes and prejudice: Their automatic and controlled components. *Journal of Personality and Social Psychology, 56*, 5-18.

Devine, P G., & Monteith, M. J. (1999). Automaticity and control in stereotyping. In S. Chaiken & Y. Trope (Eds.), *Dual-process theories in social psychology.* (pp. 339-360.) New York: Guilford Press.

Dijksterhuis, A., & van Knippenberg, A. (1996). The knife that cuts both ways: Facilitated and inhibited access to traits as a result of stereotype activation. *Journal of Experimental Social Psychology, 32*, 271-288.

Dougherty, M. R. P., Gettys, C. F., & Ogden, E. E. (1999). MINERVA- DM: A memory process model of judgments of likelihood. *Psychological Review, 106*, 180-209.

Dunn, D. S., & Wilson, T. D. (1990). When the stakes are high: A limit to the illusion of control effect.

Englich, B., & Mussweiler, T. (2001). Sentencing under uncertainty: Anchoring effects in the courtroom. *Journal of Applied Social Psychology, 31*, 1535-1551.

Eraker, S. A., & Politser, P. (1988). How decisions are reached: Physicians and the patient. In J. Dowie & A. S. Elstein (Eds.), *Professional judgment: A reader in clinical decision making.* (pp. 379-394.) Cambridge, UK: Cambridge University Press.

Fiske, S. T. (1989a). Examining the role of intent: Toward understanding its role in stereotyping the prejudice. In J. S. Uleman & J. A. Bargh (Eds.), *Unintended thought.* (pp. 253-283.) New York: Guilford.

Fong, G. T., Krantz, D. H., & Nisbett, R. E. (1986). The effects of statistical training on thinking about everyday problems. *Cognitive Psychology, 18*, 253-292.

Ford, T. E., & Thompson, E. P. (2000). Preconscious and postconscious processes underlying construct accessibility effects: An extended search model. *Personality and Social Psychology Review, 4*, 317-336.

Fox, J. (1980). Making decisions under the influence of memory. *Psychological Review, 87*, 190-211.

Frankel, Glenn. (2005, 24 July). *London Police Had Expressed "Deep Regret" for Bystander Shooting.* www.washingtonpost.com. Retrieved August 3, 2005.

Gigerenzer, G. (2000). *Adaptive thinking: Rationality in the real world.* Oxford, UK: Oxford University Press.

Gilbert, D. T. (1991). How mental systems believe. *American Psychologist, 46,* 107-119.

Gilovich, T. (1991). *How we know what isn't so: The fallibility of human reasoning in everyday life.* New York: Free Press.

Gilovich, T., & Griffin, D. W. (2002). Introduction: Heuristics and biases, now and then. In T. Gilovich, D. W. Griffin, & D. Kahneman (Eds.), *Heuristics and biases: The psychology of intuitive judgment.* (pp. 1-18.) New York: Cambridge University Press.

Harkness, A. R., DeBono, K. G., & Borgida, E. (1985). Personal involvement and strategies for making contingency judgements: A stake in the dating game makes a difference. *Journal of Personality and Social Psychology, 49,* 22- 32.

Higgins, E. T. (1996). Knowledge application: Accessibility, applicability, and salience. In E. T. Higgins and A. R. Kruglanski (Eds.), *Social psychology: Handbook of basic principles.* (pp. 133-168.) New York: Guilford.

Higgins, E. T., & Brendl, C. M. (1995). Accessibility and applicability: Some "activation rules" influencing judgment. *Journal of Experimental Social Psychology, 31,* 218-243.

Jussim, L. (1986). Self-fulfilling prophecies: A theoretical and integrative review. *Psychological Review, 93,* 429-445.

Jussim, L. (1989). Teacher expectations: Self-fulfilling prophecies, perceptual biases, and accuracy. *Journal of Personality and Social Psychology, 57,* 469-480.

Jussim, L. (1991). Social perception and social reality: A reflection construction model. *Psychological Review, 98,* 54-73.

Kruglanski, A. W. (1989). *Lay epistemics and human knowledge.* New York: Plenum.

Kruglanski, A. W., & Webster, D. M. (1996). Motivated closing of the mind: "Seizing" and "freezing." *Psychological Review, 103,* 263-283.

Krull, D. S., & Dill, J. C. (1996). On thinking first and responding fast: Flexibility in social inference processes. *Personality and Social Psychology Bulletin, 22,* 949-959.

Kunda, Z. (1999). *Social cognition: Making sense of people.* Cambridge, MA,: MIT Press.

Kunda, Z., Sinclair, L., & Griffin, D. (1997). Equal ratings but separate meanings: Stereotypes and the construal of traits. *Journal of Personality and Social Psychology, 72,* 720-734.

Lange, E. J. (1975). The illusion of control. *Journal of Personality and Social Psychology, 32,* 311-328.

Lyubomirsky, S., Caidwell, N. D., & Nolen-Hoeksema, S. (1993). Effects of ruminative and distracting responses to depressed mood on retrieval of autobiographical memories. *Journal of Personality and Social Psychology, 75,* 166-177.

Madon, S., Jussim, L., & Eccles, J. (1997). In search of the powerful self-fulfilling prophecy. *Journal of Personality and Social Psychology, 72*, 791-809.

Major, B., & Gramzow, R. H. (1999). Abortion as stigma: Cognitive and emotional implications of concealment. Journal of Personality and Social Psychology, 77, 735-745.

Mandel, D. R., & Lehman, D. R. (1996). Counterfactual thinking and descriptions of cause and preventability. *Journal of Personality and Social Psychology, 71*, 450-463.

Marion, R. (1995, August). *The girl who mewed.* Discover, pp. 38-40.

Markus, H. (1977). Self-schemata and processing information about the self. *Journal of Personality and Social Psychology, 35*, 63-78.

Markus, H. R., & Zajonc, R. B. (1985). The cognitive perspective in social psychology. In G. Lindzey & E. Aronson (Eds.), *Handbook of social psychology.* (3rd ed., Vol. 1, pp. 137-230.) New York: McGraw-Hill.

Martin, L. L. (1986). Set/reset: Use and disuse of concepts in impression formation. *Journal of Personality and Social Psychology, 51*, 493-504.

Martin, L. L., Seta, J. J., & Crelia, R. (1990). Assimilation and contrast as a function of people's willingness and ability to expend effort in forming an impression. *Journal of Personality and Social Psychology*, 59,27-37.

Mckelvie, S. J. (1995). Biases in the estimated frequency of names. *Perceptual and Motor Skills, 81*, 1331-1338.

Metcalfe, J. (1998). Cognitive optimism: Self-deception or memory based processing heuristics? *Personality and Social Psychology Review, 2*, 100-110.

Mussweiler, T., & Strack, F. (1999). Comparing is believing: A selective accessibility model of judgmental anchoring. In W. Stroebe & M. Hewstone (Eds.), *European Review of social psychology.* (Vol. 10, pp. 135-167.) Chichester, UK: Wiley.

Nisbett, R. E., & Ross, L. (1980). *Human inference: Strategies and shortcomings of human judgment.* Englewood Cliffs, NJ: Prentice Hall.

Payne, B. K. (2001). Prejudice and Perception: The role of automatic and controlled processes in misperceiving a weapon. *Journal of Personality and Social Psychology, 81*, 1-12.

Petrie, K. J., Booth, R. J., & Pennebaker, J. W. (1998). The immunological effects of thought suppression. *Journal of Personality and Social Psychology, 75*, 1264-1272.

Petty, R. E., & Cacioppo, J. T. (1986). *Communication and persuasion: Central and peripheral routes to attitude change.* New York: Springer-Verlag.

Petty, R. E., Priester, J. R., & Brinol, P. (2002). Mass media attitude change: Implications of the elaboration likelihood model of persuasion. In J. Bryant, & D. Zillmann (Eds.), *Media effects: Advances in theory and research.* (2nd ed., pp. 155-198.) Mahwah, NJ: Erlbaum.

Petty, R. E., & Wegener, D. T. (1999). The elaboration likelihood model: Current status and controversies. In S. Chaiken & Y. Trope (Eds.), *Dual-process theories in social psychology.* (pp. 41-72.) New York: Guilford Press.

Quattrone, G. A. (1982). Behavioral consequences of attributional bias. *Social Cognition, 1*, 358-378.

Renaud, J. M., & McConnell, A. R. (2002). Organization of the self-concept and the suppression of self-relevant thoughts. *Journal of Experimental Social Psychology, 38*, 79-86. Relations, 2, 161-185.

Roese, N. J. (1997). Counterfactual thinking. *Psychological Bulletin*, 121,133-148.

Roese, N. J., & Olson, J. M. (1997). Counterfactual thinking: The intersection of affect and function. In M. Zanna (Ed.), *Advances in experimental social psychology.* (Vol. 29.) San Diego, CA: Academic Press.

Rosenthal, R. (1994). Interpersonal expectancy effects: A 30-year perspective. *Current Directions in Psychological Science, 3*, 176-179.

Rothman, A. J., & Hardin, C. D. (1997). Differential use of the availability heuristic in social judgment. *Personality and Social Psychology Bulletin, 23*, 123- 138.

Rudman, L. A., & Borgida, E. (1995). The afterglow of construct accessibility: The behavioral consequences of priming men to view women as sexual objects. *Journal of Experimental Social Psychology, 31*,493-517.

Schaller, M., Park, J. H., & Mueller, A. (2003). Fear of the dark: Interactive effects of beliefs about danger and ambient darkness on ethnic stereotypes. *Personality and Social Psychology Bulletin, 29: 5*, 637-649.

Schwarz, N., Bless, H., Strack, F., Klumpp, G., Rittenauer-Schatka, H., & Simmons, A. (1991). Ease of retrieval as information: Another look at the availability heuristic. *Journal of Personality and Social Psychology, 61*, 195-202.

Schwarz, N. & Vaughn, L. A. (2002). The availability heuristic revisited: Ease of recall and content of recall as distinct sources of information. In T. Gilovich, D. W. Griffin, & D. Kahneman (Eds.), *Heuristics and biases: The psychology of intuitive judgment.* (pp. 103-119.) New York: Cambridge University Press.

Scott, D. (1999). Equal opportunity, unequal results: Determinants of household recycling intensity. *Environment and Behavior, 31*, 267-290.

Slusher, M. P., & Anderson, C. A. (1989). Belief perseverance and self-defeating behavior. In R. Curtis (Ed.), *Self-defeating behaviors: Experimental research, clinical impressions, and practical implications.* (pp. 11-40.) New York: Plenum.

Smith, A. E., Jussim, L., & Eccles, J. (1999). Do self-fulfilling prophecies accumulate, dissipate, or remain stable over time? *Journal of Personality and Social Psychology, 77*, 548-565.

Snyder, M. (1984). When belief creates reality. In L. Berkowitz (Ed.), *Advances in experimental social psychology.* (Vol. 18, pp. 247-305.) Orlando, FL: Academic Press.

Strack, F., & Hannover, B. (1996). Awareness of influence as a precondition for implementing correctional goals. In P M. Gollwitzer & J. A. Bargh (Eds.), *The psychology of action: Linking cognition and motivation to behavior.* (pp. 579-596.) New York: Guilford.

Taylor, S. E., & Crocker, J. (1981) Schematic bases of social information processing. In E. T. Higgins, C. P. Herman, & M. P. Zanna (Eds.), *Social cognition: The Ontario Symposium.* (Vol. 1, pp. 89-134.) Hillsdale, NJ: Erlbaum.

Tetlock, P. E. (1992). The impact of accountability on judgment and choice: Toward a social contingency model. In M. P. Zanna (Ed.), *Advances in experimental social psychology*. (Vol. 25, pp. 331-376.) San Diego, CA: Academic Press.

Todorov, A., & Bargh, J. A. (2002). Automatic sources of aggression. *Aggression and Violent Behavior, 7*, 53-68.

Travis, C. B., Phillippi, R. H., & Tonn, B. E. (1989). Judgment heuristics and medical decisions. *Patient Education and Counseling, 13*, 211-220.

Trope, Y., & Lieberman, A. (1996). Social hypothesis testing: Cognitive and motivational mechanisms. In E. T. Higgins & A. W. Kruglanski (Eds.), *Social psychology: Handbook of basic principles*. (pp. 239-270.) New York: Guilford Press.

Vallone, R. P., Gariffin, D. W., Lin, S., & Ross, L. (1990). The overconfident prediction of future actions and outcomes by self and others. *Journal of Personality and Social Psychology, 58*, 582-592.

Wegner, D. M. (2002). *The illusion of conscious will*. Cambridge, MA: MIT Press.

Wegner, D. M., & Bargh, J. A. (1998). Control and automaticity in social life. In D. Gilbert, S. Fiske, & G. Lindzey (Eds.), *The handbook of social psychology*. (4th ed., Vol. 1, pp. 446-498.) New York: McGraw Hill.

Wilson, T. D. (2002). *Strangers to ourselves: Self-insight and the adaptive unconscious*. Cambridge, MA: Harvard University Press.

Wilson, T. D., & Brekke, N. C. (1994). Mental contamination and mental correction: Unwanted influences on judgments and evaluations. *Psychological Bulletin, 116*, 117-142.

Wyer, R. S., & Srull, T. K. (1998). *Memory and cognition in its social context*. Hillsdale, NJ: Erlbaum.

SOCIAL PERCEPTION:
HOW WE COME TO UNDERSTAND OTHER PEOPLE

From Social Psychology, 3rd Canadian Edition by E. Aronson, T. Wilson, R. Akert, B. Fehr (2007).

Ambady, N., & Rosenthal, R. (1992). Thin slices of expressive behavior as predictors of interpersonal consequences: A meta-analysis. *Psychological Bulletin, 111*, 256-274.

Anderson, C. A. (1999). Attributional style, depression, and loneliness: A cross-cultural comparison of American and Chinese students. *Personality and Social Psychology Bulletin, 25*, 482-499.

Archer, D. (1997b). Unspoken diversity: Cultural differences in gestures. *Qualitative Sociology, 20*, 79-105.

Archer, D., & Akert, R. M. (1980). The encoding of meaning: A test of three theories of social interaction. *Sociological Inquiry, 50*:3-4, 393-419.

Archer, D., & Akert, R. M. (1984). Problems of context and criterion in nonverbal communication: A new look at the accuracy issue. In M. Cook (Ed.), *Issues in person perception.* (pp. 114-144.) London and New York: Methuen.

Archer, D., & Akert, R. M. (1998). *The interpretation of behavior: Verbal and nonverbal factors in person perception.* New York: Cambridge University Press.

Argyle, M. (1975). *Bodily communication.* New York: International Universities Press.

Aune, K. S. & Aune, R. K. (1996). Cultural differences in the self-reported experience and expression of emotions in relationships. *Journal of Cross- Cultural Psychology, 27,* 67-8

Bargh, J. A. (1994). The four horseman of automaticity: Awareness, intention, efficiency, and control in social cognition. In R. S. Wyer Jr., & T. K. Srull (Eds.), *Handbook of Social Cognition.* (Vol. 1, pp. 1-40.) Hillsdale, NJ: Erlbaum.

Barrett, L. F, Lane, R. D., Sechrest, L., & Schwartz, G. E. (2000). Sex differences in emotional awareness. *Personality and Social Psychology Bulletin, 26,* 1027-1035.

Berry, D. S., & McArthur, L. Z. (1986). Perceiving character in faces: The impact of age-related craniofacial changes in social perception. *Psychological Bulletin, 100,* 3-18.

Biehl, M., Matsumoto, D., Ekman, P., Hearn, V., Heider, K., Kudoh, T., & Ton, V. (1997). Matsumoto and Ekman's Japanese and Caucasian facial expressions of emotion (JACFEE): Reliability and cross-national differences. *Journal of Nonverbal Behavior, 21,* 3-21.

Blairy, S., Herrera, B, & Hess, U. (1999). Mimicry and the judgment of emotional facial expressions. *Journal of Nonverbal Behavior, 23,* 5-41.

Bond, M. H. (1996). Chinese values. In M. H. Bond (Ed.), *The book of Chinese psychology.* (pp. 208-226.) Hong Kong: Ox University Press.

Buck, R. (1984). *The communication of emotion.* New York: Guilford Press.

Burger, J. M. (1991). Changes in attributions over time: The ephemeral fundamental attribution error. *Social Cognition, 9,* 182-193.

Butler, E. A., Egloff, B., Wilhelm, F H., Smith, N. C., & Erickson, A. (2003). *The social consequences of expressive suppression Emotion, 3,* 48-67.

Carlston, D. E., & Skowronski, J. J. (1994). Savings in the relearning of trait information as evidence of spontaneous inference generation. *Journal of Personality and Social Psychology, 66,* 840-856.

Carroll, J. M., & Russell, J. A. (1996). Do facial expressions signal specific emotions? Judging emotion from the face in context. *Journal of Personality and Social Psychology, 70,* 205-218.

Carter, B. (2000, August 24). CBS is surprise winner in ratings contest. *New York Times,* p. A22.

Carter, B. (2003, May 19). Even as executives scorn the genre, TV net- works still rely on reality. *The New York Times,* p. C l, C7.

Davis, M. H., & Stephan, W. G. (1980). Attributions for exam performance. *Journal of Applied Social Psychology, 10,* 235-248.

Deaux, K., & Major, B. (1987). Putting gender into context: An interactive model of gender-related behavior. *Psychological Review, 94,* 369-389. Harvard School of Public Health.

DeMarco, P. (1994, September 28). Dear diary, *New York Times*, p. C2.

DePaulo, B. M., Epstein, J. A., & Wyer, M. M. (1993). Sex differences in lying: How women and men deal with the dilemma of deceit. In M. Lewis & C. Saarni (Eds.), *Lying and deception in everyday life.* (pp. 126-147.) New York: Guilford Press.

DePaulo, B. M., & Friedman, H. 5. (1998). Nonverbal communication, In D. Gilbert, S. Fiske, & G. Lindzey (Eds.), *The handbook of social psychology.* (4th ed., Vol. 2, pp. 3-40.) New York: McGraw Hill.

Dion, K. K., Berscheid, E., & Walster (Hatfield), E. (1972). What is beautiful is good. *Journal of Personality and Social Psychology, 24*, 285-290.

Eagly, A. H., & Karau, S. J. (2002). Role congruity theory of prejudice toward female leaders. *Psychological Review, 109*, 573-598.

Ekman, P. (1965). Communication through nonverbal behavior: A source of information about an interpersonal relationship. In S. S. Tomkins & C. E. (Eds.), *Affect, cognition, and personality.* (pp. 390-442.) New York: Springer-Verlag.

Ekman, P. (1993). Facial expression and emotion. *American Psychologist, 48,* 384-392.

Ekman, P. (1994). Strong evidence for universals in facial expressions: A reply to Russell's mistaken critique. *Psychological Bulletin, 115*, 268-287.

Ekman, P., & Davidson, R. J. (Eds.) (1994). *The nature of emotion: Fundamental questions.* New York: Oxford University Press.

Ekman, F, & Friesen, W. V. (1969). The repertoire of nonverbal behavior: Categories, origins, usage, and coding. *Semiotica, 1,* 49-98.

Ekman, P., & Friesen, W. V. (1975). *Unmasking the face.* Englewood Cliffs, NJ: Prentice Hall.

Ekman, P., & O'Sullivan, M. (1988). The role of context in interpreting facial expression: Comment on Russell & Fehr (1987). *Journal of Experimental Psychology: General, 117*, 86-88.

Elfenbein, H. A., & Ambady, N. (2002). On the universality and cultural specificity of emotion recognition: A meta-analysis. *Psychological Bulletin, 128*, 203-235.

Fein, 5. (1996). Effects of suspicion on attributional thinking and the correspondence bias. *Journal of Personality and Social Psychology, 70*, 1164-1184.

Fiedler, K., Walther, E., & Nickel, S. (1999). Covariation based attribution: On the ability to assess multiple covariations of an effect. *Personality and Social Psychology Bulletin, 25*, 607-622.

Fiske, S. T., & Taylor, S. E. (1991). *Social cognition* (2nd ed.) New York: McGraw-Hill.

Frank, M. G., & Gilovich, T. (1989). Effect of memory perspective on retrospective causal attributions. *Journal of Personality and Social Psychology, 57*, 399-403.

Friesen, W. V. (1972). *Cultural differences in facial expressions in a social situation: An experimental test of the concept of display rules.* Unpublished dissertation, University of California, San Francisco.

Gawronski, B. (2003). Implicational schemata and the correspondence bias: On the diagnostic value of situationally constrained behavior. *Journal of Personality and Social Psychology, 84*, 1154-1171.

Gilbert, D. T. (1991). How mental systems believe. *American Psychologist, 46*, 107-119.

Gilbert, D. T. (1993). The assent of man: Mental representation and the control of belief. In D. M. Wegner & J. W. Pennebaker, (Eds.), *The handbook of mental control*. (pp. 57-87.) Englewood Cliffs, NJ: Prentice Hall.

Gilbert, D. T. (1998a). Ordinary personology. In D. T. Gilbert, S. T. Fiske, & G. Lindzey (Eds.), *The handbook of social psychology*. (4th ed., Vol. 2, pp. 89-150.) New York: McGraw-Hill.

Gilbert, D. T. (1998b). Speeding with Ned: A personal view of the correspondence bias. In J. M. Darley & J. Cooper (Eds.), *Attribution and social interaction*. (pp. 5-36.) Washington, DC: American Psychological Association.

Gilbert, D. T., & Hixon, J. G. (1991). The trouble of thinking: Activation and applications of stereotypical beliefs. *Journal of Personality and Social Psychology, 60*, 509-517.

Gilbert, D. T., & Malone, p. (1995). The correspondence bias. *Psychological Bulletin, 117,* 21-38.

Gilbert, D. T., & Osborne, R. E. (1989). Thinking backward: Some curable and incurable consequences of cognitive busyness. *Journal of Personality and Social Psychology, 57*, 940-949.

Gilbert, D. T., Pelham, B. W., & Krull, D. S. (1988). On cognitive busyness: When person perceivers meet persons perceived. *Journal of Personality and Social Psychology, 54*, 733-740.

Grant, M. J., Button, C. M., Hannah, T. E., & Ross, A. 5. (2003). The role of ideological consistency in attitude inferences. Current Research in *Social Psychology, 9:3*, 32-49.

Gross, J. J. (1998). Antecedent- and response-focused emotion regulation: Divergent consequences for experience, expression, and physiology. *Journal of Personality and Social Psychology, 74*, 224-237.

Gross, J. J., & Levenson, R. W. (1993). Emotional suppression: Physiology, self-report, and expressive behavior. *Journal of Personality and Social Psychology, 64*, 970-98

Gudykunst, W. B., Ting-Toomey, S., & Nishida, T. (1996). *Communication in personal relationships across cultures*. Thousand Oaks, CA: Sage Publications.

Guimond, S. (1999). Attitude change during college: Normative or informational social influence? *Social Psychology of Education, 2*, 237-261.

Haidt, J., & Keltner, D. (1999). Culture and facial expression: Open- ended methods find more faces and a gradient of recognition. *Cognition and Emotion, 13*, 225-266.

Hall, E. T. (1969). *The hidden dimension*. Garden City, NY: Doubleday.

Hall, J. A. (1979). *A cross-national study of gender differences in non-verbal sensitivity*. Unpublished manuscript, Northeastern University.

Hall, J. A. (1984). *Nonverbal sex differences: Communication accuracy and expressive style*. Baltimore, MD: Johns Hopkins University Press.

Hansen, C. H., & Hansen, R. D. (1988). Finding the face in the crowd: An anger superiority effect. *Journal of Personality and Social Psychology, 17*, 917-924.

216

Hatfield, E., & Sprecher, S. (1986a). *Mirror, mirror: The importance of looks in everyday life*. Albany, NY: State University of New York Press.

Heider, F (1958). *The psychology of interpersonal relations*. New York: Wiley.

Henley, N. M. (1977). *Body politics: Power, sex, and nonverbal communication*. Englewood Cliffs, NJ: Prentice Hall.

Herzog, T. A. (1994). Automobile driving as seen by the actor, the active observer, and the passive observer. *Journal of Applied Social Psychology, 24*, 2057-2074.

Hess, U., Philippot, P., & Blairy, S. (1998). Facial reactions to emotional facial expressions: Affect or cognition? *Cognition and Emotion, 12*, 509-531.

Hewstone, M., & Jaspars, J. (1987). Covariation and causal attribution: A logical model of the intuitive analysis of variance. Journal of *Personality and Social Psychology, 53*, 663-672.

Hilton, J. L., Fein, S., & Miller, D. T. (1993). Suspicion and dispositional inference. *Journal of Personality and Social Psychology, 19*, 501-512.

Jackson, L. A., Hunter, J. E., & Hodge, C. N. (1995). Physical attractiveness and intellectual competence: A meta-analytic review. *Social Psychology Quarterly, 58*, 108-122.

Jones, E. F. (1990). *Interpersonal perception*. New York: Freeman.

Jones, E. E., & Nisbett, R. E. (1972). The actor and the observer: Divergent perceptions of the causes of behavior. In F. E. Jones, D. E. Kanouse, H. H. Kelley, R. E. Nisbett, S. Valins, & B. Weiner (Eds.), *Attribution: Perceiving the causes of behavior*. (pp. 79-94.) Morristown, NJ: General Learning Press.

Kahn, J. P. (2003a, June 5). Stewart's fans still see a shine under the tarnish. *Boston Globe*, p. Dl; D7.

Kahn, J. P. (2003b, June 7). How the mighty have fallen. *Boston Globe*, p. Dl, D7.

Kappas, A. (1997). The fascination with faces: Are they windows to our soul? *Journal of Nonverbal Behavior, 21*, 157-162.

Kelley, H. H. (1967). Attribution theory in social psychology. In D. Levine (Ed.), Nebraska Symposium on Motivation. (Vol. 15, pp. 192-238.) Lincoln, NE: University of Nebraska Press.

Kim, M. P., & Rosenberg, S. (1980). Comparison of two structural models of implicit personality theory. *Journal of Personality and Social Psychology, 38*, 375-389.

Knapp, M. L., & Hall, J. A. (1997). *Nonverbal communication in human interaction*. New York: Harcourt Brace College Publishers.

Krull, D. S. (1993). Does the grist change the mill? The effect of the perceiver's inferential goal on the process of social inference. *Personality and Social Psychology Bulletin, 19*, 340-348.

La France, M. & Hecht, M. (1999). Option or obligation to smile: The effects of power and gender in facial expression. In P. Philippot, R. S. Feldman, & E. J. Coats (Eds.), *The social context of nonverbal behavior*. (pp. 45-70.) New York: Cambridge University Press.

Leathers, D. G. (1997). *Successful nonverbal communication: Principles and applications*. Boston, MA: Allyn & Bacon.

Lee, Y., & Seligman, M. E. P. (1997). Are Americans more optimistic than the Chinese? *Personality and Social Psychology Bulletin, 23,* 32-40.

Leung, K. (1996). Beliefs in Chinese culture. In M. H. Bond (Ed.), *The handbook of Chinese psychology.* (pp. 247-262.) Hong Kong: Oxford University Press.

Malamuth, N. (1983). Human sexuality. In D. Penman & P. C. Cozby (Eds.), *Social psychology.* New York: Holt, Rinehart & Winston.

Malle, B. F, & Knobe, J. (1997). Which behaviors do people explain? A basic actor-observer asymmetry. *Journal of Personality and Social Psychology, 72,* 288-304.

Markus, H. R., & Zajonc, R. B. (1985). The cognitive perspective in social psychology. In G. Lindzey & E. Aronson (Eds.), *Handbook of social psychology.* (3rd ed., Vol. 1, pp. 137-230.) New York: McGraw-Hill.

McAllister, H. A. (1996). Self-serving bias in the classroom: Who shows it? Who knows it? *Journal of Educational Psychology, 88,* 123-131.

McArthur, L. Z., & Baron, R. M. (1983). Toward an ecological theory of social perception. Psychological Review, 90, 215-238. McArthur, L. Z. (1990). *Social perception.* Pacific Grove, CA: Brooks/Cole.

McHugo, G. J., & Smith, C. A. (1996). The power of faces: A review of John T. Lanzetta's research on facial expression and emotion. *Motivation and Emotion, 21,* 85-120.

Miller, A. G., Ashton, W., & Mishal, M. (1990). Beliefs concerning the features of constrained behavior: A basis for the fundamental attribution error. *Journal of Personality and Social Psychology, 59,* 635-650.

Miller, J. G. (1984). Culture and the development of everyday social explanation. *Journal of Personality and Social Psychology, 46,* 961-978.

Morry, M. M., & Winkler, E. (2001). Student acceptance and expectation of sexual assault. *Canadian Journal of Behavioural Science, 33,* 188-192.

Newman, L. S. (1996). Trait impressions as heuristics for predicting future behavior. *Personality and Social Psychology Bulletin, 22,* 395-411.

Newman, L. S., & Uleman, J. 5. (1993). When are you what you did? Behavior identification and dispositional inference in person memory, attribution, and social judgment. *Personality and Social Psychology Bulletin, 19,* 513-525.

Perrott, S. B., Miller, Y. M., & Delaney, M. E. (1997). Attitudes toward the mandatory arrest response to domestic battering: Gender and institutional differences from a traditional and a women's university. *Legal and Criminological Psychology, 2,* 35-49.

Pittman, T. S., & D'Agostino, P. R. (1985). Motivation and attribution: The effects of control deprivation on subsequent information processing. In J. Harvey & G. Weary (Eds.), *Attribution: Basic issues and applications.* New York: Academic Press.

Ramsey, S. J. (1981). The kinesics of femininity in Japanese women. *Language Sciences, 3,* 104-123.

Richards, J. M., & Gross, J. J. (1999). Composure at any cost? The cognitive consequences of emotion suppression. *Personality and Social Psychology Bulletin, 25,* 1033-1044.

Riggs, J. M., & Gumbrecht, L. B. (2005). Correspondence bias and American sentiment in the wake of September 11, 2001. *Journal of Applied Social Psychology, 35*, 15-28.

Robertson, T. (2003, June 8). Cries of gender, celebrity bias over Stewart. *New York Times*, p. A14.

Robins, R. W., Spranca, M. D., & Mendelsohn, G. A. (1996). The actor- observer effect revisited: Effects of individual differences and repeated social interactions on actor and observer attributions. *Journal of Personality and Social Psychology, 71*, 375-389.

Rosenthal, R., & De Paulo, B. M. (1979). Sex differences in accommodation in nonverbal communication. In R. Rosenthal (Ed.), *Skill in nonverbal communication: Individual differences.* (pp. 68-103.) Cambridge, MA: Oelgeschlager, Gunn & Ham.

Ross, L. (1977). The intuitive psychologist and his shortcomings: Distortions in the attribution process. In L. Berkowitz (Ed.), *Advances in experimental social psychology.* (Vol. 10, pp. 173-220.) Orlando, FL: Academic Press.

Ross, L. (1998). Comment on Gilbert. In J. M. Darley & J. Cooper (Eds.), Attribution and social interaction. (pp. 53-66.) Washington, DC: *American Psychological Association.*

Ross, L., Amabile, T. M., & Steinmetz, J. L. (1977). Social roles, social control, and biases in social perception. *Journal of Personality and Social Psychology, 35*, 485-494.

Ross, L., & Nisbett, R. E. (1991). The person and the situation: *Perspectives of social psychology.* New York: McGraw-Hill.

Russell, J. A. (1994). Is there universal recognition of emotion from facial expressions? A review of the cross-cultural studies. *Psychological Bulletin, 115,* 102-141.

Russell, J. A., & Fehr, B. (1988). The role of context in interpreting facial expression: Reply to Ekman and O'Sullivan. *Journal of Experimental Psychology: General, 117*, 89-90.

Sherman, J. W., & Klien, S. B. (1994). Development and representation of personality impressions. *Journal of Personality and Social Psychology, 67*, 972-983.

Sorkin, A. R. (2003, June 5). Despite shuffle, Stewart still in charge. *New York Times*, p. C l, CS.

Summers, G., & Feldman, N. 5. (1984). Blaming the victim versus blaming the perpetrator: An attributional analysis of spouse abuse. *Journal of Social and Clinical Psychology, 2*, 339-347.

Tait, E. (2005b, August 2). Missed tackles gave Argos early momentum. *Winnipeg Free Press,* p. C3.

Ting-Toomey, S., & Chang, L. (1996). Cross cultural interpersonal communication: Theoretical trends and research directions. In W. B. Gudykunst, S. Ting-Toomey, & T. Nishada (Eds.), *Communication in personal relationships across cultures.* Thousand Oaks, CA: Sage.

Uleman, J. S., & Moskowitz, G. B. (1994). Unintended effects of goals on unintended inferences. *Journal of Personality and Social Psychology, 66*, 490-501.

Wagner, A. W., Roemer, L., Orsillo, S. M., & Litz, B. T. (2003). Emotional experiencing in women with posttraumatic stress disorder: Congruence between facial expressivity and self-report. *Journal of Traumatic Stress, 16*, 67-75.

Webster, D. M. (1993). Motivated augmentation and reduction of the overattributional bias. *Journal of Personality and Social Psychology*, 65, 261-271.

Wegener, D. T., & Petty, R. F. (1996). Effects of mood on persuasion processes: Enhancing, reducing, and biasing scrutiny of attitude- relevant information. In L. L. Martin & A. Tesser (Eds.), *Striving and feeling: Interactions between goals and affect.* (pp. 329-362.) Mahwah, NJ: Erlbaum.

Wehrle, T., Kaiser, S., Schmidt, S., & Scherer, K. R. (2000). Studying the dynamics of emotional expression using synthesized facial muscle movements. *Journal of Personality and Social Psychology, 78*, 105-119.

White, P. A. (2002). Causal attribution from covariation information: The evidential evaluation model. *European Journal of Social Psychology, 32*, 667-684.

Williams, S. S., Kimble, D. L., Covell, N. H., Weiss, L. H., Newton, K. J., Fisher, J. D., & Fisher, W. A. (1992). College students use implicit personality theory instead of safer sex. *Journal of Applied Social Psychology, 22*, 921-933.

Wright, E. E, Luus, C. A. E., & Christie, S. D. (1990). Does group discussion facilitate the use of consensus information in making causal attributions? *Journal of Personality and Social Psychology, 59*, 261-269.

Yik, M. S. M., Meng, Z., & Russell, J. A. (1998). Adults' freely produced emotion labels for babies' spontaneous facial expressions. *Cognition and Emotion, 12*, 723-730.

Yik, M. S. M., & Russell, J. A. (1999). Interpretation of faces: A cross-cultural study of a prediction from theory. *Cognition and Emotion, 13*, 93-104.

Zebrowitz, L. A., & Montepare, J. M. (1992). Impressions of babyfaced individuals across the life-span. *Developmental Psychology, 28*, 1143-1152.

PSYCHO-LOGICAL DEFENSIVENESS AND TRANSACTIONAL ANALYSIS

Mastering Human Relations by Anthony Falikowski. (2002).

Atwater, Eastwood. (1999). Psychology of Adjustment (6th ed.). Upper Saddle River, NJ: Prentice Hall.

Barocas, Harvey, Reichman, Walter, and Schwebel, Andrew. (1983). *Personal Adjustment and Growth.* New York: St. Martin's Press.

Berne, Eric. (1961). *Transactional Analysis in Psychotherapy.* New York: Ballantine Books.

Hall, Calvin. (1954). *A Primer of Freudian Psychology.* New York: New American Library.

Dusay, John, and Dusay, Katherine. (1977). Transactional Analysis. Pp. 374-427 in R. J. Corsini, *Current Psychotherapies.* Itasca, IL: F. E. Peacock.

Engler, Barbara. (1985). *Personality Traits: An Introduction* (2nd ed.). Boston: Houghton Mifflin Company.

Frager, Robert, and Fadiman, James. (1984). *Personality and Growth* (2nd ed.). New York: Harper and Row Publishers.

Gilliland, Burl, Richard, James, and Bowman, James. (1989). *Theories and Strategies in Counselling and Psychotherapy* (2nd ed.). Englewood Cliffs, NJ: Prentice Hall.

Harris, Thomas. (1969). *I'm OK-You're OK*. New York: Avon Books.

Hjelle, Larry, and Ziegler, Daniel. (1981). *Personality Theories: Basic Assumptions, Research and Applications*. New York: McGraw-Hill Book Company.

James, Muriel, and Jongeward, Dorothy. (1971). *Born to Win*. New York: Signet.

Masserman, J.H. (1961). *Principles of Dynamic Psychiatry*. Philadelphia: W. B. Saunders Company.

Weiten, Wayne, Lloyd, Margaret A., and Lashley, Robin L. (1991). *Psychology Applied to Modern Life: Adjustment in the 90s* (3rd ed.). Pacific Grove, CA: Brooks/Cole Publishing Co.

IMPROVING COMMUNICATION AND BECOMING A POSITIVE LISTENER

Person to Person: Positive Relationships Don't Just Happen by Sharon L. Hanna. (2000).

Campbell, K. E., Kleim, D. M., and Olson, R. (1992). Conversational Activity and Interruptions Among Men and Women. Journal of Social Psychology, 132, 419-421.

Ernst, F. H. (1973). *Who's Listening?* Valleio, CA: Addresso' set.

Mckay, M., Fanning, P., and Paleg, K. (1994). *Couple Skills: Making Your Relationship Work*. Oakland, CA: New Harbinger.

Satir, V. (1976). *Making Contact*. Millbrae, CA: Celestial Arts.

Vogt, W. P. (1997). *Tolerance and Education: Learning to Live with Diversity and Differences*. Thousand Oaks, CA: Sage.

CONFLICT

Mastering Human Relations by Anthony Falikowski. (2002).

Johnson, David W. (1990). *Reaching Out: Interpersonal Effectiveness and Self Realization*, (4th ed.). Upper Saddle River: Prentice Hall.

Lafferty, Clayton, and Phillips, Ron. (1990). *LSI Conflict: Self-Development Guide*. Plymouth, MI: Human Synergistics.

Lussier, Robert N. (1990). *Human Relations in Organizations: A Skill-Building Approach*. Homewood, IL: Irwin.

Rahim M. A. (1983). *A Measure of Styles of Handling Interpersonal Conflict*. Academy of Management Journal (June): 368-76.

Robbins, Stephan P. (1993). *Organizational Behaviour: Concepts, Controversies, and Applications*, (6th ed.). Upper Saddle River, NJ: Prentice Hall.

INTERPERSONAL ATTRACTION: FROM FIRST IMPRESSION TO CLOSE RELATIONSHIPS

From Social Psychology, 3rd Canadian Edition by E. Aronson, T. Wilson, R. Akert, B. Fehr (2007).

Bargh, J. A., & McKenna, K. Y. A. (2004). The internet and social life. *Annual Review of Psychology, 55,* 573-590.

Bargh, J. A., & McKenna, K. Y. A., & Fitzsimons, G. M. (2002). Can you see the real me? Activation and expression of the "true self' on the Internet. *Journal of Social Issues, 58,* 33-48.

Baumeister, R. F, & Leary, M. R. (1995). The need to belong: Des for interpersonal attachment as a fundamental human motivation *Psychological Bulletin, 117,* 497-529.

Bell, J. (1995). Notions of love and romance among the Taita of Kenya. In W. Jankowiak (Ed.), *Romantic passion: A universal experience?* (pp. 152-165.) New York: Columbia University Press.

Berry, D. S. (1995). Beyond beauty and after affect: An event perception approach to perceiving faces. In R. A. Eder (Ed.), Craniofacial anomalies: *Psychological perspectives.* New York: Springer-Verlag.

Berseheid, E. (1985). Interpersonal attraction. In G. Lindzey & E. Aronson (Eds.), *The handbook of social psychology.* (pp. 413-484.) New York: McGraw-Hill.

Berscheid, E., & Peplau, L. A. (1983). The emerging science of relationships. In H. H. Kelley, E. Berscheid, A. Christensen, J. H. Harvey, T. L. Huston, G. Levinger, E. McClintock, L. A. Peplau, & D. R. Peterson (Eds.), *Close relationships.* (pp. 1-19.) New York: Freeman.

Berscheid, E., & Reis, H. T. (1998). Attraction and close relationships. In D. Gilbert, S. Fiske, & G. Lindzey (Eds.), *The handbook of social psychology* (4th ed., Vol. 2, pp. 193-281). New York: McGraw-Hill.

Berscheid, F., & Waister (Hatfield), F. (1974). A little bit about love. In T. L. Huston (Ed.), *Foundations of interpersonal attraction.* (pp.355-381.) New York: Academic Press.

Berscheid, E., & Walster (Hatfield), E. (1978). *Interpersonal attraction.* Reading, MA: Addison-Wesley.

Bird, B. (2001, January 28). Love as fleeting as a bus ride. *Winnipeg Free Press,* p. B5.

Bornstein, R. F (1989). Exposure and affect: Overview and its analysis of research, 1968-1987. *Psychological Bulletin*, 265-289.

Bornstein, R. F, & D'Agostino, P. R. (1992). Stimulus recognition and the mere exposure effect. *Journal of Personality and Social Psychology, 63,* 545- 552.

Brigham, J. C. (1980). Limiting conditions of the, "physical attractiveness stereotype": Attributions about divorce. *Journal of Research in Personality, 14, 365-375.*

Buss, D. M. (1989). Sex differences in human mate preferences: Evolutionary hypotheses tested in 37 cultures. *Behavioral and Brain Sciences, 12*, 1-49.

Buss, D. M., & Barnes, M. (1986). Preferences in human mate selection. *Journal of Personality and Social Psychology, 50*, 559-570.

Byrne, D. (1997). An overview (and underview) of research and then within the attraction paradigm. *Journal of Social and Personal Relationships, 14*, 417-431.

Byrne, D., & Clore, G. L. (1970). A reinforcement model of evaluative processes. *Personality: An International journal, 1*, 103-128.

Byrne, D., Clore, G. L., & Smeaton, G. (1986). The attraction hypothesis: Do similar attitudes affect anything? *Journal of Personality and Social Psychology, 51*,1167-1170.

Byrne, D., & Nelson, D. (1965). Attraction as a linear function of positive reinforcement. *Journal of Personality and Social Psychology, 1* 659-663.

Cate, R. M., & Lloyd, S. A. (1992). *Courtship*. Newbury Park, CA: Sage.

Cunningham, M. R. (1986). Measuring the physical in physical attractiveness: Quasi-experiments on the sociobiology of female facial beauty. Journal of *Personality and Social Psychology, 50*, 925-935.

Cunningham, M. R., Barbee, A. R., & Pike, C. L. (1990). What do women want? Facial metric assessment of multiple motives in the perception of male facial physical attractiveness. *Journal of Personality and Social Psychology, 59*, 61-72.

Dion, D. L. (2002). The social psychology of perceived prejudices and discrimination. *Canadian Psychology, 43*, 1-10.

Dion, K. L., & Dion, K. K. (1993). Gender and ethnocultural comparisons in styles of love. *Psychology of Women Quarterly, 17*, 463-473.

Dryer, D. C., & Horowitz, L. M. (1997). When do opposites attract? Interpersonal complementarity versus similarity. *Journal of Personality and Social Psychology, 72*, 592-603.

Fehr, B. (1993). How do I love thee? Let me consult my prototype. In S. Duck (Ed.), *Individuals in relationships*. (pp. 87-120.) Newbury Park, CA: Sage.

Fehr, B. (1996). *Friendship processes*. Thousand Oaks, CA: Sage Publications.

Fehr, B. (2001). The status of theory and research on love and commitment. In G. Fletcher and M. Clark (Eds.), *The Blackwell handbook of social psychology: Interpersonal processes*. Oxford, UK: Blackwell Publishers.

Fehr, B., & Russell, J. A. (1991). The concept of love viewed from a prototype perspective. *Journal of Personality and Social Psychology, 60*, 425-438.

Feingold, A. (1990). Gender differences in effects of physical attractiveness on romantic attraction: A comparison across five research paradigms. *Journal of Personality and Social Psychology, 59*, 981-993.

Fink, B., & Penton-Voak, I. (2002). Evolutionary psychology of facial attractiveness. *Current Directions in Psychological Science, 11*, 154-158.

Gao, G. (1993, May). *An investigation of love and intimacy in romantic relationships in China and the United States.* Paper presented at the annual conference of the International Communication Association, Washington, DC.

Gao, G., & Gudykunst, W. B. (1995). Attributional confidence, perceived similarity, and network involvement in Chinese and European American romantic relationships. *Communication Quarterly, 43*, 431-445.

Griffin, E., & Sparks, G. G. (1990). Friends forever: A longitudinal exploration of intimacy in same-sex pairs and platonic pairs. *Journal of Social and Personal Relationships, 7*, 29-46.

Halberstadt, J. B., & Rhodes, G. (2000). The attractiveness of nonface averages: Implications for an evolutionary explanation of the attractiveness of average faces. *Psychological Science, 11*, 285-289.

Hartup, W. W., & Stevens, N. (1997). Friendships and adaptation in the life course. *Psychological Bulletin, 121*, 355-370.

Hassebrauck, M., & Buhl, T. (1996). Three-dimensional love. *Journal of Social Psychology, 136*, 121-122.

Hatfield, E., & Rapson, R. L. (1996). *Love and sex: Cross-cultural perspectives.* Needham Heights, MA: Allyn & Bacon.

Hatfield, E., & Sprecher, S. (1986a). *Mirror, mirror: The importance of looks in everyday life.* Albany, NY: State University of New York Press.

Hendrick, S. S., & Hendrick, C. (1986). A theory and method of love. Journal of *Personality and Social Psychology, 50*, 392-402.

Hendrick, S. S., & Hendrick, C. (1992). *Liking, loving and relating.* (2nd ed.) Pacific Grove, CA: Brooks/Cole.

Hendrick, S. 5, Hendrick, C., & Adler, N. L. (1988). Romantic relationships: Love, satisfaction, and staying together. *Journal of Personality and Social Psychology, 54*, 980-988.

Hofstede, G. (1984). *Culture's consequences: International differences in work-related values.* Newbury Park, CA: Sage.

Holtz, R. (1997). Length of group membership, assumed similarity, and opinion certainty: The dividend for veteran members. *Journal of Applied Social Psychology, 27*, 539-555.

Hui, C. H., & Triandis, H. C. (1986). Individualism-collectivism: A study of cross cultural researchers. *Journal of Cross-Cultural Psychology, 17*, 225-248.

Jankowiak, W. (1995). Introduction. In W. Jankowiak (Ed.), *Romantic passion: A universal experience?* (pp. 1-19.) New York: Columbia University Press.

Jankowiak, W. R., & Fischer, E. E (1992). A cross-cultural perspective on romantic love. *Ethnology, 31*, 149-195.

Kenny, D. A. (1994). Using the social relations model to understand relationships. In R. Ether & R. Gilmour (Eds.), *Theoretical Frameworks for Personal Relationships.* (pp. 111-127.) Hillsdale, NJ: Erlbaum.

Langlois, J. H., & Roggman, L. A. (1990). Attractive faces are only average. *Psychological Science, 1*, 115-121.

Langlois, J. H., Roggman, L. A., & Musselman, L. (1994). What is average and what is not average about attractive faces? *Psychological Science, 5,* 214-220.

Lea, M., & Spears, R. (1995). Love at first byte: Building personal relationships over computer networks. In J. T. Wood & S. W. Duck (Eds.), *Understudied relationships: Off the beaten track.* (pp. 197-233.) Thousand Oaks, CA: Sage.

Lemieux, R., & Hale, J. L. (1999). Intimacy, passion, and commitment in young romantic relationships: Successfully measuring the triangular theory of love. *Psychological Reports, 85,* 497-503.

Levinger, G. (1994). Figure versus ground: Micro and macro perspectives on the social psychology of personal relationships. In R. Ether & R. Gilmour (Eds.), *Theoretical frameworks for personal relationships.* (pp. 1-28.) Hillsdale, NJ: Erlbaum.

Little, A. C., & Perrctt, D. I. (2002). Putting beauty back in the eye of the beholder. *Psychologist, 15,* 28-32.

McArthur, L. Z., & Berry, D. S. (1987). Cross cultural agreement in perceptions of babyfaced adults. *Journal of Cross-Cultural Psychology, 18,* 165-192.

McKenna, K. Y. A., & Bargh, J. A. (2000). Plan 9 from cyberspace: The implications of the Internet for personality and social psychology. *Personality and Social Psychology Review, 4,* 57-75.

McKenna, K. Y. A., Green, A. S., & Gleason, M. J. (2002). Relationship formation on the Internet: What's the big attraction? *Journal of Social Issues, 58,* 9-31.

McPherson, M., Smith-Lovin, L., & Cook, J. M. (2001). Birds of a feather: Homophily in social networks. *Annual Review of Sociology, 27,* 415-444.

Moreland, R. L., & Beach, R. (1992). Exposure effects in the classroom: The development of affinity among students. *Journal of Experimental Social Psychology, 28,* 255-276.

Moreland, R. L., & Zajonc, R. B. (1982). Exposure effects in person perception: Familiarity, similarity, and attraction. *Journal of Experimental Social Psychology, 18,* 395-415.

Morry, M. M. (2005). Relationship satisfaction as a predictor of similarity ratings: A test of the attraction-similarity hypothesis. *Journal of Social and Personal Relationships, 22,* 561-584.

Newcomb, T. M. (1961). *The acquaintance process.* New York: Holt, Rinehart & Winston.

Regan, P. C., & Berscheid, E. (1995). Gender differences in beliefs about the causes of male and female sexual desire. *Personal Relationships, 2,* 345-358.

Regan, P. C., & Berscheid, E. (1997). Gender differences in characteristics desired in a potential sexual and marriage partner. *Journal of Psychology and Human Sexuality, 9,* 25-37.

Regan, P. C., & Berscheid, E. (1999). *Lust: What we know about human sexual desire.* Thousand Oaks, CA: Sage.

Roszell, P., Kennedy, D., & Grabb, E. (1989). Physical attractiveness and income attainment among Canadians. *Journal of Psychology, 123,* 547-559.

Rubin, Z., Peplau, L. A., & Hill, C. T. (1981). Loving and leaving: Sex differences in romantic attachments. *Sex Roles, 7,* 821-835.

Secord, P. F., & Backman, C. W. (1964). *Social psychology*. New York: McGraw-Hill.

Segal, M. W (1974). Alphabet and attraction: An unobtrusive measure of the effect of propinquity in a field setting. *Journal of Personality and Social Psychology, 30*, 654-657.

Sternberg, R. J., & Beall, A. E. (1991). How can we know what love is? An epistemological analysis. In G. J. 0. Fletcher & F D. Fincham (Eds.), *Cognition in close relationships*. (pp. 257-278.) Hillsdale, NJ: Eribaum.

Stroebe, W., & Stroebe, M. (1996). The social psychology of social support. In E. T. Higgins & A. W. Kruglanski (Eds.), *Social psychology: Handbook of basic principles*. (pp. 597-621.) New York: Guilford.

Walther, J., Anderson, J. F., & Park, D. W. (1994). Interpersonal effects in computer mediated interaction: A meta-analysis of social and antisocial communication. *Communication Research, 21*, 460-487.

Werner, C., & Parmelee, P. (1979). Similarity of activity preferences among friends: Those who play together stay together. *Social Psychology Quarterly, 42*, 62-66.

Zajonc, R. B. (1968). Attitudinal effects of mere exposure. *Journal of Personality and Social Psychology, 9*, Monograph Suppl. 2, Pt. 2

Zebrowitz, L. A., & Montepare, J. M. (1992). Impressions of babyfaced individuals across the life-span. *Developmental Psychology, 28*, 1143-1152.